Babafemi A. Badejo

RAILA ODINGA
An Enigma in Kenyan Politics

To H.E Jimmy Carter,
with compliments

[signature]
27/4/2012

YINTAB BOOKS
Lagos and Nairobi
2006

Yintab Books, a division of Yintab Ltd.

TOS Benson Estate Road, Owutu
P.O. Box 1258, Ikorodu, G.P.O.
Lagos, Nigeria
Tel: 234-803 331 1235

Scripture Union Center
Off Argwings-Khodek Road
Hurlingham
P.O. Box 76386-00508
Nairobi, Kenya
Tel: 254-733 586 904

www.yintab.com

For interactive comments on this book, please go to www.badejo-on-raila.com

Cover designed by Jennifer Odallo

Copyright © 2006 by Babafemi A. Badejo

ISBN   978-37208-9-9 Hard Cover
       978-37208-8-0 Paper Back

Table of Contents

Acknowledgements

I am extremely grateful to all those who found time to see me. My special thanks go to those who made themselves readily available and from whom my knowledge became richer. These people are too numerous to list and not all of them made it to the footnoting in my work even though their respective insights improved my knowledge of Kenya.

However, my indebtedness is high to Dunera Ilako, (initially my Ophthalmologist and later a critic and editor of many versions of this work); Linda Ochiel, at a time, Media Assistant to Raila Odinga, and Anthony Ade Sekudo, a friend, and for a time, the Acting High Commissioner of Nigeria to Kenya. They all, at different times, took interest in this work and constantly counselled me to keep pressing at the doors of those who rejected my quest for interviews. This volume is testimony to the success of their counselling.

Prof. Wanjiku Kabira, then of the Constitution of Kenya Review Commission, not only shared her thoughts on Kenyan politics and insight into the constitution review process at three different sessions, but provided published materials both from the NGO she led and the Constitution of Kenya Review Commission. Dr. Willy Mutunga readily saw me at very short notice on a public holiday. He went further and eagerly gave a free copy of his seminal work and directed me to some valuable literature on my research. He not only accepted the onerous task of reading through a tedious manuscript, but also gave insights that were extremely useful. Others like Sebastian Groth, then at the German Embassy in Nairobi, and Dr. Onukaba Adinoyi Ojo, former Spokesman to the Nigerian Vice-President, shared ideas on how to improve on the quality of the work. Dr. Fred Matiagn'i, an academic at the University of Nairobi, provided many leads, valuable books and personal records of the 2002 General Elections. Professor Tade Aina with the mind of a fine Sociologist, challenged me towards substantial improvement of the penultimate draft.

Bunmi Makinwa, Prof. Raphael Omotayo Olaniyan, Christine Onyango, in different ways, went beyond friendship to lend hands in improving this work. So did Kamar Yousuf, a colleague, as well as Anne Maria Madsen of the Danish Mission in Nairobi who dutifully went through and made substantial comments on the typset version. Mary Onyango, a friend of a friend, and Salim Lone, a friend in retirement from the United Nations, both offered some last minute critique that affected the content and the overall structure of the book. Doye Olugbemi, read the penultimate draft with the mind of a Lawyer. Prof. Oye Oyediran and Prof. Ademola Salau, eagerly read through earlier drafts and offered words of encouragement. Emeritus Prof. Richard Sklar and Prof. Mike Lofchie continued to nurture me even on this task as they did about two and a half decades ago when I was a graduate student at UCLA. The encouragement and critique of the manuscript by Prof. Adebayo Adedeji, (Asiwaju of Ijebu), was also very helpful.

Patrick Quarckoo, the brain behind Kiss FM Radio Station in Nairobi, might have forgotten that he linked me to one of my main sources and easily volunteered a phone number I made good use of without disclosing his culpability. Ling Kituyi, the United Nations Medical Officer in Nairobi diverted from healing me to providing an impromptu lecture and a valuable subsequent interview on Kenyan politics from her vantage point of being a wife during a struggle that used the sitting of wives at dinner tables to fool Kenyan security agents and sell the impression of social and non-political events. Rose Muchiri, a colleague at the United Nations, was helpful with some insights on Kenyan personalities, and provided the link with one who agreed to an interview before becoming elusive after an hour of interaction. The typesetting and the design of the cover was a result of the selfless support of Jennifer Odallo subsequently supported by Winnie Oyuko. Salim Kibwana and Gabriel Munyao spent good times assisting in many respects. Winnie Kamau also spent some useful time in teaching me on computer skills that reduced the task of the publisher. Lola Abijo started but David Bell of the British High Commission, as a friend, subsequently accepted the oncrous task of trying to make this work more reader friendly.

Ian Steele, a friend and colleague readily made me smile into his camera for use in the back cover of this book. I am most grateful. May be I should also thank the unnamed lion on the front cover for giving me such a nice pose at the lake Nakuru national park.

There were many other people who were invaluable. Some of these were: Susan Kibathi, Raila's able and affable administrative assistant of many years; many of Raila's personal assistants like: Odungi Randa; George Oduor "Opondo"; George Oduor; Francis Ogola; Dave Arunga, Kennedy Ogana, Thomas Oduor and others whom I am unable to mention. They all helped in no small way to make my life easier during travels, and on some occasions when I ventured into huge crowds. I remain indebted to Michael Njeru for making it possible for me to be at the grand finale of the Orange Democratic Movement rally on the referendum at Nyayo stadium on Saturday, November 19, 2005.

Willis Leah Gondi, a Physician in Nairobi provided useful initial insights and gave a major link for my work. Ida Betty Odinga, aside from several intellectual guides and materials, tried to alter, in a positive direction, my generalistic assessment that Kenyans are hospitable at restaurants and hotels, but not in their homes. Most of my interviews with her and Raila turned into opportunities for sumptuous dishes. My appreciation is also extended to Wenwa Akinyi Odinga; Fidel Castro Odinga; Rosemary Odinga; Mark arap Too; Mirulo Okello; Jonah Bett; Mohamed Abdi Affey, Lawyer Ojwang' Agina and many others, who arranged a good number of my appointments and/or provided some useful documents.

Finally, I must thank my wife Jumoke and last child Bidemi, who accepted my "absent mindedness" during the little time we spent together in either Lagos or Nairobi, as I got tied into completing the work. Jumoke and Tokunbo, my second daughter spent time not only typing some of the work but also as guinea-pigs in providing commentary on earlier drafts, as did my other children Yinka and Adebola. In the case of Adebola, he was an important critic whose views I had to consider seriously.

Of course, I accept responsibility for any remaining errors in the book which was written in my spare time. The views expressed herein does not reflect, in any way, the views of any organization, especially the United Nations with which I am associated.

Preface

It is easy to construe the writing of a biography on a living person as hero-worshipping. But then, there are very few human beings who could ordinarily be considered as heroes. I am not the type that has heroes. Perhaps in my own time, and in Africa, I may reluctantly name Nelson Mandela, Kwame Nkrumah and Obafemi Awolowo. Mandela could be considered for his self-sacrifice while pursuing the dignity of his people in particular, and humanity in general. In the latter respect, Mandela continued from where the towering Nkrumah left off in his struggle for the emancipation of the African. Awolowo, in my Yoruba existence (the Yoruba as an ethnic group reside mainly in Nigeria; but are also found in the southern parts of many West African countries and constitute a reasonable population base of Brazil and a number of the black populations of some other countries in the Americas), was a hero. Aside from many of his far sighted achievements in the western part of Nigeria on the eve of independence, he also showed how policies could go a long way in making a difference to the lives of millions including myself that benefited from his struggle to have Yoruba children pursue Western education.

Since I do not consider myself the hero-worshipping type, I never thought I would devote any time towards writing anyone's biography. I have known and related with many whose biographies could have sold several copies. Of course, I had been intellectually attracted to the writings of a number of political and academic leaders without considering them heroes.

To start with, I must make it clear that Raila Odinga is still defining himself within Kenya and I am not, by any chance, suggesting that he is in the same league today, with Nkrumah, Mandela and Awolowo. So why write about Raila? I first met him in 1995 at an Africa Leadership Forum function in Addis Ababa, after my relocation to Nairobi from Mogadishu. Back in Nairobi, I approached Raila as a Parliamentarian, on what he could do to assist the pressure to have the current President of Nigeria, Olusegun Obasanjo, then a prisoner, released from the clutches of late Sanni Abacha who was at that time the Nigerian Head of State. He gave me audience at his AGIP House office and together with some Kenyan Parliamentarians, did his best on the issue.

I subsequently took interest in Raila's effort in popularising the West African dress style as an alternative to the European one and as "proper attire" for the Kenyan Parliament. I saw this effort as a major part of a drive towards the decolonisation of the Kenyan mind. He kept this drive up in and out of Parliament and West African clothing in Parliament received the tag of "opposition dressing." I continued to follow his activities out of my interest in politics in Africa in general, and in Kenya in particular.

Raila was an enigma to me. His courageous and daring styles, like a Simba (Lion) in the "Animal Kingdom" was without doubt. But I could not understand why after such feats in opposition politics, he abandoned the opposition to cooperate and then merge with the ruling party, Kenya African National Union (KANU). I was convinced that he would be dumped at the appropriate time by President Daniel Toroitich arap Moi. But I did not realize that instead of being dumped, he could leave KANU with more than he brought in. I did not anticipate that President Moi would dump both George Saitoti, his Vice-President for thirteen years, and Musalia Mudavadi, the Minister for Transport and Communication and latterly his Vice-President, who had been rumoured as his possible successors, and instead impose Uhuru Kenyatta, the son of the first President of Kenya.

It was a relief to see someone I knew, openly and bravely defy President Moi. A few years earlier, I had been shocked to see some KANU politicians clap on TV as President Moi said that none of them was good enough to succeed him or else he would have left power like Nelson Mandela did in South Africa. The Raila-led politics of defiance in KANU, operated under the tag "Rainbow Alliance." As Rainbow Alliance took shape, I became excited seeing Raila take advantage of an opportunity President Moi presented. However, I was worried that the Alliance would break apart over who would be the presidential candidate. As I expected the worst, it was yet another shock, suddenly to hear Raila's declaration of what became an election slogan "Kibaki *Tosha*" (Kibaki was good enough as presidential candidate) on October 14, 2002. It became clear that a coalition capable of unseating Moi's power design was in place.

I woke up a month later, on November 15, 2002, and decided that I would like to know more about Raila's role in Kenyan politics. At the same time, I also wanted to know more about the story of Kenya in terms of major contributions to the political scene in Kenya over the years. I thought such knowledge would be worth sharing with posterity. While a Kenyan audience may be saturated with the history of the struggle for independence and other details outside Raila's social and political life, I thought a concise account of those earlier events that had impacted on today, would excite an international audience, and especially a new student of politics in Kenya.

November 15, 2002, was Raila's first day back in Nairobi after a tour of Europe and America seeking support for the National Rainbow Coalition (NARC), the party that emerged from the collaboration of the Rainbow Alliance and the Mwai Kibaki- led National Alliance Party of Kenya (NAK). Rateng Oginga Ogego, at that time a Raila aide and later Kenya's High Commissioner to Canada, whom I approached to arrange a meeting for me with Raila, suggested that I should go immediately to the Jaramogi Odinga Foundation [a foundation set up in the memory of Raila's father Jaramogi Oginga Odinga] to meet Raila before a scheduled press conference. I diverted from a send-off lunch for a colleague and did just that. With jet-lagged eyes, Raila said: "Fine!" to my expressed intent to write a biography on him as an entry point into my understanding of politics in Kenya.

But that was it. It became difficult to get appointments from many Kenyans, including Raila who only sat with me 8 months later. I must thank him for all the time he subsequently gave. At the end of my interviews, I wanted to know if he knew who Raila was. He was upset as he felt he had made that clear. However, when I showed him some of the reactions to my question: Who is Raila? He decided to write his own reaction to the question. His long reaction I slightly reduced and added to this volume as: "Raila Odinga on Raila."

In doing the research on this work, generally, people gave appointments but unilaterally cancelled them without discussion or notice. It was difficult to understand this as them just being busy. In many cases, it was refined political avoidance. I tended to receive audience to indicate what I wanted to talk about and thereafter got nice rebuffs as times for a meeting shifted and continued to change until I gave up in frustration. This avoidance game probably came either out of fear of being quoted on Raila, or very strong detestation of him. At one stage, I even thought some of the people, who had said they would have to check with him, had as a result, subsequently refused to talk to me. I later found out that he had not stopped anyone from talking to me.

In spite of several efforts through aides, including Lee Njiru, and in writing, I never had an audience with former President Moi. His knowledge of politics in Kenya would have been of immense benefit. I also would have been in a position to get his side of the story on some of the events under his watch, which I have chronicled on the basis of interviews with independent observers, "victims" and secondary sources.

My intention in this work is simple. It is to tell as briefly as possible, the story of politics in Kenya and Raila's role in them. In effect, it is a desire to write two biographies in one. I make no pretence about wanting to provide a psychological profile of what made Raila tick as he went through the landmines of Kenyan politics unscathed. Neither do I seek to provide a grand explanatory framework of Kenyan politics. I leave all that to other students of the Kenyan political reality. However, I would be satisfied if students and general readers on politics in Kenya knew more of the many important aspects of the life of a person who has loomed large on the Kenyan political horizon for over two decades and shows the promise of many more years of shaping the Kenyan reality. But that should not be all. The reader should have some relief in being able to obtain some knowledge from an abridged version of politics in Kenya over the last sixty years.

To a large extent, the political history of a country is the summation of the stories of individuals who have been involved in the moulding of its political path. Such moulding could, in some cases, arise from individuals from the external environment, or put another way, individuals who, as a result of circumstances, came from outside the country and put their stamp on it. In other cases, individuals, in the process of just living their lives, shape the political history of their country of birth. Many others become important appendices and footnotes to the process of history shaped by significant individuals. Of course, over time, routine human behaviour, become institutions and structures. At times, structures and institutions, whether from within or outside a country, though still driven by individuals who dare to win, do appear to acquire lives of their own as they shape the political history of a country. There are situations in which the same significant individuals could go beyond shaping political history and create important and lasting socio-cultural and/or economic changes.

The Mau Mau struggle and its unsung heroes, set the stage for Kenyan independence. As this struggle went on, a number of individuals entered the political arena of negotiations for independence and made significant marks thereafter. These individuals provided the foundation for the political history of Kenya. Thus, any attempt to understand the political history of Kenya in the last sixty years would be incomplete without the roles of five individuals. These are: Jomo Kenyatta; Jaramogi Oginga Odinga; Tom Mboya; Daniel arap Moi; and Raila Amolo Odinga. The object of this book is to tell the story of the last of these as he moved within the imprint of the first four and defined new paths of further change.

Babafemi Adesina BADEJO, Ph.D, LL.B

Prologue

It was December 4, 2004. This was a day many people had been waiting for in the Odinga and Akasa families. It was also a political day. Planning by two families for that day, had started long before. It would be safe to say that the coming together of the two families on April 25, 2004 for the Luo *ayie* (betrothal) ceremony, marked the beginning of a formal relationship that was initiated by a young man, Amos Ndanyi Akasa, and a young lady, Rosemary Akeyo Odinga.

At the *ayie,* Amos was absent. He remained in the United States where he had been in sojourn with Rosemary. So, an arrangement was made for his friend Gabriel Okata to stand as proxy for him. Gabriel was the centre of attraction even though he knew very well that he was not the beneficiary.

Rosemary had to return to the two acre homestead of her parents, Raila and Ida Odinga, in the posh Karen neighbourhood at the fringe of Nairobi. She had to be there to respond to the question of whether she knew Amos and accepted his proposal to marry her. Rosemary came from the United States to spend about ten minutes answering that question and to fulfil her part in an elaborate three hours plus negotiation.

After the negotiation, which took place in Rosemary's absence, Gabriel Okata on behalf of Amos, led sheeps and goats into the tastefully furnished marble floored living room. He handed the animals over to the Odinga family led by Alogo Raila who stood in for late Oginga Odinga (Rosemary's late grand father). As well as exchanging other gifts, it was agreed that Amos would pay KSH 160,000 (about USD 2,100) as bride price plus 6 cows that he would deliver to Bondo, the ancestral home of the Odingas, before the wedding. Instead of the announced initial plan of having the wedding sometime in October, it took place on December 4, 2004.

A very large open space at the Kenya Commercial Bank Management Centre in Karen, had been converted into a church with enough canopies to shade people from the hot African sun. There were many priests from different Christian denominations to perform the wedding ceremony. The invitations were for an 11 am start. But guests continued to stream in long after that time. President Mwai Kibaki was invited with the First Lady, Lucy Kibaki.

The First Lady stayed away to support a social event. The fact that the President was to attend the wedding, was a surprise to many. But two years earlier, Raila had been at the forefront of the move to make Kibaki (who had twice failed to unseat former President Moi) the President of Kenya. Raila single-handedly campaigned throughout Kenya while the President was hospitalised from a motor accident he suffered during his campaign. There was a Memorandum of Understanding that Raila would become the Prime Minister through a swift amendment to the constitution, and that his party members would get 50% of the spoils after their victory. Kibaki won. Raila literally pushed Moi out of office only to be sidelined by Kibaki who gave him only the Ministry of Roads, Public Works and Housing. But loyal members of his party in the larger coalition were sidelined and short-changed. Some others who had hung on Raila's coat-tails, were given posts in a bid to reduce Raila's strength among his followers. Lieutenants who were deemed close to Raila, made it clear privately, that the Kibaki group would not trust Raila with the reigns of power. The drive for a new constitution for Kenya which had swallowed a lot of resources, became personalised.

There were constant plots and counter-plots on how to clip Raila's wings. About six months before the wedding, the President succeeded by appointing some members of the Opposition to his cabinet, to form what he called: "Government of National Unity." Rather than give Raila's party more cabinet posts, his personal portfolio was reduced when Housing was chipped away and given to Kibaki loyalist, Amos Kimunya, the Minister of Lands. Raila's ardent supporters were given lesser ministries as chosen opposition leaders, were given major posts to boost the President's parliamentary support, which Raila and his colleagues were threatening. The President did indeed have more success in Parliament immediately after the re-structuring. Nevertheless Raila invited all Members of Parliament and others from the Kenyan and International communities, to the wedding.

On the eve of the wedding, it was clear that Raila and most of his lieutenants would be at Karen. Instead of attending the wedding, Norman Nyagah, the Chief Whip of the governing coalition, sent text messages through his cell phone to many Members of Parliament deemed loyal to President Kibaki coalition, asking them to go to Mombasa for a meeting on December 4. The plan was to make amendments to the registered constitution of the coalition to seal the fate of the "opposition" group.

Thus, it was a surprise to many who felt that the Kibaki/Raila relationship was very bad, to see the President arrive at the wedding venue at 12:15 pm. The gathering stood up as a mark of respect for the Head of State.

But the major surprise, was the arrival of former President Daniel arap Moi two minutes after President Kibaki. It was a protocol coup for Moi. People who were still standing for the President when Moi arrived did not sit. Instead, surprisingly, they gave Moi a very warm welcome. Raila had pushed Moi out of office sooner than he might constitutionally have stayed, by single handedly convening an immediate post-election swearing-in ceremony which was not coordinated with the retiring President. Uhuru Kenyatta, the son of the founding President of Kenya, who was sponsored by the constitutionally-barred Moi, to run against Kibaki, had graciously accepted defeat. But there was a fear that Moi's cohorts would push Uhuru to contest the election results in court. The total public displeasure with Moi had been demonstrated at the unruly swearing-in of President Kibaki in December 2002 when he was jeered, booed and humiliated at his final official appearance after 24 years as President of Kenya. Most people would not have believed that he would attend a social event at the invitation of Raila nor that he would receive a warm reception at it. After all, before Kibaki had dealt Raila the blow over the MoU, Moi had already betrayed Raila's trust by breaking an earlier understanding to get Raila to dissolve his party and join Moi's KANU.

The wedding ceremony began at 12:30 pm. The highlight was not only that Raila and his wife, Ida, walked into the "church" with the bride between them, but that they chose to set an example by jointly responding to the question "Who gives the bride in marriage?," with "We do," thus challenging the age-old assumption that only a man could give away a bride to another man. Raila and Ida gave a political lesson in being gender sensitively correct.

The sermon was also very political. The preacher dwelt on the theme of defining happiness as wanting what you get. He used the new couple's inter-ethnic marriage to declare that Kenya was not ethnicised. He wished that Kenyans would not always suffer bad experiences after General Elections. He was concerned that the Government which had been in office for two years, was spending so much money on commissions to probe the acts of its predecessor, while the country returned to the same ills being probed.

The reception was in another part of the same compound with many canopies to accommodate different categories of people. Politically important was the fact that the parents of the new couple sat on the same table with the present and former Presidents of Kenya. Also at the top table was Britain's Lord Steele, a long-time friend of Kenya. Surprising, however, was the fact that the space of a chair separated former President Moi from President Kibaki. It was not clear if the space was for the First Lady if she showed up unexpectedly, or if it was meant to demonstrate the gulf between Moi and Mwai, who visibly avoided each other throughout. Interesting, however, was the fact that President Kibaki shared his special meal from State House with all on that table. He showed that he loved ordinary Kenyan roasted meat "nyama choma" as he enjoyed his meal to the fullest and continued for a long while as one Ambassador quarrelled with his wife who wanted him to eat food which he deemed unhygienic! A Chinese diplomat jokingly pointed out to the Ambassador, that the food must be safe if President Kibaki was enjoying it. He was not amused and decided that he wanted to leave. But his wife politely ignored him as she enjoyed her meal. When he insisted, she told him he could go, but she wanted to continue with the reception.

Raila chose not to make a speech. But his wife did pointing out that her daughter's wedding to Amos was a uniting event, not only for the couple but for the former and current Presidents as well as many politically strange bed-fellows who were in spirited discussions. She wondered why Kenya could not always be like the situation at the wedding where there is no ethnic and religious divide.

Ida was right. Politically, Kenya was and is not as things were at the wedding. It will be interesting now to trace the basis for some of the divisions of today in Kenya from around the time of the birth of the bride's father.

Chapter 01

Genesis

A new beginning began at the beginning of an end. That end saw the dawn of a new era in the world. The World changed in 1945. The year saw the end of a devastating war, which had raged from 1939. The war had become more determined and vicious from January 1945 the year that saw the end of an era and the beginning of a post-war world.

Though the Allied powers' victory over Germany was not declared until 8 May, earlier in the year, from 4-11 February, President Franklin D. Roosevelt of the United States of America, Joseph Stalin of the Union of Soviet Socialist Republics (USSR) and Prime Minister Winston Churchill of Great Britain, met at the Livadia palace in Crimea on the Black Sea. This meeting, known as the Yalta Conference, was to consider the shape of the world after the war. Unfortunately, it also marked, the beginning of what was dubbed 'the cold war'. The pre-war mutual detest by the capitalist Western countries, (especially the United States) of the Communist USSR which had enveloped Eastern Europe at the end of the war, re-surfaced. This strong hatred became a very tense situation of undeclared war. There were a number of proxy wars in the Korean Peninsula, later in Vietnam and Afghanistan, as well as a search for friends among the new independent states of Africa and Asia. This aspect of the Cold War legacy was to mould politics and the lives of individuals in many countries in Africa.

However, the Allied victory at the end of World War II, meant the beginning of the return of many unsung African heroes, including Kenyans who had been conscripted to fight for "a free world." They would later play a role in raising appropriate questions in many parts of Africa about the purpose of the war they had fought in. And if they fought for the freedom of the world, they wondered why their own countries remained colonies.

These African fighters in the World War II also saw the relative weaknesses of he *Wazungu* (white people) at the war front and realized that there was nothing different (aside from skin colour), about these people as human beings. According to Professor Atieno-Odhiambo, many of the Kenyan Africans fought against the Italians in Ethiopia and the Japanese in Burma (now Myanmar); and some of these veterans like Bildad Kaggia and Paul Ngei later joined hands with other nationalists to quicken the pace of de-colonisation in Kenya.[1] The militancy of the veterans for nationalist struggle was, according to Eric Aseka, evident in the Forty-Group, most of whose members had served in World War II.[2] The militant struggle over the appropriation of the Kikuyu lands by white settlers, many politicians and scholars agree, set the stage for the struggle of the Kikuyus (the largest ethnic grouping in Kenya) to recover their lands which had been expropriated by the colonial occupiers of Kenya. That struggle was tagged by the colonial administration as the '*Mau Mau* uprising'. The *Mau Mau* revolt, in turn, speeded up the road towards decolonisation in Kenya.

In a different way, the end of the war contributed to the accumulation of resources to fight colonialism. Jaramogi Oginga Odinga, did not go to war but fought colonialism with his intellect. As part of his many-sided struggle for a just world, he had decided that economic freedom was essential for independence from colonialism. In 1944, he with others, had set up the Bondo Thrift Association. This savings-for-investment mechanism was originally confined to the Sakwa people of Nyanza who put aside 11 shillings every month. However, Oginga Odinga saw an opportunity for expansion at the end of the war in 1945.

Oginga Odinga opened membership of the savings association to other people not originally included, in order to, among others, attract the demobilization grants and compensation sums that returning veterans had received. He urged these veterans to develop a spirit of thrift, responsibility, hard-work and savings, by telling them to avoid buying useless things in the Indian shops but to invest in the Luo Thrift and Trading Corporation (the new name for the Bondo Thrift Association) which was opened to all East Africans. Though he chose Luo as a name for the Corporation to be sure of the commitment of his immediate ethnic group, he canvassed for membership beyond Kenya into Uganda and Tanganyika.

---

[1]   E.S. Atieno-Odhiambo, *Jaramogi Ajuma Oginga Odinga: A Biography,* (Nairobi: East African Publishers, n.d.).

[2]   Eric M. Aseka, *Mzee Jomo Kenyatta,* revised ed., (Nairobi: East African Educational Publisher 2001).

Thus, in 1947, with the support of Achieng' Oneko, (one of the foremost Kenyan nationalists who was eventually incarcerated with Kenyatta by the British) it was subsequently possible, among other things, to purchase and establish a press in Nairobi that printed *Ramogi*, (the name of the Luo mythical ancestor), a newspaper involved in raising consciousness about decolonisation. Later, as the printed word increasingly became part of the anti-colonialism fight, this press printed other African publications: *Agikikuyu* in Kikuyu; *Mwiatha* in Akamba; *Mulinavosi* in Maragoli; *Radioposta* in Swahili, published by W.W. Awori; and *Mwalimu* by Francis Khamisi. According to Oginga Odinga, there was no profit in printing these African weeklies. The effort was seen as a contribution towards African independence.

In spite of Oginga Odinga's struggles, he found time to be attracted to Mary Juma Ng'ong'a, the grand-daughter of late Chief Ng'ong'a, and the daughter of ex-Chief Odima. But in his book[3], he did not refer to Mary's blunt initial reaction to him. However, Wenwa Akinyi Odinga, in a manuscript, recounted Mary's salvo to Oginga Odinga: "I am afraid I cannot accept your proposal because first, you are short, and second, you have very unattractive teeth."

Nonetheless, Mary was later caught by the persistence of a man who was bluntly told off but kept coming back. As was customary with the Luo, Oginga Odinga turned over all negotiations with the ex-Chief Odima's family to his brother and other family members. Though he saved for the cattle for the marriage dowry, it was his brother and his family that paid the cows to the bride's family. The formal marriage took place on January 23, 1943. The first son, Oburu, from this wedlock was born in October of the same year when the father, on the basis of his assumed year of birth of 1911, was thirty-two years old.

The turbulent year, 1945, that marked the beginning of the cold war, had, on 7th January, witnessed the birth of a significant child, the second son of the union of Mary and Oginga Odinga. They were, both Luos – an ethnic group that is one of the largest primordial groups in Kenya. Since people do not choose their primordial affiliation, Raila Amolo Odinga (as Ng'ong'a Molo Oburu before him and later a

---

[3] Many historical accounts about Oginga Odinga in this volume are mainly from his seminal work. See, Oginga Odinga, *Not Yet Uhuru*, (Nairobi: East Africa Educational Publishers, 1967). Other primary sources have also been useful.

third son Ngire Omuodo Agola) was automatically first a Luo and then a Kenyan, in a territory that was at that time occupied by the British.

While he was a teacher at the Maseno School, in Kenya's Nyanza Province, Oginga Odinga, in defining his identity as a Luo, had rebelled against the use of Christian names. He had been baptized and given the Christian name, Adonijah. When he was at Makerere University, his friends had called him Oginga son of Odinga. So, he wanted to be known as Oginga Odinga and not Mr. Adonijah, as his white teaching colleagues at Maseno liked to call him.

He continued this struggle against foreign names with no meaning in Dholuo (the Luo language), in the naming of his three sons.[4] Their baptism was part of the de-colonisation of the mind. Oginga Odinga refused to give his three sons strange *Wazungu* (white people) names he could not identify with. Names have deep meanings for the Luos. Oginga Odinga preferred to adopt the names of Luo role models for his sons. But the officiating priest at the baptism, Rev. Simon Nyende would not have any of such names which he must have believed were unknown and undesirable to God. Oginga Odinga explained that he preferred Ng'ong'a as the baptismal name for his first son, because Ng'ong'a was a great chief in the country and was loved by his people. He went further to point out that he had never heard that the great chief had done anything that Christians found objectionable.

The name Rayila, (another way of writing Raila) which simply means "nettle sting," was given to his second son after Oginga Odinga's grandfather who had, according to Odinga in *Not Yet Uhuru*, "combined providence with frugality." He had been too poor to afford cattle for his marriage. So living within his means, he took a widow as a wife because a widow's dowry was reasonably less. He and his wife, tilled the soil to pay the dowry. But he was a visionary. His foresight was a major lesson for his children as they grew up.[5] He had craftily dug a hole where, he and his wife kept some food for the rainy day. Indeed, when there was a famine, poor

---

[4] The name of a child is important for the Luos. Names are given on the basis of time of birth, important events or after an important person. Many a time, there are two different names for the sexes. For details, see, Jane Achieng, *Paul Mboya's Luo Kitgi Gi Timbegi,*(Nairobi: Atai Joint Limited, n.d.), pp. 104-106.
[5] For more, see, Oginga Odinga, *Not Yet Uhuru, op. cit.* p. 5.

Rayila was able to maintain his family. Amolo and Odinga were two of Rayila's nine sons. For his second son, Oginga Odinga chose three names from his ancestry: those of his grandfather, his Uncle Amolo and his own father. Hence, the second son was named: Raila Amolo Odinga.[6]

When Rev. Nyende refused to officiate using such names, Mary Odinga stormed out of the church feeling humiliated before a large crowd. But Oginga stood firm. He wrote a protest note to Archdeacon Stanway wanting to know why his children could not be baptized with Luo names. Archdeacon Stanway referred the matter to the Bishop in Nairobi. Even when it was decided that nothing in the church constitution prevented the use of African names for baptism, no African priest was willing to officiate unless names of African Christians like Khama (Sir Seretse of Botswana) were used. Ironically, it took a *Mzungu* (singular for *Wazungu*) priest's benevolence to have the children baptized with Luo names.

Though Oginga Odinga was indifferent to whether he was a Christian or not, he knew there was more to the attempts by the *Mzungu* in trying to impose his culture through such methods as giving names that only had meanings to them. Such colonization was not a civilizing one but one on which its economic mission had been documented.[7]

The Material Basis of Colonization

E.A. Brett and Colin Leys,[8] among many others, showed that the colonization of Kenya was based on crass economics. According to Leys, the incorporation of Kenya into the world economy had started with the administration of Seyid Said at Zanzibar in the 1840s. This effort was restricted to the coastal areas and hence to a reasonable mixed population of Arabs and Swahili Kenyans. Prior to the time of Sultan Seyid Said, the coast of Kenya was not strange to Arabs, Persians and Indians, long before the Chinese (1414); and then the Portuguese who were followed by other European sailors in transit to India.

---

[6] The account on the names derives from Oginga Odinga, *Not Yet Uhuru,* op.cit., p. 5.

[7] A major source on this, is, Walter Rodney, *How Europe Underdeveloped Africa,* (London: Bogle L'Ouverture, 1972).

[8] See, E.A. Brett, *Colonialism and Underdevelopment in East Africa* (London: Heinemann, 1973) and Colin Leys, *Underdevelopment in Kenya* (Nairobi: East African Publishers Ltd., 1975).

A few Indians (who were later known generally in Kenyan terminology as Asians even after the separation of India and Pakistan and which terminology would include Bangladeshis and Sri Lankans) controlled trade and credit at the Kenyan coast. Before the eve of colonization, the Indians had moved into the interior as wholesale and retail traders. There was an Indian trader at Lake Baringo in 1885.[9]

These precursors were followed by some 32,000 Indian coolies who were brought to East Africa to work on the construction of the railways. They had a relative advantage over the Africans since India got railways earlier. Some 6,700 Indian coolies, opted to remain in Kenya on completion of their task.[10] They and their families together with further immigrants resulted in the Asian population growing from 98,000 in 1948 to 177,000 on the eve of independence in 1962. Their wealth from their control of Kenyan commerce also grew in leaps and bounds. By 1961, they reportedly controlled more than 67 per cent of all locally-owned industrial enterprises with fifty or more employees.[11]

But the arrival of the Asians in relatively larger numbers about the time of colonization was a sideshow. Oginga Odinga in *Not Yet Uhuru* provided an economic explanation of the imperative of Europeans to colonize Kenya. Britain had coveted Uganda as important for its lake system and the waters of the Nile and as a means of expansion to the north through Sudan to Egypt. In the scramble for Africa, Britain had given Uganda to chartered companies as a way of claiming ownership against other Europeans. But as the chartered companies were not keen on the holdings because of the cost, Britain made Uganda a protectorate in 1893. However Kenya remained under the administration of the Imperial British East African Company until 1907.

The commercial need for transportation resulted in the decision to build a railway system which extended to Nairobi in 1899 and to Kisumu in the area of the great African lake two years later. Kisumu was christened Port Florence. It was named after Florence Patterson, wife of the Railway Engineer who reportedly killed the

---

[9]   See, Colin Leys, *ibid.,* pp. 44-45

[10]   Smith Hempstone, *Rogue Ambassador: An African Memoir* (Sewanee: University of the South, 1997), p. 75.

[11]   For this and the population estimates, see, Colin Leys, *op. cit.,* pp. 44-45.

lions known as the man-eaters of Tsavo. The railway was built with loan funds. To pay back the British Treasury for providing access to the headwaters of the Nile and to fund the administration of the territory, the project had to be made productive. The answer was to encourage White settlements on several million acres of high-altitude land close to the railway. The real scramble for land began when Lord Delamere who was in East Africa on safari, received a free grant of 100,000 acres at Njoro.[12]

The settlers were expected to invest capital on the land they received or for which they paid negligible prices, with the aim of producing crops. The railway would transport the crops to Mombasa and, on the return journey, carry imported materials for consumption in the interior. The railway would, thus repay its construction costs.[13] But the colonial design had to go beyond repayment of the cost of building the railway. Since the settler production could only thrive with cheap African labour, policies were put in place that deprived Africans, rendered them vulnerable, and gave them no choice but to work on settler farms as migrant labourers in search of cash to pay all sorts of taxes. There were also restrictions on Africans planting certain crops like coffee.[14]

---

[12] Oginga Odinga, *Not Yet Uhuru*, (Nairobi: East Africa Educational Publishers, 1967), p. 17.
[13] See, Colin Leys, *op. cit.,* p. 28.
[14] See, *ibid.,* pp. 29-36 and Oginga Odinga, *op. cit.,* pp. 104-105.

Chapter 02
The Luo in Kenya

Shared ethnic identity and loyalty could be a basis for action in the political arena. This can be either in terms of how a group looks inward to find guidance for their reaction to or relationship with others or how they interpret the reactions of other groups to themselves. Such understanding of the logic of group action, in this case, the ethnic group, has been important in politics in Kenya, as is the case in many parts of the world, especially in Africa. A number of practices and cultural ways of life of the Luo have impacted on their political existence in Kenya. These include the issue of rites of passage from childhood to adulthood, and practices like chasing away evil spirits as part of burial rites.

The Luo Boundary

As was noted earlier, being a Luo was and still is, to have an identity. Dholuo was the only means of communication of this primordial group in a country of several languages. In 1945, their shared language, among other things, welded the Luos together, at that time, in a limited space. The Luos in Nyanza were limited to the West by the presence of a large lake that had formed part of the waters that added to the provision of life to Sudan and Egypt, the direction from which the Luos were said to have migrated into their present homeland. Thus, they are referred to as part of a generic grouping called Nilotics.

This lake, for some reason, was named after some English Queen Alexandrina Victoria who was born in 1819 and reigned in England from 1837 to 1901. The far away land called England was, at that time, a figment in the imagination of most Luos. This imagined land, however, was made real by the presence of a few white-men who insisted that they were in the service of some Royal Majesty who held sway over the United Kingdom of Great Britain and Ireland. Starting first with missionaries and later soldiers and traders, they installed officials who demanded obeisance to their laws, and the payment of taxes.

But the Luos' reported first contact with white-men was not too long ago. As Paul Mboya taught in his *Luo Kitgi Gi Timbegi*, written in 1938 in *Dholuo*, and translated into English by Jane Achieng, "the Europeans first came to Mumias in 1882 and Kisumu in 1896. They went to war with the people of Uyoma in 1899. They raided cattle near Karachuonyo in 1904. The government built Karungu in 1903. Kisii was built in April 1907. Karachuonyo, Mumbo and Kabondo were transferred from Kisumu district to Kisii district in June 1908. In January of that year, a Kisii slew Mr. Northcote and the Europeans went to war with the Kisiis. Missionaries came to Kaimosi in 1902, to Maseno in 1906 and to Gendia in 1906."

Even Rhoda Kwamboka Obachi, reportedly 107 years old when she talked to Joe Ombuor as reported in the *Daily Nation* of February 28, 2003, knew and remembered the first contact with the *Wazungu* in her neighbourhood now called Kisii. She said that they had thought the new people arriving on their land were "over-grown babies" as their skins were white like the skin colour of African babies which did not change and thus they looked like over-grown babies. Trying to be protective of these "over-grown babies," people put out fires, in order to prevent them being attracted into the fires and getting burnt as infants tended to do. But not only did these *Wazungu* have Nubian porters that carried their loads to Getare (later called Kisii), they also had objects that, according to her, spat fire, or as the Luos thought, harboured thunder. According to Kwamboka Obachi, a young warrior, Otenyo, decided to prod one of the "over-grown babies" with his spear and thereby killed him on the spot. Maybe this was Mr. Northcote that Paul Mboya wrote about. Of course, the object that harboured thunder roared and floored Otenyo who also died on the spot.

So, if the Europeans only reached the great African lake with the arrival of John Speke in 1858, and the great African lake had always existed before his arrival, how dared Speke and his ilk claim he discovered a lake that the Luos called *Lolwe* or *Sango*, but was more popularly known by its Bantu name of Nyanza, and in which the Luos had fished for centuries after they settled on its plains? Similar half-truths had it that David Livingstone made a "discovery of the River Niger." Henry Stanley, who sought to name everything around the great Congo River after himself, repeated the same false claims about the Congo River. Richard Burton who was with John Speke on the 1857-59 expedition and was actually the leader, in his account acknowledged the name of the lake that his friend 'discovered' as Nyanza. He mentioned having heard about the lake. If he heard about Nyanza earlier on, then other people had told both of them about it. This being so, why should popularising an African great lake or an African great river, to the limited world of the Europeans, be called 'a discovery' as if all the Africans who had lived beside these waters, had been animals without consciousness of the existence of these waters or their environment generally?

And what gave the white men the audacity to change the name of the African lake and name it after one of their own? Did Victoria create the lake like Gamel Abdel Nasser [the revolutionary Egyptian leader] did with respect to Lake Nasser in Egypt, in order to have it named after her? And if the *Wazungu* named the lake after one of their own, why have the Luos and others in Kenya, Uganda and Tanzania agreed to continue to call it such a name? Questions like these must have bothered the critical mind of Oginga Odinga. Just as he had refused to give his three sons *Wazungu* names that had no meaning, in the immediate post war period, as he stated in *Not Yet Uhuru¹,* he also stopped calling the lake by a *Mzungu* name. He instead, restored its original name: lake Nyanza. Such is the legacy of a critical mind that Raila acquired from Oginga Odinga.

This great African lake, which had its name restored in writing by Oginga Odinga, separated the Luos from present day Uganda. In the South, the Luos shared borders with the Maasai, and what was once Tanganyika and is now Tanzania as a result of a re-birth after its union with Zanzibar. Other Kenyans like the Kuria, Kisii, Kipsigis, and the Abaluhya bound the Luo in the East and the North.

Some Aspects of Being a Luo²

There are many aspects to being a Luo whether in Kenya, Uganda or Tanzania. The Luo traditional organization of communities; their arrangements for law and order including for the breakdown of order and for war; their food; their child bearing and nurture; and their burial rites, have fascinated many Kenyans and international observers. David Parkin, for instance studied the Luos' culture to make sense of their political behaviour.³ Wambui Kimathi noted: "The Luo identity has largely been shaped by shared values born of a rich range of cultural

---

¹ Oginga Odinga, *op. cit.*

² Much of the write-up below depended on readings from a number of books and exchanges with many Luos and especially an interview with Raila on February 29, 2004.

³ See, David Parkin, *The Cultural Definition of Political Response: Lineal Destiny Among the Luo,* (New York: Academic Press Inc., 1978).

practices and activities. These provide them with unique social interactions such
as burial rituals that allow for prolonged periods of community mourning, an
outspokenness that keeps the community at the leadership of most labour unions,
and love for fun (music and football). Their linguistic uniqueness (unlike the Kikuyu
whose language is easily understood by the Embu, Meru and Kamba or the Luhya,
who have a number of different dialects) makes them more cohesive when one
considers the 'close relationship between a common language and effective political
community' ."[4]

Circumcision as a Rite of Passage

The rite of passage from adolescence into adulthood used to be important in
Kenya, as was the case in many an African setting. The rite of passage for all but
three of the 42 communities that make up Kenya, used to be in the form of
circumcision of age sets in the early teens. The exercise of removing the foreskin
of a man and the female genital cutting in women, signalled adulthood. Not to go
through the rite of passage is to be seen as still a child.

The Kikuyu referred to people who had not gone through the rites as a *kihii,* that
is, an uninitiated juvenile. Jomo Kenyatta made great play of the importance of
circumcision for both Kikuyu men and women. An uncircumcised man did not
get the status of a citizen with the rights of participation in decision-making for
society.[5]

However, the Luo, the Tesso and the Turkana, in cultural harmony with most of
the ethnic communities in Uganda, did not circumcise their men and women.

For the Luo, their rite of passage to adulthood, involved the removal of six frontal
lower teeth of adolescent males and females. The reason for doing this was to
test the courage and the endurance of the child through its ability to withstand

[4] Wambui Kimathi, "A Strategic Seclusion – Yet Again! The 1997 General Elections in Luo
Nyanza," in Marcel Rutten, Alamin Mazrui & Francois Grignon, *Out for the Count: The 1997
General Elections and Prospects for Democracy in Kenya,* (Kampala: Fountain Publishers, 2001), p. 498.
[5] For a detailed treatment of this issue that may be indicative on Kenyatta's ethnocentric mind-
set on his Vice-President Jaramogi Oginga Odinga much later in life, see, Jomo Kenyatta, *Facing
Mount Kenya,* (Nairobi: Kenway Publications, 1978), pp. 130-154.

pain. No kind of anaesthesia or pain suppressant was applied as one tooth after another was pulled out with instruments that predated the pliers.

For the male adolescent, being able to go through the process without clinging to or touching the man carrying out the operation, tested endurance. Each touch during the process amounted to an act of cowardice that was punished by a penalty of a hen to be handed over by the mother of the *coward*. To cost a mother many hen penalties was frowned upon, as the mother would then say: "I did not know I gave birth to a coward." Young girls were not so penalized. The stereotype was applied in this aspect of Luo culture, as women were not tested on courage and bravery which were regarded as the province of men.[6]

The Luos also found good use for the removal of the six frontal lower teeth. In situations when people suffered from the lockjaw form of tetanus, where the jaws become rigidly closed, they used the gap to gain access for curative medicine through the mouth.

However, in a society like Kenya, where Luos are a minority in not undertaking circumcision by cutting off the foreskin of the male sex organ, the ritual, has been exploited as a political issue. Jomo Kenyatta, the first President of Kenya would use this cultural issue to his political advantage when, in the little General Elections of 1966, he whipped up the sentiment of his people against the party of his former Vice-President, Oginga Odinga.[7] He had ridiculed Bildad Kaggia, a foremost nationalist who spent time in incarceration with him, as a traitor to the Kikuyu cause for trying to hand over power to a *kihii*. This struck a positive political cord among the Kikuyu, who continued in the same spirit in the first multi-party elections of 1992 when Kiraitu Murungi and Gitobu Imanyara, both young Meru politicians, were ridiculed for associating with Oginga Odinga, a *kihii*. Even during the referendum campaign on a new constitution for Kenya in October-November 2005, one of the foremost politicians, Simeon Nyachae, saw it fit to return to the same theme in arguing against Raila's possibilities as a leader.

Of course, as an anthropologist, Jomo Kenyatta knew that most peoples in the world did not cut the foreskin of their male adolescents. He knew that next door

---

[6]   This rite of passage started dying off among the Luos about sixty years ago.
[7]   This issue will be elaborated on later in the book.

in Uganda; most of the communities did not circumcise their men. But it was to his political advantage to use a cultural issue with no bearing on the quality of governance, to denigrate a large number of people in the country he led. But then, exploiting cultural differences at the political arena, for the purpose of hanging on to power, was not unique to Jomo Kenyatta or to Kenya. After all, colonization itself had disguised material exploitation as a cultural issue in terms of giving civilization. In effect, culture, very often, plays an important role in political behaviour.

Burial rites

Burial rites are important in many cultures in Africa. The Luos are no exception. They undertake different burial procedures for people depending on the circumstances of the death and the social standing of the dead person.[8] However, it is important to note that the burial of a person is a community affair. In this respect, the burial rites of the Luo have been seen as yet another cultural attribute with political significance.

Communal mourning and elaborate arrangements for burial in which different relations from far and wide, (including relations through marriage) participate, are avenues for social interaction. These interactions renew bonds of kinship among the Luo. The pre-burial ceremony called *teroburu*, separates a community from its enemies. *Tero*, when translated into English means "take" while *buru* literally means "dust" even though in this instance, it could also mean "evil spirit." In effect, *teroburu* is the act of taking or chasing the evil spirit away to the land of the enemy.

The Luos believed that evil spirits were responsible for deaths. Before the burial of the dead, the evil spirits had to be chased away so that the soul of the dead could rest in peace. This chasing away involved young men in the community, running with cattle as far as the neighbour's boundary. Thus, they concluded that the evil spirits had been chased to the enemy's territory. At times, the young men were engaged in battle by the enemy side. According to Paul Mboya:

---

[8]   See, Jane Achieng, *Paul Mboya's Luo Kitgi Gi Timbegi,*(Nairobi: Atai Joint Limited, n.d.), pp. 100, 107-125.

"When those people involved in the pre-burial ceremony returned home, they came back either jubilantly singing ritual songs, or carrying the bodies of their people killed by the enemy. This time, everybody wept."[9]

The community feeling of the Luo was successfully exploited by Oginga Odinga as he provided a leadership that joined others in the struggle to free Kenya from the colonial yoke.

Wife Inheritance

Though Raila, to date, is monogamous, polygamy is a common practice among the Luos. However, his brother, Oburu, with two wives, conformed to the practice among Luo men, by choosing to marry another wife. For many Luo men, however, a second or many more wives, result from inheritance.

The death of a family member constituted one of the modes of wife acquisition. A young wife, for whom dowry had been paid, belonged to the community at the death of the person who had married her. After the mourning period, the woman was given the opportunity to decide the person amongst her in-laws, she would like to continue to live with. If the woman had children, the Luos believed that the presence of a father figure was essential for good upbringing. Then there were functions like bush clearing that required a male effort. So, the Luos figured out that it was a man's responsibility to take care of the widow of the deceased. Apart from clearing the bush for her to plough, he also provided the inherited wife with protein from his hunting and fishing expeditions. He played the major role in negotiations with prospective in-laws when the children of the deceased were to be married, and served as caretaker of the deceased's estate which was divided among the children.

The inheriting in-law would normally be younger than the deceased husband. But a marriage from wife inheritance was not an irrevocable relationship. If the woman felt mistreated, she could easily approach the Elders in the community and seek an annulment of the earlier marriage and the choice of a different in-law.

---

[9] *Ibid.,* p. 107.

A woman who had reached menopause could be inherited. There might be no sex in this situation as the man only assumed responsibility in order to discharge obligations expected of a man of the household. A bunch of tobacco was given to the woman as a symbol that the giver had inherited her.

Today, the practice of wife inheritance is being opposed by many advocacy groups as a way of reducing the incidence of HIV/AIDS among the Luos. Both Raila and his father's foundation, (Jaramogi Oginga Odinga Foundation), have been involved in such advocacy by asking people to be concerned about the cause of death before rushing to inherit. Before inheritance takes place, couples are being encouraged to undertake a HIV/AIDS test to show if either of the parties is HIV positive. In such a situation, symbolic inheritance still allows a family to discharge the functions a wife needs to operate in society. Such a caring arrangement also prevents the ostracizing of an HIV positive wife.

Wife Replacement

In some circumstances it is normal, among the Luos, for a man to marry the sister of his wife. If a woman could not bear a child after marriage, her parents might give a sister in marriage to the husband. The concept of *sister* here could mean siblings or cousins. Rather than have the husband take the initiative by marrying another woman from a different community in search of children, the younger sister would come in as a co-wife, with the parents' blessing. The first child by the new wife would automatically be adopted by the elder sister. This Luo adoption arrangement tended to be harmonious.

Similarly, when a wife died and left children, her family provided another daughter to take the place of her deceased elder sister. The rationale behind this was that it would be better to have a blood relation care for the children instead of a total stranger who might not have any love for the children. A woman, in a case where her husband was sterile, would be privately allowed, with the knowledge of her mother-in-law, to approach a brother or cousin of her husband, for assistance towards conception.

The Luos, as an ethnic group in Kenya, have over time forged a common feeling of community. This feeling is continuously reinforced by many cultural practices they continue to hold on to. Such cultural bonds could, to some extent, explain the tendency of the Luos to act almost in unison on political issues.

The Luos, though very ubiquitous, in that they easily settled in many parts of East Africa, tended to continue to be wedded to their communities of origin. This sense of community among the Luos, transcends socio-cultural needs into the political arena. The Luos, unlike most other communities in Kenya, have tended to exercise the right to vote along the same party line under the multi-party system in Kenya. But a few do dissent and make a foray into other parties.

Raila Odinga, at the beginning of his life was limited in horizon by language, and in part by a vast body of water vis-à-vis other peoples next to his own Luo land. Though a few people like his own father and Nehemiah Oyoo – the father of Ida Betty Oyoo who later became Raila's wife - had gone to Maseno School and started using English, the language of the far away and imagined land, very few Luos and their neighbours used this foreign language. Kiswahili, which was to become a major inter-group language of communication in East Africa, was a language of the market in places far away from the vicinity of the Luo, and was being used at the Kenyan Coast and in the cities. However, Raila, in Kaloleni estate and at school in Kisumu, had the advantage of learning Kiswahili as he played with children from the Swahili, Luhya, Arabs, Nubians and Kumams from Uganda and Isahakias originally from Somalia.

But then, the Gikuyu (Kikuyu), the largest ethnic group in Kenya, were remote from the world of the Luos. Their languages were, and remain, as far apart, as English is to Chinese. Modern day means of communication were largely non-existent. Transportation was rudimentary as it was on footpaths and the few rough roads available to the equally few bicycles, carts and other vehicles.

But whatever limitations were placed on Raila as a result of Kenya's circumstances at the time of his birth, were drastically ameliorated when the situation of his birth is considered. When he was born, his father, had started giving momentum to the mobilization of his brethren for a new type of politics from far beyond the Luo environs. Oginga Odinga had joined the select group of a few Africans who went to Makerere University, which was then the fountain of knowledge in East Africa.

Raila's Political Training

At a very early age, as Raila, the child, was developing, he could see the tremendous organizing and mobilizing capacity of an astute politician; and the emergence of his father as a pre-eminent Luo leader beyond the limited Luo world. He saw the passion and dedication with which his father fought against social injustice. It was in the mid to late fifties period that Raila's father earned the name Jaramogi, which derived from the name of the legendary mythical ancestor of the Luos, Ramogi Ajwang'. This name signified that Oginga Odinga was following the example of the Luos' ancestral father or simply put, that he was Ramogi's man.

Ramogi's man had gone beyond the ways of his people to acquire knowledge of the ways of the *Wazungu*. This knowledge had shown him that the way the world had been organized by the *Wazungu* from far away lands, required him to aspire to a type of leadership that was far outside the largest geopolitical chiefdom of the Luos called *piny* or literally, the Luos' concept of the world. Oginga was not aspiring to being a *ruoth,* the traditional chief of a *piny.*[1] He aimed higher. His children had an early start in such new ways of doing things.

But not all his children were interested in this new life-style. Wenwa Akinyi the fourth child of Oginga Odinga, in spite of her pedigree, was not interested in politics.[2] As a child, she was deprived of privacy in her home. As early as 5 a.m., people would start arriving at their homestead to see Jaramogi. This would continue for the whole day. So it was impossible to ask Jaramogi anything private because of all the visitors who were with him. Even to ask for money for private female needs had to be done in the presence of these people. She also had to join in cooking and catering for these large numbers of people. She did not want this type of life as an adult.

In addition, she saw the tribulations of Jaramogi at close range. He was under house arrest, then in detention, then house arrest again. His transport business collapsed as, according to Wenwa, he was being witch-hunted. Then auctioneers came for the house etc. All these matters, for Wenwa, were unpleasant and she clearly did not want to be part of a profession that brought such experiences.

---

[1]   For additional details, see, Jane Achieng, *Paul Mboya's Luo Kitgi Gi Timbegi,* (Nairobi: Atai Joint Limited, n.d.), p. 1.

[2]   These accounts on her early years and Raila's derived from an interview with her on April 10, 2003.

However, for her brother Raila, who was six and a half years older, politics appeared to have been his second nature.[3] Even as a child, he displayed leadership qualities. If his siblings wanted something, they went to him. Raila could present their respective wishes to their father.

Both Oburu[4] and Wenwa attested to the fact that Raila, at an early age, was a stickler for news. Raila's desire for news, as a child, had been influenced by Jaramogi who bought his children a radio when they were in Standard 2. He encouraged them to listen to the news. Raila carried this too far. He would leave any function including school, to listen to the news. Oburu vividly remembered an incident when their primary school headmaster, Mr. Hezekiah Ougo Ochieng, who later became Member of Parliament for Bondo, asked why Raila had been absent from games on the previous evening. He answered that he had gone to listen to the news. The headmaster who then gave the boy a smacking, thought Raila's behaviour was wrong. He had independently set his own priorities without caring that he was in violation of the school rules.

Wenwa recollected that there were times when their mother would send Raila on an errand just before the news. Whenever this happened, it was horrors for her as a young six year old. Raila would order her to sit in front of the radio, listen to the news and relay to him whatever was said, when he returned. With the mind of a child, Wenwa only remembered some of the advertisements and nothing about the news. The soft delivery of advertisements she could cope with, but she could not understand the complexities of the news stories. This normally got Wenwa a beating if Raila returned and she told him that nothing was said in the news.

Raila had always been very quick to understand issues. As Wenwa puts it: "As you explained problems to him, he already understood where your story would end.

---

[3] Though Raila had wanted to run for the Langata seat in 1974 but was persuaded to leave the seat for Maurice Omwony who had just returned from a stint at the International Monetary Fund, it is noteworthy that contrary to the general impression, Oburu Oginga became a practicing politician before Raila. He contested as Councillor for Kisumu East (then Stadium) Ward and won with a landslide in the 1974 General Elections and barely lost being the Deputy Mayor. He completed his term before joining the Ministry of Planning as a Civil Servant, in 1979 where he remained until he ran for Jaramogi's Parliamentary seat in Bondo, upon the death of Jaramogi in 1994.

[4] Interview with Oburu Oginga, September 2, 2003.

This tended to make him impatient with the narrator. If he listened to the end of the story, it was because he was concerned about the narrator's feelings and was pretending to be attentive."[5] Wenwa remembered that she once travelled from her workplace in Nakuru to take a complaint to Jaramogi on behalf of people who felt uncomfortable with one of Raila's character traits, impatience. These people had started seeing in Raila, the same qualities of Jaramogi, as a young man. They were convinced that he would be his father's successor, and wanted to offer advice on how he could improve his attitude.

For example, like Jaramogi, Raila is an early riser. Jaramogi's day started at 3:30 a.m. when his tea was taken to him. Thereafter, he began to read. Thus, when his visitors, who had walked from long distances, arrived to see him, he was already awake. Whenever he was to travel to Nairobi, he left Kisumu at 3:30 a.m., joined Wenwa for breakfast in Nakuru at 6 am, and arrived in Nairobi as workers were resuming about 8 a.m. Raila is the same and works extremely hard, spending little time sleeping. He normally sleeps late and by 6:00 a.m., is at the gym, not far from the city-centre, having travelled the twenty five minute drive from his former residence in Runda.

Raila's courage, another of Jaramogi's traits, was visible when he was a child. Wenwa recalled that Raila was the only one among them who could stand up to Jaramogi. She recalled that her father was like a slave driver. He would insist every so often that everyone planted and watered trees on the homestead. One day, when this ritual was underway, everyone was present except Raila. When Jaramogi learnt that Raila had remained in bed, he stormed to him and demanded to know why he was not at the tree planting. Raila responded that he was not a slave, that the assignment was too tough, and that Jaramogi did not know how tough, because he was not participating. Jaramogi floored him and started jumping on him with his gumboots. Raila refused to cry as he took the beatings and kicks, and it was only Mary's cries that saved the situation between father and son. Raila, when necessary, always protested without fear.

Oburu and Raila had a head start in politics at the highest levels. As Oginga Odinga campaigned to realize a Luo Union and sought investors for the Luo Thrift and Trading Company, he had to travel all over Kenya and East Africa. On

---

[5] Interview, Nairobi, April 10, 2003.

these trips, either Oburu or Raila accompanied him. They met important people and listened as their dad articulated Luo interests.

Oginga Odinga, proud of the achievement of completing the Ramogi House in 1950, had invited the Colonial Governor to grace the opening ceremony. The colonial system had placed several impediments in the path of Africans to building in the centre of Kisumu which was reserved for Europeans and Asians. The overt rationale was that Africans could not own standard buildings that could befit such an environment. When the Governor would not accept his invitation, Oginga Odinga invited the Indian High Commissioner to Kenya, who presided over the ceremony and in turn, extended an invitation from the Indian Government to visit India.

He took advantage of the invitiation and travelled to India in 1952. He wrote a book, *"Dweche Ariyo e India"* on his experience. The title, of the book, which was translated from Dholuo into English by a strong Asian supporter of Jaramogi, Ambubhai Patel, was: *Two Months in India*. Oburu and Raila were keen to know what their father had written. So, they learned about Mahatma Gandhi, Jawaharlal Nehru, as well as other Indian nationalists, and the story of their struggle for freedom from British colonialism.

Later, in 1959, Indira Gandhi, deepened the knowledge of Oburu and Raila when she visited Oginga Odinga, who had by then become a member of the legislature. The position of their father, made them take an interest in the African elected members of the legislature, and what they were saying there. They met some of them in person. The first opportunity was at the end of the first Legislative Council session when Jaramogi invited a number of these leaders to Kisumu to address a huge meeting in his constituency to brief his people. It was at this meeting that he used metaphors to describe some of his colleagues in the Legislative Council. Masinde Muliro he tagged 'a sailing boat' whose destination was difficult for the white settlers to assess. Ronald Ngala from the Coast he saw as 'a young hippo', who secretly measured his footprints on that of his father, and when he realized that he had achieved equality, challenged his father to a duel. Tom Mboya, the Labour Union activist he tagged 'a rabid black dog' that barked furiously, biting all in his path. Lawrence Oguda, on the other hand, he saw as 'a black dog' that seldom barked but bit dangerously. Bernard Mate was tagged 'the philosopher' as Daniel arap Moi was described as 'the giraffe that saw from far.'[6]

Another opportunity arose in 1958 when Jaramogi invited Alan Lennox-Boyd, the British Colonial Secretary to Bondo. Aside from political speeches, this occasion was also a display of Luo culture by way of music. *Orutu,* a one string African violin was used in the entertainment. The women, in a separate effort to that of the boys, sang *ohangla* as they danced in circles shaking their instruments. The girls sang and danced to the *bodi* a round steel ring on a drum which produced an interesting mix of steel and drum sounds when hit. Of course, the ubiquitous one-man band that played at beer parties, provided the *dodo* music. The Luo trumpeter was also there with his *abu,* the long round gourd which is blown at one end.

Then in 1959, Jaramogi brought Humphrey Slade, the Speaker of the Legislative Assembly to Kisumu. Oburu and Raila were not only excited to see Humphrey Slade introduced to Luo culture through food and attire; they learned new political words in English as they listened to Slade, and then heard Ojino Okew, Oginga Odinga's Personal Assistant, translate Slade's speech.[7]

Motherly Grooming

Raila's being has, most of the time, been understood in terms of the impact of Jaramogi Odinga on his life. But as Wenwa rightly noted, he was also a product of Mary Odinga. His down-to-earth lifestyle was due to Mary's influence. She brought up her three older sons to cook, clean and care for their younger siblings. According to Oburu, Mary believed that her sons must be trained all round. She refused to treat them literally as kings as many male children were treated vis-à-vis their female siblings who carried out all household chores. She would deliberately call the boys her daughters and at times her sons.

The responsibility for cooking was shared among the three boys. If Raila cooked the stew, Oburu cooked the Ugali (maize meal made into a hard mash), and Agola

---

[6] Oginga Odinga, *Not Yet Uhuru,* (Nairobi: East Africa Educational Publishers, 1967), p. 145.
[7] Much of the account here benefited from the recollections of Oburu Oginga in an interview in Nairobi on September 2, 2003.

washed the dishes. But Oburu and Agola never liked the idea of Raila cooking the main dish as he liked his food hot and spicy which they did not. When Raila cooked the main dish, the other two boys shed tears as they ate, while Raila laughed. They preferred him to cook the Ugali.

The children often trekked six kilometres to buy ground maize for Ugali. This discipline was to help the boys later in life. As Oburu stated: "In Germany, whenever I visited Raila or he visited me in Russia, we cooked. Before marriage we did not depend on house helps."[8] Mary's children also did the gardening and worked on the farm from their early days. They were taught how to plough using hoes as well as modern implements. They also knew how to harvest and preserve maize.

Mary Odinga's bluntness was noted earlier over Oginga Odinga's proposal of a love relationship. This quality of Mary's was also attested to by Ida Betty Odinga, Raila's wife who stated: "She had a strong personality. The people in her village respected her. She was not the type that would say 'may be' or 'perhaps.' She was point blank even if it hurts."[9]

Mary's bluntness was to rub off on Raila. As a child, he never hesitated to tell things as they were. This trait was to continue into his life as a politician. One of his colleagues, Otieno Kajwang', the MP for Mbita Constituency noted: "Sometimes, I think he is too honest for a politician. He puts his cards on the table and keeps his side of the bargain. He is most unsuspecting and has been horrified that people he thought were his friends, could turn against him."[10]

Mary reportedly had a hot temper like Jaramogi. Even Oginga Odinga made this point about himself and his wife in *Not Yet Uhuru*. As he puts it: "Like me, she is hot-tempered, though her temper cools fast."[11] Corroborating Oginga Odinga, both Wenwa and Fidel Odinga, Raila's first child, attested to her being able to spank a child and immediately turn around and be very loving. As Fidel puts it: "Grandmother was a very harsh lady, a disciplinarian of some sort. But she was

---

[8] *Ibid.*
[9] Interview, Nairobi, June 4, 2003
[10] Interview, Nairobi, April 11, 2003
[11] Oginga Odinga, *op. cit.,* pp. 53-54.

harsh and loving."[12]   Wenwa noted that this attribute of blowing up fast and cooling down equally fast, runs in both sides of her family, that is, Jaramogi and Mary shared this attribute. And like Mary, most people around Raila agree that he is hot tempered. But his rage is normally followed immediately by a rapid cooling process.

Wenwa, in her unpublished manuscript, recounts an instance illustrating the temper and rage as well as the quick cooling aspects of Raila, especially in his pre-detention time. She noted that Raila used to be a fast and reckless driver, but none of his passengers dared to criticize his driving. One evening, when Beryl, another sister, and Oburu were driving with Raila on Ngong Road, Nairobi, they forgot the unwritten rule and criticized Raila's driving. He stopped the car, left Beryl and Oburu in it and walked away. Oburu, a learner driver who had just returned from his studies in Europe, had to use the first gear to drive the car at snail speed to Raila's house where they were staying. They were surprised when they got to Raila's house and found "a sheepish looking Raila already in bed speaking normally as if nothing had happened."[13] This attribute, for Wenwa, could explain why Raila found it easy to work with former President Daniel arap Moi in spite of what he went through during the Moi repressive years.

Mary was not one who would be afraid to take anyone on when she felt wronged. She was going on a journey and approached the Headmaster of Maranda School, Mariko Otombo and sought permission for Oburu and Raila to stay home to look after their siblings, (Wenwa and Achieng) while she travelled for a day.[14] The Headmaster granted the request. But on the first day at school after her return, the same Headmaster, who had given permission, caned Oburu and Raila for being absent. Raila, as a non-conformist, took exception to the teachers' instructions that pupils must thank them with a salute after being spanked. So, on this occasion, Raila neither saluted nor said, "thank you, Sir!" Oburu complied and did what was expected of him. Raila got another round of beatings and still refused. He received the third round of beatings and again refused to oblige with the expected ritual but instead walked out, saying he should not be beaten for nothing, and went home. Oburu remained in school.[15]

---

[12] Interview, Nairobi, April 8, 2003

[13] Interview, Nairobi, April 10, 2003

[14] This story was told in Wenwa's unpublished manuscript.

[15] Interview with Oburu Oginga, September 2, 2003.

When Mary learnt of the punishment, she took off on her bicycle the following day to the school and openly challenged the Headmaster to a duel in front of the pupils. Of course, the Headmaster did not accept the challenge, but he was shamed in front of his pupils, as one who was afraid of being beaten by a woman. Just like Mary, Raila is not known to run away from a fight. He may bide his time, but he does not accept being trampled on.

Mary also had a natural flare to pull people around her. In spite of her short temper, many people wanted to be with her. Even when she told some women off in the village as a result of her temper, they still waited for her to cool down. She was a leader. Many a time, when Jaramogi was away from the homestead, Mary held fort and received all visitors without any feeling of the absence of Jaramogi. She was, according to her children and grandchildren, a very kind woman. Wenwa, for instance, pointed out how Mary would give out all the food in the house to visitors, and subsequently go to bed without eating.

Raila, like Mary, was constantly described by siblings, offsprings, subordinates and colleagues, as being extremely kind and generous. For example, Linda Ochiel who once worked as Raila's Media Assistant, claimed that she had never seen someone who cared so much about other people. Fidel says that: "He rarely turns down people who come to him for assistance. He is supportive of so many people. He is very generous." Wenwa said that Raila is "somebody whose support you can rely on when you need it. He is very sympathetic."[16]

On Raila's decision-making style, many of the people interviewed for this book emphasized the fact that he is a voracious reader on many subjects. His decisions tend to be influenced by knowledge drawn from far and wide. As the 2002 general elections drew near, a dialogue with Raila on the rigging of elections, took him from Mexico to South Africa and beyond, to learn about means of responding to different types of poll rigging.[17] Raila reads widely while researching issues he needs to decide on. Some of the research that has informed his decisions, also came from Think Tanks.

---

[16] Interview, Nairobi, April 10 2003.
[17] An informal breakfast chat with Raila on Sunday, October 20, 2002

More importantly, however, is the fact that he consults a lot. Willis Leah Gondi, a Nairobi physician who, at times, took care of Raila's health, stressed that Raila normally criss-crossed the country to consult the youth and the elders on major issues, before he took a position. Wenwa noted that Raila is close to the Luo Council of Elders and constantly consults them. In addition, when in the country, he makes sure that he goes to the University of Nairobi Academic Staff Club, as a former member, at least once in a week to listen to the views of the "eggheads" from all over Kenya on national issues.

Elementary Education

Jaramogi Oginga Odinga did not need to be preached to on the importance of having his children go to school. Raila initially attended Kisumu Union Primary School. Then from 1955-62 he was at the Maranda School, (which his father had attended), to complete his primary and intermediate education. According to Raila, Jaramogi had moved him and Oburu out of Kisumu to make them learn the ways of their people in a rural setting.

However, this transfer was traumatic for Raila. First was the dramatic change of environment. Maranda School was three miles from his home so Oburu and Raila had a forced exercise of six miles each day. Initially since both parents remained in Kisumu, Raila and his brother had to live with uncles and aunts.

More disappointing, however, was the fact that the new school decided that Oburu and Raila would start in a class three years behind their level of attainment in Kisumu. Raila could not understand this. He saw that the children in the rural school were much older and heftier than he and his brother, but could not understand why they should be punished because those older pupils had not started school sooner. He could not understand why his father did not interfere with the school's decision. But then, he remembered that they had to cross a stream to get to school, and sometimes, he and Oburu who were comparative tiny-tots, had to depend on the older kids to carry them across. Two of his classmates, were Edwin Otieno Aliwa, now a Quantity Surveyor and Ogendi Odero, now a retired teacher.

The teachers were strict with Oburu and Raila who saw this as revenge by the teachers for Oginga Odinga's strictness, when he had taught many of them. If they were five minutes late, the teachers would not accept the argument that they had to wait at the stream until they could be carried across. The path to school, was also muddy. Though their lateness was due to nature, Oburu and Raila, like other children, were punished by having to cut grass.

Oburu said that Raila was usually first in his class; and Raila remembered being punished because he once came third in his set. The teacher saw this as encouragement for Raila to excel.

Life in rural Bondo was harsh. The chores were many. They had to draw water for household use from the river. They fetched firewood, which provided the fuel for cooking. They tended the garden and were made to look after cattle, goats and sheep. During the planting season, they were deployed, with other children, to take turns in watching over newly planted maize. Squirrels, if unchecked, dug out the maize seedlings and ate them. As the maize grew, they had to stop rabbits from eating up the new plants. And at maturity, if care was not taken , monkeys would eat the maize cobs.

In effect, maize, a staple food, had to be protected throughout the day. They also had a share of night watch to protect the maize from pigs which normally dug up anything, in search of food. They rung bells or beat drums, to scare the hogs away from farms. As tiny kids, Raila and Oburu did not undertake their chores separately. As they worked together, a strong bond grew between them.

During the school holidays, Oginga Odinga sent the duo to the homes of Luo Elders. He wanted Oburu and Raila to learn Luo history and culture in the footsteps of these elders including Joel Omer who became the Luo *Ker* (patron) after Jaramogi; John Paul Olola, one of the pioneers of the independence movement in Luoland; and Paul Mboya, a foremost source of written accounts on Luo culture.

The Journey to Higher Education

What would ordinarily have been a simple act of going to school, where a scholarship for a quality education was available was later read within the cold war legacy. Oginga Odinga had narrated how he had used his visits to the socialist countries in 1960 to solicit and receive many scholarships for Kenyan students to compensate for what he described as the retarded education facilities in Kenya.[18] These scholarships to the Soviet Union, Yugoslavia, North Korea, Bulgaria, Czechoslovakia, Hungary, and the German Democratic Republic, resulted in an airlift that produced over a thousand Kenyans highly skilled in Medicine, Engineering and the Sciences. As part of that movement of Kenyan students to the Eastern bloc, Raila, at age 16, went to the German Democratic Republic. These scholarships were different from those sourced from the United States by Tom Mboya, a younger politician from the same ethnic stock as Jaramogi, who subsequently became Jaramogi's avid competitor.

Raila's father, on his return from his visits "behind the iron curtain" in 1960, had his passport seized and all his belongings impounded at the airport. According to Raila, Oginga Odinga had to rely on two passports: one from Kwame Nkrumah and the other from Gamel Abdel Nasser for his travels in those days.[19] To keep Kenya within its own sphere of influence, and more importantly to protect British capital in Kenya, the colonial government clearly wanted to prevent any contact between Kenyans and the socialist countries, which at that time was seen as going behind the iron curtain.

Even before Oginga Odinga had his passport impounded, in 1959 the colonial authorities had prevented three Kenyan youths: Odhiambo Okello, Wera Ambitho and Abdulla Karungo Kinyairo from sailing from Mombasa to Europe. Okello and Ambitho had scholarships to study in Italy. The three determined young men smuggled themselves out of Kenya and for three months travelled through Uganda to Khartoum, Sudan. In Sudan, they tried to open a Kenyan office to publicize the socialist countries and the anti-colonial struggle in Kenya and the rest of Africa. The failure to achieve this in Sudan saw the young Kenyans continue to Cairo to the warm embrace of Gamel Abdel Nasser, who had earlier welcomed three other Kenyans on the same route in their search for education. Odhiambo Okello and his colleagues went on to open Kenya's Cairo office. Another Kenyan, Othigo Otieno, who had reached Britain to study, strayed from that goal, and opened Kenya's London office. These two offices were to be instrumental in making arrangements for Kenyans to study abroad. It was the Cairo office and in particular Odhiambo Okello, that handled Raila's travel.

---

[18] See, Oginga Odinga, *Not Yet Uhuru,* (Nairobi: East Africa Educational Publishers, 1967), pp. 187-188.

[19] Interview with Raila, Nairobi, 22 June 2003.

Oginga Odinga in canvassing for external scholarships for Kenyans, especially in Eastern European countries and in India, worked closely with the Cairo and London offices to achieve this. The Cairo office working with B.F.F. Oluande K'Oduol, (Jaramogi's Personal Assistant in Nairobi), arranged the travel of many Kenyans on scholarships. Three scholarships were granted to Odhiambo Okello's full brother Mirulo Okello and half-brother Oudia Okello and Raila Odinga, a cousin to Oudia.[20]

Okuto Bala, Jaramogi's long-time business associate in Luo Thrift and Trading Corporation (LUTATCO), took Raila from Maranda School to Kisumu. The following day, Raila was driven to Nairobi by the late D.O. Makasembo, then the KANU Chairman for Central Nyanza District. Raila met Mirulo and Oudia Okello at the office of BFF Oluande K'Oduol, and stayed at K'Oduol's house as his travel arrangements were made. Israel Agina, a nephew of BFF Oluande K'Oduol, and now a close associate of Raila's, remembered that his first meeting with Raila was when he came for the night to BFF Oluande K'Oduol's house seeking his travel document.

Raila never tried to get a passport from Gill House where Sikhs, who controlled Kenyan immigration before independence, had already refused Oburu's application. Mirulo and Oudia Okello, and Raila left Nairobi for Dar-es-Salaam on a Dar-es-Salaam Motor Transport (DMT) bus service from the OTC (Overseas Trading Company) bus station. The journey took 24 hours. The following morning, they were received by Dola Othman, a Regional Commissioner (equivalent to a Provincial Commissioner in Kenya) of independent Tanganyika. Tanganyika had secured self-government status on May 1, 1961, and independence followed on December 9, 1961. Nyerere's forward looking orientation in support of the overall growth and development on the African continent, made the new Government in Tanganyika friendly, not only to freedom fighters, but also to Kenyans who could not get travel documents from their country's colonial government. Dola Othman took the trio to the Nyerere-led Tanganyika African National Union (TANU) headquarters. Oginga Odinga had an understanding with Julius Nyerere to provide Kenyan youths with travel documents.

---

[20] Much of the account in this section depended on the recollections of Eng. Mirulo Riako Okello in an interview in Nairobi on July 22, 2003 and subsequent reactions by Raila.

At TANU HQ, the trio had the unique opportunity of meeting Julius Nyerere who received them warmly. He gave them a brief speech that Mirulo re-cast as: "I wish you well wherever you are going to. All we want in Africa is to see that our people are educated. Even me here, I was in Scotland and I read, I read, I read. I did not marry a *Mzungu* but I married books. When I came back to Tanganyika, I married Maria. That is what I want to see of you people. Come back with knowledge. Feel at home, you are in the good hands of the people of Tanganyika."

They were hosted in a prestigious International Hotel for five days as their travel documents were processed. They were given the same travel documents that Tanzania provided to South Africans, Namibians and Rhodesians who lived under other repressive administrations. Thus they became Tanzanians in their search for education. Interestingly, they travelled to Cairo on a Boeing 707, which transited Nairobi's Embakasi airport. While on transit, they met K'Oduol. Jaramogi had travelled to attend a conference in Belgrade, Yugoslavia. They had to travel incognito or else they would have been arrested at the Nairobi airport.

They landed in Cairo in the middle of the night only for Raila Odinga to be detained and quarantined because his inoculation had not matured for travel. Wera Ambitho, who had met them, argued in vain with the authorities on behalf of Raila. But his fluent Arabic fell on deaf ears. Raila had to remain behind in quarantine for three days. The Okello brothers were driven by Mr. Ambitho to Zamalek Estate in Cairo, where Kenya's office and residence were located. They did not realize that a few hours before their arrival, Oginga Odinga and Odhiambo Okello had just returned from the World International Conference on Disarmament in Belgrade. According to Mirulo, Oginga Odinga was shocked to see him and exclaimed: "Mirulo, and how did you come?" Mirulo said that he had come with Oudia and "Aluo" (a corrupted form of a nickname-*Wuod Luo*-meaning "son of a Luo," which Jaramogi had given Raila) who had been detained for the immaturity of his vaccination. Mirulo was surprised about the reaction of Oginga Odinga who said: "it's ok, if it is just that. It is good for Raila to know that there is law in Cairo." He asked Mirulo and Oudia to go and sleep as he would see "Aluo" later that morning.

On his way out of Cairo on the following day, Jaramogi told his son that he was now a man and should not cry. He asked him to understand that there were laws that must be applied. He told him he was lucky to be in the hands of Messrs Okello and Ambitho, and should proceed to study. Raila completed his quarantine in the company of a Japanese diplomat who had been similarly detained. They were in a room like in a hotel.

The Kenya office in Cairo took charge of and dispersed the trio. The decision was that Mirulo would go to a University in Moscow, Oudia to Prague University in Czechoslovakia, and Raila to the German Democratic Republic. When Mirulo and Oudia flew to their respective destinations, Raila stayed in Cairo for about two months before leaving. He had the experience of a life-time.

According to Raila, the Cairo office decided that he was to travel by ship. But the ship was at Alexandria on the Egyptian coast. So Raila and three others who were scheduled to go to the German Democratic Republic, had to travel by road through the desert. His other colleagues were: Moses Kiprono arap Keino (a fellow Kenyan who was later to become Speaker of the Kenyan parliament before his death), and two Zambians, John Muchinga and Yona Shimwanza, both of whom had been sponsored by Zambia's UNIP. UNIP, the movement that led the struggle for Zambian independence, like KANU in Kenya, also had an office in Cairo. So did other African movements such as the ANC and PAC from South Africa; SWAPO from South-West Africa (later Namibia); FRELIMO from Mozambique etc.. These offices were supported by the Nasser government and funds from the Afro-Asian Solidarity Movement which came out of the Bandung Conference of 1955. The Afro-Asian Solidarity Movement was a collaboration towards the decolonisation of Africa by Heads of Government like Kwame Nkrumah of Ghana, Sekou Toure of Guinea, Jawaharlal Nehru of India, Sukarno of Indonesia, Gamel Abdel Nasser of Egypt and Joseph Bros Tito of Yugoslavia,. It was supported by the Governments of the People's Republic of China, the Union of Soviet Socialist Republics, the German Democratic Republic among others.

The cargo ship chosen to carry Raila and his colleagues, was the *Stubbenkammer*, which at 20,000 tonnes, made it a big ship then and even now. The *Stubbenkammer* loaded and discharged cargo from port to port. After Alexandria, the next port of call was Latakia in Syria where During the loading and discharging, Raila and his friends took the opportunity to visit Damascus.

As ship's passengers, they were entitled to supplies of cigarettes and wines etc. which they did not use, but were easily exchanged for money at ports of call. The residents of adjacent towns and cities wanted to try foreign goods and eagerly waited to purchase them. With the proceeds, it was possible to travel.

On the way to Damascus, Raila was excited when he passed the spot where Saul, in the Bible, had reportedly seen the light, and later became Paul. His excitement was heightened because his Uncle with whom he lived when he was in the primary school in Bondo, constantly told the story of Saul becoming Paul. At that time, his conception of the World did not include the place of Saul's transformation and similar places which he thought were in heaven. He sent a postcard from Damascus to his Uncle announcing his feat.[21]

From Latakia, the ship embarked on the same route that, according to the Bible, Paul, the Apostle had taken to Rome. But the Cuban Missile Crisis had broken out. This was a tense twelve-day period for the world in 1962. The cold war which had started at the end of the Second-World War, was accompanied by the craze for the acquisition of nuclear weapons by the two major powers: the United States of America and the Union of Soviet Socialist Republics (USSR or Soviet Union). The revolution led by Fidel Castro Ruz and Che Guevara, against the American-backed Batista government in Cuba ended in a closer relationship between that Island country next to the United States, and the Soviet Union. Under President Dwight Eisenhower of the United States, the Central Intelligence Agency (CIA) planned to have Cuban exiles, supported by anti-Castro elements at home, work for the overthrow of Castro, such that the United States would not be linked with the coup. In January 1961, before leaving office, President Eisenhower broke diplomatic relations with Cuba. However, it was his successor, President John F. Kennedy, who approved the CIA invasion plan. On April 15, 1961, the US forces attacked and destroyed part of Cuba's Air Force. 1500 Cuban exiles, armed by the United States, landed at Bahia de Cochinos (Bay of Pigs) at the Southern tip of Cuba. Castro's forces were waiting for them and defeated them. The fighting ended on April 19 with 100 dead and many captured. The Bay of Pigs battle was a humiliating fiasco for the United States of America.

But the Bay of Pigs was not to be the last confrontation between Fidel Castro and the United States under President Kennedy. On October 15, 1962, an American U-2 spy plane over Cuba revealed the presence of many SS-4 nuclear missiles on the island. The following day, President Kennedy summoned his Executive

---

[21] These accounts are based on interviews with Raila Odinga on June 22, 2003 and February 15, 2004

Committee to consider the threat directly next door. The missiles were determined to be capable of striking 1,000 nautical miles from Cuba. This meant that the Soviet Union could hit Washington DC and several American cities. There were indications that missiles capable of going about 2,000 nautical miles were also being deployed. Andrei Gromyko, then the Foreign Minister of the Soviet Union met President Kennedy in Washington on October 17, 1962 and denied the presence of any Soviet missiles in Cuba. However, Kennedy decided on a naval blockade on Sunday October 21, 1962.

Raila and his colleagues were unaware of this global tension. However, on October 22, 1962, as they moved near to Cyprus en route to Malta, there was a big scare on board as it was announced that the American President was going to make an important address to the world on the British Broadcasting Corporation (BBC). American troops all over the world had been placed on alert. The Captain of the *Stubbenkammer* had been a captain of a warship in Hitler's German navy and sensed the implication of what was happening.

When the announcement came, President Kennedy made it clear that the presence of Soviet missiles in Cuba was unacceptable, and called for their removal. He declared that any missile launched from Cuba against any nation in the Western Hemisphere, would be seen as an attack on the United States by the Soviet Union. He then announced a naval blockade on Cuba. Among other measures, he instructed American troops to board and search any ship thought to be carrying offensive military equipment to Cuba.

The Captain of the *Stubbenkammer* and his crew became scared as one of the American warships the US seventh fleet in the Mediterranean, followed the *Stubbenkammer*. The US ship signalled the *Stubbenkammer*, wanting to know its identity, crew and passengers on board, and the nature of its cargo. Raila Odinga and his colleagues followed the Captain into the signals room as he replied. Nevertheless, the US warship followed them all night with her guns aimed at the defenceless cargo ship.

The response of the leader of the Soviet Union, Chairman Nikita Khrushchev, was not a capitulation. He insisted that the Soviet Union was capable of defending its interests, would not be intimidated or blackmailed by imperialist forces, and would continue to support Cuba.

The tense situation ended on October 28, despite Fidel Castro's plea to Khrushchev two days earlier to prepare for a nuclear first strike against the US should Cuba be invaded. Khrushchev announced the dismantling of the missiles in exchange for a US agreement not to invade Cuba and to remove its own missiles from Turkey. Though a war that could have resulted in mutually assured destruction (MAD) and serious harm to the world, was avoided, this was an eye opener to Raila Odinga about international politics. It also marked the beginning of his knowledge of the role of Fidel Castro, and his admiration for the revolutionary.

The *Stubbenkammer* continued its journey and stopped in Malta. Here Raila and his friends met an African-American who had served in the US Army during the Second World War and had chosen to settle in Malta. He told them a lot of exciting stories about the war. From Malta, the ship went on to Tunis without stopping in Tripoli. From Tunis, they stopped in Algiers before moving towards Gibraltar.

Beyond Gibraltar, they had to pass through the Bay of Biscay, a vast inlet of water on the Atlantic Ocean, bordered by France in the North and East, and by Spain in the South. North-west winds and strong currents, made the Bay of Biscay difficult to navigate. This problem of navigation, over time, led to superstitious reactions by sailors as they approached this Bay. Sailors had similar superstitions about other places like the Bermuda Triangle, the Cape of Good Hope, Tierra Del Fuego and the Magellan Strait.

Raila Odinga and his three friends, as new comers to the sea, underwent an initiation ceremony before passing through the Strait of Gibraltar. This was meant to make them appear to spirits as fish and thereby prevent harm to the *Stubbenkammer* and the people on board. On this special occasion, the ship was anchored at sea. The four people to be initiated played a game of hide and seek with the crew. They had to wear anything but decent clothes. When found, they were each arrested and dragged to the deck. They were made to sit on a stool as one of the crew drew water from the sea. The water was poured over the initiate and one of the crew put hot pepper in his mouth. The initiate was then made to crawl through a pipe. Half way through, water was released from the opposite end. At the end of the pipe, the initiate was hit in the chest with a rubber baton and then seated before the Captain who baptized him with the name of a fish. Raila was named *Seenadel* meaning Sea needle. The four initiates were given certificates of initiation and told they were now fish and not human beings as they had passed through the Strait of Gibraltar.

However, the initiation did not help the turbulence that the *Stubbenkammer* faced at the Bay of Biscay. Navigation is normally difficult and dangerous because of the prevailing north-western winds and strong currents. The waves would throw the ship very high and then down. Waves at the Bay of Biscay could rise well above 50 metres. So those on the ship could neither eat nor drink for two days. Anything they took in, was immediately vomited. Raila and his friends thought it was the end of the world for them. But they survived and passed through the English Channel and up the Thames River to London.

Raila was excited. He looked forward to seeing dockworkers who he had assumed were black people. He could not believe that white people did such jobs. But he saw differently as they berthed. The dockworkers were white and they were speaking the London Cockney English dialect, which he could not understand.

Raila and his friends, as usual decided to explore London during their three-day stay. They went looking for the KANU office in Africa Unity House in South Kensington. The house was bought by Ghana's first President Kwame Nkrumah, who at that time, was known as *Osagyefo or* the Saviour. Nkrumah had the house used as emergency accommodation for African students and as offices for the coordination of liberation efforts in Africa. On the recommendation of Oginga Odinga, Othigo Otieno who was studying in London was given the job of managing the Africa Unity House.

Otieno received the four new faces well. They also met a lady, Eta Kirui, the first Kalenjin woman to study Nursing in Britain. Having finished the first stage of her course, she was under pressure to return home. But she wanted to continue her training. Otieno had secured a place for her to study Advanced Nursing in the German Democratic Republic (GDR). She and Moses, a fellow Kalenjin who had known of her, got close. Ms. Kirui went to the GDR before Raila and his friends. But Moses followed her and they were married. Raila was Master of Ceremonies at the wedding.

The ship went from London via Rotterdam and Denmark to Rostock in Germany where the new students took a train to Leipzig. That year, the winter was the coldest for about fifty years: a rude introduction for a young man brought up in a very warm part of Kenya.

Education in Eastern Germany

On arrival in the GDR, as Wilfred Aput Adhoch pointed out,[22] a new student joined others from various parts of the world for a three to six month induction course in Leipzig, about life in Germany and to learn German. Raila passed his language test.

He had wanted to study history, but his father would not hear of it and wrote him a strong note to the effect that if he wanted to read history, he need not have travelled so far. For Oginga Odinga wanted his son to be a medical doctor. So the choice was made for Raila. He began with Mathematics, Chemistry, Physics Biology and Latin in addition to more German studies. The programme was intense. The day started at 6 am to be ready for classes, which began at 7am and went on till 6pm with a one-hour break. After another break, they had two to three hours of evening tutorials with Teaching Assistants. On Saturdays, classes ended at 1 pm.

The holidays were short: two weeks in winter and four in the summer. Every four months, the students sat exams to decide if they were to move to a higher level until the German University entrance examination called *"Arbitur."*

Raila started at the Herder Institute High School. Moses Keino and the two Zambians, who were older and had been in school longer, went on to higher classes. Keino and Muchinga studied Economics and Shimwanza preceded Raila in Medicine. Keino was to return home to enter politics; John Muchinga rose to become Zambia's Permanent Representative to the UN; and Shimwanza retired as a Senior Doctor in Zambia.

However, Raila was not to become a doctor. He was not amused when his class went on excursion to do practicals in human anatomy at a hospital in Jena, where he saw live operations on humans and was shown different organs. He had to watch senior students playing with cadavers. Although he was very disturbed, his teachers told him that was usual and that 95% normally got used to the experience.

---

[22] Wilfred Aput Adhoch, a German trained Engineer from Dresden University retired from Kenya Railways. He gave the author an interview on the German Democratic Republic's education system as a contemporary of Raila Odinga on August 12, 2003 in Nairobi.

That night, Raila did not sleep well and became convinced he was one of the 5% that would not adjust. The following day he asked to be allowed to either change subject or return to Kenya. He had spent three to four months as a medical student.

Raila decided to study Engineering, and although he had been taking Mathematics and Physics, he now had to add Additional Mathematics, Technical Drawing/Design and Practical. He had to work extra-time in order to catch up with his set; and a special teacher helped him with Technical Drawing on Sundays from morning till mid-night. As well as other students from the Middle East, South America, Africa and Southeast Asia, there was a Swiss, Mr. Ruhti. Coming from the German part of Switzerland, he had a language advantage, and was the only one who spoke better German than Raila. He had also done University entrance examination in Switzerland before being ordered to join the Raila set. He was thus more advanced and helped Raila.

Other African students included Aniche and Obi Egbunike from Nigeria; Yalla Eballa and Elinge Yeme, both from the Cameroon; Toure from Guinea; Quist from Ghana; Gastone from Congo; and El-Mammy from Senegal. There were also Shaheen from Syria and Boubakar from Morocco. They were all older. Only a Peruvian, Nunez was about the same age as Raila. Neither of them could enjoy the social life of the older students because of the strict rules that prevented under eighteen-year olds access to nightclubs. Raila remembers that they sometimes pretended to be older to enter nightclubs.

He later went on to Magdeburg College of Advanced Technology (Otto von Juericke) now the University of Magdeburg. This University specialized in heavy engineering, machine building, production technology and chemical engineering. Here Raila had only two other African students as contemporaries. Generally, there were very few foreign students at Magdeburg, and many of these were from the Middle East and Asia (mainly Vietnamese and Indians). Raila, whose mastery of the German language was as good as that of those whose mother tongue was German, put it to good use at Magdeburg.

Beginning of a Political Career

Aside from his acknowledged leadership at home, Raila began his political career in Germany. It was usual for students from different parts of the world to have area-based student associations. Frau Jung, the Registrar of Foreign Students, inducted Raila into the University world. Raila and a Sudanese student called Osman, announced that they would form an African Students' Association. But his first shock on African political reality came when Ms. Jung told him that Osman, although black, was also an Arab and could not be part of his Association. So Raila formed a one-man African Students' Association.

He also joined the Kenyan Students' Association which brought together Kenyans in Germany and had existed before his arrival. He later became the Secretary and then the Chairperson. Oburu Oginga who also became the General Secretary of the Kenya Students' Association in Russia, joined with his brother to form the Kenya Students' Union for Eastern Europe, which became part of the larger Federation of Kenyan Students in Europe. Raila travelled a lot to establish contacts with other Unions. He made some of these trips without visas and was, sometimes incarcerated at airports. But he was determined that Kenyan students would be part of the 1968 World Youth Congress in Sofia. On this, he worked closely with another Kenyan, Muturi Mukiria, who was in Warsaw, Poland. He was subsequently elected Chairman of the Federation and Muturia became the Secretary.

By the time the Kenya People's Union (KPU) was formed by Oginga Odinga in 1966, Raila, without being asked, opened a Liaison Office in Germany and allied the KPU with other fraternal organizations. He became the Secretary of the Party in Europe.[23] Since no printer would print the KPU manifesto in Kenya for fear of negative reaction from the Jomo Kenyatta regime,[24] and since the Kenya government had seized the passports of the KPU collaborators, the task of getting the manifesto printed in London, fell on young Raila. Pranlal Seth, who was Oginga's Lawyer, Osumba Langi, a Kenyan resident in the UK at that time, and Douglas Rodgers who was the editor of the "Africa and the World" magazine raised funds and supervised the undertaking.

Against all the odds, Raila got the finished manifestos to Berlin. But he had to rush back to take his exams, so he left them at the Afro-Asian office in Berlin from where they were picked up by Were Olonde, a KPU member who had flown

---

[23] These accounts depended on interviews with Oburu Oginga and Raila Odinga.
[24] There will be a more detailed treatment of the KPU later.

in from Entebbe, Uganda. Since the manifestos were banned in Kenya, KPU activists in Uganda moved them by boat to Bondo, from where Oginga Odinga's Bus Service distributed them to different parts of Kenya.

While in Germany, Raila had become interested in the writings of Karl Marx and Lenin, among others. Prof. E.S. Atieno-Odhiambo who fled into exile from the University of Nairobi in August 1988 and is now at Rice University in the United States, remembers that his first meeting with Raila in 1965 was devoted to a dialogue on such writings. He and Raila engaged in a two-day discourse on Marxism-Leninism and compared the political realities of East Germany with Kenya's.[25]

Raila was also keen about the role of Fidel Castro. As noted earlier, his first knowledge of Castro was during the Cuban missile crisis. Then came the Vietnam war. The Vietnamese, had suffered under Chinese imperialism. They resisted and threw the Chinese out at different times. But the French came in 1861 and incorporated the entire sub-region including Laos and Cambodia under French colonial rule in what was known as French Indochina.

The French thrived until 1930 when Ho Chi Minh established the Indochinese Communist Party to fight French imperialism. However, during the Second World war, the Japanese took control of Vietnam. In response, Ho Chi Minh set up the Viet Minh as a nationalist resistance movement for independence. He gained control over the whole of Vietnam in what was known as the August revolution in 1945. But the French would not accept this and attacked in 1946, eventually to be defeated by Ho Chi Minh's forces in the Battle of Dien Bien Phu in 1954. But the country was divided, and as in the case of Korea, the north was pro-communism and the south pro-western capitalism. Ho Chi Minh led the North. Bao Dai, for about a year held sway over South Vietnam and was replaced in 1955 by Ngo Dinh Diem who was assassinated in a coup in 1963. Ho Chi Minh's support of a National Liberation Front in South Vietnam, displeased the Americans.

The escalation of American involvement began in July 1964 when US ships on reconnaissance in the Gulf of Tonkin shelled some villages in North Vietnam and the Ho Chi Minh government retaliated by attacking USS Maddox, a United

---

[25] Interview with E.S. Atieno-Odhiambo, July 8, 2003.

States Navy's destroyer on August 2nd. The United States Congress' Gulf of Tonkin Resolution five days later, authorized President Lyndon B. Johnson to deal with the North Vietnamese. He used this opportunity to start a war that was never formally declared by the United States. This war was to continue for almost a decade until 1973 when the US was defeated and had to end its military involvement.

Raila was in school in Germany with many young Vietnamese, Laotians and Cambodians. The experience related to him by these students, and the accounts by even American veterans who despised the role of their country, could not endear a young man with Raila's background, to American policies in these countries. At one point, he lived with a student who had escaped from prison in South Vietnam and who told him shocking stories about the role of the Americans. He heard about Prisoners of War being thrown into a tiger's den and similar horrors. These stories were reinforced at an international conference on Vietnam in Helsinki, Finland in 1968 when several people including US military deserters corroborated these accounts. There was the use of Napalm Bomb and other chemicals (like agent orange) and biological weapons to kill Vietnamese people and destroy their vegetation and hence livelihoods.

Fidel Castro stood out as a strong voice against the American operation in Vietnam. The South American students in Germany told Raila about the gallantry of Castro, Ernesto Che Guevara and others in bringing what was initially to be nationalist change to Cuba. The American reaction pushed Castro towards the Soviet Union.

Then Raila read Castro's defence, entitled: *History Will Absolve Me,* at his trial after he was captured in his first attempt to overthrow the Fulgencio Batista y Zaldiva regime which had usurped power with army backing in 1952. In July 1953, Castro, his brother Raul and about 150 others, tried to seize the Moncada military barracks in Santiago de Cuba, which was the base for 1000 military personnel. Many were killed but Castro was captured and jailed for 15 years, only to be part of a Batista's general amnesty in May 1955. Joining hands with Che Guevara, an Argentine revolutionary, Castro eventually drove Batista into exile in January 1959.

Castro visited the German Democratic Republic when Raila Odinga was a student Raila had the opportunity of listening to Castro, and was impressed. He became convinced that Castro and Che Guevara were more relevant (compared to Communist Eastern Europe) to the situation in Kenya, and so became more of a Castroist, rather than a Communist.

But Raila's student life was not all politics. He related to other students academically as well as socially. In addition to Osman, the Sudanese student, there was another black student, Douglas Scot, a fourth year Engineering student from Guyana. Scot was very warm towards Raila, and shared his experience and his vast English and German literature with Raila.

Raila was the only foreign student in his class. His roommate in the Hall of Residence was a German named Roland Obst, who improved Raila's German and deepened his understanding of German culture.

Roland, like Raila, was a good footballer. This was a passion into which Joab Omino (later a political and trusted friend in Kenya) had initiated Raila during his Kisumu days. With Roland, Raila joined the Magdeburg FC in which Roland played number 6 and Raila number 11.

Roland Obst had a motorbike, and on many weekends, Raila joined him on a trip to his home in Nord Hausen, a region with the highest peak in Germany called "Broken." They climbed this peak many times.

Raila had enough time for the main reason for being in the German Democratic Republic. In 1969, he graduated with a Master of Science Degree in Mechanical Engineering with a focus on Special Field Production Technology. He returned to Kenya in time to witness the Kisumu Massacre in October 1969.[26] He returned to Eastern Germany in 1970 but he did not stay for long, realizing that he could not continue with the Ph.D programme for which he had registered. His father was in detention with his associates who had formed the Kenya Peoples Union (KPU, more on this later). His elder brother had started his Ph.D programme. Thus, he felt the need to return home and take charge of the family and his father's business interests. Before returning, he went to Britain, to canvass support for the release of the KPU members. On return to Kenya, in May 1970. he started teaching at the University of Nairobi.

---

[26] The Kisumu massacre is elaborated in this book.

In 1972, still seeking a Ph.D, Raila was admitted to read Mechanical Engineering at the University of Denver in Colorado. He applied to the University of Nairobi to be granted leave of absence to pursue the opportunity. But his Head of Department, Professor Harris, a British national, rejected his request, arguing that the Mechanical Engineering Department was short staffed and could not spare him.

This increased Raila's frustration as a Lecturer at the University of Nairobi. This feeling was not limited to Raila. Other Africans had similar experiences. The workload was very heavy, the Africans were sparsely represented in the Faculty, and there was no active effort to seek out bright students for further training. Between 1956 and 1970, Raila was only the third African to join the Department of Mechanical Engineering. He was preceded by Philip Githinji and Ngeso Okolo. Out of 56 scholars in the entire Faculty of Engineering (the oldest Faculty in the University that started in 1956 as the Royal Technical College), only 7 were Africans. In these circumstances, Raila was convinced that he could not stay in the academic world for long.

Chapter 04
The Inheritance

To understand the role of Raila Odinga in the politics of Kenya, it is necessary to undertake a brief foray into how Kenyans organized themselves for decolonisation. This process generated a number of legacies that influence political interaction in Kenya today.

Africans, in general, were not represented in the colonial arrangements for their governance. The only way out for them was to form political and welfare associations. These became the initial pressure groups that manifested Africans' concerns over how they were being ruled. On June 7, 1921, Harry Thuku, a clerk at the Treasury in Nairobi, set up the Young Kikuyu Association to oppose the colonialism which had dispossessed Kikuyus of their lands, and to protect Kikuyu cultural practices. The Young Kikuyu Association changed its name to the East African Association to have a wider appeal, but was disbanded in favour of the Kikuyu Central Association when Harry Thuku was detained and later deported to Kismayo.

Jomo Kenyatta, who had been associated with this ethnic-based organization from 1924 until 1926 joined it formally, and became Secretary-General in 1928. In December 1921, in Western Kenya, anti-colonial activists among the Luos and the Luhyas, formed the Young Kavirondo Association, which was re-named Kavirondo Taxpayers Welfare Association[1] by Archdeacon Owen, to make it more acceptable to the colonial government. Such were the beginnings of anti-colonial pressure in Kenya. These pressures increased after World War II, as many more organizations were formed all over Kenya as platforms for the struggle against colonialism.

Dedan Kimathi later became the foremost military leader of the armed uprising against the expropriation of Kenyan lands and denial of freedom by the colonial administration. The followers of Kimathi in what was dubbed the *Mau Mau*

---

[1] Much of these accounts can be found in Eric M. Aseka, Mzee Jomo Kenyatta, (Nairobi, East African Educational Publishers, 2001)

Uprising, came from the Kikuyu , although the Maasai lost more land, and others like the Luhya also lost some. But the Luos were not, in the large part, affected by the problem of expropriation of land by the colonial authorities.

However, the Luos contributed to decolonisation through political organization and milder forms of protests. In furtherance of his goal to go beyond his immediate environs Oginga Odinga was a great organizer not just in Nyanza. He had expanded the business horizon of the Luo Thrift and Trading Corporation, by travelling throughout East African urban areas seeking investors. But he went beyond business and also encouraged the building of Luo Union branches in these areas. The Luo Union had existed in Nairobi when Oginga Odinga was a child. But with his business travels in time, he united Luos in Nyanza with those elsewhere in East Africa. According to Atieno-Odhiambo, in 1953 these various Unions formed an umbrella body, *Galamoro* Luo Union (East Africa), and Oginga Odinga was elected the first President and *Ker*.

In 1957, Jaramogi Odinga's ability to mobilise, was very evident as he ran for one of the eight legislative seats for Africans. He ran against Beneiah Apollo Ohanga, a Luo who had replaced Walter Odede, the African nominated to the legislature in 1952. Odede had been detained in 1953 for trying to drag the Luo into the *Mau Mau*. Ohanga became a Minister in 1954. But despite Ohanga's advantage of incumbency, he was beaten by Oginga Odinga who was elected to represent Nyanza Central constituency. He joined seven others in the first legislature with elected Africans. They were: Masinde Muliro, (Nyanza North); Lawrence Oguda, (Nyanza South); Tom Mboya, (Nairobi); Ronald Ngala, (Coast); Bernard Mate, (Central Province); Daniel T. arap Moi, (Rift Valley) and James Nzau Muimi (Eastern Kenya).

Thus, at an early age, Raila at the feet of Oginga Odinga, had begun to learn politics in addition to English and other modern ways of gaining knowledge. Observing the ups and downs of Oginga Odinga in Kenyan politics was part of the making of Raila as a politician. He watched as his father mobilised the Luo, and made alliances with other Kenyans. These Kenyan leaders who were also mobilizing their respective ethnic groups were also teachers, whose sons (very few daughters), knowingly or unknowingly, were also getting a foundation in politics.

Learning at the feet of a family precursor, or taking advantage of a popular family name, has been a major legacy for many Kenyans in the quest for public office. Aside from the recent effort of former President Moi in jump-starting Uhuru Kenyatta in the belief that the legacy of Jomo Kenyatta was enough, Moi's son Gideon was given the same automatic rights to Baringo Central constituency that the father had held for over forty years. The same could be said of Simeon Nyachae's inheritance from his father Chief Nyandusi; Musalia Mudavadi from Moses Mudavadi; Katana Ngala from his father Ronald Ngala at the Coast; and Michael Kijana Wamalwa from his father Senator Wamalwa. The Nyagah "boys," Joseph and Norman, could be said to be reaping from the seeds sown by Jeremiah Nyagah their father. However, other studies could find it worth the effort to assess the role of each of these in building and contributing to politics in Kenya beyond the legacy of a popular name within an ethnic group.

Politicisation of Ethnicity

Kenya is made up of about 42 different ethnic groups, some of which could be seen as separate nationalities forced together by different historical circumstances. The reaction to colonialism that started on the basis of ethnic association, could be said to be the beginning of the politicisation of ethnicity. Trust at the political arena started on the basis of primordial realities. This mode of articulation had been fostered at the economic level for the Kikuyu who wanted their lands back. In contrast, it was easier for Archdeacon Owen to transform the response among the Luo and Luhya into a welfare association, to remove an original desire to be a political pressure group.

Ethnic stereotyping also played a role in the destruction of political trust in the interactions of the various Kenyan ethnic groups. In a commentary on the problem of building trust for a better understanding in Kenya, late Prof. Katama Mkangi examined the role of stereotyping in Kenya.[2] He argued that Kenyans laugh at stereotyping without paying attention to the fact that such stereotyping influenced national leaders when they had to make decisions. For example, the Kenyan stereotype for the Coast people is that they are lazy. Then along came former NARC Minister for Local Government, Karisa Maitha who, on the basis of such stereotyping had apparently concluded that he "cannot find qualified Coastarians

---

[2] *East African Standard,* Wednesday, April 16, 2003, p. 13.

to offer positions in government, or chairmanships and directorships in commissions and parastatals."[3] Other examples from Mkangi include: the Akamba being unsophisticated, the Luos being arrogant and the Kikuyus being deceitful. Others have added that Luhyas are either "diplomatic" when being charitable or in stronger terms seen as unreliable liars.

There was also the problem of stereotypes as a result of differences in culture and attitude to life. That Luo men do not circumcise and go through the necessary initiation process that ordinarily accompanies circumcision, some politicians have exploited to tag Luo elderly politicians as boys who cannot rule over men. But this did not hamper political collaboration when necessary and only became used as manipulative propaganda during subsequent hotly contested elections. The perception was that the Kikuyu were as greedy over material wealth as the Luo loved good life without commensurate hard work. But although arrogance did not, on its own, create political tension, it was early defined as a fact in political propaganda, and exploited for the purpose of garnering votes.

The importance of stereotyping could also be seen in the extent to which it affects national leaders in their attempts to build alliances and collaborate towards a greater Kenya. At times, social myths become realities and truths in the minds of uncritical people. These myths have affected political interaction among politicians of Oginga Odinga's generation, and it affected and continues to affect the political realities that Raila and his generation have to contend with.

Far more fundamental, however, has been the move beyond stereotyping into the active politicisation of ethnicity. The politicisation of ethnicity in Kenya is like an albatross around the neck of every politician, in spite of the attempt by some to pretend, for political advantage, that they are above the use of their primordial being. Raila, like most of his colleagues, inherited this problem from the first generation politicians who in turn blamed colonial policies for aggravating ethnic differences into political conflicts. However, as Kiraitu Murungi rightly noted: "We cannot pretend that ethnicity is not an important factor in Kenyan politics. It is part of our historical and social reality."[4]

---

[3] Ibid.

[4] Kiraitu Murungi, "Ethnicity and Multi-Partyism in Kenya," Thoughts on Democracy Series (Issue III), A Kenya Human Rights Commission Publication, Nairobi Kenya, February 1995, p. 1.

Kiraitu Murungi recounted a number of explanations that had been put forward to explain the politicisation of ethnicity. These include: exploitation of ancient tribal hatreds and primitive tribal animosities; colonial policies of land expropriations; uneven distribution of social benefits like schools, which created the social conditions for today's ethnicity-based political conflicts; unscrupulous exploitation of ethnic feelings by politicians to gain advantage; and the continuing importance to most Kenyans, of the clan and social lineage as a means of survival. Finally, there is a rational economic explanation, based on the argument that when the elephant dies, the nearest grass grows tallest, implying that an ethnic group whose sons are in power, benefit more than those out of power.

An analysis of which of these academic explanations best deals with the Kenyan political reality is beyond the purview of this work. It is enough, for our purpose to note that the problem exists and to describe how politicians have, in turn, reacted to the fact of politicisation of ethnicity.

Dalmas Otieno, a politician who served the Moi Government as MP and Minister from 1988-1996,[5] shared some thoughts on the problem of ethnicity in Kenyan politics. He argued that in the African situation, when "nationalities" cohabit in a nation-state, the large ones which could almost subsist on their own, tend to want to shape the nation-state in their own image, to serve their parochial interests. Leaders within the respective nationalities, marshalled the positions of their nationalities as what was desirable for the whole country. Jaramogi, especially with the early assassination of Tom Mboya, became the sole articulator of the Luo position as Kenyatta did for the Kikuyu; Paul Ngei for the Kamba; Masinde Muliro for the Luhya; Ronald Gideon Ngala for the Coast; Jeremiah Nyagah for the Embu; and Chief Nyandusi for the Kisii etc. Otieno noted that even Mwai Kibaki, President of Kenya, played the same game. Mrs. Jael Mbogo almost defeated Kibaki in the race for the Bahati Parliamentary seat in Nairobi in the 1969 General Elections.[6] To avoid another unsuccessful race, Kibaki returned to Othaya, his home, for the 1974 elections. He was also associated with a tribal journal of the GEMA (Gikuyu, Embu, Meru Association).

---

[5] Interview with Dalmas Otieno, Nairobi 21 February 2003.
[6] See, "Keny@40: 1969," p. 9, A *Daily Nation* Supplement, in *Daily Nation*, August 14, 2003.

This situation resulted in a clash of nationalities or ethnic groups, as efforts were made to realize nation-states in African countries. But the importance of nationalities in the lives of the people, was a variable of the overall performance of the central authority. Where the central authority remained weak, there continued to be a feeling of security for the nationalities as communities, rather than at the level of the nation-state. A quarrel between a buyer and a seller at the market place easily became a fight of two communities. In the urban slums, an outbreak of insecurity normally resulted in: 'each unto his community.' Thus, the resultant fight became a Luo-Kikuyu or Kikuyu-Luhya or Luhya-Luo etc., affair. Until the centre can mean the same thing to all, each individual naturally falls back on his community. This emotional need for the community, and cohesion in such a situation, is what a typical politician exploits by accentuating community feeling and sustaining such feeling vis-à-vis other communities, to maintain a support base for political bargaining.

Of more substance is the competition for power, which leaders within ethnic groups have tended to articulate parochially and to manipulate as ethnic rivalries. On Luo-Kikuyu rivalry, the only reason for this, according to Jaramogi, in a response to a question Otieno Kajwang' had asked, was nothing more than competition for power.[7] As Raila argued, Kikuyu elites feel only the Luos can challenge their hegemonic designs on Kenya.[8] The Luos and the Kikuyus are separate and relatively homogenous communities. Of course the extent of the exploitation of this homogeneity as basis of political action would vary among the two ethnic groupings.

The situation with the Luhya is different. For the Luhya, their dialects are not as similar as is the case with the Luos. Even with similar language, some of the Luhya are not from the same root. They have sub-ethnic groups that are almost different nationalities on their own. The Bukusu, for instance, have fundamental differences with the Maragoli. The Samias in Busia who are closer to Tesos, have experienced cultural hybridisation with the Luos just as the Tachoni in Webuye are more akin to the Kalenjin.[9] Though the Luhyas readily claim to be the second

---

[7] Kajwang' illustrating his view with a response he claimed he got from Jaramogi in an interview with the author, Nairobi, April 11, 2003
[8] Interview, May 9, 2004.
[9] Interview with Ling Kituyi, Nairobi, March 9, 2003, first addressed my mind to these differences.

largest ethnic group in Kenya, their internal differences, have probably tended to hamper the possibility of achieving more with respect to national leadership. In effect, the Luo-Luhya or Luhya-Kikuyu rivalries, have never been at the same level as that of the Kikuyu-Luo.

Development of the Luo-Kikuyu ethnic differences, has not been a linear affair.[10] From all indications, the Kikuyus started organizing as Kikuyu political entities in reaction to the loss of their lands under colonial Kenya. Since the Luos did not lose similar lands in their own areas, the difference in interest was clear. Kikuyus organizing as Kikuyus could be understood. But then, Harry Thuku's plan to build beyond Kikuyu as the basis of organization, was not to be, as Jomo Kenyatta and others consolidated a Kikuyu Central Association.

Earlier, a clear exception to this trend of ethnic consolidation as a basis for political action, was Tom Mboya. He was born a Luo, as a result of parentage. But his birthplace was in the heart of Kamba land. He grew up amongst Kamba children and spoke their language, and had several experiences that made him first a Kenyan. Rather than return to run for elections in Rusinga Island, his ancestral home in Luoland, he built his base among the workers in Nairobi from the beginning to his end. Mboya abhorred the politicisation of ethnicity. As he cautioned:

> The man who tries to live so within the confines of his tribe, not so much revering its customs as discriminating against other tribes, represents the kind of tribalism of which Africa must beware. The Luo who thinks nothing good can come from other tribes or continuously protects a person merely because he is a fellow Luo; the Kikuyu who thinks it only suitable to meet other Kikuyu and disregards merit and ability in other people because and only because they do not belong to his tribe; this is negative tribalism which cannot allow for unity. That we are born of different tribes we cannot change, but I refuse to believe that, because our tribes have different backgrounds and culture and customs, we cannot create an African community or a nation.[11]

---

[10] Aside from many written materials on this subject, the author benefited immensely from the insights from interviews with Tony Gachoka a journalist and popular political commentator on July 25, 2003 and Dr. Fred Matiang'i, a University of Nairobi academic on August 8, 2003.

[11] Tom Mboya, Freedom and After, (Nairobi: East African Educational Publisher Ltd., 1986), p. 70. See also, Edwin Gimode, *Tom Mboya*, (Nairobi: East African Educational Publishers Ltd., 1996).

It was ironic that Tom Mboya, according to most accounts, had to lose his life on the basis of such ethnic chauvinism. The assassination of Mboya accentuated the Kikuyu-Luo ethnic rivalry.[12]

The reinforcement of immediate primordial differences between the Luo and the Kikuyu probably first began when the British started deporting Kikuyus from Nairobi, to control the *Mau Mau* upsurge in the city. As the Kikuyu left, the Luo began to fill the opportunities for employment and petty businesses operated in council shops and kiosks. This degenerated into bad feelings between the two communities.

Using his clout in the Luo Union in 1954, Oginga Odinga gave an important message to the effect that organizing as a Luo, must not be at the expense of the greater goal of being a Kenyan. Nairobi Councillor, Ambrose Ofafa, a Luo and treasurer of the Luo Union, was assassinated by *Mau Mau* fighters in Kaloleni. Councillor Ofafa had been accused of collaborating with the colonialists, as he was one of the Africans who, when Kikuyus were being deported from Nairobi, took over shops previously used by Kikuyu tenants. The newspapers, without evidence, concluded that this killing represented a Kikuyu or *Mau Mau* plot against the Luo. The British colonial administration, trying to take advantage of the development, urged the Luos to join the Gikuyu Home Guards. This, according to Oginga Odinga constituted an encouragement to Luos to avenge Ofafa's death.[13] Oginga Odinga travelled to Nairobi from Kisumu and succeeded in thwarting such a volatile relationship between the Luo and the Kikuyu. He managed to make the Luos see what had brought about the actions of the *Mau Mau* fighters. Rather than kill fellow Kenyans in revenge, Oginga Odinga diverted what would have been negative energy into a positive one, by proposing that Luos should build a memorial in the name of Ofafa instead of killing fellow Africans in his name. The memorial was completed in 1957 in Kisumu and the Ofafa Memorial Hall also served as the headquarters of the Luo Union.[14]

Both Tom Mboya and Oginga Odinga have detailed other acts they carried out in their efforts in support of the cause of the *Mau Mau* freedom fighters. They also

---

[12] More on the rise and fall of Tom Mboya is to follow in this volume.

[13] See, Oginga Odinga, *Not Yet Uhuru,* (Nairobi, East African Educational Publishers, 1967), pp. 132.

[14] For more details, see, *ibid.,* pp. 132-134.

fought against the detention of Jomo Kenyatta from 1952 to 1961, which was a major sacrifice by Jomo Kenyatta and other freedom fighters who were removed from socio-political life for almost a decade. But Oginga Odinga and later, Tom Mboya, working with others, refused to compromise on who was to lead Kenya into independence. They kept the spirit of Jomo Kenyatta alive. Whatever might have remained of anti-Luo feeling among the Kikuyus, must have dwindled if not completely evaporated, as Jaramogi Oginga Odinga refused the offer by the British to assume the leadership of Kenya at the expense of the detained Kenyatta. It was thus understandable that Oginga Odinga became the first Vice-President to Kenyatta and it became clear that the Luo and the Kikuyu could work as one towards national integration and development in Kenya.

The Luo-Kikuyu collaboration was a scare to other ethnic groups ranging from the Luhyas to the Mijikenda, the Kalenjin, the Maasai, the Somalis etc. As would be seen later, this scare resulted in the formation in 1959 of the Kenya National Party (KNP), led by Masinde Muliro, and including other ethnic groups. The KNP was eventually transformed into the Kenya African Democratic Union (KADU), bringing together many of the district associations and better still, ethnic political associations and parties, which the colonial policy of restricting parties to the district level from 1955–1958, had forced. Mboya and Odinga had rejected the multiracial thrust of the KNP and tried unsuccessfully to register the Kenya Independence Movement. The Kenya Independence Movement was eventually transformed into the Kenya African National Union (KANU). While KADU sought the recognition of the ethnic differences in a federalist or regionalist arrangement for independent Kenya, KANU wanted a strong centre with the regions as agents of the central government to be known as Provinces. Eventually, KANU won as KADU dissolved itself as a result of the policies supported by Mboya and Odinga in the KANU government of Kenyatta.

Not only did the Luo-Kikuyu dominated KANU put an end to *majimboism* (federalism) or regionalism, but Muliro's biographer pointed out that Oginga Odinga's obstruction of the movement of Trans Nzoia district from the Rift Valley to Western Region after a successful negotiation by Masinde Muliro, led the Luhyas to avoid Odinga's party at the 1992 multi-party elections.[15] However, Raila contended that this biographer had distorted facts as the transfer of Trans

---

Simiyu Wandibba, Masinde Muliro, (Nairobi: East African Educational Publishers, 1996), p. 19.

Nzoia was based on a signed agreement between Honourable Daniel arap Moi as the President of the Rift Valley Regional Assembly and Honourable Wafula Wabuge as the President of the Western Regional Assembly. For Raila, it was this agreement that was gazetted and that Oginga Odinga was not involved.[16]

There were other cleavages in the new government of Kenya. The Kenyatta Presidency and the so called "Kiambu Mafia" made up of the Kikuyus who surrounded the President, are generally claimed to have used Mboya to weaken Oginga Odinga. Tom Mboya, who was more socialized in the individualistic and materialistic approach to politics of the Kikuyu, who were strong on accumulation, was against Oginga Odinga's communal basis for politics that in Kenya, was generally considered as communism. This ideological difference between the two Luos, was manipulated into a bitter rivalry under Kenyatta until Oginga Odinga was dealt a blow in 1966.

Power going to Jaramogi Oginga Odinga after Kenyatta, was perceived as power to a Luo rather than to a capable Kenyan. While it is not clear if Tom Mboya was indeed being used, or if he had his own grand plan that involved getting his Luo rival out of the way, for him to be the main contender for Kenyatta's seat, the plot did not end there, as Mboya was subsequently assassinated.

The Luos saw a clear pattern in the marginalisation of Oginga Odinga and subsequently, the elimination of Tom Mboya. In a short time, the two foremost Luo politicians were off the national political scene.

The Luos' reaction to Mboya's assassination, had been evident even before the visit of President Jomo Kenyatta to Kisumu in October 1969. The events during that visit, which are explored later in this book, saw a swift reaction resulting in the detention of many Luo leaders including Jaramogi Oginga Odinga. For four days prior to the detention, he was under house arrest with his family, including Raila. The party he led after his forced resignation from KANU was banned leaving KANU with the legacy of a single-party which it enjoyed until the end of 1991.

---

[16] Interview with Raila Odinga, January 05, 2006. See also Raila's press statement as published in *Daily Nation,* October 19, 2005.

The Communism Albatross

As earlier pointed out, ideological differences and ambition within KANU, saw a heightening of the rivalry between Oginga Odinga and Tom Mboya. The legacy of the cold war led to a perception that Odinga was a Communist with allegiance to the Soviet Union and Communist China, while Mboya was seen as epitomizing the virtues of capitalist free enterprise, and allied to the United States of America.

Part of the simplistic illustrations of this dichotomy was with respect to student airlifts in the 1960s. Though Jaramogi had started seeking educational opportunities for Kenyans from wherever he could, much earlier than the perceived competition with Tom Mboya, emphasis is normally placed on the fact that he sent many to Eastern Europe. The fact that many more secured scholarships to India after he signed an Agreement with the Indian Cultural Association, was hardly ever mentioned.

The massive airlift of Kenyan youths to the spheres of influence of the major protagonists in the cold war, in search of education, was much related to the visionary zeal of Jaramogi. However, it is needless to state that these two different spheres of influence and ideologies, took active parts in shaping the course of Kenya's political history. Nonetheless, the fact was that Jaramogi sought education for young Kenyans of all ethnic groupings, from wherever he could get assistance.

That Raila was one of the beneficiaries of the airlift to Eastern Europe has been noted. This act of going to school in Eastern Europe was to haunt Raila for a long time, especially during the cold war. Even recently, when Raila has espoused private enterprise, his stress on social justice continues to scare other competing leaders. But this was really an inheritance from Jaramogi who had been similarly tagged a communist to hurt him politically. Jaramogi summed up his own frustration as follows:

> The allegation 'communism' has always been a convenient weapon. During the colonial times, Kenyatta was termed a Communist, and the freedom struggle was labelled Communist-inspired. Politicians have made use of the anti-communist smear not because they hold confirmed political views but to use a stick to beat those campaigning for real consultation with the people against corruption in public life. I ought to know. I am not a Communist but I have

been a constant target of anti-communist forces for all the years of my political history.[17]

Going further, he noted:

> I am incensed at all these declarations of 'fighting communism' when the target is really African liberation, African independence, and the right of Africans to make policies for their own countries.[18]

In effect, the false division placed on Jaramogi and Mboya, was part of an age-long style that started with colonial policies that divided all Kenyans along primordial lines. This division made control easy as whites, for the large part, expropriated African lands and forced them into the labour market on the large scale farms and miniscule industries. Starting with proto-nationalist associations, Kenyans, with the assistance of their kith and kin who had returned from World War II, improved their organizational capabilities. When political agitation by Jomo Kenyatta and Oginga Odinga among other, was not yielding enough, the military efforts of Dedan Kimathi and his comrades became a supplement.

The politicisation of ethnicity in Kenya by the colonialists resulted in a division between the Luo, led by Jaramogi Oginga Odinga, and the Kikuyu, led by Jomo Kenyatta. Then another dichotomy arose between Tom Mboya and Oginga Odinga. This time it was not sold as ethnicity, but as ideological difference. The assertion of ideological difference and personal leadership ambitions, accentuated the struggle between Mboya and Oginga Odinga. Mboya, an ally of Jomo Kenyatta, succeeded in sidelining Oginga Odinga. However, as soon as Tom Mboya fulfilled his historical role, he paid the ultimate price.

---

[17] Oginga Odinga, op. cit., p. 294.
[18] *Ibid.,* p. 295.

Chapter 05

Enter Ida

Ida started life on August 24, 1950 as the daughter of Nehemiah and Rosa Oyoo. While Nehemiah was a Luo, Rosa was born into a Luhya family from Buchero village in Khwisero Constituency of Kakamega District. Rosa became the first woman to be registered as a nurse from her area in 1934. She was trained on the job by the Church Missionary Society which ran the Kakamega General Hospital. Here she met Nehemiah, a young medic[1] from Gem constituency in Siaya district of Nyanza province. Their love affair was briefly interrupted when Nehemiah was transferred to Nairobi to work in the King's Rifle Hospital (now known as Kenyatta National Hospital).[2] However, Nehemiah would not give up and arranged for the transfer of his girl friend to Nairobi. They were married in 1936 after Nehemiah had parted with 25 cows as dowry. This was a lot in those days.

The union was blessed with six children. They were, in order of seniority: Nick Olwande Oyoo; Lynn Mary Yaya; Peter Ogada Oyoo; Ida Betty Odinga; Clarice Auma Oyoo and Eunice Atieno Sigei. The two male siblings of Ida have since died.

Nehemiah worked in many places in Kenya. Two days before Ida's birth, he was moved from Eldoret to Karbanet where Ida was born. Nehemiah was transferred to Migori in the mid-fifties to start a health centre. He took Ida along, leaving the older siblings with Rosa. Ida, as a result, started formal schooling in Migori in 1957. Nehemiah bought land in Migori and started a new home in which Rosa still lives. He did not live long thereafter. His death of suspected food poisoning in 1959, changed things. Rosa became a single mother and Ida's role model as she observed the determined hard-work of her mother in bringing up so many children without gender discrimination.

---

[1] A medic in Kenyan parlance implies a medical assistant. In the colonial times, these individuals gave prescriptions on ailments and carried out minor surgical operations in District Hospitals and supervised a number of dispensaries.

[2] This account benefited from an interview with Gibson Shiraku, Rosa's brother on April 25, 2004.

Ida went to Ogande Girls High School, near Homa Bay and for Advanced Level, she proceeded to Highlands School (now Moi Girls' School), Eldoret. She had wanted to study Mathematics, Geography and Biology at the Advanced Level. But she had to take Geography, Botany and Zoology under the policy of the school allowing only students who had gone through Secondary school in Alliance and Highlands, to take Mathematics. The school, according to Ida, had a bias that students from any other school, would not be able to cope with the demands of Mathematics.

As well as seeing her mother as a role model, Ida admired Ms. Mary Churchill who had spent over thirty years teaching in Kenya as Headmistress in many schools including at her Secondary School (Junior High School), where they met. Mary Churchill, for Ida, was an icon in Girls' education in Kenya as she encouraged, moulded and devoted her life to Kenyan girls. Ida felt Mary Churchill put extra effort into shaping her for the simple reason that she was young; good in academics, sports, games, and drama. She was generally outstanding. In addition, Mary Churchill was probably influenced in her attitude towards Ida because she had been Headmistress at Ng'iya Girls Secondary School and knew Ida's sister, Lynn there. Two American Peace Corps volunteers also remained in Ida's memory from Secondary School. The two ladies were Irene Hyatt from Atlanta and Patricia Thornton from Chicago. Though she did not know him at that time, Johnnie Carson, an Ambassador of the United States of America to Kenya from 1999 to 2003, was a Peace Corps volunteer in a nearby school.

In September 1971, Ida realized an ambition she developed at age 8, to go to University. This ambition had arisen out of a career visit to her school in 1958 by Thomas and Douglas Odhiambo and one Onyango, when she was in Standard 2. The trio, who were students at Makerere University, were to talk to senior students because teachers felt that younger students would not understand undergraduates. However, a teacher invited Ida to join in . She was mesmerized by the students, and during question time she wanted to know if girls attended Makerere University. When they replied in the affirmative, Ida asked if any of the girls were from Kenya and was told that most of the girls were from Uganda and none from Kenya. But they emphasized hard work as the yardstick to enter a University. She then resolved to work hard to go to a University, and at the University of Nairobi, she studied Geography and in 1974, graduated with a Bachelors of Arts with Education.

Ida's first meeting with Raila was on an evening in Nairobi, in 1972. Ida, an Undergraduate at the University of Nairobi, was in the company of her friend, Debra and Debra's Uncle, Mr. Ngeso Okolo. Ngeso had stopped to talk to Raila on Uhuru Highway. Ida took no notice of the person Ngeso spoke to. Then came another chance meeting at Brunner's restaurant, which, at that time, was famous in Nairobi. Ida was lunching with her brother, Peter and his girl-friend Noella. Raila was at lunch with Ngeso at the same restaurant. Ida stepped across to greet her friend's Uncle. She noticed that Ngeso reacted as if he did not know her well and introduced her to Raila as just one of Debra's friends.

Though Ida believes that Raila made a mental note of her at this meeting, Raila does not. He is sure that he became aware of Ida during a chance meeting at Peter Oyoo's residence with a relative of his, the late Okach Ogada Ondiek. Okach was one of the youth-wingers Jaramogi had sent on a short course on cooperative movements in the German Democratic Republic. On his return, he married Anna Omulo, Ida's cousin.

But Raila was no stranger to the family. He had earlier met Nick Oyoo, Ida's eldest brother in Eastern Europe, when both were students. Nick who was studying in Krakov, Poland, came to Germany on a visit and requested Raila's assistance to buy a used car. Raila, with his language skills travelled to West Berlin with Nick and helped him select a good Mercedes 200. In thanking him, Nick had joked that Raila deserved one of his sisters.

Raila had also known Peter independently as the most successful salesman at Marshall's (the Peugeot sales outlet in Nairobi). On that visit to Peter in the company of Okach, Raila vividly remembered that he was introduced to a young Ida who was in pinkish trousers and white blouse, as she emerged from the kitchen to be introduced. Subsequently, Okach suggested that they all went out for a drink. Lyn, Ida's elder sister, Peter and his wife Noella, all agreed. For Raila, that day marked the beginning of his interest that was to be concretised later in Kisumu when Ida was on a research project in the town and stayed at Okach's residence.

Ida was not Raila's first experience with women. He had a close relationship with the late Eudia Odonde who was popularly known as "Dodge." They remained in correspondence throughout his stay in the University. By the time she finished Senior High School, she went to study in Addis Ababa where her sister and brother-in-Law resided. She fell ill in Addis Ababa and had to return home, eventually marrying a former Nyanza MP as a third wife, before she died. As a student in Germany, Raila also had a deep relationship with Hilder, a German, also a student at Magdeburg, who specialized in Chemical Engineering and Production Technology.

By the time Raila met Ida, he did not have a steady relationship with any woman. They became very close friends and enjoyed each other's company as they drove in the country-side with Ida explaining her other love, the topography and vegetation of Kenya. Of course, they also discussed current affairs. On one such drive from Kisumu to Bondo in 1972, Raila, without a prior discussion, decided to stop at his home. Ida was taken before Jaramogi who was in his office in the house. Ida, who was wearing trousers, felt ashamed that she was not "properly" dressed to meet such a *Mzee* (respected elderly man). Jaramogi asked who Ida was. She gave her name and asserted that Jaramogi would not know her family. But when she said she was the daughter of Nehemiah Oyoo, Jaramogi exclaimed that Nehemiah was his classmate at Maseno, and that when he went to Makerere, Nehemiah went to training school as a medical assistant and subsequently died at Migori. Ida was surprised.

Subsequently and without Ida's knowledge, Jaramogi contacted Ida's paternal Uncle B.F.F. Oluande K'Oduol who had been a student at Maseno School when Jaramogi was on the staff, and whose expulsion with four other students Jaramogi had unsuccessfully fought against. He was later Jaramogi's collaborator as the Registrar of Lumumba Institute in Nairobi. Jaramogi and Mary (Raila's Mother) were eager to get Raila married for the simple reason that his immediate younger brother, Agola (now deceased) was not only married but had two children at the time. BFF Oluande K'Oduol went into discussions with Rosa.

Following Luo tradition, Raila and his family went to Rosa's residence to perform the betrothal ceremony known as *Ayie*. Raila was also accompanied by Okach and Bill Okoro, another friend. In demonstration of his commitment, Raila produced the gifts, and Ida was brought before the two families to say if she consented to a life long relationship with Raila. When Ida said yes, she had to leave the meeting room and before she knew it, cows had been exchanged without her even knowing how many cows were involved.

Ida and her friends had thought that it was better to finish at the University and work for at least two years before considering marriage. Raila had wanted to finish a Ph.D before marriage. But Jaramogi and Mary Odinga rushed the process. Ida's concession was for the marriage to take place a week after her 23rd birthday so that she could add another year on the record and feel more mature. Her wedding at St. Luke's in Kisumu had many Luos and a number of Luhyas.

The first decade of marriage was a close family life for Ida and her family. The couple had a first child (a boy), on November 2, 1973. His birth gave the opportunity for Raila to choose a hero's name for his son as is the practice for many a Luo. Unlike his father whose heroes were Luo, Raila's reality was larger. He chose his hero from Cuba in the person of Fidel Castro who was a hero of many young people in the world of the 1960s and 1970s.

The tell-tale signs of Raila being a committed political activist, were very clear including from the naming of his son. But Ida insisted that she never wanted a politician for a husband. Raila as an Engineer made her feel that he was different from his father. Ida did not see any inclination towards politics and cannot say precisely when Raila became a politician. Although Raila was attached to his father and felt most comfortable at his feet and could be with him for hours, Ida never saw a politician in the making.

Raila's University friends, with whom he exchanged political ideas, included Professor. Atieno-Odhiambo of Rice University; Fred Owino; Okoth Ogendo; Wandiga; Simiyu; Fred Okacha; George Anyona; Michael Kijana Wamalwa and Vincent Otieno. But Ida did not see the growth of a politician taking place in her husband.

Ida the Teacher

Immediately after graduating from the University of Nairobi in May 1974, Ida Odinga started teaching at the Highway Secondary School, off Mombasa Road in Nairobi. She was appointed Head of the Geography Department and taught sixth form boys and a few girls. Some of the boys were older than her and looked down on her on the first day. They demanded her credentials to teach in form six. She disarmed them all and won their confidence when they realized she had been to one of Kenya's elite schools and had graduated from the University of Nairobi. Most of the students were Asians and only about ten percent were girls. But her memorable stay at Highway Secondary School was short-lived as she was moved to Kenya High School at the beginning of 1976.

Kenya High School was, at that time, still dominated by a European cultural outlook. The students were mainly Africans from elite families and with uppity attitudes. The staff was evenly distributed among Africans, Asians, Europeans and Arabs. The school was headed by Ms. Burns who had been Ida's Headmistress when she was an Advanced Level student at Highlands School. Ida taught Geography and General Paper but spent a lot of time in extra-curricular activities, including organizing St. John's Ambulance and the Red Cross. However, her most important activity was to set up a Kenya-German Students Exchange Programme in 1981. Ida turned the chance of a meeting with a German tour entrepreneur and tourist guide into an exchange programme.

The arrangement was simple. Kenyan students went to Germany for a month in August and stayed with German families with children of the same age. The German children repeated the same arrangement in Kenya during the month of December. The parents paid the airfares for their children. In Germany, the Kenyan students visited camp sites, universities, industries (ship-building, chocolate factories etc.), and took boat rides on the River Rhine. The Kenyan students took their German friends to the coast and rural Kenya showing the geographic formations and wild-life. The programme lasted two decades.

A creeping problem of the time, when Raila moved to the Kenya Bureau of Standards, was that he became a workaholic, leaving home early and returning late. However, Sunday was a family day spent with about six other families. Ida remembers especially the Atieno-Odhiambo and Fred Owino families. With pride, she expressed her excitement when, at the graduation of her daughter, Rosemary Odinga in Washington D.C. in May 2002, all the kids of those days came with their parents to felicitate with Rosemary.

Chapter 06
Graveyard's Peace and Stability

"Jomo Kenyatta had aspired to be both 'father of the nation' and the paramount chief of the Kikuyu people, ... His whole political life in the post-independence era was a struggle to come to terms with these conflicting yearnings. Much as he may have wanted to play the first role more seriously, he had to contend with the demands of the Kikuyu and to some extent, the Meru and Embu, who felt that the colonial government had made a deliberate effort to silence them due to Mau-Mau. Since they had fought the colonial government and, in their view, driven it out, it was time for them to receive their due, euphemistically called 'the national cake'. Kenyatta had to deliver to his core constituency on a priority basis or lose credibility altogether."

Githu Muigai, "Ethnicity and the Renewal of Competitive Politics in Kenya," in Harvey Glickman, ed., *Ethnic Conflict and Democratization in Africa*, (Atlanta: African Studies Association, 1995), p. 173

"the death of Jomo Kenyatta on August 22, 1978, marked a turning point in Kenyan history. There followed an out-pouring of emotion throughout the country, eulogies from around the world, and a great display of funeral ceremony. Personal tributes, hymns and Christian pronouncements were beamed by radio to all corners of Kenya. The corruption and heavy-handed rule that had marred Kenyatta's last years seemed forgotten. In death, he was again the Father of the Nation, the Mzee, the honoured leader."

N. Miller & R. Yeager, *Kenya: The Quest for Prosperity*, (Boulder, Colorado: Westview Press, 1994)

The beginning of the multi-party struggle in Kenya, predated the birth of Raila. Kenya, towards, and even for a year after independence, was an example of a budding multi-party democracy. But this experience was short-lived as a de-facto single party order ruled Kenya until 1982 when it became a de-jure arrangement.

The first African organization in Kenya that could truly be called a political party, was the Kenya African Union (KAU). The associations of the 1920s referred to earlier, were banned in the inter war years by the colonial authorities. KAU arose immediately after the war as an expression of the ferment in the African communities over dissatisfaction with the governance of Africans without them having a voice in the process. The KAU of 1946 was multi-ethnic and multi-regional. Its leaders had acquired some level of Western education; and some had participated in the Second World War and had no problem in standing up for African rights. Though Jomo Kenyatta was the foremost leader in KAU, there were many others including Achieng' Oneko, Bildad Kaggia, Oginga Odinga, Fred Kubai, Paul Ngei, etc. Even one of the biographers of Dedan Kimathi Waciuri, the foremost *Mau Mau* leader, pointed out that KAU deliberations presented Kimathi with a political training ground as the forests of Mount Kenya and Aberdares provided the real test ground.[1]

The deterioration in the lives of the indigenous Kenyans in the urban and rural areas, and the White Highlands, which had been expropriated from Kikuyus, Maasai and others, and which had led to various complaints in the pre-war years, continued after the war. This led to confrontation when some Africans decided to take to the forest in the war of liberation dubbed the *Mau Mau* uprising by the colonial administration.

A decision to clamp down on the *Mau Mau* resulted in a colonial approach that lumped KAU together with *Mau Mau*. As a result, many Kenyans were arrested on 20-21 October 1952. Jomo Kenyatta, the foremost KAU leader and Achieng' Oneko, Bildad Kaggia, Fred Kubai, Paul Ngei and Kung'u Karumba were also arrested.

These leaders were charged with being members, and managing or assisting with the management of an unlawful society known as *Mau Mau*. They were further accused of conspiracy to compel oathing by people and causing general disaffection towards the Colonial government. Their trial lasted from December 3, 1952 to April 8, 1953 when the magistrate found them all guilty on all charges and sentenced them to the maximum penalty of seven years with hard labour. On completion of the sentence, they were to be put under house arrest at the mercy of the

---

[1] Tabitha Kanogo, *Dedan Kimathi: A Biography,* (Nairobi: East African Educational Publishers, 1992), p. 6.

Colonial government.[2] This marked the beginning of the sacrifice that subsequently put Jomo Kenyatta in the enviable position of being the symbol of Kenya's independence and eventually the founding father of independent Kenya.

After imprisoning the leadership of KAU, the colonial administration banned the party in June 1953, and restricted party formation to the district level. As a result, everal district level parties were formed, reflecting the ethnic realities. Ronald Ngala as a Mijikenda saw fit to reform and chair the Mijikenda Union (after he was elected to the Legislative Council in 1957) to work alongside the Kilifi African Peoples Union (KAPU), which he had earlier founded with Sammy T. Omar, and used it to fight for his election. He left the wider-based Mombasa African Democratic Union (MADU) formed by Francis Khamisi in 1955. Ngala returned to his larger Mijikenda group with a party he used for the campaign against Francis Khamisi among others. In a similar move, Moi assembled his ethnic grouping into the Kalenjin Political Alliance.

This move by the colonial authorities could be seen as having aided the continuation of politics based on past use and exploitation of ethnicity in Kenya. Though the initial struggles of Kenyan leaders was on the issue of representation for Africans against the total dominance or pre-eminence of Europeans and, to some extent, Asians, as independence loomed, political pressure was diverted towards ethnicity. The drafters of a new constitution for Kenya, did not miss this point in their analysis on constitutional development in Kenya when they stated:

> The divisions among Africans were in part, the result of restrictions and prevented them from establishing country-wide political parties. Parties were district based and inevitably they tended to attract strong ethnic or tribal following.

> Tribal consciousness was stimulated, and a common nationalism was hindered, by the colonial policy of using the tribe as the unit of administration and the restrictions on the movement and communication among Africans.[3]

---

[2] For details, see, among others, S.N. Waruhiu, *From Autocracy to Democracy in Kenya: Past Systems of Government and Reforms for the Future* (Nairobi: S.N. Waruhiu, 1994), pp. 27-32.

[3] Constitution of Kenya Review Commission, *The Main Report of the Constitution of Kenya Review Commission,* Nairobi, Kenya, September 18, 2002, p. 15.

As the struggle for power started when independence appeared possible, aside from settler parties like Michael Blundell's New Kenya Party (NKP) with what Jaramogi termed a deceptive multi-racialism plea, and Group Captain Briggs' United Party that sought regionalism as a way to divide Africans,[4] two groups came into contention in the African Elected Members Organization (AEMO). On the one hand was the Masinde Muliro-led multi-racial Kenya National Party (KNP), formed in 1959 with the support of Ngala, Moi, Nyagah, Khamisi, Mate, Towett, Ole Tipis, Muimi, D.I. Kiamba, one European and six Asian elected members of the Legislative Council. The other group saw the remaining six AEMO members joining with eleven district associations to form the mono-racial (largely Luos and Kikuyus) and unregistered Kenya Independence Movement (KIM) with Oginga Odinga as president, Tom Mboya as secretary and Julius Gikonyo Kiano as chairman.[5]

The attempt to have an umbrella party to articulate the interests of all Africans, resulted in a meeting on 27 March 1960 in Kiambu. This meeting agreed to form a committee to draft the constitution of the Kenya African National Union (KANU). Ronald Ngala and Daniel arap Moi who had been elected Treasurer and Deputy Treasurer in absentia, rejected the positions. Seeing KANU (which had now absorbed the KIM members) as a Kikuyu-Luo party, they joined with others at another conference on 25 June 1960 at Ngong to form the Kenya African Democratic Union (KADU) which included Masinde Muliro's KNP. In effect, "both political parties that oversaw the birth of the independent Kenyan state reflected ethnicism."[6]

Given the fear of the two majority ethnic groups by KADU members, it was not surprising that KADU preferred a federal governance structure, referred to as *Majimboism*. KANU, understandably, would have nothing to do with KADU's fight for *Majimboism*. Put differently, federalism based on seven regions plus Nairobi, and a weak centre, was anathema to KANU. On the contrary and at the instigation of settlers, the smaller ethnic groups that had enjoyed relative autonomy in their respective areas, with their own parties in control, did not want to hand their power over to what they saw as a Kikuyu-Luo alliance called KANU. Though

---

[4]   See, Oginga Odinga, *op. cit.*, pp. 164-165.
[5]   See, Simiyu Wandibba, *Masinde Muliro: A Biography* (Nairobi: East African Educational Publishers, 1996), pp. 13-14.
[6]   Githu Muigai, *op. cit.*, p. 167.

Oginga Odinga and Tom Mboya had been suspicious of each other, they were united against KADU's philosophy. That KADU membership was open to the settlers did not endear it as a party to leaders like Oginga Odinga who argued that *Majimboism* was a settlers' plan to undermine genuine independence for Kenya.

Kenyatta at the Mantle

However, the April 1963 independence constitution was negotiated and agreed on the position of KADU. Regionalism was agreed and a bicameral legislature was put in place. The upper house called the Senate was to take care of the interests of the regions. KANU saw this concession as the price it must pay if KADU was to accede to independence.

With the triumph of KANU in the May 1963 elections that ushered in self-rule, and KANU's subsequent control of the apparatus of power at the centre, the days of KADU were numbered. Oginga Odinga and Tom Mboya saw to it that KADU became unviable, and the rump of its leadership that had not already crossed the carpet, ended up in KANU on the first anniversary of republican government in 1964.

The merger between KADU and KANU saw Moi, among others, achieve a larger goal of having access to a truly national party as he looked beyond his Kalenjin base for national leadership. In effect, Moi and other leaders achieved a much larger playing field for his leadership aspirations. In exchange, Moi sacrificed the Kalenjin wish to stop Kikuyu expansion into the fertile lands of the Rift Valley.[7] Much later, Moi rewarded the Kalenjin elite with capital accumulation.

Importantly, however, the admission of the relatively conservative KADU leaders strengthened the hands of Jomo Kenyatta's conservative wing of KANU, which wanted to reduce Oginga Odinga's influence.[8] This conservative wing included Tom Mboya; Ronald Ngala; Daniel T. arap Moi; Jeremiah Nyagah and Bruce Mackenzie. Oginga Odinga was allied with Bildad Kaggia, a former *Mau Mau* activist and Achieng' Oneko.

---

[7] See, *ibid.,* pp. 166-170.
[8] See, Ngugi wa Thiong'o, *Detained: A Writer's Prison Diary* (Nairobi: East African Educational Publishers, 1981), pp. 51-56.

Oginga Odinga in *Not Yet Uhuru,* detailed his tribulations as he sought a more egalitarian Kenya. These problems included the murder of his Asian friend and collaborator who was an avowed communist, Pio da Gama Pinto on February 4, 1965. Pinto was one of the few Asians who fought for the African voice like Makham Singh, Pramla Seth, Ambu Patel and others. These Asian pioneers, like the Mau Mau warriors were marginalised. Pinto's assassination was an early message to the Asian community to leave politics to Kenyatta and his friends, and face commerce. But more importantly, and probably what finally caused Pinto's murder was his intellectual support to Oginga Odinga's efforts.

As time went by, Oginga Odinga's political marginalisation was carefully planned and executed. After re-organising the KANU party branches, a new KANU constitution, approved by the KANU Parliamentary Group rather than the party conference, was put in place in what was effectively a party coup. This constitution replaced the largely (at this time), decorative position of Oginga Odinga as KANU vice-president with a party vice-president for each of the seven provinces, and one for Nairobi.

Thus, at the only party Conference, held at Limuru in March 1966, Odinga was demoted. Downgraded, Oginga Odinga, Achieng' Oneko and Bildad Kaggia, who saw his victory as party vice-president for Central Province, turned into defeat in favour of James Gichuru, all left KANU. Earlier, Bildad Kaggia had been dismissed as an Assistant Minister of Education for criticizing the slow pace of Africanisation of the civil service and the resistance to making land available to the people. Oginga Odinga resigned from KANU and the Government on April 14, 1966, and announced the formation of the Kenya People's Union (KPU) a week later. Achieng' Oneko quit the government the following week to join the new party.

The KPU, led by Oginga Odinga, sought to raise the level of Kenyan political debate beyond ethnicity. As David Throup and Charles Hornsby pointed out, "the KPU's goal was to create a more left-wing party, to oppose the growing conservatism and Western orientation of the KANU leadership, and to try to replace the persistently ethnic basis of politics with a cleavage based on ideological, class or socio-economic grounds."[9]

[9] David W. Throup & Charles Hornsby, *Multi-Party Politics in Kenya: The Kenyatta & Moi States & the Triumph of the System in the 1992 Election,* (Oxford: James Currey, 1998), p. 13

Ironically, Oginga Odinga had supported the marginalisation of KADU towards a one-party state only to become a casualty of that development. A constitutional amendment forced twenty-nine KPU Lower House and ten Senate members to return to the electorate in their respective constituencies, for a renewal of their mandate. The argument was that they were deciding to move away from the party their constituency members had endorsed, and needed a re-affirmation from the people that they still supported them in Parliament as members of another party. The by-elections for this purpose, were tagged "Little General Election" and resulted in nine members of the KPU (seven were Luos) being returned to parliament.[10]

Though some would suggest that the coming into existence of the KPU meant a return to multi-partyism, the KPU with a tiny Parliamentary Party Group, could not be described as an opposition. A situation of overwhelming disproportional strength of KANU compared to KPU could not, rightly, be termed as a two-party situation, far less as multi-partyism. In effect, there was a *de-facto* one party situation in Kenya despite the creation of the KPU which claimed to be seriously ideologically different[11] but did not have the strength to affect either the policies of KANU, or the politics of Kenya.

Repression as Governance under the Kenyatta Regime

The KPU was tolerated for three years. However, within this period, many of the KPU leaders were jailed. In addition, several administrative and legal impediments were placed on the way of the party. For instance, its ability to hold meetings at the branch level, was hampered. Delay or refusal to register many of its branches, meant that the KPU could not sponsor candidates from such branches for elections. However, before returning to the harrowing experience of those who dared to voice dissent, it is worth looking at the enforcement of stability for accumulation under Kenyatta.

---

[10] See among others, Nick G. Wanjohi, *Political Parties in Kenya: Formation, Policies and Manifestoes,* (Nairobi: Views Media, 1997)

[11] The KPU was avowedly socialist, at least in rhetoric, as its manifesto opined on the need to nationalize productive assets and give land to the tiller in Kenya. KANU on the other hand was capitalistic in utterances.

Jomo Kenyatta's struggle for the independence of Kenya had been noted. His arrest on October 20, 1952 and subsequent imprisonment, represented a major sacrifice for the independence of Kenya. He acquired a father figure image in Kenya. He was a respected larger than life figure. He was a persuasive orator who easily swayed people. And Kenyatta provided a stable environment in Kenya which experienced significant economic growth.

However, Kenyatta's father of the nation image, tended to make analysts avoid any critical assessments of his regime, especially with respect to human rights. Many Kenyans faced repression under Kenyatta's watch. In the aftermath of Oginga Odinga's break-away from KANU to form the KPU, many of his associates were detained, some for very long periods.

At independence, Kenyatta assumed the mantle of leadership, first as Prime Minister before very rapidly becoming a President with enormous executive powers. He held sway over the *de facto* one party state with his KANU as the only party after they had first seduced and then given KADU the kiss of death.

Apart from three years of military operations known as the *shifta* wars which brutalized the irredentist moves of ethnic Somali Kenyans, President Kenyatta's rule over Kenya enjoyed stability. It is a fact that stability is a *sine qua non* for the economic well-being of a nation. Kenyatta's period in office experienced positive economic growth and economic development in Kenya. Coffee, the main export crop of the country, attracted high returns for the country and its farmers. The Kenyan economy grew at an average of 6.0 per cent in the 1960s and 6.6 per cent in the 1970s.[12] Many would argue that this economic performance was the result of a positive international environment for Kenyan commodity products,[13] and, of course, massive foreign aid. However, the story was more than that. Kenyatta encouraged private accumulation by many of his co-elites and especially by

---

[12] See, Colin Leys, *Underdevelopment in Kenya: The Political Economy of Neo-Colonialism*, (Nairobi: East African Educational Publishers, 1975) and Musalia Mudavadi, *Rethinking Development in Africa in the 21st Century: The Case Study of Kenya*, (Nairobi: East African Educational Publishers, 2002).

[13] See, for instance, Mudavadi, *ibid.*

members of his family and Kikuyu ethnic kins.[14] In addition, a growing Asian community in Kenya at independence, used the profit margins they had accumulated to move rapidly into industrial investment. The Asian population accounted for "over 67 per cent of all the locally owned industrial enterprises with fifty or more employees."[15]

A concerted effort was made to encourage Africans into a competitive mode on industrialization and commerce. An Africanisation programme was embarked upon. With assistance from the German government, the Kenya Industrial Estates as a concept was set up as an example. Raila Odinga joined this programme and became both a beneficiary and a benefactor.

The positive environment in Nairobi and Kenya as a whole, attracted the United Nations to make Nairobi the Headquarters of two of its large programmes: United Nations Environment Programme (UNEP) and United Nations Centre for Human Settlements (UNCHS), i.e., HABITAT both with almost the status of Agencies.

However, Patrick O. Asingo, in a contribution to a volume on Kenya, suggests that Jomo Kenyatta, the founding father of Kenya was only a great leader on three occasions in his entire career and leadership of Kenya. These were: in 1961 when he was released from detention; in 1963 when he led Kenya to independence; and in 1978 when he died.[16] This may sound too harsh a revision of history, but it may not be too far from the reality. In Kenya, there is a tendency to over-dramatize deaths in office and by so doing, to wash the slate clean.[17]

It is worth examining the issue of detention of Kenyans without trial, or their imprisonment under spurious charges under Kenyatta, as the prelude to actions perfected under the regime of his successor.

---

[14] See, David W. Throup, "Kenya: Revolution, Relapse, or Reform?" CSIS Africa Notes, Number 3, November 2001, p. 2.

[15] Leys, *op. cit.,* p. 45.

[16] See, Walter O. Oyugi, Peter Wanyande and C. Odhaimbo-Mbai, eds., *The Politics of Transition in Kenya, from KANU to NARC,* (Nairobi: Heinrich Boll Foundation, 2003), p. 36.

[17] Similar was the situation on the death of Vice-President Michael Kijana Wamalwa in 2003.

Detentions under the Kenyatta rule

The first casualties of the detentions under the rule of the father of the nation, were members of the Kenya People's Union (KPU). As the party was taking shape, Dennis Akumu, who had left KANU for the new KPU, was involved in a rally at Nairobi's Madaraka grounds.[18] According to Akumu, the rally "was so successful that we, the organizers, were the first beneficiaries of the newly passed Detention Act, which was introduced in Parliament by Mboya."[19] The success of the rally resulted in the detention on August 4, 1966 of Akumu and six others: Ochola Mak'Anyengo, Oyangi Mbaja, Opwapo Ogai, Oluande K'Oduol, Rading Omolo and P. P. Ooko. Dennis Akumu and Rading Omolo were the first to be released a year later. But others were not as lucky.

Late Oluande K'Oduol recorded the harrowing experience in an autobiographical manuscript. They were kept in solitary confinement and allowed out for only an hour each day. Each inmate defecated and urinated in one bucket and emptied as well as washed the bucket clean in the morning in a daily ritual. When K'Oduol's mother was murdered by thieves during his detention, he pleaded to be allowed to attend the burial. But the Kenyatta government rejected his plea. He was incarcerated for four years.[20]

About three weeks after the arrest of the Dennis Akumu group, another set of arrests of KPU leaders took place on August 22. Among the new set was the Private Secretary of Jaramogi Oginga Odinga, Mrs. Caroline Okello Odongo, an African American who was married to Tom Okello Odongo MP, a brilliant economist and KPU leader. Daniel arap Moi as Minister for Home Affairs, alleged that Caroline Okello Odongo was a conduit for the funnelling of funds to the KPU from external sources for the subversion of the Government of Kenya. She was the only occupant of the female wing of the Kamiti Maximum Security Prison.[21]

---

[18] See, Dennis Akumu's chat as reported by Kwamboka Oyaro, "Keny@40: 1968-1969," A *Daily Nation* Supplement, p. 12, in *Daily Nation*, August 14, 2003.

[19] *Ibid.*

[20] See, B.F.F. Oluande K'Oduol, Cultural and Political Evolution in Kenya: an autobiography, unpublished manuscript dated 12/12/1994, pp. 75-77

[21] Interview with Israel Otieno Wasonga Agina, Nairobi, May 27, 2003.

Jaramogi Oginga Odinga himself did not escape. He was briefly detained on his return from Uganda to Kenya on October 7, 1966. Moi accused him of having gone to Uganda to receive funds and announced that the Government would not tolerate any in-flow of funds for subversive purposes. Jaramogi responded in Parliament that he had gone to Uganda to consult Lawyers about the detention of nine members of KPU.

Nationalist Bildad Kaggia, who, with Kenyatta, had been detained at Kapenguria by the colonial authorities, had a repeat experience in independent Kenya. His ideological political commitment to land re-distribution in favour of the landless, made him an able collaborator of Jaramogi Oginga Odinga. On April 10, 1969, Kaggia was found guilty of holding illegal meetings. He received a one-year sentence that was subsequently halved by Acting Chief Justice Farrel. Kaggia, the accomplished nationalist, was to remain in jail until October of the same year.[22] He was deliberately made to serve his term in his constituency, Thika, where he had to cut grass publicly, so that his constituents could see his pitiable state.

Other KPU leaders were even dealt with outside Kenyan territory. Were Olonde, who had transported the KPU manifesto from Germany to Uganda and put them on the boat for Bondo, was kidnapped by Kenyan secret agents and transported into Kenya for torture.

But he was not the only victim of this type of brigandage by the Kenyatta regime. Ochola Achola, who was KPU Youth Leader, had, with Kimani Waiyaki, (the first African Town Clerk of the City of Nairobi, who became KPU's Publicity Secretary), slipped into exile when things got too hot for KPU members. They were both kidnapped from exile and tortured in Kenya. Ochola Achola, was detained in 1968, and on his release in 1970, had become a completely different person. He never spoke to anyone for more than twenty years. People initially thought he was pretending. He died in 1997.[23]

This repressive style of the regime of the father of the nation, was clearly evident in the story of the early life of one young Kenyan. On January 28, 1969, the Kenyan Foreign Minister, Chiedo M.G. Argwings-Kodhek died on the Nairobi

---

[22] See, "Keny@40: 1968," p. 4, A *Daily Nation* Supplement, in *Daily Nation,* August 14, 2003.
[23] Interview with Raila Odinga, February 15, 2004.

road, subsequently named after him. His car had, reportedly been involved in a lone accident at the junction of what were Hurlingham Road and Wood Avenue and had overturned. As soon as Jaramogi learnt of this mysterious death, which many Luos saw as one of the many political killings under Kenyatta, he cut short his visit to Tanzania and returned to Kenya. Accompanying him on the trip was a 19 year old assistant, Israel Otieno Wasonga Agina.

Those were the days when Jaramogi was operating under the KPU. As a result, he was under constant surveillance and psychological harassment. At the border, according to Israel Agina, a large contingent of uniformed and plain-clothes policemen, was waiting for Odinga's party. The policemen thoroughly searched their vehicle and personal belongings. During this process, they discovered photographs and personal notes which Israel Agina had written. These items and some of Agina's books were taken away. And on February 6, 1969, Israel Agina was arrested from the KPU offices along Monrovia Street, Nairobi by John Bell who later became the Director of the Criminal Investigation Department. He was accused of being a professional revolutionary trained in North Korea. It was also alleged that he was found in possession of seditious documents related to plans to arrest President Kenyatta, overthrow his government and supplant it with KPU as a revolutionary party.

Israel Agina pleaded not guilty to the charges. He stated that his private notes had shown that he was not happy with the Kenyatta regime for having reneged on the aspirations of Kenyans who had been under British bondage for over 70 years. He saw the continuation of the same bondage under Jomo Kenyatta who, for him, had abandoned the freedom fighters and other patriots, and colluded with home guards to entrench neo-colonialism.[24] For the contents of his private unpublished notes, and without any further evidence or action by him suggesting that he planned to carry out a coup, Israel Agina was handed a four-year jail term.

Alleged Political Killings

Pio da Gama Pinto had blazed the trail on what Kenyans generally believed as political murders as a mode of governance under President Kenyatta. While the

---

[24] Interview with Agina, Nairobi, May 27, 2003.

death of CMG Argwings-Kodhek in a lone car crash was seen by some as an accident, many, especially among the Luo community saw this death as symptomatic of the attempt to eliminate prominent Luos. This reasoning was buoyed by the assassination of Tom Mboya on July 5, 1969 in the doorway of Channi's Pharmacy on the then Government Road (now Moi Avenue), in Nairobi. [25] A 30-year old Kikuyu man, Nahashon Isaac Njenga Njoroge was arrested and charged with Mboya's murder. On his arrest, he reportedly asked the police why they had come after him, leaving 'the big man.'

Though Israel Agina spent most of his time in jail in solitary confinement, one of the people he shared neighbouring cells with, was Nahashon Njenga. According to Agina, Nahashon Njenga maintained that he had no reason to kill Tom Mboya as Mboya had personally helped him, and he would be the last person to harm a person who had been kind to him. He claimed that he was framed. However, he was unable to explain to Agina why he thought he was being framed. Agina could not establish whether Nahashon Njenga was a murderer. He also wondered if Nahashon Njenga was not telling the whole truth because, immediately after Mboya's assassination, he had taken the Kikuyu oath of secrecy at Kenyatta's Gatundu residence under the President's supervision in his other role as the Kikuyu Paramount Chief. Whatever, the truth, Agina was unable to help history, as Njenga was moved to the condemned prisoners' cells block after his trial.

Though Nahashon Njenga was hanged for the assassination of Tom Mboya, the public accused the Kenyatta Government of being responsible.[26] Despite a sense of national loss that Kenyatta tried to put up, the Luos held the Kikuyu responsible for the assassination, and riots in Nairobi, Kisumu and Homa Bay showed the reaction, as Kikuyu shops were looted in Nyanza.

The Repressive De Facto One Party State

The strong Kikuyu-Luo relationship at independence which had scared other Kenyans into forming KADU, and pressing for and realizing *Majimbo* in the

---

[25] Other deaths included in the category of political assassination under the watch of the father of the nation, would include, JM Kariuki, Kungu Karumba etc. It is beyond the efforts in this book to establish the veracity of many of these claims

[26] Edwin Gimode, *Tom Mboya*, (Nairobi: East African Educational Publishers, 1996), pp. 47-52.

independence constitution, was at an all time low. The demotion of Oginga Odinga that resulted in his resignation from the enviable post of Vice-President, was enough humiliation for the Luos. But having another light of Luo pride permanently eliminated in the assassination of Mboya, took anti-Kikuyu feelings among the Luo to a higher level. The feelings of the Kikuyus towards the Luos were no different. Everybody unto his own ethnic group was the overwhelming feeling.

The crisis that accompanied the assassination of Mboya came to a head on October 25, 1969 when President Kenyatta was visiting Kisumu to open the New Nyanza General Hospital, built by the Soviet Union and commonly known as the Russian Hospital.

Raila remembered that presidential visit.[27] He had arrived in Kenya from Germany, on 24 October 1969 via Entebbe. He chose Entebbe, not only because it was closer to Kisumu, but also because the immigration and customs officials there were friendlier than in Nairobi. In those days of the East African Community, he took an internal flight from Entebbe to Kisumu.

As he approached the town in a cab driven by a familiar old man, they met a Ministry of Information vehicle announcing the Presidential visit on the following day. The cab driver said that the Luos were apprehensive of the Presidential visit and suspected there were ulterior motives behind it.

On the same evening, Jaramogi Oginga Odinga arrived from Nairobi, soon to be followed by other KPU MPs like Tom Okello Odongo, Luke Obok, Achieng Oneko, and Okuto Bala. They were joined by local leaders in Kisumu and a discussion ensued. According to Raila, those who spoke, claimed to have information that the Presidential visit had been planned to discredit the KPU; that there would be provocation; and any melee resulting therefrom, would be blamed on Jaramogi and his supporters. It was suggested that Jaramogi stayed away from the ceremony. But Jaramogi would not agree, arguing that if he stayed away and there was any trouble, he would surely be accused of having been involved in its planning. So it was decided that Jaramogi would attend, but that the people would be urged to be peaceful during the Presidential visit.

---

[27] Interview with Raila Odinga, Nairobi, July 21, 2003.

People lined the road as the Presidential convoy arrived from the Kakamega end of Kisumu town. Jaramogi Oginga Odinga was waiting at the entrance of the hospital to receive the President. As the convoy arrived in town, the President was standing in his limousine waving his fly-whisk as his entourage gave the KANU one finger salute, shouting "Jogoo," (Cockerel) the symbol of KANU. Those welcoming the President responded with the thumb salute of the KPU and shouted "Dume," (meaning Bull) the symbol of the KPU. According to Raila, the Presidential police escort started shooting at the crowd:

> At first, I thought it was fire-crackers. Then all of a sudden people were falling down screaming as others ran away. At that time, we took-off and ran towards the hospital in search of Jaramogi. I realized he was in the crowd and ran back to get him and we took cover inside the building. As they fired, they threw tear gas. The commotion went on for about 15 minutes. When it subsided, we came out.[28]

President Kenyatta went straight to the podium and was surrounded by his Ministers. Jaramogi took his seat opposite. In his public address, as Raila remembered, President Kenyatta blamed Jaramogi for having organized his people to come and shout at him, referring to the people as insects that should be ground into flour for maize meal. Jaramogi's response that the people were hungry and as a result had become noisy, did not go down well. The words of an irate Kenyatta on this occasion as translated from Kiswahili were:

> Now, I want, before opening this hospital, I want to say a few words; and I will start with the Kiswahili proverb which states that "the thanks of a donkey are its hind kick." We have come here to bring you luck, to bring a hospital which is for treating the citizens, and now there are some writhing little insects, little insects of the KPU, who have dared to come here to speak dirty words, dirty words. I am very glad to be with my friend Odinga, who is the leader of these people here. And I wish to say, if it were not for the respect I have for our friendship, Odinga, I would have said that you get locked up today... so that we see who rules over these citizens, whether it is KANU, or some many little insects who rule over this country ... On my part I do say this, if these people are dirty, if they bring about nonsense, we shall show them that Kenya has got

---

[28] *Ibid.*

its government. They dare not play around with us, and you Bwana Odinga as an individual, you know that I do not play around. I have left you free for a long time because you are my friend. Were it not so, you yourself know what I would have done. It is not your business to tell me where to throw you; I personally know where. Maybe you think I cannot throw you into detention in Manyani because you are my special friend ... And therefore today I am speaking in a very harsh voice, and while I am looking at you directly, and I am telling you the truth in front of these people. Tell these people of yours to desist. If not, they are going to feel my full wrath. And me, I do not play around at all .... They are chanting *Dume, Dume* – Bull, Bull. Your mothers' cunts, this *Dume, Dume*. ... And me, I want to tell you Odinga, while you are looking at me with your two eyes wide open; I have given my orders right now: those creeping insects of yours are to be crushed like flour. They are to be crushed like flour if they play with us. You over there, do not make noise there. I will come over there and crush you myself.[29]

The President after threatening Jaramogi Oginga Odinga, perfunctorily opened the hospital and took-off. Raila claimed to have seen the police escort continued shooting as they left. A stray bullet hit and killed Alnoor Dahya, an eight year old Asian child, the only son of Abdul Dahya, a former Deputy Mayor of Kisumu, in his house 30 metres from the scene. Abdul Dahya claimed he was the only person of Asian origin to publicly support Jaramogi Oginga Odinga's KPU.[30] Odungi Randa, a former political detainee who was the KPU branch secretary in Nyanza was at the scene. He mused:

"I think those renewed shootings were meant to clear the way for the Head of State, who was said to be at risk. But why they were directed at people and not in the air still puzzles me."[31]

The crowd hurled stones and insults at President Kenyatta. Two people were killed at the market, about a kilometre from the scene. Another two were shot dead at Ahero, 25 kilometres away, and the same number were murdered at Awasi

---

[29] See, E.S. Atieno Odhiambo, "Ethnic Cleansing and Civil Society in Kenya, 1969-1992," unpublished paper, pp. 4-7. The speech given in Kiswahili was translated in the paper.

[30] See, "Keny@40: 1969," p. 12, A *Daily Nation* Supplement, in *Daily Nation*, August 14, 2003

[31] Odungi Randa's interview with Agai Yier, *ibid.*

about thirty miles away. According to Raila Odinga, all this was for waving the thumb sign.[32]

At the end of the melee, there were different accounts of the number of people killed. While Atieno-Odhiambo recorded the official count as claiming that thirteen people had been killed, Raila remembers counting over 40 dead bodies before he left the scene. His estimate was that over 100 were killed in what he referred to as the "Kisumu Massacre."[33] Raila's estimate was corroborated by B.A. Ogot, the respected Kenyan historian.[34]

As the President's convoy reached Kericho, he announced a 6 pm to 6 am dusk to dawn curfew in Kisumu. By 1 a.m., Jaramogi's residence was surrounded by General Service Unit policemen. All residents, including Raila, were placed under house arrest for four days. In the course of their arrest, they learned that KPU leaders had been arrested and detained on the first night.

On the fifth day, Jaramogi's Aide-de-Camp (ADC) when he was Vice-President, was the officer chosen to lead a convoy of two land-rovers that took Jaramogi to detention. The KPU was formally banned. Jaramogi spent one and a half years in detention, but Achieng Oneko was not released until Ocotber 16, 1975, six years later. Wasonga Sijeyo was detained for almost a decade.

Within twelve weeks of the banning of the KPU, the Kikuyu leadership became openly ethnic as they rallied all adult males among the GEMA (Gikuyu, Embu and Meru Association) and the neighbouring Kamba, into a mass oathing reminiscent of the *Mau Mau* era, to keep the Presidency in their community.[35]

Oginga Odinga's troubles in the bitter factional struggles with Kenyatta and Tom Mboya that resulted in the creation of the KPU, engaged Raila Odinga's keen interest even as a student in East Germany. He was enthused by the creation of

---

[32] Interview with Raila Odinga, *op. cit.*

[33] *Ibid.*

[34] See, B.A. Ogot, *Building on the Indigenous,* (Kisumu: Anyange Press, 1998), p. 282.

[35] E.S. Atieno-Odhiambo, *Jaramogi Ajuma Oginga Odinga: A Biography,* (Nairobi: East African Educational Publishers, n.d.), p. 25 and Eric M. Aseka, revised ed., *Mzee Jomo Kenyatta,* (Nairobi: East African Educational Publishers, 2001).

the KPU and surprised at the rapid change to the constitution which reduced the KPU to a rump of its membership. Raila was shocked at the assassination of Tom Mboya. But it was the banning of the KPU and the detention of its leaders, that probably marked the watershed in Raila Odinga's decision to become a politician. In an October 2002 interview he gave to *Finance,* a Kenyan journal, Raila made this point very clear when he stated:

> The eventual proscription of KPU and detention of its leaders have been the driving force in my political career. I needed to counter the government's refusal to accept challenges to its rule and stem out the rapid reversion of the constitutional opposition to its ethnic bastion.[36]

However, it would still take about one and a half decades before the impact of Raila would begin to be felt on the Kenyan political scene, when he was locked up and subsequently joined his father and others in, the struggle for multi-party democracy.

With the KPU out of the way, there was no need for an academic debate on whether Kenya really had more than one party. It was a Kikuyu opponent of Kenyatta, J.M. Kariuki, a wealthy veteran *Mau Mau* fighter, who reacted . He tried to register a new political party, the Socialist Party, before the 1974 general elections, but was denied. He voiced his strong displeasure against the continuous sidelining and marginalization of Oginga Odinga, and his prevention in 1974 from standing for election under KANU. JM Kariuki was to lose his life not long after this push for multi-party democracy and political tolerance.

As the experience of JM Kariuki[37] and others further illustrate, it is important, to note that the assassinations, repression and detentions under Kenyatta, were not limited to Luos and KPU leaders. Koigi wa Wamwere, who sought the Nakuru North parliamentary seat in the 1974 General Elections but lost to Kihika Kimani, a GEMA kingpin, was, without the offer of any reasons, detained under the Preservation of Public Security Act on September 26, 1975.

Martin Shikuku, a Member of Parliament for Butere constituency and critic of the Kenyatta regime had made an intervention on October 9, 1975 in which

---

[36] *Finance,* 31 October 2002, p. 25.
[37] The JM Kariuki murder will be discussed later in this volume.

among other things he said: "Any Member who brands other members as rogues is trying to kill Parliament the way KANU was killed."[38] Kihika Kimani demanded clarification of this remark but Jean Marie Seroney, a Nandi leader and Deputy Speaker, ruled that: "A Member cannot be asked to substantiate the obvious." This resulted in a walk-out of Parliament led by Vice-President Moi, who insisted that: "KANU is not dead." On October 15, 1975, Martin Shikuku and Jean Marie Seroney were picked up from Parliament and detained for years without any official reason, for daring to express their minds.[39]

George Anyona, a Member of Parliament for Kitutu East constituency had his time in detention in May 1977. In Parliament he had tabled confidential documents in support of his motion seeking a parliamentary select committee probe of contracts awarded by Kenya Railways. Vice-President Moi announced his detention on May 5 without reasons other than a claim by the Government that the confidential documents had been stolen.

Another popular illustration of President Kenyatta's detention era was Ngugi wa Thiong'o's 1977 novel, *Petals of Blood,* which examined the poor state of the lives of the Kenyan lower class after the much-touted independence. For this, Ngugi was detained in 1978 under Kenya's Preservation of Public Security Act. This experience resulted in another book, *Detained: A Writer's Prison Diary,* published in 1981.

The excesses of the Kenyatta era must be blamed on the President since the buck definitely stopped at his table. The forces surrounding Kenyatta, especially his immediate so-called "Kiambu Mafia" from his ethnic group, could often be cited as accomplices. However, the tendency to leave out Daniel arap Moi, who was rewarded with the Vice-Presidency on January 5, 1967, should be re-examined. Andrew Morton, in his public relations account on Moi, extensively quoted Shariff Nassir and John Keen, to illustrate the problems of the period and allocate responsibility.[40] Sharriff Nassir, a strong politician from the coast, who was also detained under Kenyatta, reportedly told Morton:

---

[38] For this and other quotations and more details on these detentions, see, Keny@40 1975, A Daily Nation Supplement, Week 06/20, *Daily Nation,* September 4, 2003 p. 10.

[39] See, Andrew Morton, *Moi: The Making of An African Statesman,* (London: Michael O'Mara Books Ltd., 1998), p. 148

[40] *Ibid.,* p. 150.

"There was a real mood of repression in those days. You could never talk in front of Kenyatta. I remember he once called MPs together and told them: 'If you talk my bird will take you away.' After the murder of Kariuki I was very much in fear of my life. It was such a dangerous time and people didn't know how much Moi could do or how long he could last. The terror was such that you were never able to sit down with three people without knowing who was who. You were afraid it might get to Kenyatta and you would be jailed."[41]

In a similar argument, Morton reported John Keen, a popular Maasai MP as having said:

"It seemed that Governor Renison's words that Kenyatta would be leader until darkness and death were coming true. It was an ugly atmosphere. We never knew when we were going to be picked up and thrown behind bars. It was a period of suppression. The Kikuyu dominated the police force, the provincial commissioners were like little governors, the country was gripped by fear and nobody could say anything. This was an era of political exploitation – ivory poaching, coffee smuggling and so on. The rich were getting richer and the robbers were falling out over the spoils. Moi couldn't do anything because the Kikuyu were very powerful politically, economically and administratively. He didn't stand a chance. Only his tolerance and sober attitude enabled him to win through. Many other people would have resigned a long time ago."[42]

The impression of the period created by Morton, was of a democracy with a peace loving Vice-President Moi, who was helpless in the excesses of the Kenyatta regime. However, it is reasonable to assume that Vice-President Moi, as the political head of the police and of internal security, as Minister for Home Affairs, should accept some responsibility for detention orders bearing his signatures. The 'Kiambu Mafia' did not place a gun at his head to detain Kenyans, and to go to Parliament, to emphasize that democracy was essential for the survival of, as well as peace for Kenya, as he did on JM Kariuki's assassination.[43]

It is enough from Ngugi's experience that Daniel arap Moi could not claim to be an innocent Vice-President who was pushed aside as people ended up in detention without trial.

---

[41] *Ibid.*
[42] *Ibid.*
[43] See, *ibid.,* p. 149.

Chapter 07
One-Party State by Legal Fiat

The change of the Constitution has been blamed on the coup-makers, but it is Parliament which buried democracy ... We knew we were wrong, but we could not stop it ... We had no courage to stop it. It was the death of our own potency; we knew how impotent we were. We walked out of that House in shame and that change marked the most shameful chapter in our history.

Koigi wa Wamwere, *Sunday Standard*, May 9, 2004, p. 17

Raila Odinga became a lecturer in the Faculty of Engineering at the University of Nairobi at the same time as Atieno-Odhiambo came to teach there in May 1970. They lived in the same block of apartments next to the School of Law. Raila was in Apt. No. 4, Atieno-Odhiambo in No. 6. They had both been hired as Junior Faculty. As pointed out earlier, the two young men had previously engaged each other in political discussions. So, this pre-occupation continued.

However, they were not part of the mainstream of political activists at the university in those days. Reflecting on university campus politics of the time, James Orengo who was once President of the University of Nairobi Student's Union, said that Raila was not active in engaging students.[1] For Orengo, Raila could not, be compared with lecturers like Ngugi wa Thiong'o, Micere Mugo, Okot p'Bitek, or Taban Lo Lyong, who were active in the moulding of student thinking. Raila, who was lecturing at the University of Nairobi, at the height of the Kenyatta regime, was, according to Orengo, a side-line smooth operator.

Nonetheless, Orengo recognized Raila's strong interest in public affairs as very evident. Unknown to Orengo, however, Raila engaged on a daily basis, in serious discussions on the quest to change the Kenyatta system. Raila, no doubt, was not talking tough like the campus Marxists. At best, he could be described as having been a social democrat operating under the rubric of the banned KPU whose

---

Interview with James Orengo, Nairobi, June 7, 2003.

leaders were in detention. As Atieno-Odhiambo says: "When the KPU leaders returned from detention in 1971, Raila and a team were holding fort as young leaders with strong advocacy of social justice ideas."[2]

Discussion Group

The discussions that marked the beginning of Raila's role in Kenyan political life took place at regular meetings at the residences of Jaramogi Oginga Odinga, Luke Obok and Raila himself.[3] With the 1974 General Elections on the horizon, the political meetings became more intense as Jaramogi and other KPU members rejoined KANU, which was the *de facto* single party in Kenya and tried to stand for election under this party, the only available platform. However, the KANU decision makers including Jomo Kenyatta; Mbiyu Koinange, the President's brother-in-law; and Robert Matano, the acting Secretary-General for nine years after Tom Mboya was assassinated, concluded that former KPU members could not be trusted to pursue KANU ideals to the extent of allowing them to stand for elections. Of course, the principal difference between the KPU and KANU had been how to produce and distribute wealth in Kenya. While the KANU leaders under Kenyatta opted for unbridled acquisition of wealth under a capitalist regime, Jaramogi and the KPU leaders, with a few others like JM Kariuki, were seen as socialists. They argued for re-distribution of wealth, especially land, in favour of the landless poor.

The advocacy of socialist ideals in Kenya received a filip as younger Kenyans returned from studies abroad. These intellectuals like Anyang' Nyong'o, Ooki Ooki-Ombaka etc., formed a fairly coherent and disciplined discussion group that became intimately involved with young Parliamentarians like Peter Olo Aringo and George Anyona. Aringo had returned to Kenya with a Masters Degree from Canada and in 1974, stood for Alego constituency in Siaya District, which

---

[2] Interview with Prof. E.S. Atieno-Odhiambo, Nairobi, July 8, 2003.
[3] The account in this chapter benefited from interviews with Prof. E.S. Atieno-Odhiambo, Prof. Peter Anyang' Nyong'o, Nairobi, August 22, 2003 and Patrick Sumba, Nairobi, April 2, 200? Patrick Sumba, as a young man returned to Kenya from studies in the United States in February 1974 and bonded with Raila politically and was to play a significant role in the struggles that Raila engaged in from mid-1970s through to the failed coup attempt of 1982 after which time he went into exile for almost two decades.

he secured with the blessing of Oginga Odinga.[4] George Anyona was also elected as the MP for Kitutu East constituency in the same Elections. His radical and general anti-establishment politics earned from Charles Njonjo, the title of leader of "the seven bearded sisters." He was no stranger to detention under the Kenyatta regime.[5]

This nascent radicalism in the universities was heightened by the murder of Josiah Mwangi Kariuki.[6] JM Kariuki was a wealthy Kikuyu who started off as the Private Secretary of President Kenyatta. However, he was subsequently perceived as a threat to the Kenyatta regime as he spoke out strongly against corruption and sought the same redistribution of wealth in land as was advocated by Jaramogi Oginga Odinga, Bildad Kaggia and the young bloods arriving on the political scene.

The attempt to frustrate JM Kariuki's return to Parliament in the 1974 General Elections as MP for Nyandarua North failed. JM, upon realizing that Kenyatta was weakening, used his enormous wealth to secure grand relationships that transcended his Kikuyu group and cultivated a broad based national following. However, on March 2, 1975, soon after the opening of Parliament by President Kenyatta, he disappeared only for his body to be found in the Ngong Forest, a week later. He was apparently murdered by people from within his own ethnic group. As John Keen put it: "The hyenas have eaten one of their own."[7]

With JM Kariuki out of the way, the Kikuyu elite around President Kenyatta, who were largely from his Kiambu sub-division within the larger Kikuyu whole, were still worried about any other threat to one of their own succeeding the ageing President. This group, generally dubbed the "Kiambu Mafia" among Kikuyu leaders in KANU, started a movement intended to change the constitution to remove the clause that provided automatic ascension to the Presidency by the

---

For additional information on Peter Oloo Aringo, see, *The Weekly Review,* October 18, 1991, pp. -10.

See, *The Weekly Review,* February 21, 1992, pp. 13-15.

For more details on JM Kariuki's murder, see, David W. Throup & Charles Hornsby, *Multi-Party Politics in Kenya: The Kenyatta & Moi States & the Triumph of the System in the 1992 Election,* (Oxford: James Currey, 1998), pp. 19-20, Andrew Morton, *op. cit.,* pp. 148-149 and *Sunday Standard,* April , 2004, pp. 16-17.

Andrew Morton, *op. cit.,* p. 149.

Vice-President in an acting capacity for 90 days.[8] The fear of the "Kiambu Mafia" was that the acting President would have an incumbency advantage. Since Moi, a Kalenjin was the Vice-President, the group wanted Moi stopped so that the Presidency could remain in the house of Mumbi.[9] The main members of this group included Dr. Njoroge Mungai, the President's nephew; Mbiyu Koinange the President's brother-in-law; Kihika Kimani, MP for Nakuru North and national organizing secretary for GEMA; and Njenga Karume, a young entrepreneur from Kiambaa and a strong leader of GEMA. GEMA was meant to be a cultural welfare organization to weld these sub-ethnic groups into a single whole for political action.

As a back-up to the Change-the-Constitution strategy, the "Kiambu Mafia" were also planning to corner KANU party leadership positions, as another way of stopping Moi. The opportunity was planned for the KANU party elections fixed for April 1977. This would have been the first party election since the 1966 Limuru conference at which Jaramogi was cut to size, as a prelude to his resignation from the party and his position in government as Vice-President. Jaramogi decided run for Vice-President of KANU (a position reintroduced in the amended constitution) as a way to return to the political limelight. Also in the race were two Kalenjin Members of Parliament, Taita Toweet and Daniel Toroitich arap Moi, the Vice-President of the country.

However, just before the election was to take place, Robert Matano, now the Secretary-General of KANU, announced the cancellation of the polls, ostensibly because of the ill heath of President Kenyatta. The elections were called off at the eleventh hour as some delegates had already arrived in Nairobi. This decision estranged Jaramogi further as he and his supporters saw the development as part of the scheme to continue to keep him out of the political process.[10]

---

[8]   Details on the "Change the Constitution" movement, see, Andrew Morton, *Ibid.,* p. 154-158.
[9]   Mumbi is the legendary mother of the Kikuyu. In effect, it means Presidency should be occupied by no one but a person from the majority Kikuyu ethnic group. Of course, many in this move wanted to preserve and protect the phenomenal wealth they had acquired through what Andrew Morton described as fixing the administrative system. They wanted one of their own to the reins of power and were merely using house of Mumbi to garner popular support.
[10] Interview with Patrick Sumba, Nairobi, April 2, 2004.

Jomo Kenyatta eventually died of a heart attack on August 22, 1978. By the time he died, the succession was smoothly wrapped up by President Daniel Toroitich arap Moi who had built a counter support among other Kikuyus like Charles Njonjo and Mwai Kibaki, the Finance Minister who hailed from Nyeri and hence was not part of the "Kiambu Mafia." Even the plan to use trained private militia known as the *Ngoro'ko* unit to forcibly wrest power from Moi failed.[11] On taking power, Moi was anxious to mobilize support as quickly as possible after his swearing in. He particularly wanted Jaramogi's support. Jaramogi came out publicly and gave qualified support, expressing the hope that Moi would lead Kenya towards a new beginning and away from the practices of the Kenyatta era, by listening more to the desires of Kenyans.[12]

However, using the same argument as in 1974, KANU leaders once again prevented Jaramogi and the KPU leaders from participating in the 1979 General Elections. George Anyona was also barred from contesting his Kitutu East seat. This produced violent reactions from University students who demanded justice for the KPU leadership and Anyona. The Moi regime's reaction was systematic repression of the intelligentsia in the University, to reverse the radicalism that had intensified since the assassination of JM Kariuki.

But the situation of ferment did not help the lot of Jaramogi and the KPU leaders. The best they could do was to sponsor parliamentary candidates. One of these was Phoebe Asiyo. As a young woman and chair of *Maendaleo Ya Wanawake* (a women's development organization), Phoebe, accompanied by some other women (one woman per province), visited Kenyatta in detention at Maralal in 1960. Unlike men who flew in to see him, she and her team drove in two land-rovers and took fruit and flowers to him. As a gardener, Kenyatta appreciated the women's gesture and actually cried.[13]

Phoebe began life as a teacher and worked later as a Social Worker. In the latter role, she was in charge of women's prisons and saw through the prison decentralization that allowed women to be quartered separately. She was on the Kenya delegation at the UN from 1966 to 1975, and served on the Human Rights

For details, see, Andrew Morton, *op. cit.*
Interview with Patrick Sumba, April 2, 2004.
Interview with Phoebe Asiyo, Nairobi, July 2, 2003

Commission. She served on the sub-commission responsible for minorities' affairs and the status of women. Under the persuasion of Jaramogi (her father Joel Omer was a friend of Jaramogi and had succeeded Jaramogi as Luo *Ker*) among others, she stood for the Karachaunyo parliamentary seat in the General Elections of 1979, and won.

Birth of **Wakombozi**

The KPU leaders had some success through the use of surrogates, and one rigging by an incumbent was challenged in court. In Ugenya constituency Bishop Ondiek Oluoch ran against Mathews Ogutu for the parliamentary seat. Mathews Ogutu was the immediate past MP and had been a cabinet Minister under the Kenyatta and Moi Presidencies. The poll was counted four times before Mathews Ogutu was declared the winner by 13 votes. Bishop Ondiek Oluoch challenged the result and the court ordered a repeat of the contest. However, the court also barred Oluoch from participating in elections for five years as he was said to have been involved in some irregularities himself.

This development brought James Orengo into the race. Orengo's sister is married to Bishop Ondiek Oluoch. He had been on the ground in support of Bishop Ondiek Oluoch's race. So, he knew the terrain and could expect the support of the strong Legio Maria sect in Ugenya, which had been founded by Bishop Ondiek Oluoch's father. After initial reluctance by Jaramogi Oginga Odinga towards his candidacy, on the grounds that Orengo was a young man who had not built house in Ugenya, Jaramogi was persuaded.

Orengo, in addition, had the support of a group of young men who had been meeting informally. This group included Raila Odinga; Okach Ogada, an activist cousin of Raila's; Atieno-Odhiambo; and Sumba. These youthful politicians named their group *wakombozi* meaning liberators. Orengo clearly remembers the role of Raila during this race. As he notes:

> "My next close encounter with Raila was during my contest for the Ugenya
> Parliamentary seat in a by-election in 1980. When I wanted to run for Parliament,
> Oginga Odinga did not support me initially. Some people around him did not
> want me as an unmarried, young person without a home in the village. Others
> had told him that I was not pro-Luo in the University. I went to him and pointed
> out that he was a national leader who had supported people who later turned

against him like my opponent, Mathews Ogutu who had been Minister in Kenyatta and Moi governments. After this, Jaramogi decided to support me and campaigned for me in my constituency. Raila also came to help in my campaign."[14]

Orengo, with the blessing of Jaramogi and the support of Raila and the *wakombozi,* defeated Mathews Ogutu.

The next port of call for the *wakombozi,* was the 1981 by-election in Karachaunyo. Phoebe Asiyo's election success had been challenged by David Okiki Amayo, the immediate past Member of Parliament and a political kingpin in the constituency as well as a personal friend of President Moi.

According to Patrick Sumba, Raila and the *wakombozi,* "mobilized a strong support that saw Phoebe win with a landslide over a candidate who enjoyed the full support of President Moi who campaigned vigorously at Karachaunyo."[15] She held the seat from 1979 to 1997, when she retired in favour of Adhu Awiti, one of Raila's close political colleagues.

It was another by-election in Nyeri that saw the *wakombozi* acquire a national outlook. This was the Nyeri by-election in which the late Wang'ondu wa Kariuki ran against Nderithu Githua, Kanyi Waithaka and Wachira Moto among others. The by-election was occasioned by the arrest and imprisonment of Waruru Kanja, a radical Member of Parliament and ex-*Mau Mau* detainee on charges of violation of exchange-rate regulations, by the Attorney General, Charles Njonjo.

Anyona joined the original members of the *wakombozi* to plan for this by-election. He had been barred by KANU leaders from running in his constituency for the 1979 General Elections. He threw his support behind Abuya Abuya who won the seat and became the MP for Kitutu East. Others in the Nyeri by-election campaign team were Koigi wa Wamwere, another thorn in the flesh of KANU, Orengo and Mwashengu wa Mwachofi, the MP for Wundanyi constituency. But this time in Nyeri, the *wakombozi* and their candidate lost.

Interview with James Orengo, Nairobi, June 7, 2003
Interview with Patrick Sumba, April 9, 2004.

The efforts of the *Wakombozi* and their association with Jaramogi was clear. In addition, President Moi could not but recognize that Jaramogi remained the undisputed political head in Luoland after Moi's candidates had been floored in Nyanza. As if to make up for the estrangement of Jaramogi from the political process, by denying him the KANU platform to run in two consecutive General Elections, and possibly to consolidate his grip on politics further, President Moi appointed Jaramogi as the Chairman of the Cotton Seed and Lint Marketing Board. He also made him a life member of KANU.

Apparently, President Moi asked Jaramogi for his support, and in exchange, suggested he would be allowed to run for the Bondo seat if the incumbent were to resign to cause a by-election. Accordingly Hezekiah Ougo, who had won the Bondo seat resigned. While the by-election was being planned, in April 1981, Jaramogi was invited to a fund-raising meeting in Mombasa. At this meeting, Jaramogi spoke and announced that President Moi had approached him urging that they work together, hence his intention to contest the Bondo seat. He said he agreed because he believed Moi was an honest man and, unlike Kenyatta, was not a land grabber.[16]

Though what he said reflected the truth of the post-independence period, KANU leaders went up in arms. They accused Jaramogi of having besmirched the memory of the late President who was father of the nation. President Moi denied that he had approached Jaramogi who, under pressure, had to resign the chairmanship of the Cotton Seed and Lint Marketing Board. Again, he was barred from contesting the Bondo by-election.

Many Kenyans, including those close to Jaramogi, felt that his statement in Mombasa was untimely and tactless. However, he argued on the basis of a Luo saying to the effect that if someone is returning to a homestead he had left a long while ago, he does not enter without first throwing stones into the homestead to test what sort of creatures had occupied the space. He said when he threw stone, what emerged were snakes, lions and all manners of vicious animals. He felt he would rather be outside KANU if they remained untruthful and if Moi would not stand by his words in public.[17] For him, nothing had changed in KANU

---

[16] Patrick Sumba in an interview on April 2, 2004 recounted the private brief that Jaramogi gave him and Raila on details surrounding this issue. See also, Andrew Morton, *op. cit.,* pp. 184-18

Raila and Sumba who had been privately briefed by Jaramogi, returned to Nairobi to brief a meeting of the *wakombozi* which included Anyona;, Salim Lone, a feisty Kenyan journalist of Asian origin; the late Dr. Ooko Ooki-Ombaka; and Shadrack Guto. An invitation was then extended to Anyona, Oyangi Mbaja and Abuya Abuya to visit Jaramogi in Kisumu. Raila also attended this meeting at which Jaramogi told them that there was no alternative but to form another political party. In fact, according to Raila, Jaramogi insisted on dictating to them the text of the launching statement for the new party at that meeting.[18]

This marked the beginning of the move towards the realization of a political party. In the second half of 1981, the group, which included Anyona, Raila, Oyangi Mbajah, Anyang' Nyong'o, Atieno-Odhiambo, David Mukaru Ngang'a, a University of Nairobi lecturer, and Patrick Sumba, among others, started preparing a party manifesto using the KPU manifesto as a guide. They also worked on a party constitution. Then came the debate on the choice of a name for the party. The group wanted to be broad in the choice of name so that they could attract many of the people who were dissatisfied with the KANU order. But they wanted to give a sense of being progressive. Though Anyona wanted the party called socialist, he realized that there could be varying degrees of socialist orientation and saw the need to accommodate all. Raila had argued in support of calling the new structure the Social Democratic Party. However, he agreed with the suggestion from Salim Lone to the effect that they should use Alliance instead of Party. This was in recognition of the diversity of their group which included Traditional African Socialists, Scientific Socialists and Social Democrats.

In February 1982, Jaramogi sent a special message to the Tanzanian President, Mwalimu Julius Nyerere about the formation of the party and the general need for change in Kenya The lot fell on Salim Lone to deliver the message.[19]

The Kenya African Socialist Alliance (KASA) had been conceived. The problem now was how to execute the delivery. Shadrack Guto and Ombaka, who were

---

[17] Jaramogi in the brief to Raila and Sumba was most pained by the fact that Moi denied that he had approached him.
[18] Interview on May 9, 2004.
[19] Interview with Salim Lone, Nairobi, November 23, 2004.

Lawyers, developed cold feet arguing that a resolution by delegates was required for registration.[20]

However, there remained the question of how to get registration. The KASA promoters decided that it would be tactful simply to go to the Registrar's office, hand in the registration documents and obtain a receipt from clerks at the desk. After getting the receipts, they planned to call a press conference at the Norfolk Hotel. At the press conference the interim Chairman would show their receipt as proof of registration of KASA. But this plan could not be executed. Two days before the planned submission of documents to clerks, President Moi at a public rally in Kiambu announced that a bill was to be introduced in Parliament to make Kenya a de jure one party State.

Anyona and Sumba decided to mobilize University students against the bill. On May 29, 1982, at the Serena Hotel, the duo met student leaders including Maurice Justice Adongo, (who later went into exile in Canada); David Murage (who later became MP for Gatanga); and Rateng Oginga Ogego, now Kenyan High Commissioner to Canada. A plan was hatched to call an international conference at which, a demand for a referendum would be made, using the argument that the issue of a de jure one-party state required popular discussion/referendum. The student leaders were charged with responsibility for mobilizing support among students.

The duo of Anyona and Sumba agreed to meet the following day at the Intercontinental Hotel and then proceed to meet the students at their campus. Anyona stayed the night at Lone's residence. In the morning, Anyona and Lone parted ways. Lone had an appointment with Maina wa Kinyatti, an activist University Lecturer who was working on getting Jaramogi and Kaggia to re-engage strongly to build a winning alliance for a democratic Kenya. But he remembered that Anyona was indiscreet with his use of the phone as he spoke about KASA and other plans, without concern for the phone being bugged.[21]

Sumba arrived on time only to learn that Anyona who had arrived at the Intercontinental Hotel slightly earlier had been picked up by security agents. Abuya

---

[20] Interview with Raila Odinga, Nairobi, January 5, 2006.
[21] *Ibid*

Abuya's car that he drove to the Hotel was outside. On the advice of waiters, Sumba quickly left.

Sumba, Prof. Alfred Otieno Osanya and Atieno-Odhiambo went to the airport to receive Raila Odinga who was returning to Nairobi from Kisumu on the afternoon flight, and informed him that the Chairman of the intended party had been arrested earlier in the day.

Apparently, Anyona had been tricked by a journalist who worked for the Special Branch, who had invited him to come to the Intercontinental Hotel for some information. He went there before his scheduled meeting with Sumba but the journalist did not show up. He was taken from the Hotel to his residence and a search yielded the Constitution and Manifesto of the KASA.

Though Raila was still determined to launch KASA with the remaining colleagues, on June 3, 1982, the Government published two Bills seeking to make Kenya a one-party state. These were: The Constitution of Kenya (Amendment Bill), 1982 and the Election Laws (Amendment) Bill, 1982.[22] It was unclear if the forestalling of KASA arose from the activities of the Kenyan intelligence or if Jaramogi Oginga Odinga, while giving a talk in London, had let the cat out of the bag, as Andrew Morton alleged.[23]

On June 9, the Kenyan Government, led in Parliament by Vice-President Mwai Kibaki, the Leader of Government Business, moved a procedural motion to reduce the fourteen day period of publication of a Bill to six days.[24] On clearing this impediment, Throup and Hornsby noted that "legislation (drafted by Charles Njonjo's legal adviser Paul Muite), was rushed through the National Assembly by Vice-President Mwai Kibaki to make Kenya a *de jure* single-party state."[25] The amendment's main clause (which was to become the infamous section 2A of the Constitution) stated: "There shall be in Kenya only one political party, the Kenya African National Union."

---

[22] See, Daily Nation, Friday, June 4, 1982, p. 1.

[23] Morton, *op. cit.,* p. 185.

[24] See, Hansard of the Kenyan National Assembly, 9th June 1982, pp. 75-76.

[25] Throup and Hornsby, *op. cit.,* p. 31. However, Paul Muite, in an interview with the author in Nairobi on February 21, 2004, stated that he had nothing to do with the draft of Section 2A.

Charles Njonjo, the Minister for Constitutional Affairs, after a first reading, proceeded to speak by leave of the House. In a re-writing of historical facts, he stated:

> "We have been independent since 1963, under one political party. We have organized a number of elections since 1963 – and by-elections – and the candidates who participated in all these elections came in with KANU tickets. Therefore, we are doing nothing new. In fact, Kenya has been a one-party-state since that time. It has been a *de facto* and what we are doing by amending the Constitution is really legalizing what has been taking place all this time, by making Kenya a *de jure* – one party."

Kibaki and Njonjo made all the "debate" on the Bill except for interruptions of applause from the House; an intervention by Nicholas Biwott, the Minister for Regional Development, Science and Technology, who hastened the Bill along; and an irritant from Orengo who interrupted Njonjo. Njonjo had suggested that the President of Kenya was to look after the majority of Kenyans and Orengo wanted it stated that the President was to look after all Kenyans. Trying to ignore the intervention, Njonjo continued, but the uproar in the House forced him to state: "the President shall look after all the people in this country, whether they are black, blind, short or whether they are bearded."[26]

All 158 members present voted in favour of the Bill on the second reading. The Speaker, Mr. Fred Mati, in a further setting aside of the rules, committed the Bill to a committee chaired by Moses arap Keino. In no time, arap Keino reported back that they had approved the Bill without amendment. The Third Reading took place immediately while some MPs left. This time 151 members were present including Koigi wa Wamwere who had joined the sitting. They all voted in favour with neither a nay vote nor an abstention. The amendment had been passed in an hour and 45 minutes.[27] President Moi assented to the Bill making it a Constitutional Law on June 17, 1982.

Raila accepted defeat by this move. He was reported by President Moi's chronicler as having said: "The political competition had outsmarted us."[28] The reality of a *de jure* single-party state, nonetheless, reduced the options available to many Kenyans, including Raila Odinga and his father. The avenue for party competition had been closed to them.

---

[26] *Ibid.,* p. 85.
[27] See, *Daily Nation,* Thursday, June 10, 1982, p. 1.
[28] Andrew Morton, *op. cit.,* p. 186.

Chapter 08

Discontent Resulting in Failed Coup

Having started with a ban on the official opposition party, KPU, in October 1969, the KANU regime closed all channels for open discussion of public affairs. The free speech and free association stipulated in our constitution was curbed. The mass media was put under censorship. To discuss the government in public could lead to charges of sedition, and detention or a jail sentence. Kenya became a closed society. It was only through rumour-mongering that Kenyans (with the exception of the executive and a few of his close associates) could pass on information about what was going on in the government.

James Waore Dianga, *Kenya 1982: The Attempted Coup – the consequence of a one-party dictatorship,* (London: Pen Press Publishers Ltd., 2002), p. 48, fn. 51.

By the 1982 constitutional change, the Kenyan government justified war against itself.

Koigi wa Wamwere, *Sunday Standard,* May 9, 2004, p. 17.

A spate of coup d'etats and coup attempts had dominated the political scene in Africa from the 1960s to the 1980s. Kenya failed to escape this means of changing government through the barrel of a gun.[1] However, the 1982 coup attempt went beyond planning. It was executed by a group of discontented junior military men in the Kenyan Air Force. This discontent was based on a perception, rightly or wrongly, that the Moi government did not care about non-commissioned officers. The Air Force plotters were largely from the Luo ethnic group, and were equally

---

[1] There had been claims of an earlier plan to topple the Kenyatta government by killing the President and Vice-President in 1971 by some Kamba politicians and military men to pave way for the ascension to power of Chief Justice Kitili Mwendwa, a Kamba. On this, see, David W. Throup & Charles Hornsby, *Multi-Party Politics in Kenya: The Kenyatta & Moi States & the Triumph of the System in the 1992 Election,* (Oxford: James Currey, 1998), p. 17.

unhappy with the political developments which had marginalized the Luos in the affairs of the nation. Other civilians in Kenya who were disenchanted with the dictatorship that had enveloped Kenya provided assistance to the coup planners.

The *Sunday Standard,* a foremost Kenyan newspaper in its March 14, 2004, edition, like many other newspaper accounts over-time, named Raila Odinga "as the central civilian accomplice of the coup plotters." The following account draws from this and other newspaper publications and probing interviews with many Kenyans who were involved in many aspects of the coup attempt. It is important, however, that in spite of what looks like his obvious facilitation of the coup, Raila Odinga, throughout the interview for this work, neither admitted nor confirmed a role in the planning of the coup attempt. Thus, the public will have to wait for Raila's autobiography for a final word on his role.

Planning a Coup

The beginning of the plan to overthrow the government of President Moi could be traced to discontent in the military forces that became evident in 1980. This discontent found articulation in a Senior Private, James Waore Dianga who had joined the Kenya Air Force on September 2, 1977. This junior Air Force man saw a lot of corruption in the procurement of air force equipment. Worse was the failure of the Moi regime to meet the needs of junior military men in the provision of barracks and basics like food.[2] In addition, the military men could see the repression that was taking place in the wider society, as KPU leaders and others went in and out of detention, while KANU leaders continued their accumulation.

Waore Dianga concluded that something needed to be done to change the situation. He started talking to his junior colleagues in the Air Force. One recruit to his line of thinking, was Senior Private Hezekiah Ochuka Rabala, reportedly a charismatic leader among his contemporaries at Eastleigh Air Force Base. However, Waore Dianga was arrested on January 15, 1981 and by April, he faced court-martial. He was not tried for treason as the military could not trace his accomplices and concluded that one man could not overthrow a government. So, he was accused

---

[2] For a detailed account on factors that led to the planning of a coup by a participant who claimed to be the brain on the enterprise, see, James Waore Dianga, *Kenya 1982: The Attempted Coup – the consequence of a one-party dictatorship,* (London: Pen Press Publishers Ltd., 2002).

of making preparations between December 15, 1980 and January 15, 1981 to commit an act of sedition, that is to say, to overthrow by unlawful means the Government of Kenya. He was sentenced to three years imprisonment.[3]

Senior Private Hezekiah Ochuka waited for a while after the imprisonment of Waore Dianga. He resumed with the plan to overthrow the government of Daniel arap Moi in mid-March 1982. Ochuka saw a general worsening of the situation of Luos in Kenya. Jaramogi Oginga Odinga was prevented from standing in the Bondo by-election. Luos were under-represented in the armed forces and were not promoted, with Major Opande as the highest ranking Luo in service. There was a marginalisation of Luoland with respect to development and there were shortages of schools and teachers. The junior Air Force men lacked proper accommodation and stayed in leaky tents.

Other political reasons that Ochuka gave in his confession during his trial, included the lack of proper presidential elections in Kenya since independence as people who showed interest in running against Kenyatta, like Ronald Ngala, were, according to Ochuka killed, thus scaring off any other ambitious politicians. He felt parliamentarians were not allowed to air their views as detention hovered over their heads.[4] The rumour that the Kikuyu were planning their own coup to remove President Moi and replace him with Vice-President Mwai Kibaki hastened the planning of the Luo junior military men led by Ochuka. They were worried that a successful Kikuyu coup would not augur well for Luos.

Snr. Sergeant Pancras Okumu Oteyo, Sergeant Joseph Ogidi Obuon and Snr Private Ochuka had their first meeting at the Eastleigh base swimming pool on March 28, 1982. The plot began in earnest. By mid-April, Ogidi Obuon made contact with Jaramogi Oginga Odinga and briefed him on their plan to overthrow the government of President Moi. This visit resulted in the involvement of John Odongo Langi generally referred to as Oginga Odinga's "security man." Langi had been trained in Czechoslovakia. He lived in Kisumu where he ran a small

---

[3] For details, see, *ibid.*

[4] For details, see, "Ochuka spills coup secrets," *East African Standard,* Monday, March 15, 2004, p. VI. For an account on the course of the coup itself and consequent developments, see a special report in the *Daily Nation,* Thursday, August 1, 2002, titled: "Blood, Bullets and Tears: 20 years later, how the August 1 coup bid changed Kenya,"

shop. He was part of the group, unemployable as a result of the Kenyatta and Moi paranoia against those close to Jaramogi, who had military training. Langi would be one of the main civilian links between the military coup planners and the Kenyan society outside the barracks. The other person with a similar background to Langi was Opwapo Ogai. Opwapo was in the Kenyan Army and was sent for training in Kazakhstan only to return and be rejected from re-absorption. He eventually died in exile in Sweden in 1993.

On May 2, 1982, Ochuka, having obtained the voting rights of all those he had recruited in Nairobi because they could not travel to Karatina, near Nyeri, met Oteyo and Ogidi at the Three-in-One Bar. They met as the People's Redemption Council which was agreed to comprise: S/Pte Hezekiah Ochuka Rabala who was elected chairman; S/Sgt Pancras Okumu Oteyo; Sgt Joseph Ogidi Obuon; Sgt Samuel Opiyo; Sgt. Richard Obuon; Cpl Fenwick Chesori Odera Obedi; Cpl Ombok; and Captain Agola. Half of the membership of the Council reportedly met Oginga Odinga. Ochuka, the chairman, reportedly informed Oginga Odinga that they had no politician in their plan. He went further to make it clear that "the government that would follow would be purely military, and no civilians would be in the ruling council." Interestingly, though Ochuka made it clear that he was the one to become President and not Jaramogi Oginga Odinga, the old man blessed the coup and provided some financial support.[5] In effect, Jaramogi Oginga Odinga wanted change in Kenya but not necessarily power by any means, as his critics claimed.

Two other civilians associated with the coup plotters, were Raila and Patrick Sumba, also known as "Paddy Onyango." They had been frustrated by efforts which suppressed any alternative means of political expression in Kenya outside the tightly controlled KANU apparatus. The pervasive discontent in Kenya reached its high point with the constitutional amendment that made Kenya a one-party state. This development left many civilians who were very dissatisfied with the state of affairs with no other choice other than to go underground.

---

[5] See, *East African Standard,* March 17, 2004, p. 14. Patrick Sumba in an interview on April 9, 2004 suggested that there were some embellishments in the Ochuka confessions as Ochuka needed to play to the government gallery in the hope that his life would be spared as he had been assured.

Shortly after the detention of Anyona, Raila briefed Sumba on the ferment in the military and the efforts of the Ochuka group to overthrow the government of President Moi. The two agreed that there was a basis for collaboration with the Ochuka group. They were happy that there was a viable option to the one party state which Moi had imposed on Kenya. They agreed that given the nature of the "project," information management was crucial, that they would operate with others on a need to know basis.[6] They decided to avoid a large open planning group. Raila was to be the contact point with the military men in relaying views on important issues.

For example, there was a need to decide if the coup should take place when President Moi was in Kenya or outside. The Ochuka group preferred to act when President Moi, who at that time, was the Chairman of the Organisation of African Unity, would be handing the Chairmanship over to the Libyan leader Muammar Ghaddafi. Raila and Sumba came to the conclusion that it would be better for President Moi to be in Kenya to avoid his rallying external support and being returned to power by external forces. The military group of Ochuka agreed.

Another issue was the extent of damage. Raila and Sumba pushed the position that even though it was naïve to think a coup could be executed without blood, bloodshed if any, would need to be minimized. They argued that Kenyan popular support would be essential after the coup and they should not be perceived as a bunch of reckless and heartless people. They wanted to be seen as agents of positive change. This sentiment was conveyed to the military. The military was committed to minimum human collateral damage.

There was also the issue of the day on which to carry out the coup. With the commitment to minimum collateral damage in terms of human life, it had to be on a day of minimum human movement and activity. Hence, the choice of a Saturday night leading to Sunday was agreed with the military. Details of purely military matters were held with Langi and Opwapo.

The night of July 31, 1982 was set as the date to strike. Raila had been tasked with the provision of a command post. For this, he secured an apartment on Ngong

---

[6] Interview with Sumba, ibid.

Road belonging to Professor Alfred Otieno fondly called Osanya (who knew nothing about what his apartment was to be used for). The military were then to move all the required communication gadgets to this operational headquarters.

Sumba who was a Public Affairs Executive with Kenya Shell Company Ltd also presented a weekly sports programme on the Voice of Kenya as a freelance. So, he was to provide adequate intelligence on the taking of the TV House. He was also to undertake reconnaissance on all the residences of diplomatic missions that members of the Moi regime could run into.

On Saturday 31 July, there were intense movements and rearrangements were made. The organizing group first met in Umoja and then regrouped at a joint in Shauri Moyo Estate. Ochuka who had earlier briefed Raila, provided a similar briefing to Sumba and Opwapo. Later that night, they all congregated at the command post on Ngong Road. The process began when Ochuka finally came to the command post. He ordered that a few people would remain at the command post. These were basically experts in communication.

The attempt to take over the Moi Government began at Embakassi military base. The only reason why Embakassi was chosen, was because the Armourer, who had agreed to cooperate with the plotters, was based there. He was to open the armoury for the insurgents to take weapons with which they were to capture Eastleigh, Langata and Kahawa barracks.

Opwapo led the group that stormed Embakassi. They went into the base as civilians. Although as they opened the armoury, the alarm went off, they took their weapons as planned. They ordered the duty officer to surrender. He did. On interrogation later, the duty officer rightly described Opwapo as a civilian who must have been very highly trained.

Opwapo's team bombed the normal line of communication between Embakassi and the Department of Defence (DoD). However, as they tried to exit at the gate, they were challenged. The resulting exchange of fire alerted the Embakassi police who rang police headquarters when the firing persisted. The police headquarters, wanting to know what was happening, contacted the Department of Defence headquarters.

Opwapo's group moved quickly and captured Eastleigh Air Force base. But the alert that started from Embakassi led to a counter plan, and the group that was to take Langata Barracks was ambushed and crippled.

As the operation began, Ochuka, Raila, Sumba and Oteyo all left the command post to survey developments at the targeted installations. They were parked outside Broadcasting House as it was being taken over by Ochuka's forces from Embakasi. They then drove to Langata, switched on the transmitters and by 6 am the first announcement was broadcast. Later in the morning, Ochuka, Oteyo, Raila, and Sumba drove to Eastleigh Air Force Base. Ochuka and Oteyo went inside and ordered Raila and Sumba as civilians to remain outside.

As they waited outside, they saw the people of Nairobi in a celebration, the type of which had never been seen before. When Ochuka and Oteyo did not come out, Raila and Sumba decided to move to town. They stopped at the house of one of Raila's acquaintances in Parklands. Suddenly, just after 11 am, the music of the old regime was back on air and they realized that something had gone wrong, and that the regime had retaken control of the Voice of Kenya. They went out to find out what was going on. They went to the house of Raila's sister, Dr. Wenwa Akinyi in Chiromo campus to monitor what was happening. She found out that her brother had been involved in the coup attempt after they got to her, distraught.[7]

At some point they called the command post and asked Opwapo to take Sumba's car to Dr. Akinyi's house and pick them up. On the way, Opwapo driving with Pr. Private Ogidi Obuon, ran into an army ambush. They were shot at, the bullet missed; but they were captured and taken to the Department of Defence. Ogidi knew there was no way out for him, but decided to save Opwapo by claiming that he had hijacked Opwapo to drive him. They were taken in and Ogidi taken away. In the evening, an old man had Opwapo released by claiming he was a friend with whom he watched football. As it became clear, things had crumbled, Raila and Sumba began planning how to escape from Nairobi.

However, General Musomba, in an interview in Nairobi on November 18, 2003 was not too clear on whether she had had earlier contacts with one or more of coup plotters.

What Went Wrong?

On August 1st 1982, the now retired General Joseph Musomba, commanded the Second Kenyan Brigade. He had started his service in the army in 1965 when he was sent to Moyale after being commissioned as Lieutenant. He found himself in the *shifta* war. During the Ogaden war between Ethiopia and Somalia, in 1977, he was the Kenyan Director of Operations. Initially, the Kenyans believed that the build up in Somalia would result in a second *shifta* war, and Musomba was involved in planning a response if Somalia attacked Kenya. Although there was a mutual agreement between Kenya and Ethiopia for a joint reaction if Somalia attacked either of them, Kenya did not support Ethiopia in the Ogaden war.

On the morning when President Moi appeared to have lost power, Musomba was woken up at 1 am by the late George Kimeto, the Provincial Intelligence and Security Officer.[8] Musomba's command base was in Gilgil, but he slept in Nakuru. He was informed by Kimeto that the President had lost communication with Nairobi and wanted to know what was happening there. Musomba quickly found that the Army communication network was still functioning. Having established that a coup d'etat by some Air-force officers was in progress, he spoke to President Moi, received his instructions, and began to deploy his own forces to counter the coup attempt. He blocked the road to Nakuru at Gilgil, and sent troops to Nairobi and Nanyuki.

At 3.15 a.m. President Moi called Elijah Sumbeiywo, Commander of the Presidential Police Escort[9] and told him what had happened. Sumbeiywo immediately called his brother, Major Lazarus Sumbeiywo. Since Moi knew about the efforts of Musomba and those of General Mohamud Mohamed, the Deputy Army Commander, in Nairobi, he refused to leave his Kabarak home. The two brothers forced the President into Lazarus' Peugeot 204 car to take him to safety initially outside the country, but later in the bush. Subsequently, the President was returned to Nakuru State Lodge as reports filtered through, that the coup was being crushed.

---

[8] Interview with General Musomba, *ibid.*
[9] See, Andrew Morton, *op. cit.* pp. 187-189 and *Sunday Nation,* August 1, 2004, p. 13, for account among many that had been given by Elijah Sumbeiywo over time.

By mid-day, the President insisted that he must return to Nairobi. Musomba received the order from his superiors (and not Elijah as he later claimed),[10] to escort the President to Nairobi with 100 men and two armoured cars.

In Nairobi, Musomba took over from General Mohamed, at the *Voice of Kenya* where Mohamed had rallied troops (mainly cooks, suppliers, education instructors and other non-regular armed men) from the logistics base in Kahawa and succeeded in retaking the broadcasting house. For three weeks, Musomba carried out a mopping-up operation in Nairobi to find the other plotters. But Ochuka and Oteyo had grabbed an aircraft and flown to Tanzania.

Musomba's next order was to Chair the Courts-Martial that tried the coupists. His memory of those trials before he handed over to Joseph Kibwana (who about two decades later became the Chief of General Staff of the Kenyan army), was that the leaders of the attempted coup d'etat had connections with Raila and the Jaramogi family.

On the claim see, ibid., p. 13. Musomba maintained he had nothing to do with Elijah in a phone interview with the author on August 1, 2004.

Chapter 09
Seasons of Incarceration in Daniel's Dens

The Prelude

Scholars and commentators alike often suggest that the 1982 coup attempt changed a good and benevolent President Moi into a dictator with the hallmark of human rights abuse as people were jailed without trial or faced Kangaroo courts. The facts do not support this thinking.

Under President Moi, it was dangerous to be a teacher with a critical mind. The ominous signs had started in July 1980, when he banned the University Staff Union which had been registered on April 19, 1972 as a Union, after its previous existence as an Association.[1] He made clear that his government having improved the wages and welfare packages of the Union of Kenya Civil Servants and the University Staff Union, he could not understand why they should continue politicking.[2] According to Anyang' Nyong'o, this ban was followed by the detention and harassment of leaders in the Universities; a situation that led to his fleeing Kenya in December 1981 after having been arrested a number of times.[3]

Wanyiri Kihoro gives a good account of the repression of the pre-coup period in his *Never Say Die*.[4] In 1979, Kihoro sought election as the MP for Nairobi's Bahati constituency, veering off his main calling as an Estate Valuer. He lost and returned full-time to his job. On June 8, 1981, he took his sick mother from Nyeri to Nairobi to see a cardiologist on June 11. But, before taking her to the hospital he went to his office planning to return home to collect her. He did not see his mother for three weeks, because waiting in his office were security men who took him through a gruelling three hours search. Despite begging to be allowed to take his sick mother to hospital, for six days, he was moved between five police stations

---

[1] Willy Mutunga, the Secretary-General of the University Staff Union, in an interview on October 20, 2003, stated that the USU was officially banned on July 19, 1980.
[2] See, *Sunday Nation,* July 20, 1980.
[3] Interview with Anyang' Nyong'o, August 22, 2003.
[4] Wanyiri Kihoro, *Never Say Die: The Chronicle of a Political Prisoner,* (Nairobi: East African Education Publishers Ltd., 1998), pp. 28-32.

and on June 17 he was charged with being in possession of a seditious publication. Apparently, the Moi regime wanted to punish Kenyans who had circulated reports of repression in Kenya to other African Heads of State, who were to visit Kenya in mid June for the 19th Annual Meeting of the Organisation of African Unity.

Chief Magistrate Fidahussein Abdalla remanded Kihoro in custody for 14 days while waiting for consent to prosecute from the Attorney-General. This was contrary to Section 72 of the Kenyan Constitution which said that an accused must be brought before the courts within 24 hours of arrest, or be released. On June 30, Kihoro was released on bail and the case was withdrawn by the police one and a half months later. His mother's condition had deteriorated when he was in jail, and she died of cardiac arrest on October 22.

Three months later, Kihoro went to London with his wife Wanjiru and daughter Wangui, to study Law. Six months after his return to Kenya in January 1986, he was back in the welcoming hands of the Moi torture apparatus. During his months in detention, he experienced the *Nyayo House* degrading torture experience as human beings were put through the life of amphibians in a room turned into an acquarium with water from a high pressure hose giving a feeling Kihoro described as aqua thrashing.[5]

According to Kamoji Wachiira, the routine detention of University lecturers and other government critics, began after the publication in 1981 of *CheChe: In-Dependent Kenya* and *Pambana a year later*.[6] The late Wang'ondu wa Kariuki, a journalist, according to Willy Mutunga, blazed the trail when he was arrested on May 15, 1982. He was charged with possession of seditious publication, *Pambana*, a radical underground publication issued by the Twelfth December Movement.[7] Wang'ondu was jailed for three and a half years. Wang'ondu was defended by Mirugi Kariuki an activist lawyer and associate of Koigi wa Wamwere. In August 1982, Koigi was detained and subsequently imprisoned. Mirugi Kariuki, in turn started his own series of incarcerations in November 1982. He had been bold

---

[5] For more on this experience and the general description of the torture chamber known as *Nyayo House* (named after a Government of Kenya multi story building of the same name in Nairobi), see many pages of *ibid.*

[6] Kamoji Wachiira's reaction to a written interview in January 2005.

[7] See, *Daily Nation,* June 11, 1982, p. 40

enough to announce that he would contest the by-election to fill Koigi's Nakuru North parliamentary seat which had been declared vacant. For this and other sins against the Moi regime, Mirugi would spend a total of 1984 days in custody between 1982 and 1995.[8]

Stephen Muriithi, the former Deputy Director of Intelligence was detained on May 27, 1982 and Anyona, whose detention, as we noted earlier, had started under the Kenyatta regime, was re-incarcerated by the Moi regime three days after Muriithi, simply because he wanted to form a political party. He was not released until 1984 and was back in detention in July 1990, this time in the company of Edward Oyugi, Augustine Njeru Kathangu and Ngotho wa Kariuki all of who were arrested at Mutugi Bar and Restaurant at Dagoretti Corner, allegedly for holding an illegal meeting to plot the overthrow of the Government. After a year in remand, they were jailed for seven years, until their release on bail, pending appeal, in early 1992.[9]

Using his *Madaraka* day address on June 1, 1982 (a holiday marking self-government), President Moi made this move towards repression clear when he said: "I want to make it clear that we shall not allow a few individuals who regard themselves as revolutionaries promoting foreign ideologies to be disrupting our education and training programmes."[10]

Challenging this repression, John Khaminwa, a Nairobi Lawyer who had appeared in court on June 2, 1982 to argue the application for *habeas corpus,* filed by Mrs. Esther Mokeira Anyona, seeking the production of her husband in court, was himself detained a day later.[11]

Maina wa Kinyatti, a University of Nairobi lecturer, documented his own arrest on June 3, 1982 by the Special Branch (Kenyan political police). During interrogation, he was informed that he was: a communist; a producer of anti-government leaflets on campus; a polluter of the minds of children; a helper to Koigi wa Wamwere to write critical parliamentary speeches, and to Oginga Odinga

[8] Interview with Mirugi Kariuki, July 21, 2004.
[9] For additional details, see, *The Weekly Review,* February 21, 1992, pp. 13-15.
[10] See, *Daily Nation* June 2, 1982, p. 6.
[11] See, *Daily Nation,* June 4, 1982, p. 1.

and Anyona to write the constitution of their Socialist Party; and an organiser of university students. He was also accused of working with Ngugi wa Thiong'o, Koigi wa Wamwere and others, to overthrow the KANU regime etc. Maina wa Kinyatti was in remand for four and a half months before being sentenced on October 18, 1982 to six years imprisonment at the end of what he saw as a Kangaroo trial. He was freed on October 17, 1988 having served the full term.[12]

Al-Amin Mazrui and Kamoji K. Wachiira were picked up on June 7, 1982 after thorough searches of their homes.[13] They were accused of corrupting young minds. Recounting his experience, Kamoji said:

> I was handcuffed, hooded and thrown into a Landrover for Kamiti Maximum detention wing, not far from the deathrow wing. Soon after we were shipped to Shimo-la-Tewa, then I was secretly shifted solo to Hola (a world famous death camp which we termed the Dachau of Kenya in memory of the Mau Mau detainees routinely mowed down there by guards in the fifties). Hola was the Government's punishment camp for political detainees one a time – in total solitary. Our punishment was due to wives lawsuit. After nine long months alone in the desert camp, I was moved to Kamiti's isolation wing for almost a year and a half before release in late 1984.[14]

Following quickly on the heels of Kamoji and Alamin was Willy Mutunga, another radical academic who was the Secretary-General of the University Academic Staff Union from 1979 till it was banned in 1980. He was picked up on June 10, 1982.[15] He was accused of being a member of the Twelfth December Movement as well as participating in the production of the movement's publication, *Pambana*. Postage stamps that were found on him during a search were read by the security apparatus as being used for the mailing of *Pambana*. Appearing before the late Senior Resident Magistrate, Mr. P.N. Tank, on June 12, 1982, accused of being in possession of a leaflet deemed seditious and headlined: J.M. Solidarity Day: Don't be fooled: Reject these Nyayos," he was remanded in custody at the Nairobi Industrial Area Remand

[12] For details on his life in prison, see, Maina wa Kinyatti, *Kenya: A Prison Notebook* (London: Vita Books, 1996)
[13] See, Daily Nation, June 9, 1982, p. 1.
[14] Kamoji Wachiira, *op. cit.*
[15] See, *Daily Nation,* June 11, 1982, p. 1. Late Dr. Katama Mkangi, lecturer in Sociology and UASU Assistant Chairman who was with Willy Mutunga on that day was also arrested but released.

Prison. His request for bail was denied. After appearing in court for the mention of his case four times in the two and a half months in remand, he was served with his formal detention on July 29, 1982. He was shifted around many prisons and experienced harsh conditions, until his release on October 20, 1983.

In support of the crack-down on academics, Charles Njonjo, the Constitutional Affairs Minister told Parliament during the debate on the Election Laws (Amendment) Bill No. 11 in June 1982, that detention was constitutional in Kenya and could not be challenged in any court. This hard-line position was reiterated when he was reported in newspapers on 17 June 1982, as having expressed the position that all academics teaching Marxist and other "foreign ideologies" should be jailed without trial.[16]

As this clamp down was on before the coup attempt took place, it would be wrong to suggest that repression under Moi was merely a reaction to the failed coup. Nevertheless, it would be right to say that a very bad situation became worse in the aftermath of the failed putsch. Raila's incarceration on August 11, 1982 was in this category.[17] He was in detention for almost a decade with two short-lived interruptions. He returned to join the multi-party struggle in the early 1990s.

Raila Odinga's First Period of Detention

According to Musomba, the Privates who planned the coup, admitted that they had received Luo traditional blessing and encouragement from Oginga Odinga to carry out the coup attempt.[18] Musomba also claimed that Raila was mentioned by the Privates as having given assistance towards the execution of the failed coup.[19] Sgt. Joseph Ogidi Obuon, one of the ringleaders in the coup attempt who was subsequently executed for treason, reportedly claimed that Raila had given the plotters money and had promised to canvass support for them from

---

[16] See, the *Nation* and *Standard* of that date.

[17] Many Kenyans like Koigi wa Wamwere and countless number of students were taken in also after the failure of the coup.

[18] Jaramogi was placed under house arrest in Kisumu in the aftermath of the failed coup.

[19] For additional details, see, *The Weekly Review*, June 21, 1991, pp. 20-21 and *The weekly Review*, June 28, 1991, pp. 9-11.

neighbouring countries. Snr. Pvt. Hezekiah Ochuka who led the coup, corroborated the claims of Obuon at his court martial after his extradition from Tanzania where he had fled with Sgt Pancras Oteyo. On the basis of those accounts, it was a question of when, and not if Raila would be picked up for interrogation.

As the coup attempt crumbled, and with the failure of Opwapo to arrive, Raila and Sumba remained at Wenwa Akinyi's University apartment at Chiromo in Nairobi.[20] The military were everywhere. There was a general crack-down on all who had been critical of the Kenyan Government. Raila and Sumba with Odongo Langi decided to move out of Nairobi and head for Kisumu, the capital of their ethnic community. They borrowed Wenwa's Volkswagen.

Just before the escarpment, they met the 5th Battalion column from Gilgil. They stopped and the Commander of the troops approached the car. As he approached, however, Langi who was in the back seat instinctively reached for his fire-arm which he had carried without the knowledge of the other two in the car. Seeing this, Sumba cautioned him against trying to be a hero, and he slid the gun under the front passenger seat occupied by Sumba.

The Commander asked if the trio knew what had happened in the country. They responded in the affirmative but pleaded that they were rushing to a funeral in Nyanza. Since they looked harmless in a Volkswagen, the Commander allowed them to pass. Having survived this check-point, and knowing that they would meet more troops if they stayed on the main road, they turned off towards Narok. This circuitous route turned out to be the longest trip any of the trio had had to Kisumu from Nairobi. In addition, it rained heavily and the road was awful. But Raila and Sumba took turns to drive all night. They got stuck in the mud a few times but succeeded in extricating themselves. They had been driving since about 6 pm of August 1st and were in Litein at about 8 a.m. They left Nairobi with a full tank and only re-fuelled once. They went to Kericho and took the road through the sugar belt to Kisumu .

At Litein, they monitored the situation and heard on the radio that there were still pockets of resistance. It was not like it was over. On arrival in Kisumu, they

---

[20] Much of the account that follows depended on interviews with Raila Odinga, Nairobi, July 21, 2003 and with Patrick Sumba on April 9, 2004.

went to Dr Odhiambo Olel who practiced medicine in Kisumu and was a close ally of Jaramogi Oginga Odinga.

They spent the day and night in Kisumu but did not reach Jaramogi Oginga Odinga as they concentrated their effort on monitoring events in Nairobi and the rest of the country. Although clearly, President Moi had been reinstated, the regime was not in full control of the country. There was still confusion and even pockets of resistance.

Raila, Odongo Langi and Sumba could have escaped to Uganda via Lake Nyanza. But they decided not to take this option. Odongo Langi was to stay in Kisumu as the others returned to Nairobi on August 3rd . They wanted to return and see if military colleagues could still be helped by rallying elements still resisting and/or to arrange an escape with them. They decided that they could not simply leave Kenya at that time.

As Raila and Sumba approached Nakuru, they saw that there was a major road-block at which identification was being demanded. Sumba had his in his pocket, but Raila was not carrying any form of identification. So, they decided that Raila would find his way into Nakuru and take the train. On arrival at Nairobi railway station the following day, Sumba picked Raila up.

In Nairobi, the duo learned that Ochuka and Oteyo had fled and that Ogidi Obuon and many of their friends had been arrested. They knew that the net was closing in on them and expected that the military officers would put all the facts together and come after them.

Raila heard of the death of a relative, an activist and a very close friend, Okatch Ogada Ondiek, who was killed on the night of the coup. The circumstances of Okatch Ogada's death remain unknown. One version suggested that he was a guest at the Ambassadeur Hotel and had stepped out of the Hotel only to be shot by rampaging Kenyan soldiers. However, the second more plausible version, was that being an activist, Okatch Ogada came out of the Hotel intending to find Raila, and with his clenched fist signifying power to the people, the soldiers executed him in cold blood. Whatever, the case, his death reflected the excesses of the Moi regime on the day of the coup.

Raila spent the night of August 5, in his house at Kileleshwa. The following day, he was in town joining the arrangements for the burial of Okatch Ogada. At a fund raising for the funeral in Kaloleni Hall, he was told that Special Branch officers had been looking for him. So, he began to cover his tracks as he moved.

On August 10, Raila met with Sumba and they both decided to flee Kenya the following day. It was agreed that Agung'a, Raila's driver would pick Sumba up from the 680 Hotel at 1 pm on August 11.

Raila decided that it would be better for him to stay away from home overnight. He decided to sleep in the house of the late Dr. Oki Ooko-Ombaka, an activist lawyer. Agung'a dropped him at Ooko-Ombaka's house and was instructed to keep watch at Raila's residence and alert him if the Special Branch came searching.

Police officers visited Raila's Kileleshwa residence on August 10 and were told that Raila had travelled. They left but returned in the early hours of 11th August and insisted on searching the house. Raila's driver (who he claimed later to have learned, was working for State Security) told them not to bother and volunteered to take them to where Raila Odinga was.

At Ooko-Ombaka's residence, at around 6 am., Raila heard the distinct sound of his Peugeot 504 car on which he had altered the muffler. There was knocking on the door and Raila woke Wycliffe Oduor Ombaka, his host's junior brother who was sleeping in an adjoining room to get the door. As the door opened, Agung'a, was the first to come in. He told Raila that "these people" wanted to talk to him. The people identified themselves and demanded that he came along with them. Raila told them he would see them later as he had some things to do. They insisted and he had no choice but to follow them.

Raila was taken to the Central Police Station and was booked in the office of the Officer-in-Charge. He was transferred to the Nairobi Area Special Branch office, on the first floor of a building opposite the Central Police Station and was handed over to Senior Superintendent Josiah Rono, the officer-in-charge who interrogated him on his role in the events of August 1st.

Raila's position was that he knew nothing. He decided to be silent on whatever he knew for the sake of people who had been arrested. He recorded a statement and was taken back to the Central Police Station for custody and locked up.

Meanwhile, Agung'a went to the 680 Hotel and told Sumba that his boss had been picked up that morning. As soon as the driver told him this, Sumba left without saying a word. Why did Agung'a not hand Sumba over to State Security? No one knows.[21] Since he did not know the details of the escape plan, Sumba briefly went to the house of Arthur Nyamogo, a cousin of his, and from there left for Mombasa to attend the Annual General Meeting of the Amateur Athletics Association, where he took the risk of contesting for the post of Public Affairs of the Association. He eventually disappeared into Nyanza where he remained in hiding for a few weeks before, with the assistance of Jaramogi Oginga Odinga escaping to Uganda to begin a nineteen-year exile of which seventeen were in Sweden.

On the second day of his arrest, Raila was taken back to the Special Branch offices for further interrogation. He realized they were asking the same questions to cross-check what he was saying with what those who had been arrested earlier had said. On the third day when he returned for interrogation, Inspector Rono and his team became rough. They told Raila that they had instructions from above to do whatever they liked with him, including killing him, if he did not cooperate. Rono charged at Raila, broke the leg of a table in the room and started to hit him with it. Raila fell and Rono stepped on his groin. Thereafter, Inspector Rono's subordinates joined in hitting and stepping on Raila.

After this experience, he was transferred to Kilimani police station in Nairobi. He was joined there by student leader Paddy Onyango and Adongo. He spent two days at Kilimani and was transferred to Nairobi's Muthangari police station for torture. The Nyayo House Torture Chambers were yet to be built.

At Muthangari, the police removed Raila's pullover (August is usually cold in Nairobi), his shirt and shoes. They poured water inside a room. The door of the room had been sealed with rubber material to prevent water from escaping. The cold water was up to Raila's ankles. He could not sit and had to stand all night. In the morning, he realized that Titus Adungosi, a former student leader, was in the cell opposite. Adungosi told Raila that he had been tortured since August 1 when he was arrested as one of the students celebrating the coup attempt, and that his

---

[21] Agung'a died a while ago.

tormentors wanted him to confess even to what he had not done. Raila advised him to stand firm and refuse to break up.

Raila was taken to C.I.D Headquarters on Milimani Road, Nairobi, where he met Otieno Mak' Onyango, an Assistant Editor at *The Standard.* He was interrogated by Chief Inspector Mwangi and a bulky *Mzungu,* whom he later knew as, the late Patrick Shaw who was a teacher at Starehe Boys School and a police reservist. It was a long interrogation and he made a lengthy statement. Raila and Mak'Onyango were transferred to the General Service Unit (GSU) Headquarters at Ruaraka, in the outskirts of Nairobi, where they met Prof. Alfred Vincent Otieno, a former University of Nairobi don, who had also been arrested. The trio were kept in different cells for the night.

The following day, on August 19, 1982, Shaw came for him and he was returned to the CID station to face further interrogation and made another lengthy statement before being returned to the GSU HQ. According to Raila, at 11 pm that evening, his cell was invaded by a group of GSU officers led by Mr. Ben Gethi, the Police Commissioner who was accompanied by Mbuthia, the Commandant of the GSU. He was subjected to rough interrogation including being beaten-up in an attempt to extract a confession. Gethi was drunk and had a roasted goat leg which he chewed as he ordered his officers to assault Raila and company.

Gethi ordered that Raila be given pen and paper and commanded him to write all he knew about the coup. Gethi told him to write a confession addressed to "Uncle Ben" asking for mercy. But Raila refused to implicate himself. Instead, he wrote that he knew that Charles Njonjo, the powerful Minister of Constitutional Affairs was involved in a plan to overthrow Moi. Gethi, a close associate of Njonjo tore up Raila's statement four times. The substance of Raila's repeated statements as summarized before the Judicial Commission of Inquiry that probed Njonjo read:

> I stated that I had received information to the effect that Mr. Njonjo had made plans to overthrow the Government of Kenya with the aid of South African and Israeli mercenaries and the General Service Unit. To this effect, substantial amount of arms had been smuggled into the country. Some of these arms were kept somewhere in the Aberdares and the said coup was planned to take place on the 5th August, 1982. I also stated that the same source had said that several

South Africans and Israeli agents had come into the country to make arrangements for the coup.[22]

Two days after his assault on Raila, Gethi was relieved of his post in the "public interest" and jailed by President Moi. Apparently, he could no longer be trusted and he was replaced by Bernard Njiinu.[23] But Njonjo was not carpeted until June 29, 1983 when he was suspended as Minister and an inquiry set up to look into several allegations that bordered on compromising the security and integrity of the Kenyan State and conspiracy to overthrow President Moi. The Commission of Inquiry believed the testimony of Raila, and on the basis of this and other evidence adduced before it, concluded in the affirmative on most of the allegations against Njonjo

On the day before Gethi was fired, Shaw visited the GSU Headquarters and gave instructions that the three detainees could now mix, as they had all made their statements. Raila spent five weeks there in addition to the week in different cells after his arrest.

Raila recollected that one afternoon in late September, he, Otieno Mak'Onyango and Prof. Alfred Vincent Otieno were taken to court and charged. They were all charged with treason. After the charges were read, they were taken to Kamiti Maximum Security Prison on remand. At Kamiti, they met Captain Olak Diego who had been an air force Captain before he retired to work at the Directorate of Civil Aviation at Wilson Airport in Nairobi. He had been arrested for knowing about the coup plot and not reporting on it. He was charged with misprison of treason (concealing of information about a treasonable offence). They became a quartet at Kamiti.

At Kamiti, they were specially treated and referred to as "capital remand" prisoners with a big red letter "C" on their "Kunguru" shirts depicting that status. They were to receive capital punishment if found guilty and were not to mix with others on remand. Each one of them was in his own cell for 24 hours except for

---

[22] Hon. Mr. Justice C.H.E. Miller, E.B.S, Chairman, *Report of the Judicial Commission appointed to Inquire into Allegations Involving Charles Mugane Njonjo, (Former Minister for Constitutional Affairs and Member of Parliament for Kikuyu Constituency)*, November 1984, p. 29.

[23] For details, see, *Sunday Nation* March 2, 2003, p. 1, ff.

brief excursions to the toilet. Every day, porridge was thrown in as breakfast, *"Ugali and Sukumawiki"* (a hard maize meal mix and a vegetable dish) as lunch, and *Ugali* and beans as supper. It was not long before they became emaciated from poor diet and lack of daylight. Though Kamiti was very cold, they had one blanket to put on the floor, and another to cover themselves. They had no shower until they were on the way to court two weeks later for the mention of their case. They were also given civilian clothes for the court appearance.

Since Ida Odinga had no knowledge about legal representation, she consulted Jaramogi Oginga Odinga who decided that the late S.M. Otieno, a prominent criminal lawyer, would represent Raila. Retired Justice Kwatch (then a Lawyer) represented Prof. Otieno and Lawyer Owegi represented Mak'Onyango. Sharad Rao, the Deputy Public Prosecutor led the case before Chief Magistrate Abdul Rauf. On the first appearance, Sharad Rao said that investigations were incomplete and requested a two-week adjournment. This was granted and began a routine of coming for mention every two weeks.

At Kamiti, their health deteriorated. They began to feel dizzy and when the doctor came round, he recommended that they be given an additional blanket each and allowed brief daily access to sunshine.

As the routine of bi-weekly mention in court continued, a group of friends in the United Kingdom and Europe came to the conclusion that higher profile representation was needed for Raila and his co-accused. These friends raised funds and hired the services of a British Lawyer, Desmond Da Silva, QC (Queen's Counsel). When Da Silva got involved, the Kenyan Government entered a *nolle prosequi* (legal withdrawal of the charge) as the State no longer wanted to prosecute.

However, the *nolle prosequi* was not just the result of the personality and stature of Da Silva. President Moi was determined to put the inner core of the planners of the coup to death.[24] Raila had been charged with treason, a capital offence, on the basis of the confessions of military men like Ogidi Obuon. As a civilian, he could not be tried by a court-martial. However, under the Kenyan Criminal Procedure Code, when the offence is treason, the evidence of an accomplice must be

---

[24] The explanation here has depended totally on the accounts of Murithi Mutiga, Douglas Okwatch and David Makali, "How Raila escaped the noose," *Sunday Standard,* March 14, 2004, p. 11-12.

corroborated by an independent witness. In other words, the evidence of ten accomplices could not convict without the corroboration of a witness who was not a participant. Since there were no such witnesses, the Chief Justice, A.H. Simpson, advised the Attorney-General Joseph Kamere and President Moi against prosecution. The bringing of a Bill to Parliament to amend the law to try Raila, met with an outcry both in Kenya and in Britain. Nonetheless, it was passed.

Raila's formal detention started on March 23, 1983 as the withdrawal of the charge did not result in freedom for him and the two others accused with him. They were re-arrested in the court cells, taken to Langata police station till midnight and then transported to Nairobi Area Police Headquarters, where Provincial Police Officer, Kilonzo, served them with detention orders.

They were subsequently transferred to Kamiti Maximum Security Prison's segregation block. Captain Olak Diego left after he received a sentence of 10 years. So, the remaining trio occupied the segregation blocks until 20 October 1983 when Prof. Otieno was released. On the following day, the other two were transferred to Mombasa's Shimo-La-Tewa prison which they had visited in June with Prof. Otieno, to face a Review Tribunal. This Tribunal was only concerned with the physical state of the prisoners every 6 months. According to Raila, they found the Review Tribunal a useless Kangaroo arrangement; but they took advantage of the occasion to get out of segregation.

Mak'Onyango was transferred to Manyani and Raila stayed in solitary confinement at Shimo-La-Tewa prison from 1984 till March 1986. Angered by what he saw as wrongful confinement, Raila sought to know why he was being detained by filing a suit in February 1986. The suit was filed by Gibson Kamau Kuria and Kiraitu Murungi (two activist Lawyers who subsequently fled to the USA as Government clamped down on multi-party advocates), and sought a detailed answer for the grounds of Raila's detention; his immediate release, and a declaration that his right to have his case reviewed by an independent and impartial tribunal under the Kenyan constitution, had been adversely impaired. Other orders sought from the court included payment of damages for the breach of Raila's constitutional rights as well as the provision of a mattress, bed, radio, television set, newspapers, trousers, shirts, shoes and that he, like other prisoners, be allowed access to relatives and friends.[25]

---

[25] *Ibid.*

The travesty that was justice during the Moi era played itself out as the Chief State Counsel took issue with the suit on the basis of legal technicalities arguing that: "an application such as this could not be brought by way of notice of motion but by a plaint with pleadings as provided under the civil procedure rules." Kuria counter-argued that the suit had been properly filed.

Acting Chief Justice Madan dismissed the case, citing a written submission from Raila to the Detainees Review Tribunal, dated 25 October 1983 in which Raila had stated that there were sufficient grounds to warrant his detention. Justice Madan ignored the power relationships in Kenyan prisons that made people write or sign whatever their tormentors wanted. He treated a forged letter of what Raila had purportedly written in detention, as a freely entered into agreement with the Moi Government that he deserved to be detained. The fact that Raila was denied appearance before the court was never questioned. He was not impressed that Raila's suit now wanted a review of the whole process of his detention within the constitution of Kenya. Madan ruled that: "to ask the court under these circumstances to make a declaration that [Raila] Odinga's right given by Section 83(2)(a) of the Constitution has been contravened is a limping and pedantic peroration."[26]

In March 1986, following the court ruling, Raila was moved from his solitary confinement at Shimo-La-Tewa to Manyani prison at the coast as a punitive measure. Raila regarded this prison as the most difficult and went on hunger strike for five days.

He continued his hunger strike until Kilonzo came with the Deputy Commissioner of prisons, Mr. Valai. They told him that they would order that he be force fed if he continued with the hunger strike. Kilonzo and Valai were accompanied by a doctor who prescribed a medicine for Raila ostensibly to ameliorate Raila's poor state of health.

---

[26] As quoted in *Ibid.* The case of Naomi Waithira Mbaraka Karanja v. The Attorney General, High Court Miscellaneous Application No. 193 of 1987 reported in S.N. Waruhiu, *From Autocracy to Democracy in Kenya: Past Systems of Government and Reforms for the Future* (Nairobi: S.N. Waruhiu, 1994), pp. 112-115 contains accounts on undue pressure from the Presidency through the Chief Justice that led to the departure of Justice Schofield from Kenya.

According to Raila, he took the medicine only to have his blood pressure shoot up with pain in his hands. One side of his arm started going darker. He complained. But the warders thought he was pretending. Then pimples filled up his hands and he started shouting every night that his body was reacting to a medicine he had been given in jail and that if he died, the State should be held responsible.

It took Ida's smuggling of a medicine to him to have an improvement on his health. He was transferred to Kamiti prison in July 1986 and within months to another maximum security prison at Naivasha where he spent 1987 alone in a block meant for 300 prisoners. He did a lot of farming in the compound using a variety of seeds: tomatoes, onions, maize, cabbages and carrots, given to him by prison officers. He ate some of his produce raw, got assistance to roast maize and gave some to other prisoners and warders.

Aside from farming, after his first year in detention, Raila received books from Ida. The books were normally censored. Out of ten books sent, five might survive censorship. Sometimes Ida re-sent the same books with new ones and some that had earlier been rejected, made it. This told Raila that the censorship was being done by semi-illiterates. Raila found the Naivasha prison library well stocked with books donated from the United States and Britain, and for the first time, he had access to knowledge beyond the Qoran and the Bible. He read the Bible from Genesis to Revelation and he had a teacher of the Qoran at Shimo-La-Tewa prison. This helped him to appreciate Islam.

Letters between him and his family were heavily censored and at times took more than six months to be delivered. He was denied access to radio and newspapers as he was not to receive current news while in detention. The warders were not to speak to him.

The Experience of one of Raila Odinga's Business Associates

Among the many other Kenyans who were detained, in the aftermath of the coup attempt was a business associate Israel Otieno Wasonga Agina who had also been detained under Kenyatta's regime. On his release, he was hired at East Africa Spectre in May 1973. Ten years after his first stint, the police came for Israel Agina at the East Africa Spectre premises in 1982. Luckily, he was standing behind the receptionist when the Special Branch officers, pretending to be his friends, said they wanted to see him. They told the receptionist that they knew him and claimed to have had drinks with him the night before. Agina pre-empted any additional word from the receptionist, by quickly stating that Mr. Agina was yet to report at work as he normally came late. After his baptism under Jomo Kenyatta, he wanted to avoid jail and fled to Uganda without telling his wife that he was leaving, telephoning her only after he had been officially accepted as an exile in Uganda.

He subsequently returned only to start his detention without trial on September 3, 1986. He was alleged to be a member of a clandestine organization called Kenya Revolutionary Movement helping Kenyans to get military training in Libya and Tanzania. He was accused of being anti-government and working to remove the government by unconstitutional means.

On the basis of this accusation, Agina spent 96 days in the Nyayo House torture chambers. He claimed that while he was at Nyayo House, he spent four days of each week continuously standing in water. He was not fed as his tormentors denied him water and food, to save him from having to use the toilet. Throughout the four days, the cell was kept completely dark, and he only knew it was dawn of a new day through the hearing of the sounds of the shoes of women reporting to work and of many vehicles on the road. On the basis of this, he marked each day on the wall.

While in the water, Agina claimed he could hear his captors having sex with Koinange Street prostitutes, who, he gathered were normally raped and then chased away without payment. This was additional psychological pressure.

After each water session, he was taken to the roof top, where there was sunlight, holding cells and a conference room. He was interrogated by men with whips, batons, *pangas,* and, of course, pistols. He was beaten, and told that his captors had Presidential authority to deal with him however they liked including killing him if he did not tell the truth.

Since Agina, unlike some of his fellow captors, refused to confess to what, (according to him), he did not do, he was sent to Naivasha Maximum Security Prison for three months of solitary confinement. He wondered why his co-detainees like late George Katama Mkangi were allowed freedom of interaction with others while he was in solitary confinement. Agina knew Katama Mkangi was allowed to play volley-ball.

He was transferred in March 1987 to Kamiti Maximum Security Prison where he joined other detainees like Mirugi Kariuki and Ngotho Kariuki. Here he was only in solitary confinement for three days before he was mixed with other prisoners. Life was better at Kamiti as he also had access to the Bible and the Quoran which he analysed politically. Occasionally, non-political novels were allowed from family members and which detainees shared.

While in Kamiti, Agina's wife, Elizabeth died of high blood pressure and goiter on July 1987 at the Misericordiae Hospital. In a press release on 4 August, Ida Betty Odinga announced the death of Elizabeth pointing out that her condition had deteriorated badly since Agina's detention in September 1986.[27] Agina was neither informed nor allowed to view his wife's body before burial. He learned of her death and burial from a letter from his 11 year old first son, Salvador Omondi Otieno Agina.

Release from First Detention

February 5, 1988 was an eventful day for Raila Odinga and Israel Agina. That morning, Raila was told to pack his belongings and was driven from Naivasha to the Nairobi Area Police Headquarters. There, he met a number of old friends and acquaintances. In all, there were eight other detainees: Israel Agina; Herbert Lusiola; Jackson Waga Ngola; Ngotho wa Kariuki; George Katama Mkangi; Nicodemus Benedict Obiero; Patrick (Paddy) Ouma Onyango; and Paul Ong'or Amina. They were driven to State House where they were taken to a large room. Kilonzo asked the detainees to select one among them to thank the President when he came to set them free, and he advised them to be of good behaviour. Since Raila was the "dean" of his co-detainees, he was chosen. He told Kilonzo he would speak on the understanding that he would not express thanks.

When President Moi arrived, Raila spoke about the conditions in detention describing it as inhuman, and saying that it should be unnecessary to detain any Kenyan without trial. He stressed the need for due process of law in Kenya. Moi then set the detainees free.[28]

---

[27] *Daily Nation,* August 4, 1987.
[28] Raila's account at an interview with the author on July 21, 2003.

Raila was driven to Kenya High School where his wife, was a teacher, for a re-union with his family: Fidel, who was then 14; Rosemary 10, and Raila Odinga Jnr. who was 8.

Before his arrest he had been Deputy Director at the Kenya Bureau of Standards, a post he lost. On his release, he returned to East Africa Spectre Ltd., as Managing Director.

The Second Detention

During a six-month break, Raila tried to rebuild his life and re-organize his business.[29] But he was, arrested again on 14 August 1988. Israel Agina followed on Raila's heels. But although their detentions were gazetted, they were never charged or brought before any law court.

Nyayo House had been built, but what happened in the basement was hidden from Kenyans and the rest of the world. Raila was in the infamous torture chamber in this building for ten days. Of this experience, he stated:

> I spent 10 days standing in water. That is when you know how long the night is. The cell was like a tank. It had automated doors that closed tight. Water would reach the legs. They would pour cold water on you at midnight and at 5 am. Then they would blindfold you and take you to the interrogation room on the 24th floor. When the blindfold was removed, you found yourself before a row of five or six well-dressed men sitting on a raised platform. It was a very terrifying scene. Mr. George Anyona said he saw them and thought they were from the moon.[30]

In a further description of how the Nyayo House interrogators operated, Raila recalled that detainees in Nyayo House were normally naked during interrogation. The detainee was usually under flood-light while the interrogators sat in partial darkness. The detainee could see fresh blood on the floor with broken wood all over the place as if a battle had just ended. The interrogators would then be

---

[29] The account here is based on an interview with Raila on July 27, 2003

[30] *Sunday Nation,* January 26, 2003, p. 12

smoking and eating roast chicken before a detainee who had been starved for weeks. In Raila's own words:

> They [interrogators called *Wazee*, meaning elderly men] would start by telling you that they thought you were there by mistake, that the sooner you confessed everything, the better, so you could leave. As they did so, they would be smoking heavily while munching roast chicken. The sight of the food would make the starved prisoner say anything in order to be freed as quickly as possible so he could feed.[31]

Raila was transferred on rotation to the familiar environment of Kamiti, Naivasha and Shimo-La-Tewa. Israel Agina and Raila, though in solitary confinement, realised that they shared the same block at Naivasha for some time during their second detention. Though they could not see each other, they communicated by shouting at night. With the assistance of some warders, they even shared fruits brought by Ida. For Agina, the assistance of some warders told him there were good ones among their captors.[32] This non-visual interaction lasted for about three months before Agina was transferred to Manyani prison to stay in solitary confinement for the rest of his detention.

Raila was accused of planning clandestine activities against the legally constituted Government of Kenya, and that he had engaged in subversive activities which necessitated his detention. Ida's attempt to secure his release through a writ of *Habeas Corpus* (a legal order which if granted, forces the authorities to produce the accused in court), forced the Kenyan authorities to serve Raila's detention order.

The rumour was that Raila had been mentioned in a number of sedition cases. In the trial of a Nakuru businessman, Gibson Maina Kimani, Raila was alleged to be behind a Kenya Revolutionary Movement planning a guerrilla attack on the country. *The Weekly Review* quoted comments from Dr. Robert Ouko (who was assassinated much later) and Dalmas Otieno, both Luos and Moi functionaries, which lent credence to the rumours. Dr. Ouko issued a statement: "We ask the people of Kenya to regard Raila as an individual who has gone astray and not to associate

---

[31] See, *ibid.*
[32] Interview with Israel Agina, Nairobi, 27 May 2003.

his subversive activities with any section of the Luo community." Dalmas Otieno as Minister for Industry, reportedly said that Raila had been conducting himself in a manner prejudicial to the security of the state, but that he had influenced only "a few insignificant" people.[33]

Agina was released before Raila on June 6, 1989. On his release, Agina suggested that his detention was really a vendetta against Jaramogi Oginga Odinga and made a plea that his natural relationship with Jaramogi should not be denied him. He stated: "We are blood-related and the Odinga family are my business associates. Nobody will deny me this right as a free Kenyan."[34] Agina claimed he had been detained for allegedly joining a clandestine Kenyan Revolutionary Movement and facilitating the travel for military training in Libya of some unnamed Kenyans. He denied being a subversive or doing anything that he had been accused of. Recalling the scars of this period, Agina reportedly said: "It not only affected my family but also occasioned the death of my wife."[35]

Agina subsequently re-married his late wife's sister, Ethel Truda Akello, a graduate of the University of Nairobi, who added two sons and two daughters to the four boys by Elizabeth. For him, this showed that struggle for a just cause does not preclude family life.[36]

Release from Second Detention

Raila, was released on June 12, 1989 and characteristically, in an interview with *The Weekly Review,* said that he was not bitter with the Government. He returned to making sense of his life from where he had left off. However, changes were taking place in the world at large, and in Kenya. The Berlin wall subsequently came down and in Kenya, a number of new leaders had started to speak out boldly. Many of these leaders came from the Church and the Law Society of Kenya. One was the late Bishop Henry Okullu. These courageous new political leaders especially Charles Rubia and Kenneth Matiba, added strength to the protests of the better known Jaramogi; Masinde Muliro and Martin Shikuku.

---

[33] Both Luo MPs were reported in *The Weekly Review,* June 28, 1991, p. 11.

[34] The *Standard,* Wednesday, June 7, 1989, p. 10.

[35] *Sunday Nation,* January 26, 2003, p. 13.

[36] Interview with Agina, Nairobi, May 27, 2003.

Charles Rubia and Kenneth Matiba, former members of President Moi's cabinet emerged in early 1990 and in an unprecedented move, called for the repeal of Section 2A of the Kenyan Constitution to allow the formation of other political parties. The reaction from the establishment was, as expected, sharp and threatening. The two leaders were instantly transformed into tribalists who wanted to plunge the country into chaos by the introduction of ethnic politics. A countrywide campaign was orchestrated to demonise them as enemies of the Kenyan people. KANU sponsored political rallies where, the effigies of the leaders were publicly burnt.

Raila knew Matiba fairly well as they had worked together in the administration of football in Kenya in the 1970s. Matiba urged Raila to join the crusade for the repeal of Section 2A. Raila was asked to get a statement of support from Jaramogi. Matiba and Rubia were worried that they could be arrested and felt a statement from the leading veteran opponent to one party rule could save their skin. Raila arranged a meeting with Jaramogi at which Matiba and Rubia pledged their full support to his cause for change, and promised to work with him and support him for the Presidency when the time came. Jaramogi issued a strong statement on the principled ground that Kenya should have a multi-party system.[37]

The Rubia, Matiba and Raila group then decided to organize a public rally at Kamukunji to test popular opinion on support to multi-partyism. Their appleation for a permit was rejected. Nevertheless, they decided to go to Kamukunji on 7th July (Saba Saba) with or without a permit. In the absence of a proper political mobilization machinery, they decided to use informal channels. Matiba used his contacts in the Matatu (private mass transport vans) industry. Raila used his in football circles.

Raila Odinga's Third Stint

When the Government realized that the public had been mobilized to endorse multi-partyism by attending the rally, the security apparatus moved to arrest the leaders. Rubia and Matiba were picked up on July 4, 1990 and Raila on July 5. A number of other multi-party activist lawyers associated with the trio, like Dr. John Khaminwa, Gitobu Imanyara and Mohammed Ibrahim were also arrested

---

[37] Much of these accounts were based on interview with Raila, July 27, 2003.

but released a few weeks later. Imanyara was re-arrested and charged with sedition. But Rubia, Matiba and Raila remained in detention. Raila was again taken to Kamiti Maximum Security Prison, then Naivasha and finally Shimo-La-Tewa.

Raila, should have known that as the clamour for multi-party democracy grew, using his AGIP House offices as a meeting point was enough reason for an intolerant government to jail him. But a week before his release, he filed a court application seeking to know why he was being detained and challenging the constitutional validity of his detention. He claimed in his application that the real reason for his detention was to get at his father for leading the demand for multi-partyism in Kenya, and daring to write an open letter to Moi that was critical of the political atmosphere in Kenya.[38]

The Final Release

Raila was not released until June 21, 1991 after Rubia and Matiba had been released on health grounds. Rubia went to hospital on his release and Matiba was released while in hospital having suffered what was said to be a mild stroke.[39] Ida, with the assistance of Lawyer Japheth Shamalla called attention to the situation of Raila claiming that he was also sick and needed to be released as detention had aggravated his diabetes. Earlier, Shamalla claimed Raila was suffering from chest, waist and back pains, and heart palpitations, and needed to be seen by his doctor.[40]

President Moi quickly condemned detainees who "feigned illness in order to be released." He claimed that an X-Ray of Raila had shown that he was not ill. Ida replied that Raila's illness could not be diagnosed by X-Ray, and that the State had refused to carry out the blood and urine tests recommended for her husband since May 19. But as *The Weekly Review* noted, the Government had accepted sickness as a basis for release when it freed Gulabchand Shantil Shah, imprisoned for stealing millions of shillings.[41]

---

[38] Reported in *The Weekly Review*, June 28, 1991, p. 11.
[39] For details, see, *The Weekly Review*, June 21, 1991, p. 20.
[40] *Ibid.*
[41] *Ibid.*

Raila and Matiba had again asked the courts to order their release. They asked the court to review the constitutional validity of their detention and to order their immediate release. This was not to be. Raila was released on what appeared to be health grounds. He then had tests at Nairobi hospital and asked for the return of his passport which had been withheld for almost a decade so that he could go to England for further tests. But this request fell on deaf ears.

The Raila periods in jail were for being accused of involvement in opposition to as well as an attempt to overthrow a regime the Luos (and many non-Luos) deemed oppressive and against Luo interests. This act of "bravery" (as the Luos saw it), marked the beginning of Luo endearment to Raila as a courageous leader ready to take bold risks and suffer courageously for the interest of all. This perception was further strengthened by the later detentions.

Chapter 10
The Impact of Raila's Incarceration

Any confinement represents a life-long memory for most human beings. The depravity, solitude and the hopelessness, generally takes its toll on a person wanting freedom. A long period in jail gives the prisoner another problem. Society moves on. The changes in society are sharper for someone emerging from long-term incarceration.

After the coup attempt, President Moi and those around him decided to go strong on all forms of opposition to prevent a repeat performance. He purged the civil service, cabinet and party hierarchy. Senior civil servants were required to be life members of KANU and promotion depended on the extent of expressed loyalty to the President and his Nyayo ideology of "peace, love and unity."

The move to arrest University lecturers in the pre-coup days, intensified. Those lecturers who did not want to go to jail, pledged loyalty to the President as part of their ethnic groups. Student movements were also cowed as the State took close interest in who became student leaders. Academic freedom suffered.

A loyalist core group vetted politicians according to the extent of their loyalty and whether they were pro or anti-Nyayoism. Public expression of loyalty was not enough and MPs easily lost their seats if they were deemed disloyal. The procedure was simple. Members of a constituency sub-branch of KANU would denounce their MP and express their dissatisfaction by passing a vote of no confidence. When this vote of no confidence was sent to the district level, suspension would be confirmed and the "errant" politician would be referred to KANU headquarters for expulsion from the party. After expulsion was confirmed, the MP lost his seat under section 40 of the Constitution.[1] This section prohibited people from being MPs if they cease to be members of a party that had supported them into parliament. They would have to seek a new mandate in a by-election. But in a one-party regime, there was nowhere to go.

---

[1] See, Laws of Kenya, *The Constitution of Kenya,* Rev. Ed. (1998), (Nairobi: Government Printer, 1998), p. 25.

As part of the changes, KANU instituted the *Mlolongo* nomination system under which party members, at the constituency level had to queue behind the individual or the portrait of the individual they wanted to represent them. The longest queue signified support for the owner of the photograph as the nominated candidate. A candidate securing 75% of votes at the nomination stage did not have to face a Parliamentary secret ballot to become an MP. The right was automatically conferred. When the queue cleared, there was no evidence of whose line was longest other than what core Nyayoists announced. In effect, the real decision on the nominee was that of the core Nyayoists.

When he was released from his first detention, Raila was amazed by these changes.[2] Parliament was dissolved on the day of his release. He went to political rallies and was shocked to see how Kenya had been transformed, and found the change too much to stomach. Attending his first campaign rally he found the shouts of praise of the President revolting. Sycophancy had reached astronomical proportions with Kenyans being made to shout: *Mtukufu Rais juu, juu, juu zaidi* (high, high, to the President up to infinity .... This was the equivalent of *Heil Hitler* in the Nazi era).

At a personal level, he realized that fearing victimisation and persecution, some of his friends and even relatives were avoiding associating with him. Many stopped visiting him and his family at the Kenya High School, to avoid registering at the gate as his visitors for fear of being subsequently followed by Kenyan intelligence. He stopped visiting friends and relatives at work since they were normally questioned by the police and/or employers after his departure. Some people lost their jobs because he had visited them at work.

Ida saw some differences in her husband on his release. He was always in a rush, feeling that he had lost valuable time when he could have achieved a number of things. He had major plans for East Africa Spectre that he could not achieve.

Ida felt that the temper and impatient streak of the pre-detention Raila had substantially changed. "These days, he allows people to develop their point even if he knows what they are saying cannot work. He started behaving more like his father as he grew older."[3] She recalled a moment in 1978 when auctioneers visited

---

[2] Interview with Raila Odinga, Nairobi, September 28, 2003.

[3] Interview with Ida

and removed everything in Oginga Odinga's house ostensibly for a National Bank loan which he had obtained to purchase commercial buses. The bank had recalled the loan and auctioneers followed swiftly. Ida had thought the old man would react strongly but he was calm and consoled others like Ida. A similar situation was when Raila was arrested for treason and Jaramogi stayed very calm contrary to his younger day's temperamental image (which he acknowledged in *Not Yet Uhuru*). Ida, believed that prison changed Raila into a determined calm person.

When Raila was released, Wenwa Akinyi knew that her brother would be different. She had seen the example of her father who, after being released from detention asked his children why they had not gone to church on a Sunday. This was strange as he did not normally encourage his children to go to church. When the children pointed this out, Jaramogi replied that he had some reflections in prison where the Bible was the only book he could read every day.

Wenwa felt that the impatient streak in Raila became apparent, in the initial stages of his freedom. This impatience was most noticeable when he wanted information. Raila, realized he became an information freak after his release. In his defence, he parried:

> If you have been in confinement for 6 years, to be up to date, you require a lot of information. It's not information that could be given in a day. You normally would get impatient with somebody treating you as if you ought to have known because he or she knows.[4]

According to Wenwa, Raila also appeared eager to do many things at the same time. He became more appreciative of freedom and quality of time with his family. Whereas he had previously taken favours for granted, he was now more appreciative of what people did for him. For Wenwa, Raila's imprisonment was like dying and then being reborn.

The Effect of Raila's Detention on Family Members

Raila's going in and out of jail had its impact on many family members. Ida led the second exchange programme of 25 Kenyan students to Germany in 1982.

---

[*] Interview with Raila Odinga, September 28, 2003.

She was at a camping site near the German – Denmark border when she saw a television programme in a camper's caravan showing the map of Kenya. This was strange. Germans would not normally air news on Kenya. But the German camper spoke no English and there was no way of Ida knowing that a coup had been attempted in her country.

Though she could not have imagined that this coup attempt would change her life, she was worried when she learnt from her sister Lynn Yaya that many people had been killed including Okach Ogada Ondiek. She had no reason to be bothered about Raila's safety since he had reportedly gone to Nyanza. She stayed on to take responsibility for the 25 students, rather than rush back to her kids on the advice of Lynn.

On 11 August, she took the students to a chocolate factory in Lubec and visited old churches and castles. On impulse she phoned home only to learn that Raila had been arrested. There was another teacher, Mrs. Grace Ochieng on the trip, to whom she handed over responsibility and rushed back to Nairobi, arriving two days later.

The questioning and rough search at the airport told her that the situation was tense. This was her first experience of the stigma she would carry for ten years for being an Odinga. At the Special Branch police office, she was told that Raila was being held. She waited all day but was not allowed to see her husband, and was asked to return the next day.

On reaching home, she found that two land-rovers full of security people had followed her. They had weapons including machine guns and demanded to search the house. She asked what they were looking for and they retorted that they would pick what they were looking for when they found it. She was too shocked and confused to ask for a search warrant, which, she insists, she would have done today. She and her children heaved a sigh of relief when the search that had turned everything into a garbage heap ended after five and a half hours. The security men left with several books and many family pictures.

Ida went to bed only to be woken up by the same policemen the following morning saying they had returned to complete their work. Ida asked to be allowed to go into her room to change from a dressing robe and be properly dressed. Though they consented, they immediately followed her into the room as she was trying to take off her dressing robe. They asked her to continue with her dressing but they would be around as they thought she was trying to hide incriminating evidence. They even searched inside the ceiling board, leaving with more books and photographs which were never returned.

Ida did not see her husband until he was charged in September 1982, and remanded at Kamiti Maximum Security Prison. At the first meeting, she saw that Raila had lost a lot of weight and had a puffed face. But his spirit was very strong. At the daily meetings that followed, Raila was behind a four feet high wall topped with barbed wire. They spoke to each other across the barbed wire with policemen listening. Ida had been instructed to speak only in English or Kiswahili. She also saw him at the two-week court appearances to mention his case; but was instructed to speak only about the children, family and business. Sometimes, she managed to speak to him about how he was being represented.

During his formal detention, Ida's visit rights changed. She could only see Raila once in six months. Sometimes that right was denied and she had to wait a year. For Ida, seeing Raila depended on the mood of the officer in charge of detained and restricted persons.

The visits took place either at the Nairobi Area Police Headquarters, when Raila came by road or at Wilson Airport when he came by air. Where he was being held determined the mode of transportation. The meeting room had a long table. Ida sat at one end and Raila at the other. The police swarmed on either side of the table with some observing, some taking notes, and others listening. The Officer-in-Charge was also present. Towards the end of the detentions, Ida won a relaxation that let her bring food that was shared by all, including the policemen.

Ida did not like the idea that the police had a duty to regulate what they discussed during visits. Anybody whose name was mentioned was later invited for questioning. Care had to be taken not to mention names or incidents that could get innocent people harassed.

The absence of a bread-winner, friend and husband was difficult for Ida. At the beginning, she fared badly. She did not know where and how to pay her electricity and phone bills and learned the hard way that she needed to reduce her use of these. Raila had previously bought meat from the Kenya Meat Commission and she cooked it. Now she had to order and did not know that she must pay immediately at the point of collection. She later realized that she could go to butcheries at a cheaper rate. Her earnings were miniscule compared to her needs. She had been barred from seeing Jaramogi after the first week of his house arrest. And when he started providing some financial support to Ida, she still had the problem of budgeting. The family cars were seized by the police for a year as exhibit. For a while, it was difficult to handle simple issues like dropping her children to school until Jaramogi came to her rescue with a small Toyota car.

Ida's professional life suffered too. She had applied to take a Masters degree programme at the University of Nairobi and was to have started in September 1982. But she never got back to school. Instead, she used all her energy to teach the children in her class and became so popular that by 1988 she had twice the number of pupils of 1982.

Despite her hard work, Ida was retired "in the public interest." A letter of retirement addressed to Mrs. Ida B. Oginga, and signed by one Mrs. S.N. Kinyua on behalf of the Secretary of the Teachers Service Commission, was delivered to the Kenya High School on 12 September and given to Ida on the same day in spite of the error in her name. She was required "to hand over any property belonging to the school not later than 12th September, 1988."[5] In effect, she had less than six hours to vacate her government accommodation at the Kenya High School. It was clear to her that she was being victimized because, with legal assistance from Dr. John Khaminwa, she had taken the state to court seeking the release of her husband who was re-arrested about six months after his first release in February 1988. She had taken the case to press for his release or for him to be taken to court rather than detention without trial.

The Kenya National Union of Teachers (KNUT) led by the late Ambrose Adey Adongo did not lift a finger in support of Ida, a member who was being victimized. Everyone knew Ida's problems were related not to her work but to her marriage to Raila.

However, the late Bishop Alexander Muge who Ida had never met, galvanized many Kenyans and others to protest about Ida's dismissal. Many pleas and representations were sent to President Moi and as a result of this local and

---

[5] Ida shared copies of her letters with the author.

international pressure (including from Amnesty International), Mr. J. Kang'ali, Secretary, Teachers Commission wrote to Ida on September 23, 1988 stating that: "The Teachers Service Commission has carefully reviewed its decision on this matter and having taken into account your previous record of service as a teacher, it has been decided that you be reinstated back to the teaching service, on humanitarian grounds." Washing its hands of the possibility of any claims from Ida, the letter continued: "The Teachers Service Commission wishes you to note that your reinstatement back to teaching service is purely on humanitarian grounds, therefore, the Commission will not accept any responsibility on any expenses or inconveniences that you may have been caused by its earlier decision to retire you in public interest." She was not to return to her students at the Kenya High School or even teach. Her letter informed her that she had, initially, been seconded to the headquarters of the Ministry of Education. She became an Education Officer at the Ministry in Jogoo House. She was deployed in the school administration department and put in charge of Board of Governance. This included the writing of speeches for the Minister, Permanent Secretary and Directors.

Ida was invited to the October 1988, prize giving day at the Kenya High School, both as a former teacher and in her new position as Education Officer. As fate would have it, her car was blocked at work and she arrived at the ceremony an hour late just when Mrs. Githinji, the Permanent Secretary at the Ministry of Social Services was giving her speech as the Guest of Honour. Ida's former students spotted her arrival and rushed out to meet her. The speech was suspended. The girls were screaming: Winnie! Winnie!! Winnie!!! referring to her as the Winnie Mandela of Kenya.

Ida's action was read as intended to embarrass Mrs. Githinj and the Education Permanent Secretary and the Police Commissioner told Ida that she was never to step into the Kenya High School again.

Ida's spirit was not cowed by such threats. She remained actively involved in pressing for Raila's release each time he was arrested, by writing to those in authority challenging the behaviour of the State in detaining Raila. In a letter dated April 5, 1991 the late Hon. Justice M.G. Muli, at that time the Attorney General, Ida wrote:

Dear Justice Muli,

In the light of your recent comments regarding the principle and condition of detention without trial in Kenya I would request you to clarify the following points:

1. Why is it that up to now Raila has not been told specifically what it is that he did to warrant detention without trial? Would you not agree that general reference to his "involvement" or "association" with persons is not specific at all? How can he change if his offences are not specified? Is it impossible for the authority to be specific? Could it be lack of real offence on Raila's part?

   Does the law regarding detention require that a detainee's offending actions be spelt out or does it only say that generalized accusations are all that it takes for one to be detained?

2. Even accepting that the Review Tribunal is not the detaining authority, why is it that the same review tribunal only demands confessions and plea for mercy from him and not his request that he be told his specific offence?

3. Why can the authorities not allow Raila the facilities to sign the requisite affidavits to validate his application to challenge his detention in the High Court? Is it because the authority wants to deny Raila a legal recourse? He is not allowed to sign affidavits. Without signed affidavits his case cannot be heard. This is a "catch-22" technicality. Why do it to him?

4. You say that the world must accept that "detention" is legal in Kenya. Granted but do you personally accept the morality and legitimacy of:

   a) "Apartheid" which is legal in South Africa?
   b) The law that Bokassa enacted to transform the Central African Republic into his Empire?

   1. He is held in solitary confinement in a small cell?
   2. His sole diet is Ugali [maize-meal] and half cooked cabbages?
   3. He has no bed, and his entire bedding consists of one thin blanket on cold cement floor?
   4. He is forbidden any source of information including newspapers and radio?

5. He is dressed in calico prison garb without underclothing?
6. He is denied the ordinary opportunity to be seen by our family doctor?
7. My application to see him takes inordinately long time?
8. Whenever granted, the visits take place in an intimidating atmosphere and security officers record anything said?
9. His eyesight is now damaged due to continuous but inappropriate cell lighting?
10. His cell has no sanitary toilet facilities and he is forced to use cans which he has to empty?
11. In your opinion as A.G., how much detention is "enough"?
12. Is Kenya signatory to the U.N. international Bill of Human Rights – containing the Universal Declaration of Human Rights whose article 5 states: **"No one shall be subjected to torture or to cruel, inhuman or degrading treatment or punishment,** or The International Covenant on Civil and Political Rights whose article 9(4) states: **"Anyone who is deprived of his liberty by arrest or detention shall be ENTITLED to take proceedings before a court, in order that that court may decide without delay on the lawfulness of his detention and order his release if his detention is not lawful?"**

In 1988 I was sacked from my teaching job after I filed a—*habeas corpus*—application for Raila Odinga to be produced in court. This, no doubt, was a punitive action intended to deter me from exercising my legal and constitutional rights. Following a public outcry against this action, I was reabsorbed into the civil service on "humanitarian grounds" and transferred to the Ministry of Education Jogoo House offices.

I sincerely hope that the issues I am currently raising will be looked into within their own constitutional merits, and no untoward action will be taken against me or my person as past experiences have shown. Further, I hope your answers to my questions will be more specific than those so far given to Raila as your records no doubt show.

Thank you for your time.

Obediently
Signed

Ida did not receive a reply from Attorney-General Muli who was later replaced by Hon. Amos Wako. Congratulating Wako on his appointment, Ida wrote on May 24, 1991, calling his attention to the tribulations of her family in the last ten years during which Raila had been detained without due process or trial in an open court. She stated: "I do not and I will not accept as fair the principle of detention without trial. Consequently, any law brought about to give detention a legal force is immoral and has no legitimacy." She went further to appeal to the new Attorney-General to use the freshness of his untainted views to ensure the release of Raila, Matiba and Rubia and "thereafter hasten to cause the repeal of the detention act." She went on to conclude that by such an act, Wako "will have done our beloved country greater service than you will be able to immediately comprehend and you will be deserving of more gold and silver medals than the earthly powers can ever present you with."

Wako, like Attorney-General Muli before him did not respond to Ida's entreaties. However, he sent her an official Christmas and New Year greeting card significant for the quotation in it from Amos 5:24 in the Bible which reads: "But let justice roll down like waters and righteousness like an ever flowing stream."

Although Raila was released before Wako's greeting card was sent, Ida's experience had politicised her and she continued to take an interest in the plight of those who remained in detention. Matters came to a head for her on March 11, 1992. Three days before, mothers of political prisoners, had been in the basement of the All Saints' Cathedral Church on the third day of a renewed hunger strike to press for the release of their sons. They included the mothers of Koigi wa Wamwere, Mirugi Kariuki and Rumba Kinuthia among others. Ida claimed she felt the need to encourage the women as she remembered the depressing days of her mother-in-law, Mary Odinga, over the detention of her son. While she was with the mothers, the press took her photograph. Her picture by Hudson Wainaina was given prominence in the *East African Standard* newspaper of the following day with a caption: "PLOT THICKENSÖ" She was described as the wife of FORD activist Raila Odinga, who was comparing notes with the mothers on hunger strike.

In the afternoon of the same Sunday, Ida went to the Church of the Province of Kenya (CPK) to conduct a *"Harambee"* (fund raising to support a cause). Peter Anyang Nyong'o who was to have chaired this *Harambee* was travelling in Europe and had persuaded her to represent him and donate 7,000 Kenyan shillings on his behalf. The fund-raising was to assist in bringing home, the body of Caroline Aluoch, a Kenyan woman who had been living with a Ugandan man Farrouk Okullu, before she died mysteriously in London in November 1991. Caroline Aluoch hailed from Anyang' Nyong'o Kisumu Rural Constituency which was represented in parliament by Wilson Ndolo Ayah, the Kenyan Foreign Affairs Minister. Not much money was being realized at the "Harambee." Ida donated 2,000 shillings and commented that repatriation of the body of a Kenyan citizen abroad should receive Government assistance. She lamented that it was a shame that Caroline Aluoch's body was still lying in London four months after her death, and suggested that Aluoch's family should see Wilson Ndolo Ayah, the Foreign Minister.[6]

On March 10, 1992 *The Standard* reported the events under the title: "Raila's wife hits at Govt." In effect, Ida, a government employee had made the headlines on two consecutive days at functions which were not pro-government.

By lunch time, on March 11, Ida was again given a letter of retirement in the public interest, by the Deputy Director of Education, Mr. Sitima. Mr. J. Kang'ali, Secretary, Teachers Service Commission, told Ida that that day was her last day of service and she was retired with effect from 12th March, 1992. This time, she was offered a month's salary in lieu of notice.

Ida left the Ministry of Education, went to the Agip House office of the Forum for the Restoration of Democracy (FORD) and offered her services. She took the plunge into full time politics and was at the FORD offices beyond the 1992 elections, working directly under Jaramogi until he died in 1994.

Fidel clearly remembers August 1st 1982 although he was then only ten years old. The holidays were just beginning. His mum had gone to Germany on some exchange programme and one day, he recollected waking up to gun shots at their Kileleshwa residence near State House. The maid told him that the Government had been overthrown. Fidel did not remember the day his father was arrested. But he only saw him once or twice between August 1 and his arrest. Many people kept coming home asking for him and there were many intimidating phone calls.

This account depended on interview with Ida Odinga and *The Standard,* March 10, 1992.

For him, the return of his mum saw even more strangers in the house who were tearing the whole place apart in search of what he could not figure out then but now understands to be seditious papers.

During Raila's first six years of detention, Fidel, and his siblings never saw their dad except his being called all sorts of names in the newspapers. They all missed the role of a father in their lives. They had to believe their father existed but without being able to see him or to feel his fatherly presence.

There was the locking up in a cell of Raila Odinga Jnr, aged three. Ida left him in the care of her maid, Mary Mudoro as he was feverish and could not go to school. Police, as they did with many domestic helps of the Odinga's, came to interview Mary Mudoro. They invited Mary to the station and since she had no one to leave Junior with, she went with the sick child. During Mary's interrogation, the child kept crying and the police decided to lock both of them up until the crying subsided. But Junior did not stop crying and later in the day, they were released with the police returning on another day when Ida was home. Mary, unlike other domestic help, did not run away from police harassment. She remained strong until she succumbed to diabetes and high blood pressure in 1992.

At school, it was not easy for the three children. According to Fidel, he and his two siblings were treated differently. Some students said nasty things about Raila to them. They called Raila names like criminal, prisoner etc. All three were at Kilimani Junior Academy but three years into Raila's detention, they were transferred to Consolata Primary school. Although separated from an environment that they had become used to, Fidel later understood that Ida could not afford Kilimani Junior Academy. He knew only that she was searching for another school, until one day she came and moved them to Consolata. They had no choice in the matter. It was another sacrifice for the children of a detainee.

On November 5, 1984, Mary Odinga died at age 60,[7] while Raila was in detention Ida was convinced that her mother-in-law died of depression that started with Raila's detention and Jaramogi Oginga Odinga's house arrest in 1982, followed by an accident in late 1982 when Raila's younger brother, Agola, knocked down and killed a cyclist. For this, Agola was jailed in 1983. He was diabetic and could no

---

[7] She was born in July 1924.

cope in jail. Without special food, his health deteriorated and he was released on health grounds, only to die five days later.

Ida saw the strong Mary lapse into depression as she grieved over the lot of her family. She recalled a visit to Kisumu in 1984, when she found that Mary had not eaten for a while and had refused to get out of bed or even lift up her head to see people around her. When Ida entered Mary's room, she refused to lift up her head but saw Ida's legs and said "those legs are 'Nyar Gem's' (Ida's nick-name) legs." She responded to Ida's plea for her to get up and eat and Ida felt this was the result of her new hope in seeing Raila in Ida.

Raila's siblings also suffered from the detention of their brother. Wenwa Akinyi recounted how she had been in University in Norway for her doctorate degree when Raila was arrested and detained. Wenwa would rather put Raila's detention behind her, but she provided some insight into that period of his life. Her memory of her experience of visit rights of Raila as detainee, was no different to Ida's. She said:

> Seeing Raila required an application to the Officer in Charge of detained and restricted persons, who at that time was late Philip Kilonzo. Later, applications went to Kinoti, his successor. After a letter for visitation request had been sent, one had to wait for about six months or longer. And when a decision to allow a visitation had been made, it was never communicated until the day that the visit was to take place.

On suppression of access to information, Wenwa remembered two incidents in which they were shut up. She was telling him about a new disease in the world called HIV/AIDS, how it was common in homosexuals but was spreading to heterosexuals. The police ended the discussion by saying that Raila was not supposed to know about that. Any reasonable person would wonder why information about HIV/AIDS was a threat to President Moi. During his last stint in detention, Raila's daughter, Rosemary Odinga had accompanied the visitation team. She began by saying how excited the family had been when they learnt of the release of Kenneth Matiba and Charles Rubia, as they had thought Raila's would follow soon, all three having been arrested at the same time. The policemen jumped on Rosemary, shouted at her and shocked the little girl who could not understand what she had done wrong.

When Mary Odinga died in 1984, Wenwa was home, having rushed to Nairobi on the day before, only to see her mother in a coma, from which she never recovered. Wenwa pleaded with the police to allow Raila to attend the funeral. But they refused. She then asked that at least he should be informed. Still they refused. However, Raila whom many see as having very good instincts, later told his family that he knew when his mother had died because he had had a dream which convinced him she had passed away. And he cried. When a smuggled note told him about his mother's death, it was no longer news.[8]

Wenwa Akinyi found each parting from Raila very painful. She always felt bad that they were returning to freedom as Raila, looking pitiful, was surrounded by policemen and being taken to an unknown destination as a captive. However, Wenwa who, like Raila had studied in East Germany, sometimes parted with a sentence in German to pass a short message that she knew Raila would build up given his rapid understanding. Since the police would not know what she had said.

Like most prisoners around the world, there were people who collaborated by taking messages to and from Raila. He devised a communication code for his family. For instance, Wenwa Akinyi was SWA in all communication. SWA meant Sister Wenwa Akinyi, and she took advantage of the German language they shared, to send messages she knew would evade the strict censorship applied by the prison authorities.

The Torture Chamber

On February 11, 2003 the NARC Government, allowed the public to glimpse the experience of Raila and others like him who were prepared for their detention or time in jail by State operatives at Nyayo House. Raila himself revisited this part of his past on 13 February; with other former detainees including Israel Agina; Lawyer Patrick Lumumba and Wanyiri Kihoro, a former Nyeri Town MP.

Many Kenyans found the stories about Nyayo House torture chambers unbelievable, and could not understand why their Government could have done

---

[8]   Raila informed the author that this sixth sense, while he was in jail, was not limited to the death of his mum as he knew of other cases concerning friends and relations.

such things to Kenyans. One such Kenyan was Mohamed Abdi Affey, former Assistant Minister for Foreign Affairs and Member of Parliament for Wajir South. Affey was also a member of the task force President Moi set up to review why KANU lost in the 2002 General Elections. At a press conference on 16 February 2003, Affey resigned from the task force, from KANU and all leadership positions in it, and expressed shame at being in a party which had carried out what was found in the basement of Nyayo House.

Chapter 11
Flight into Exile

G oing into exile was a normal response to repression in Kenya since the days of Kenyatta. Raila had the opportunity to rush into exile on August 2, 1982. He had just collaborated with the architects of a failed coup and knew that Moi's intelligence apparatus would be on his trail. He did not on that day, but returned to Nairobi and chose to leave on August 11, 1982. But he was caught and put in detention.

After his first release, he was detained twice more. When it became clear that his life was threatened, Raila decided to borrow a leaf from the reggae lyric: "He who fights and runs away lives to fight another day." Raila went into exile in a risky venture that was not as comfortable as hitherto believed. But many preceded Raila.

Ngugi wa Thiong'o was one of Raila's predecessors who went into exile in 1982. He did not plan it. He had gone to Britain in June 1982 to launch his books: *Devil on the Cross,* and *Detained: A Writer's Prison Diary.* Recounting events, Ngugi wa Thiong'o stated:

> While in Britain I learnt of the government's plans to arrest me on my return, imprison or even eliminate me. It was Moi as the Vice-President who in 1977 signed papers for my detention without trial. It was his government which on March 12, 1982, sent three truckloads of armed policemen to raze down the Kamirithu Open-Air Theatre. [1]

Ngugi reminisced about many Kenyans who lost their lives or were maimed or exiled. He stated: "I cannot help but think about all the people that perished in Moi's jails, simply because they wanted to see the end of the culture of silence, fear and division. There were those grouped around 'Mwanguzi' and 'Pambana'

---

[1] See, *Sunday Nation,* January 26, 2003, p. 14. David Musila, at that time the Central Provincial Commissioner and now Deputy Speaker in the 9th Parliament supervised the demolition of Ngugi's cultural centre. See, Sunday Nation, August 1, 2004, p. 6. Kamirithu Open-Air Theatre was Ngugi's pet project in Limuru, Kenya.

way back in the 70s and 80s. There were those grouped around 'The December 12 Movement' in the early 80s. And there were those around 'Mwakenya' and other underground forces."[2]

Ngugi stayed out of Kenya from June 1982 throughout Moi's period in power. He returned after twenty-two years for a one-month holiday in July 2004. On that occasion, he stated:

> "I hope Kenyans will never forget the ideals for which so many lost their lives. I hope they shall never stray from the path of unity in their struggle for economic, political, cultural and psychological empowerment of all Kenyans."[3]

However, this holiday was a traumatic experience for Ngugi and his wife, Njeeri wa Ngugi, who were attacked less than two weeks into their stay. Njeeri was raped during the ordeal as Ngugi was beaten with a pistol butt, and had his face burned by a cigarette butt. Njeeri courageously used her experience to draw world-wide attention to the cases of many women and infants who were brutalised without the State being able to stop the horrible trend.[4] Ngugi as strong as he was in his days of standing against oppression, refused to be detracted from his programme and continued with the public lectures arranged by his publishers as part of his home-coming.

Salim Lone, the activist collaborator of Anyona and others, followed on the heels of Ngugi. On June 19, 1982, a woman who claimed to be working for an Assistant Commissioner of Police approached him and told him that she loved the Magazine *Viva* that he produced, and for that reason she was warning him that he was about to be arrested. She gave him so much information that reluctantly, he believed her. A week earlier, he had been visited by Special Branch who accused him of distributing *Pambana*. Fortunately, he was in Germany on the date they alleged he had commited the crime. His passport made it easy for him to escape. In 1981 he had been tried with Wangari Maathai, the fearless activist who was the first Kenyan lady to earn a Doctorate and who normally led environmental causes with her

---

[2] *Sunday Nation,* January 26, 2003, p. 14.
[3] *Sunday Nation,* August 1, 2004, p. 5.
[4] For details, see the *Daily Nation* and *East African Standard* especially on Monday and Tuesday, August 16-17, 2004.

Green Belt Movement NGO and subsequently became the 2004 Nobel Peace Prize winner, for publishing an interview in which she accused the judiciary of being corrupt. He was given 3 months or a fine of 1,000 Kenyan shillings, which he paid. But Wangari who did not have the option of fine, went into jail for six months. Lone remembered other brushes he had had with the Kenyan authorities.

Arguments, especially from his wife, Patricia Lone who worked with him on *Viva,* persuaded Lone to take a break. He went to London where he called on Bethwel Kiplagat, the Kenya High Commissioner, and at that time, a confidant of President Moi. Lone regarded Kiplagat as an old friend and told him he was on the run to avoid arrest. His fears were confirmed when Kiplagat pulled a telex from his desk that set out the charges against Lone. He was said to be an accomplice of Ngugi in his anti-regime efforts and a publicist of dissidents such as Micere Mugo.[5] Kiplagat reportedly called Nairobi and was assured that if Lone behaved well in future, he would be forgiven. But his wife and friends prevailed on him that he should not walk into a trap. At the coup attempt on August 1, 1982, Patricia Lone was picked up and her home ransacked in a search for dissident materials. It took the intervention of the American Embassy for her to be released and she left to join her husband in exile.

That was not the end of Lone's plight. He had joined the United Nations while in exile. In 1986, Elijah Mwangale, the Foreign Minister came to New York for a meeting. He met Lone and urged him to return to Kenya as his sins had been forgiven. He decided to check out the situation with his two sons. Like Ngugi would do several years later, he took a suite at the Norfolk Towers. Five days after his arrival, he was visited by a Special Branch officer who asked Lone to come with him to the police station for a few questions. Lone refused and called Abraham Kiptanui, the State House Comptroller saying that he was about to be arrested. Kiptanui's reaction confirmed that there was such a plan. He promised to look into it. Lone enjoyed visiting old friends like Koigi wa Wamwere. But two days before his departure, he was picked up at 4 a.m, was taken to the Central Police Station and dumped into a cell with drunks for an hour. Blind folded and driven around, he found himself at Shauri Moyo Police Station where he briefly shared a cell with a young man who claimed to have killed someone. Blind folded again,

---

[5] The account in this section benefited from an interview with Salim Lone, Nairobi, November 23, 2004. Micere Mugo's experience will be reported next.

he ended up in what he later knew was Nyayo House. He was tortured by being taken to the balcony of a high building and threatened with being pushed over before he was pulled back. A panel of twelve men accused him of smuggling guns for *MwaKenya,* an underground movement. He was also accused of trying to revamp the organisation which was said to be dying at the time. As well as being named as an accomplice of Ngugi and Koigi wa Wamwere and others, he was said to be the Libyan pointman in Kenya. At the end of the day, he was dumped at the General Post Office Building and told not to travel and not to speak a word about his arrest. But the press already knew and the UN Chief of Security and the Country Representative of UNICEF, the organisation he worked for, on the instruction of Kofi Annan, then UN Head of Personnel, had become involved in his case and arranged for him to leave Kenya on the following day.

Subsequently, the Moi government revoked the citizenship he had acquired from his grand parents who had settled in Kenya almost 50 years before he was born. He remained stateless until 1992 when Tom Ogada, Kenya's Permanent Representative in Geneva was embarrassed that UN staff members in Geneva had added Kenya to the list of bad Governments which had ill treated their colleagues. Pressure on Moi from Western governments also forced him to ease up. Attorney-General, Amos Wako, sent Lone an application form to regain his nationality. He did.

Other exiles before the coup of 1982 included Micere Mugo a lecturer at the University of Nairobi. She was one of those who stood for a better society under Moi. But her ideas were not acceptable to the authorities and she was put under surveillance.[6] Special Branch and CID officers camped in front of her house and office at the University. She was seen as a subversive intending to cause disaffection against the Moi government. She fled to the United States, a week before the 1982 coup, and remained in exile with her two children. She returned briefly in 2003 after the change of government and Moi's retirement.

James Orengo was President of the University of Nairobi Students Union in 1972-73. The Union's affiliation with the International Union of Students in Prague, allowed him to travel several times to Eastern Europe. His radical politics leaned ideologically towards Jaramogi Oginga Odinga.

---

[6] For her account, see, "Midweek," *East African Standard,* Wednesday, June 11, 2003, p. 1.

He was one of those Charles Njonjo had tagged the "Seven Bearded Sisters" in Parliament. For Njonjo, the "Seven Bearded Sisters" were radical MPs who behaved like an official opposition despite Parliament being a one-party outfit. These MPs became an unacceptable problem for KANU. When Koigi wa Wamwere and Anyona went into detention, two of the "Sisters," Chelagat Mutai, and Orengo, fled into exile. The former Eldoret North MP, Chelagat Mutai, fled to Tanzania in October 1981.

Mutai was the leader of a number of MPs accused of a variety of politically motivated offences. It is not clear if Orengo falls into this category. In July 1982, he was arrested and accused of forgery and stealing a client's money. While out on a bond of KSh. 50,000, he jumped bail.[7] He fled to Tanzania through Uganda, and eventually went to Zimbabwe.

Orengo, returned to Tanzania to study for a Masters in Law, but was arrested in Dar-es-Salaam. A deal had been worked out under which Tanzania and Kenya were to exchange people evading the law from their respective countries. Orengo was exchanged at the Kenya-Tanzania border in November 1983 and taken to Kamiti Maximum Security Prison for three weeks before being transferred to Naivasha Maximum Security Prison, where he was detained.

The Government subsequently dropped the criminal charges against him. On the day of his release in April 1984, he was driven to Kisumu. The authorities insisted on driving him all the way to Nyanza. In Kisumu, they asked where he should be dropped and he opted for the residence of Grace Onyango, the MP for Kisumu Town constituency and first Mayor of Kisumu. The release was the result of a bout of cerebral malaria, which the State probably thought he would not survive. When he reached his home in Ugenya he was taken to hospital unconscious. The intervention of Jaramogi, got him better medical care in another hospital. He survived, later to join Raila in the struggle for democracy.[8]

---

[7] See, Macharia Munene, *The Politics of Transition in Kenya, 1995-1998,* (Nairobi: Quest and Insight, 2001). P. 66.

[8] Much of these accounts depended on interview with James Orengo, June 7, 2003.

Raila's Turn to go into Exile

The Moi State had seen to many Kenyans going in and out of exile. Raila took his turn when he fled from Kenya in October 1991. In an undated press statement, Ida detailed the circumstances that led family and friends to pressurise Raila to flee the country. It said:

Due to persistent threat to the life of my husband, Raila Odinga, organised by the Kenyan Police he has had to go into hiding.

It will be recalled that during a physical attack on him outside the gates of our home last month, the rear windscreen of his car was smashed with stones that were aimed at him. Days later, a bucketful of human faeces was deposited on our backyard at night by unknown person(s).

Persons introducing themselves as policemen harassed Raila's Company employees; police surveillance on Company premises, and our residence was beefed up, culminating in the police instruction on 3rd October, that Raila should report to Central Police Station. It was ominous that when he reported to the Central Police Station, no officer at that station knew anything about his requirement to report.

On 4 October 1991, a rowdy and rude group of uniformed and plain clothed policemen, numbering about twenty attempted to forcefully gain access to our house in an attempt to get Raila. They only left after I convinced them that he was truly away. Since then, the police have been telephoning our house every night and leaving death threat messages for Raila.

The latest telephone message that the police will shoot him if they catch up with him is the most terrifying of them all. The police have created a lot of fear in our children with these threats. The children freeze every time the phone rings or whenever there is a knock on the door. The children have become very nervous. Last week, our daughter Rosemary broke down in class, as a result of these police threats. She had to be comforted by teachers and classmates. I am afraid our children cannot take it anymore. I therefore appeal to the police to stop it for the sake of the children. They are innocent and they have absolutely nothing to do with the current political atmosphere now prevailing in the country.

For the past 10 years, our children have known no peace. To them, unlike most children, the language of peace and love are foreign languages that they do not understand. I appeal to the Kenya Police to go about their duty without harassing my children. In this country, all children are supposed to occupy a special place in the hearts of the leaders.

It is very clear to me that the bands of police hounding Raila are not ordinary policemen. I say this because never before have I heard policemen leaving death messages to the people they intend to arrest. May be the tactics have changed! When they say openly that 'he will see fire' or 'he will see what he had never seen before' and 'he will never see the sun again'. All these messages mean the same thing that they will kill him. Raila has witnessed unprintable things in the hands of the police, the only thing he has not gone through is death. So the message they are trying to relay is very clear.

Raila has made his political beliefs very clear and I am sure that he is being harassed for those beliefs.

Lastly I want to state very clearly and in no uncertain terms that if something happens to Raila, my family will hold the police wholly responsible.

But Raila Odinga's escape from Kenya was not uneventful. As will be pointed out later, Raila was involved in the formation of the Forum for the Restoration of Democracy (FORD), and his AGIP House offices doubled as Headquarters for the new venture.

The FORD Young Turks and the famous six elderly men on the board began to mobilize Kenyans and intended to hold a rally at the Kamukunji grounds. As the days went by, nationwide, tension grew. Raila remembers that Alan Eastham[9], of the US Embassy told him that they had intelligence that the Moi government was panicky and was laying all the blame for the tension on Raila as the man behind FORD. Eastham told Raila that he should expect to be arrested two days before the rally they were planning for October 5, 1991. The Moi government had concluded that Raila no longer feared detention and Eastham warned that they could do him physical harm or assassinate him. The advice was that Raila should take care.

---

[9]   Alan Eastham and his role in the formation of FORD will be examined shortly.

On Thursday morning, October 3, 1991, the police went to the 4ᵗʰ floor AGIP House (Eastern Wing). But Raila had left his office a little earlier and gone to Orengo's office on the 2ⁿᵈ Floor in the Western Wing. As he was talking to Orengo, Raila's long standing Secretary, Susan Wairimu Kibathi, phoned to say that the police had visited the office looking for him. Susan knew policemen even in disguise. She had been with Raila for some time and the previous year, had seen him arrested by armed officers. She was worried and Raila could sense danger from her tone on the phone. While discussing the matter with Orengo, Raila had another call from his factory on Likoni Road Industrial Area, that the police had come there looking for him. Israel Agina, the Technical Director at the factory on Mombasa Road called to say that a land rover full of police officers had come there looking for him and that their demeanour was arrogant.

Raila and Orengo decided that the answer was to bring as many of the progressive lawyers, journalists and the media to AGIP House. Seven other lawyers who immediately answered the call, included: Japheth Shamalla; Mohamed Ibrahim; Kathurima M'Inoti; K. Mussili; Ms. Martha Njoka; Ms. Matha Kome and GBM Kariuki.[10] Anyang' Nyong'o and representatives of BBC, AFP, Reuters, Kenya Television Network, and the two major Kenyan newspapers: *Daily Nation* and *East African Standard* were also present.

With such popular support, Raila was emboldened to phone Mr. Kinoti, the then Provincial Police Officer (PPO) for Nairobi. He asked what was happening and why the police were looking for him as he had not committed any crime. The PPO, on the phone, stated that he was ignorant of the development and suggested that Raila and his team got in touch with the Officer-in-Charge of Central Police Division (OCPD) at the Central Police station. The group, with Raila, decided to march to the Central Police. According to Raila, the OCPD fled from the station through the back door when he heard that such a large group was with Raila to see him. They found the Deputy OCPD who also expressed ignorance. The group left with a request that the police communicate with them in due course on why they wanted to see Raila.

As they left the station, Raila, realizing that it was Thursday, remembered Eastham's advice which also suggested the possibility of physical harm if not assassination. Raila and some of his close colleagues including Orengo and Anyang' Nyong'o,

---

[0] See, *Daily Nation*, Friday October 4, 1991, p. 28.

decided it was too risky to play games "with a desperate enemy." They decided that Raila should go underground. The day was spent at Orengo's residence, and that night a brainstorming session concluded that it would be careless and irresponsible for Raila to remain there or go to the home of any of their usual supporters. Anyang' suggested the residence of a friend of his, known to be discrete and trustworthy, as the best option.

This friend was Dr. Mukhisa Kituyi who had been an activist in his student days at the University of Nairobi and had been expelled with Otieno Kajwang' and others for their roles in student unionism. Mukhisa went to Makerere University before going to Norway where he married Dr. Ling Kituyi. Driven by Anyang', Raila met the couple and their children on the night of October 3, 1991. He was given a room and stayed with them for a week. As Raila was the only one in when everyone left for work or school, he took the opportunity to read as much as he could.

On his first night at the Kituyi residence, a large contingent of policemen went to Raila's residence at Kileleshwa in Nairobi. When they knocked violently on the gate, the gateman for the set of apartments in the compound, refused to open it, until the police became furious and identified themselves. When he opened the gate, they slapped and kicked him, and frog-marched him to Raila's apartment. They rang the bell and commanded Ida to open the door. Ida's inquiry as to who they were, was answered by the gateman who told her they were armed police. She refused to open and told them Raila was not home. They continued to bully her as she pretended to search for the key, but used the time to call the press. She asked the gateman to count the number of police officers loudly. When he reached 17, he was beaten up and Ida was told that she should tell her husband that if he was man enough, he should come to the police station and he would know who they were.[11]

The next day, Jaramogi called a press conference at Raila's residence. He pleaded with the Kenyan authorities to leave his son alone:

> I appeal to the Commissioner of Police to put a stop to this nonsense. I appeal
> to the Head of the Special Branch, whose professional duty is to advise the

---

[11] Aside from Ida's reminiscences, an account on this incident is in *Daily Nation,* Saturday October 5, 1991, p. 1 and p. 28.

Government on political matters as they relate to the security of society, to advise against the Gestapo behaviour.[12]

In the circumstances, Raila and his collaborators decided that he should leave the country for a while, and to postpone the Saturday rally. They then began making arrangements for Raila to leave Kenya.

The first option they named "the Kuria route." Gibson Kamau Kuria, an activist lawyer fled the country using the US Embassy as conduit for his departure. Learning that he was about to be picked up on July 7, 1990 (*Saba Saba day*, i.e., 7th day of 7th month in Kiswahili) and remembering the torture he had suffered previously, Kuria slipped into the American Embassy into the welcoming hands of Smith Hempstone, the "rogue" maverick American Ambassador. Hempstone who had begun to speak out on the deplorable human rights situation, and for democracy in Kenya, granted Kuria asylum, but had to deal with a not too happy State Department over the development. The US Government eventually secured safe passage for Kuria from the Kenyan Government. The Ambassador personally ensured Kuria's safety by accompanying him into the plane.[13]

A plan was made for Raila to be taken to the US Embassy avoiding roadblocks that had been set up to look for him. The final advice to those arranging Raila's departure was that he should be taken to the Embassy without any prior information. The task of disguising Raila fell on Dr. Ling Kituyi, a medical practitioner. She altered his beard and hair, fixed him with short-sighted reading glasses that made it impossible for Raila to see. He was driven by Mukhisa Kituyi. A second car, driven by Joe Ager with Anyang' Nyong'o, followed at a distance, in case things went wrong.

Raila arrived at the United States Embassy, walked straight in and was ushered through after identification. Ambassador Smith Hempstone was on leave and was not in town. Raila had an audience with Michael Southwick, the Deputy Chief of Mission, and a career diplomat, who later became US Ambassador to Uganda. Raila explained his story. After more than half an hour, he was taken to

---

[12] *Sunday Nation,* October 6, 1991, p. 20.
[13] See, Smith Hempstone, *Rogue Ambassador: An African Memoir* (Sewanee: University of the South Press, 1997), pp. 105-112.

the basement for another meeting with Southwick. Raila was told that the Embassy had asked their Government what to do. Washington had approached President Moi who had said that the Kenyan Government was looking for Raila in connection with some crime he had committed. President Moi had assured Washington that Raila would be accorded due process. Their view, therefore, was that it was safe and there was nothing to fear. Raila protested that he had committed no crime and that secondly he was surprised that despite what had happened, they could rely on President Moi's assurances. Raila was told that a car was ready to take him to any place of his choice.

Raila still cannot understand what happened and why Eastham did not come to his rescue. He felt betrayed. But he was unaware of the problems caused by Kuria's asylum. The US State Department was determined to maintain a good relationship with the Moi Government despite the activism of Ambassador Hempstone on the ground. In his memoirs, Hempstone did not give any clues as to why Raila was turned down. But it sounds reasonable to deduce that a free passage for Raila by the US Government would have worsened the existing tension. The US decided to avoid dealing with a legitimate asylum claim and took the risk of throwing Raila back on the streets.

Raila decided not to return to the Kituyi residence as he knew he could be followed in the car provided by the Americans. He got off at the residence of Anyang Nyong'o, who on his arrival from work was surprised to find Raila. Paul Muite was called and they decided that Raila should sleep at the Loresho residence of Gordon Jalang'o Anyang'o, a relative of his. He stayed there for another week.

While underground, Raila issued a statement in which he expressed fears for his life. He claimed he was in danger because of his political beliefs and his proposals for a peaceful transition to multi-party democracy in Kenya.[14] President Moi chose an interview with *Visnews* on the eve of the Kenyatta Day national holiday, to announce that no-one was harassing anyone in Kenya. For him, the Constitution of Kenya clearly stipulated that the country is a one-party State. He claimed that those detained were in detention for breaking the laws of the land.[15]

---

[14] See, *Daily Nation,* Wednesday, October 16, 1991, p. 28.
[15] See, *Sunday Nation,* October 20, 1991, p. 1.

Other Kenyans did not see the situation along Moi's lines. The Catholic Secretariat, which had been sympathetic to the plight of Kenyan activists, took Raila's fears and experience very seriously. Archbishop Okoth was instrumental in making the plans for his evacuation from Nairobi in disguise. On the night before his departure, he moved to the residence of Clarice Auma Oyoo, his sister-in-law. This provided him with an opportunity to see his children before going into exile. Rosemary Odinga remembers that night. She recognized her father despite his disguise. She remembers Raila promising never to go back into detention.[16]

On the morning of his departure, Raila was collected by Father Mak' Opiyo and a white American nun. They were in their religious dresses. Raila, also dressed as a Reverend Father, sat behind them wearing sun glasses and clean-shaven. He read a newspaper as they passed through all the roadblocks. The reverend fathers and nun were waved on at every road block. At Kisumu, they went up the hill to the Catholic Station where Raila was booked in as Father Augustine from Machakos. He was there till evening before being transferred to Rangala Mission in Ugenya, where again, he was introduced as Father Augustine and he stayed till midnight when a vehicle came from Jaramogi to take him to Bondo. He stayed indoors most of the following day until his father came around 2 am.

The arrangement was for him to leave by boat. Simon Chiambe Oloo, a local businessman in Bondo, made the arrangements for his escape across the lake. The boat was procured and diesel was purchased. At 4 pm, he went to Lake Nyanza. At Olago beach, he boarded the boat with a single outboard engine, which was owned and driven by the late Hezron Orori. The lake was very rough and Hezron had to collect other passengers from his tiny home Island called Ndeda. The passengers were Ugandans who knew the terrain fairly well on the Ugandan side. They set sail from Ndeda at about 8pm when the lake had calmed. With Raila and Hezron, there were two Ugandans, one of Hezron's many wives going to Uganda for treatment and one of Hezron's helpers.

The boat moved slowly using only the moon and stars for navigation on an initially calm night. They moved parallel to the Coast at first passing several islands on the Kenyan side. After two hours, Hezron announced that they were in Ugandan waters, Raila heaved a sigh of relief. Shortly after, however, there was a heavy storm.

---

[6] Interview with Rosemary Odinga, Nairobi, July 20, 2003.

Though Raila had been on a ship while travelling to Eastern Europe, this was the first time he made a long journey on the Lake. It was very cold and Hezron's sick wife began to shiver badly. Raila lent her his jacket and became cold himself. He remembered that Simon Chiambe Oloo had given him a bottle of vodka for the journey. This soon got rid of the cold.

Four hours later, they arrived at the Island of Sigulu, one of those annexed by former Ugandan dictator, Idi Amin in 1973. Before then, the Island was Kenyan with a Kenyan population. Hezron had another home in Sigulu. This settlement of Kenyans, Ugandans and Tanzanians welcomed Raila and company for the night. The next day, using Hezron's influence, Raila secured Ugandan papers including tax certificates, which were more important than an ID *"misolo"* and showed that he had paid taxes in the last five years. His new name in the documents was Joseph Ojiwa Wadeya and Father Augustine was no more.

Having gotten the documents, they left at around 3 pm and moved along many Islands. Due to heavy rains, they stopped at one of the Islands and continued later, arriving at the mainland just before midnight in Busoga District of Uganda. Early the following day, they hired bicycles to take them to where they could find motor transport, and they went by Matatu to Iganga and from there through Jinja and Owen Falls and on to Kampala. Showing his Joseph Ojiwa Wadeya papers, Raila passed through all the roadblocks to Kampala.

Coincidentally, on October 24, 1991, when Raila had barely arrived in Kampala, his driver, James Omol, and his Personal Assistant/Guard, George Opondo Oduor were driving to East Africa Spectre in Industrial area. Just before they got there, the car was stoned and severely damaged.[17] But the occupants escaped unhurt. This was a repetition of an earlier incident at Raila's residence in Kileleshwa on 10 September.

When he got to Kampala, Raila immediately found a friend, Shem Luanga, who had been Chief Accountant at East Africa Spectre. He changed money to pay Hezron for the transportation, and contributed to the cost of treating Hezron's sick wife. Raila then went to Shem Luanga's residence at Mukono Satellite town of Kampala and Shem reported to the UNHCR Country Representative for

---

[17] See, *Daily Nation*, Friday, October 25, 1991, p. 3.

Uganda, Ahmed Sayyid Farah, a Somali national. Farah could not believe that it was Raila who had come.

UNHCR reported Raila's arrival to the Ugandan Authorities who informed the Kenyan Authorities without Raila's knowledge. He was in his bed two days later, listening to BBC news when it was announced that a leading Kenyan wanted by the Kenyan government had escaped to Uganda. The same day, Kenyan newspapers carried a Government statement that reported that Raila had escaped into Uganda seeking political asylum and that the Ugandan authorities had rejected the request and handed him over to the UNHCR.[18] Jaramogi Oginga Odinga was quick to defend his son's decision to go into exile. He pointed out that Raila had been complaining of many ailments and wanting to go abroad for medical attention, but the State had held his passport. He said that Raila was constantly "being pestered and harassed."[19]

The Ugandan government had decided that to help restore relations with Kenya, they should inform the Kenyan authorities. The Ugandan Deputy Foreign Minister, Agard Didi made the point clear when he stated that Uganda would not do a "tit for tat," with Kenya which in the past had harboured Ugandan dissidents.[20]

UNHCR told Raila to be careful and to remain under-ground as Kenya had sent security men to search for him and repatriate him. However, he was lucky that the Ugandans, did nothing more to help them.

His positive identification was made at the residence of the Permanent Secretary for Local Government. He met the Chief of Intelligence, Jim Muhwezi, who assured him that he would be given full protection and that the Ugandans would make it possible for him to have safe transit, as he could not stay in Uganda much longer. As the situation became more difficult, Raila moved from Shem Luanga's to Farah's residence for increased safety.

The UNHCR Uganda office sent messages to several countries looking for one to host Raila Odinga. The responses from the United States, Great Britain and

---

[18] Reported in *Sunday Nation,* October 27, 1991, p. 1.
[19] See, *ibid.*
[20] See, *Daily Nation,* Thursday October 31, 1991, p. 40.

Germany were similar. They were either consulting or processing his papers. Eventually, Norway with which Kenya had broken relations because the Norwegian Ambassador had gone to visit Koigi wa Wamwere at Kamiti prison, granted the asylum request. Norway also accepted Raila because two of his sisters: Ruth Adhiambo Odinga and Caroline Akinyi Odinga, were studying there. And Wenwa Akinyi Odinga, had previously acquired her Ph.D in Norway.

Dr. Steve Chebrot, Ugandan Minister for Local Government had lived in Kenya during his own exile. Raila had known him well. Chebrot made the arrangements for Raila's departure for Norway. He was given a passport that was only valid for the journey. Raila had spent two weeks in Kampala.

To leave Kampala, a disguise was necessary as Raila could be abducted by the Kenyan security men in Uganda. Farah and Raila were not going to take chances. Farah got Raila a *Kanzu* dress with a fez and jacket like those Ugandan Muslims wear. So, he became Haji Omar, who was going to Mecca on Pilgrimage.

His first attempt to enter the airport through a designated entrance failed and he missed the flight. The next Sabena flight was in another four days, so Raila stayed underground. At the second attempt, he got through the security entrance and took his flight to Brussels. When he greeted an old friend who had boarded the same flight in Nairobi she failed to recognize him, as a result of his disguise. He changed flights in Brussels and arrived safely in Oslo. Ruth Adhiambo Odinga who was at the airport with her sister Caroline Akinyi to receive their brother did not recognize him as they walked past.[21]

Raila moved into Ruth's small flat and settled quickly into life in Oslo. The Norwegian Government gave him a passport that allowed him to travel to all countries of the world except Kenya. Initially he worked in the offices of the Norwegian Human Rights Commission.

With small budgets for his activities, he flew to London, Bonn, Brussels and Stockholm. He opened FORD offices manned by other committed Kenyans resident in these countries and built a network to mobilize Kenyans abroad in support of the movement for change. He remained in touch with people at home,

---

[21] Interview with Ruth Adhiambo Odinga, Nairobi, June 18, 2003.

regularly issued statements on developments in Kenya and gave interviews to the BBC as the effective voice of the opposition party outside Kenya. This became strategically important for the movement, as he created a voice and an international link, and used it to champion the cause and mobilize support. Raila fled to fight another day and he returned to join the last leg of the multi-party campaign for the 1992 General Elections.

Chapter 12
A Hundred Flowers Finally Bloomed

Raila Odinga played a pivotal role in the struggle that subsequently realized a multi-party order for Kenya in the 1990s. But he did not act alone. There were many other Kenyan heroes. However, the enactment of Section 2A delayed the push for multi-partyism by almost a decade. It was not until February 1991 that Jaramogi decided to take the bull by the horns by announcing the formation of the National Democratic Party (NDP) which was the first concrete attempt to challenge Section 2A as the established order.

While Raila was in his third detention, Jaramogi and some other colleagues, including Paul Muite who had been the lawyer for Matiba and Rubia, decided to apply for the registration of the NDP. The registration was refused by the Registrar-General who cited Section 2A. Jaramogi and his colleagues went to court. Their application was rejected. Raila Odinga's release from his second spell of detention took place as the court rejected the case for registration of the NDP. James Orengo was the young lawyer who had represented the NDP.

On the day of the ruling, Raila, out of detention, organized a number of youths to go to court to support Jaramogi. Posters were prepared on the need for multi-party democracy and the repeal of Section 2A etc. When the ruling was given, they protested loudly and marched defiantly out of court with Jaramogi. In a show of people's power, the youths marched through the streets to Jaramogi's office at AGIP House.[1]

This march was a defiant challenge to the Moi regime. A loss in court was being challenged on the streets and the popular desire for a multi-party democratic order was being articulated. This could arguably, be seen as a turning point for the strategy that eventually forced the Moi State to accept the need to remove Section 2A from the Constitution.

---

[1] This account depended on Raila Odinga's memory of the events at an interview with the author on July 27, 2003.

Jaramogi decided to appeal against the court ruling. It was not clear if he thought he would win against the government. But Orengo, his lawyer advanced other reasons for being in court. According to Orengo:

> Though I knew we did not stand a chance to be registered, we decided to use the visits to the Registrar-General, the Attorney-General and the courts merely to seek publicity as a way of fighting injustice and raising the level of consciousness of the people on the need for democracy in Kenya.[2]

Whatever the case might have been, Raila differed with his father. He was hesitant and told Jaramogi that going to court, played into the hands of the establishment that controlled it. It would lend the appearance of legitimacy to the repressive acts of the government. Raila believed it would be an exercise in futility.

However, other events were taking place in the struggle for multi-partyism. One was the desire to create an organizational structure to mobilize and articulate the wishes of the opposition. This eventually became known as Forum for the Restoration of Democracy (FORD).

Throup and Hornsby, on the origins of FORD suggested that it dated back to a dinner in May 1991 involving Sir David Steel, the former leader of the Liberal Party in Britain. Steel who was raised in Kenya towards the end of colonialism when his father was a Missionary, continued to show a deep interest in the country. Throup and Hornsby further suggested that the idea of operating as pressure groups came from Steel, who pointed out that critics of the KANU government could operate in the format of the Civic Forum movements in Czechoslovakia and East Germany which brought down the Communist dictatorships through a coalition of civic associations, local activists, the Churches, intellectuals etc.[3] However, Raila and Orengo suggested otherwise.

On Raila's release from detention he was visited by Masinde Muliro who came to his office to congratulate him on his struggles and release, and offered to work closely with him. Raila met Martin Shikuku at the Norfolk Hotel at an American Embassy reception in honour of visiting Judges from the United States.

---

[2] Interview with James Orengo, June 7, 2003.
[3] See, David W. Throup & Charles Hornsby, *Multi-Party Politics in Kenya: The Kenyatta & Moi States & the Triumph of the System in the 1992 Election,* (Oxford: James Currey, 1998), p. 76.

At the reception, Raila remembers meeting an Embassy Political Officer. That was the beginning of his relationship with Alan Eastham, a big middle-aged man. Talking to Eastham, Raila realized that he had much sympathy with the opposition cause. Leading Eastham, as the United States Ambassador to Kenya, was Smith Hempstone – a journalist by profession, who was appointed Ambassador by George Bush Senior. Hempstone had cast diplomacy aside and disagreed very strongly with President Moi over his repressive policies.[4] Moi saw Hempstone as interfering in Kenya's internal affairs.

Eastham and Raila agreed to meet for lunch at a Chinese Restaurant in a red brick house at APIC Centre in Westlands. It was normally agreed by the two that they would meet at the red brick house. And they did several times. From the first meeting, Eastham made an impression on Raila and reinforced his view that the time had come for the various groups in the opposition to form a common front to work together as a pressure group. Eastham told Raila that the diplomatic community in Kenya knew that the opposition strength in Kenya was considerable but fragmented and ineffective. Opposition unity, would give more credibility, and with it, the necessary support asked of the international community.

Raila shared his thoughts with Orengo, who was Jaramogi Oginga Odinga's lawyer in the appeal against denial of registration of NDP. He convinced Orengo that an appeal was an exercise in futility, and urged him to help him to persuade Jaramogi to abandon the thought that he would get justice on appeal. They were successful.

Raila introduced Eastham to Orengo and they decided to use what would appear like a harmless dinner to discuss the idea that had crystallized at the Red Brick House. A dinner was arranged at Orengo's residence and included their wives to make the meeting appear innocuous.

At dinner, Orengo pointed out that a pressure group could be formed under the Laws of Kenya without seeking registration if the membership was not more than nine. According to Betty Murungi, this dinner marked the birth of FORD.[5]

---

[4]   See, Smith Hempstone, *Rogue Ambassador: An African Memoir* (Sewanee: University of the South Press, 1997).

[5]   Interview with James Orengo at his Lonhro House office, June 7, 2003. Betty Murungi, Orengo's spouse and her sister Rose Muchiri joined the tale-end of this interview.

Raila and Orengo briefed Jaramogi, and decided to look for eight others to join Jaramogi in the pressure group. Between July and September 1991 they convened meetings of Young Turks to plan the way forward. This initial group comprised: Paul Muite, Raila, Orengo, Anyang' Nyong'o and Joe Ager. They were joined later by Mukhisa Kituyi and Gitobu Imanyara. The Young Turks decided to approach veteran politicians whom, unlike themselves, the system would find it difficult to arrest. They believed that President Moi would hesitate to detain older politicians, some of whom were his contemporaries. But they also knew that they would still be the engine to pull the train of multi-party democratisation in Kenya.

Drawing from each of Kenya's provinces, they initially identified the following:

Western	Martin Shikuku
Nyanza	Jaramogi Oginga Odinga
Rift Valley	Masinde Muliro and Charles Murgor
Nairobi	Charles Rubia or Dr Munyua Waiyaki
Central	Waruru Kanja or Kimani Wanyoike
Coast	Morris Mboja
Eastern	Mzee Kioko
North Eastern	Ahmed Khalif Mohammed

Charles Murgor declined the offer from the Young Turks. Munya Waiyaki pointed out that he was working for an international organization, which required him to travel and feared he would lose his passport if he became involved. Kimani Wanyoike said that his wife was heavily pregnant and he did not want to cause her anxiety. Rubia said he was unwell and could not join. Ahmed Khalif Mohammed and Mzee Kioko were also not available. Morris Mboja declined on the grounds that he had too many debts and feared the State would move in on him. Dennis Akumu was supportive but did not want to play any leadership role. Matiba was recuperating in England. In his place, the Young Turks brought in Philip Gachoka. Martin Shikuku secured the acceptance of George Nthenge from Eastern Province and Ahmed Salim Bamahriz, a farmer from the Coast. At the end of the search, the famous six became: Jaramogi Oginga Odinga, Martin Shikuku, Masinde Muliro, Philip Gachoka, George Nthenge and Ahmed Bamahriz.

They drafted a launch statement which was rejected by Masinde Muliro for being too radical. He suggested that they needed a non-radical name for the group.

Raila started discussing a name with Paul Muite three days before returning to Masinde Muliro with Orengo. Names ranging from League, Movement, and Front were considered at a brainstorming session. Orengo introduced "Forum for the Restoration of Democracy" abbreviated to FORD. This was exciting to Masinde Muliro: FORD was a catchy word popularised by the Ford Motor Company which he had patronized all his life.

They decided that pressure for the repeal of Section 2A of the Constitution would be FORD's focus. Their strategy was to engage with the government and sensitise the people. They applied to hold a rally at Kamukunji grounds and gave the required 14 days notice. There was no response. They decided that if the State still refused to respond for another fourteen days, they would hold the rally with or without permission on October 5, 1991. They began mobilizing people. As the day drew near, there was tension in the whole country. The rally was called off when Raila went underground on his way to exile in Norway.

According to Orengo, after Raila went into exile, another attempt was made to have a rally at Kamukunji on November 16, 1991. They were refused a licence, but went to court knowing full well that the court would rule against them. Orengo advised that it was better to withdraw the case to avoid having their hands tied by an adverse ruling. So the case was withdrawn and planning for the meeting continued. On the eve of the rally, Jaramogi was arrested and taken to Siaya. Muite who had hidden in the house of a foreign diplomat on the previous night was also arrested on the day of the rally.[6] As police prevented people from going to Kamukunji grounds, Muliro, Shikuku, Orengo and Gachoka, joined by US, Swedish and German diplomats, led an agitated public through the streets of Nairobi.[7]

Germany recalled its Ambassador in protest over the arrests, and donors took the opportunity to send a clear signal to the Moi regime when they met in Paris from 25-26 November, to review aid to Kenya by suspending balance of payments

---

[6]   Throup and Hornsby, *op. cit.,* p. 79.
[7]   *Ibid.* According to Hempstone's account, *op. cit.,* the British Government under High Commissioner Sir Roger Tomkys avoided the opposition. However, his successor, Sir Kieran Prendergast started building contacts with the opposition as he still gave Moi the benefit of the doubt. He was instrumental in ensuring wider international engagement when the General Elections of 1992 were held.

support and all quick disbursing aid to Kenya for six months. This and domestic pressures pushed KANU. Throup and Hornsby described the situation thus:

> This decision, despite all the warning signs, deeply shocked the government .... Kenya, the long-term favourite of the West, was being treated as one of Africa's pariah regimes. Beset by mounting domestic and international pressure for multi-party democracy, the revelations at the Commission of Enquiry into Ouko's death, reaction against the Kalenjin call for *majimboism,* and the continuing opposition of the main Churches and the LSK, the Moi regime felt hopelessly beleaguered. The Paris Group's decision to suspend aid the same day as Biwott and Oyugi were arrested broke the regime's resolve.[8]

An emergency KANU delegates' conference on December 3, 1991, debated whether Kenya should opt for multi-partyism. At a party National Executive meeting before the delegates' conference, the sentiment was against abolition of the single party-state. Former Vice-President, Mwai Kibaki argued persuasively that ending the monopoly of KANU would kill Kenya. It would be for him, "akin to cutting a fig tree with a razor blade."[9] At the delegates' conference, most delegates also spoke against the abolition of the one party state. Kalonzo Musyoka, the National Organizing Secretary of KANU opposed the change to multi-partyism, arguing that Kenya would be torn apart by ethnic rivalries. For him, the choice was "between KANU and violence."[10] However, President Moi was realistic. He knew and felt the impact of the pressure from the Western partner countries. He summed up: "It is prudent that we allow those in our country who want to form their own parties to do so. But these parties must not be tribally based, but must be national."[11] He announced his intention to repeal Section 2A.

---

[8]   *Ibid.* pp. 84-85. Robert Ouko, then Kenyan Foreign Minister had been found shot dead on February 16, 1990, three days after he was last seen alive. Nicholas Biwott, a very close ally of President Moi and Permanent Secretary for Internal Security, Hezekiah Oyugi were arrested on 25 November as suspects. But they were subsequently released. *Majimboism* was a call for federalism and riddance of non-Kalenjins from the rift valley. Throup and Hornsby suggested that this call could be seen as Biwott's attempt to rally his and Moi's Kalenjin ethnic group behind himself.

[9]   Andrew Morton's rendition. See, Andrew Morton, *Moi: The Making of An African Statesman,* (London: Michael O'Mara Books Ltd., 1998), p. 245.

[10] See, Throup and Hornsby, p. 87. In an interview with Kalonzo Musyoka on March 13, 2004, he informed the author that he was merely articulating the party position as the party's Organizing Secretary.

[11] Morton, *op. cit.,* p. 245.

His recommendation was unanimously adopted, and two days later, a bill was introduced in Parliament. The repeal came into effect on December 10, 1991[12] and FORD was registered as a party on December 31st. On January 18, 1992, FORD held first rally at Kamukunji, this time with Government approval,

At this first rally, Jaramogi introduced what FORD stood for, with an onslaught on KANU, which he described as perpetuating: "repression, corruption, violence, unaccountability and incompetence."[13] On the economy, Jaramogi reflected the current situation in the world by affirming that, "FORD supports a competitive market economy and economic liberalization, and will dismantle parastatals and reduce government intervention in economic affairs."[14] He also pressed for enquiries into the murders of Dr. Robert Ouko and Bishop Muge both of whom he suggested were killed to cover up corruption.[15] The move into FORD from KANU became a bandwagon.

However, according to Throup and Hornsby, Mwai Kibaki and several other Kikuyu leaders, wanted to stay and reform KANU. But their efforts were blocked by the Kalenjin inner core surrounding President Moi, actively supported by Joseph Kamotho, a Kikuyu and Secretary-General of the party, and Elijah Mwangale, a Luhya MP who had come into limelight in his forthright role in chairing the investigation into the murder of JM Kariuki.

By Christmas in 1991, Mwai Kibaki had made no progress in seeking reforms in KANU and it was speculated that he was about to be fired by President Moi. He made the first move by resigning from the cabinet on the pretext of dissatisfaction with the rigging of the 1988 KANU elections, and the dissolution of the Commission of Enquiry into Ouko's death. Two days later, he announced the formation of the Democratic Party of Kenya. Many prominent Kikuyus and others like John Keen from Maasailand followed Kibaki into the new party.[16] The

---

[12] For details, see, ibid., pp. 84-88.

[13] *Ibid.,* p. 100.

[14] *Ibid.,* p. 101

[15] *Ibid.,* p. 101. Bishop Alexander Muge, a vociferous critic of the government had died in an accident on 14 August 1990. Since he had been threatened by Minister of Labour Peter Okondo not to visit Busia or he would not return alive and he did but died on the way back, there was a feeling that the accident with a run away milk truck had been staged. For details, see, *ibid.,* pp. 66-67

[16] For details, see, *ibid.,* pp. 94-100.

Kikuyu elite who had transformed themselves into a wealthy entrepreneur class under Kenyatta, felt that the opportunity had come to return to power. They were not ready to concede leadership to Oginga Odinga whom they still saw as the most prominent left-winger in post-independence Kenya.[17]

A number of minor parties were also registered: Johnstone Makau's Social Democratic Party (SDP); Harun Mwau's Party of Independent Candidates of Kenya (PICK); Mohammed Akram Noor's Labour Party Democracy (LPD); and Mukaru Ng'ang'a's Kenya National Democratic Alliance (KENDA).

The alleged seditious document in the possession of George Anyona at the Mutugi Bar and Restaurant when he was arrested in July 1990, was the manifesto of his Kenyan National Congress. When he was released, he renounced any local leadership post reserved for him in FORD, and seeing himself as a national figure, tried to register the Kenya National Congress. But the name had been registered by another group, so he settled for Kenya Social Congress (KSC).

Though some of the leaders of these small parties went beyond merely using the parties for bargaining purposes with other parties by fielding candidates in some parliamentary constituencies and being in the Presidential race themselves, they were not taken seriously.

Fractionalisation within FORD

Just as the stage appeared set for a three way run for State House by Moi's KANU, Odinga's FORD and Kibaki's DP, FORD began fracturing. According to Raila, the original FORD was a pressure group to push KANU to accept multi-party democracy. Membership was thrown open without concern for ethnic background. However, as it appeared that FORD could remove KANU from office, ethnic caucuses began to divide the party. Raila claims that a GEMA caucus of politicians from the Mount Kenya area, met at Matu Wamae's Ngong Hills Hotel. The AFC caucus was named after an Abaluhya football team. They met in offices purportedly provided by Musikari Kombo, who at the time was not even a member of FORD but provided support aimed at protecting Luhya interests in FORD. The Gor

---

[17] *Ibid.*

Mahia Caucus represented Luo interests, and was organized around Professor Ouma Muga. They met at a club in Milimani Estate. These divisions polarized relationships and heightened ethnic tensions.[18]

Aside from the ethnic tension, the choice of a presidential candidate became another bone of contention. Party leadership had been shared by Jaramogi as party Chairman, Masinde Muliro as Vice-Chairman, and Martin Shikuku as Secretary-General. Previously, a party leader would automatically be the presidential candidate. To be transparent, FORD decided to select a presidential candidate. But the leadership split over the method of selection.

The division centred around whether the selection should be made by party delegates or by a direct primary election. Those around Jaramogi argued for the former method, and Martin Shikuku the latter. Masinde Muliro tried to reconcile the two groups.[19] The Secretariat split and Martin Shikuku and his group moved into Muthithi House offices donated by Jimna Mbaru and furnished by Raila's East Africa Spectre, to be used by a think tank. The Jaramogi group remained at AGIP House where East Africa Spectre had surrendered its offices for the party but continued to pay rent.[20]

The Jaramogi group argued that it was impractical to opt for primaries due to pressure of time and a hostile environment in which KANU could easily divide the party by rigging. They argued for democratic nomination by representative delegates. Shikuku's position was best put later by Matiba as "let the people decide."

By the time Matiba had recuperated from his mild stroke, matters had worsened in FORD. While in London, Matiba had maintained that he would not run as President,[21] but returned to Kenya as a presidential candidate. He had been

---

[18] This account depended on interview with Raila Odinga, September 28, 2003.

[19] For details, see, Throup and Hornsby, op. cit.

[20] The East Africa Spectre was a financial back-bone for FORD. As Ling Kituyi observed in an interview with the author: "Money collected at FORD for membership cards went into East Africa Spectre. But the East Africa Spectre supported the party more than what membership brought, as it paid staff and supported some of the party cadres. The problem if any, was that of accounting."

[21] Interview with Raila. Kiraitu Murungi recounted the same experience with Matiba in London. See, Kiraitu Murungi, *In the Mud of Politics,* (Nairobi: Acacia Stantex Publishers, 2000), p. 35

persuaded that he was the best candidate, as the more populous Kikuyu would never support Jaramogi Oginga Odinga who "was never circumcised and as such remained a boy."[22] In a critique of this position that might seem trivial to many observers, Raila placed the responsibility for the disintegration of opposition unity on some leaders whom he saw as "opportunists" who introduced ethnicity by claiming that uncircumcised leaders could not rule. As he put it, "we suffered defeat in our quest for multi-party democracy at the time because of ethnicity, but what the forces did not understand is that all these communities have been intermarrying and the women do not complain when they end up with uncircumcised men."[23]

Masinde Muliro and Prof. Wangari Maathai, tried hard to heal the rift in FORD. Their attempt at reconciliation after a court injunction stopped the Shikuku side from a membership recruitment drive, was dealt a fatal blow when Masinde Muliro collapsed and died on August 14, 1992 at the Jomo Kenyatta International Airport, on his return from a trip to London.

The split in FORD was concretised as two distinct parties. Those on the Matiba-Shikuku end became known as FORD-*Asili* (*Asili* is a Swahili word implying original). However, a number of leaders on the Matiba-Shikuku side further split away as they became irritated with what they saw as Matiba's intolerant style. They included Titus Mbathi, a former prominent civil servant who had also served as Minister of Labour, Charles Rubia, Kimani wa Nyoike, and Maina Wanjigi among others. They took over the Kenya National Congress (KNC) which was registered in February 1992 by Onesmus Musyoka Mbali, a Nairobi businessman.

---

[22] As noted earlier, the issue of circumcision has been a trivial ruse by the Kikuyu elite in election propaganda to easily capture the attention of uncritical simple minded voters especially in the rural areas where male circumcision is crucial as initiation for the transition from being a boy into adulthood and qualified the new entrants into decision-making status.

[23] See, *East African Standard,* Thursday, July 17, 2003, p. 2. But the issue was not women or even the ability to make decisions. Oginga Odinga had been Vice-President and his abilities were not in question. The issue was the fear of the Kikuyu elites for their wealth accumulation under the Kenyatta regime and their perception that Oginga Odinga would be more interested in policies of wealth re-distribution.

FORD-Kenya Leadership Positions

The refusal of the Registrar-General to grant the name FORD to the Jaramogi Oginga Odinga faction of the original FORD, led them to change the name to FORD-Kenya.

The "Young Turks" had chosen a party structure that at the national level, could accommodate the divergent groups and communities making up the party. Filling the party positions saw the beginning of acrimony among the "Young Turks" as individual ambitions came to the fore. Significantly, this process could be said to mark the beginning of the souring of the relationship between Raila and Muite.

Muite had argued that since Jaramogi was to be the Chairman of FORD-Kenya, Raila should automatically be barred from any national leadership position in the party. Raila knew that Muite's opinion was held by some of his other colleagues. He accepted that although he need not be a national official of the party, he felt that it would be un-befitting for him while campaigning for the party, to be seen only as the Chairman's son.

The dilemma the party faced was understandable. The Yoruba people of Nigeria have a proverb that says: "An elephant and its offspring do not trumpet at the same time." But a different way of looking at the problem would be to ask whether the son of a philosopher should not philosophise when he is able, just because his father is a philosopher. The fundamental role of Raila in the realization of FORD-Kenya with the other "Young Turks" who had merely conferred the leadership on older seasoned politicians, was not in doubt. If this was so, should Raila only be a cheer-leader to his father in a FORD-Kenya that he had played a major part in creating? Raila obviously did not think so. Fortunately for him, neither did other party members.

Anyang' Nyong'o provided a way out of the dilemma by suggesting the post of Director of Elections. This would be a highly visible post during the campaigns but less so, if not totally abolished, after the elections. So, in addition to the positions of: Chairman, First and Second Vice-Chairmen, Secretary-General and two Deputies etc., it was agreed that there would be a post of Director of Elections and two Deputies.

Jaramogi became the Chairman. But there was a problem over the position of First Vice-Chairman because of the death of Masinde Muliro. James Osogo was initially proposed and Paul Muite was to take the post of Second Vice-Chairman as originally agreed. However, at the stadium, Muite, an astute lawyer from the Kikuyu ethnic group, expressed preference for the First Vice-Chairman's post and forced a ballot in which he defeated Osogo.

Michael Kijana Wamalwa who had wanted to be in the race withdrew when he realized that the crowd was rooting for Muite. Wamalwa approached Raila for help, asserting that Raila's popularity would be helpful if Raila nominated him as Second Vice-Chairman. Raila obliged and Wamalwa was elected.[24]

The post of Director of Elections had been created, ostensibly to accommodate Raila. However, he believes that his opponents pressured Mzee Waruru Kanja to run against him. Kanja was a close friend of Jaramogi, and had been an MP and a cabinet minister. He was one of the most non-tribal Kenyans and a former *Mau Mau* fighter who had been sentenced to death during the emergency period but was reprieved by the Queen. After the banning of the KPU in 1969, he campaigned with Jaramogi's picture alongside his own on his posters, although it was not popular to associate with Jaramogi at the time.

Raila had respect for Mzee Waruru Kanja and could not stand against him although he was convinced he would win. He therefore withdrew in favour of Mzee Kanja and became Deputy Director of Elections.

The December 29, 1992 General Elections

The Lang'ata constituency, which Raila captured for FORD-Kenya in 1992, was and remains, cosmopolitan and ethnically diverse. It is made up of: the posh Karen neighbourhood with middle to upper class Kenyans and expatriates; the highly populated Kibera slums; Mugumoini; and the middle class Nairobi West. The Luo, Nubians, Luhya, Kikuyu, Kisii, and many other communities, are present in varying degrees.

In the 1992 General Elections, Raila overwhelmingly won the Lang'ata seat by polling 24,261 votes (43.2 per cent) against Kimani Rugendo of FORD-Asili, who took 13,430 votes (23.9 per cent); Philip Leakey of KANU who collected

---

[24] Interview with Raila Odinga, September 28, 2003.

11,901 votes (21.2 percent) and Mwangi Maathai who represented the Democratic Party but came a distant fourth with 6,282 votes (11.2 percent).[25]

When Raila chose to run in the Lang'ata constituency, he was taking a risk. He could easily have sought a secure parliamentary constituency in Luo Nyanza. But he demonstrated that he did not have to rely on ethnicity to serve Kenya. While virtually all Luos could be presumed to have voted for him in Lang'ata, it is safe to assume that he needed more than Luo votes to win. In this respect, he was and remains different from many Kenyan leaders who normally return to the safe security of their respective home bases to contest elections.[26]

Raila's father chose the safety of his Bondo constituency in Siaya district to run for Parliament. His only competition was William Odongo Omamo who had been a Minister under President Moi and was fighting on a KANU ticket. Jaramogi had 22,292 votes, 94.52% of the total. Omamo received only 1,292 .

In spite of the strong showing of Raila and Jaramogi, Ford Kenya won only 31 seats in Parliament. FORD-Asili had a similar number. Mwai Kibaki's DP could only manage 23 seats, and KNC, KSC and PICK had one seat each. President Moi's KANU took 100 seats. This changed when KANU regained the Bonchari seat from the DP in a by-election. In addition to its 100 seats, KANU could also count on 12 MPs in a winner takes-all situation that only changed just before the 1997 General Elections.

In the Presidential election, President Moi led the pack with 1,970,771 votes. He was followed by Kenneth Matiba with 1,419,308 and Mwai Kibaki with 1,040,997 votes. Jaramogi got 959,088 votes and was a distant fourth to Moi. Nonetheless, when parliament convened, Jaramogi, on the strength of parliamentary seats, became the leader of the official opposition.

The opposition had paid dearly for its disunity. The long struggle to change the Moi Government had been sacrificed at the altar of personal ego and ethnic

---

[25] Kimani Njogu, "The culture of Politics and Ethnic Nationalism," in Marcel Rutten, Alamin Mazrui & Francois Grignon, *Out for the Count: The 1997 General Elections and Prospects for Democracy in Kenya,* (Kampala: Fountain Publishers, 2001), p. 399.

[26] Former President Moi, President Kibaki, Michael Wamalwa, Simeon Nyachae, Uhuru Kenyatta, etc. always returned home for their parliamentary electoral contests.

chauvinism. Though KANU was reported to have played an active role in dividing the opposition and used its incumbency power to engage in electoral sharp practice in marginal areas, the final blame must rest at the feet of the opposition, who it might be expected from such an outcome to bring them back together. President Moi succeeded by building on the alliance of smaller ethnic groups which he had held since his KADU days, and defeated the ethnic chauvinists who saw their large ethnic groups as the means to electoral victory.[27]

The Split in FORD-Kenya

The result of the General Elections of December 1992 did not support the theory that Muite would get the support of the Kikuyu in such large numbers that FORD-Kenya could win the elections with Jaramogi becoming the President and Muite his Vice-President. Split ticket voting whereby an ethnic group supported its own for the Presidency on the platform of any party he had chosen (or in the case of KANU, supported President Moi), but did not follow party loyalty and instead supported another local ethnic candidate for the parliamentary seat on the platform of another party (or vice-versa), took place in twenty-one constituencies during the 1992 General Elections.

Muite's constituency was one in which voters split their vote. While Muite, running on the FORD-Kenya platform, won 38,416 representing 71.97% of total votes cast in his Kikuyu constituency of Kiambu district, the voters split their Presidential votes overwhelmingly in favour of Kenneth Matiba, another Kikuyu. Matiba had 46,277 of the total 53,137 votes and Jaramogi had a paltry 3,246. The same happened in the ethnic Somali Lagdera constituency of Garissa district where Mohamed Farah Maalim of FORD-Kenya, an ethnic Somali, got 2,735 votes representing 51.03% of votes cast to win the parliamentary seat, and President Moi of KANU beat Jaramogi by a wide margin of 4,039 votes to 1,249. Similarly, the Meru, in Imenti South constituency voted for Kiraitu Murungi, an ethnic son, on the platform of FORD-Kenya but showed preference for Mwai Kibaki an ethnic cousin in the presidential race. Here Oginga Odinga got only 1,578 votes against Kibaki's 35,576.

---

[27] See, Throup and Hornsby, *op. cit.* pp. 453-532 on a detailed analysis on why KANU won.

It has been suggested that the failure of members of FORD-Kenya from the Gikuyu, Embu and Meru Association (GEMA) areas to get serious support for FORD-Kenya in the presidential, and many parliamentary elections, led to grumbling in the party, especially from the Luhya and Luo members who argued that Paul Muite did not enjoy enough support from his community to justify his holding such a major post as First Vice-Chairman in FORD-Kenya.[28] Similar, it was claimed, was the situation of Gitobu Imanyara who was the Secretary-General of FORD-Kenya but failed to win the parliamentary seat (which KANU clinched) in his Imenti Central Constituency where Jaramogi trailed Mwai Kibaki and Moi.[29]

According to Farah Maalim, the GEMA members of the party were sidelined from party functions. They were under pressure to leave. A power struggle ensued and Gitobu Imanyara, who was voted out as party Secretary-General by the National Executive Committee on September 17, 1993, resigned two days later. But the popular belief in Kenya is that Muite, Kiraitu, Farah Maalim and Robert Shaw all resigned their posts, allegedly over the "gift" of two million shillings to Jaramogi by Kamlesh Pattni of Goldenberg International Limited. Kamlesh Pattni, was embroiled in a major controversy over the alleged disappearance of some 61 billion shillings from the Kenyan Treasury, as commission for bringing Kenya foreign exchange for Gold and precious mineral exports.[30]

For Farah Maalim, however, his resignation with the GEMA party members had nothing to do with the Pattni/Jaramogi affair. Jaramogi apparently did not know that Pattni was linked with the Goldenberg scandal. The money was given to the party for by-election contests. Farah Maalim believes that "Jaramogi was scrupulously an honest person." Farah Maalim resigned from FORD-Kenya in sympathy with the GEMA party officials as a reaction to what he saw as tribalism

---

[28] Interview in Nairobi, on October 30, 2003 with Mohammed Farah Maalim, who was MP for Lagdera Constituency, Garissa District during the seventh Parliament. In an interview with Paul Muite on January 21, 2004, he claimed that Raila Odinga championed this ethnic trend in the party.

[29] Raila, in an interview on May 9, 2004 contested this claim and suggested that Imanyara and Muite lost interest in the party and were not showing up at the Secretariat to carry out their respective tasks. In addition, the party, according to Raila had supported Imanyara to set up his publishing outfit from its meagre resources only for him to turn one of his publications, *Nairobi Weekly*, against the party and its chairman in a Goldenberg propaganda. These issues led to the removal of Imanyara and reaction to quit the party by some of his friends.

[30] The Goldenberg scandal will be re-visited in the next section.

in the party, and the fact that Jaramogi was cooperating with KANU without consulting either the party leadership or the Party Parliamentary Group.[31] Muite agreed with Farah Maalim. He said:

> I did not leave FORD-K because of Goldenberg. I left it because I saw it had no future given the steering of the party away from a national entity towards an ethnic institution.[32]

As a result of these resignations, FORD-Kenya was reduced largely to a party for the Luhya of Western Province (particularly the Bukusu sub-group) and the Luos of Nyanza Province.

Mwangaza Trust as Muite's Answer to FORD-Kenya

The formation of Mwangaza Trust, according to Willy Mutunga, could be traced to August 10, 1993 as a reaction to the resignations of Muite and others from FORD-Kenya.[33] Mwangaza Trust also signified a collaboration of Kenyans in the NGO world with politicians. The idea was to come up with a "second organizational structure" that could implement the ideals of FORD-Kenya in a national, non-sectarian and non-ethnic manner.

The founding Trustees were: Crispin Bokea, Wachira Maina and Sheikh Ahmed Munir. Since they were not politicians, the registration of the Trust did not attract the interest of Kenyan Intelligence. Registration was granted on November 3, 1993. But this was to change with the appointment of new Trustees immediately after registration. These included: Paul Muite; Peter Anyang' Nyong'o; Kiraitu Murungi; Richard Maore; Oki Ooko-Ombaka; Mohamed Farah Maalim; Joe Ager; Adelina Mwau; Wanjiku Kabira; Muturi Kigano; Willy Mutunga; Makau Mutua; Maina Kiai; Stanley Ngaine; Agnes Chepkwony; Khadija Abdalla; Robert Shaw and Mohamed Ibrahim.[34]

---

[32] Interview with Paul Muite, January 21, 2004.

[31] *Ibid.*

[33] See, Willy Mutunga, Constitution-Making from the Middle: Civil Society and Transition Politics in Kenya, 1992-1997, (Harare and Nairobi: MWENGO and SAREAT, 1999), pp. 140-141.

[34] See, *ibid.,* p. 140.

Within a fortnight of its registration, a workshop on the vision and activities of the Trust was held from November 12-14, 1993. The activist nature of the meetings of the Trust throughout 1994 attracted the attention of the Moi Administration and it was no surprise when the Permanent Secretary, Ministry of Lands and Settlements deregistered the Mwangaza Trust on January 19, 1995. The reason given was that the Trust had engaged in political activities.[35]

Before some of them went back to their ethnic parties, the members, tried to form a political party with the name Safina, which applied for registration in June 1995, but got the Government's nod of approval only in November 1997, i.e., just about a month before the 1997 General Elections. A new entrant into Safina in 1995 was Richard Leakey, the son of the two great anthropologists: Louis and Mary Leakey. He had been removed from the Kenyan Wildlife Service by the Moi Administration. He was to return to the Moi Administration later as Head of the Civil Service. But Muite continued to keep the flag of Safina flying by becoming one of its two MPs in the ninth Parliament.

The departure of Muite and others from FORD-Kenya, however, was nothing compared to the acrimony that gripped the party in the aftermath of the death of Oginga Odinga.

The Demise of Jaramogi

The death of the party Chairman, Jaramogi Oginga Odinga on January 20, 1994 was a watershed for FORD-Kenya. It was not only important that an icon was lost, but that the party structure was not well developed to handle the leadership succession. With his death, some party members like Anyang' Nyong'o,[36] argued that Jaramogi should be succeeded, on an interim basis, by a college of leaders that would enable all the constituent units to have their respective interests accommodated. Other members moved that Michael Wamalwa, successor to Paul Muite as the first Vice-Chairman, should become the Party Chairman.

---

[35] *Ibid.,* and interviews with Wanjiku Kabira, Nairobi, February 21, 2003 as well as with Paul Muite, Nairobi, January 21, 2004.
[36] Interview with Prof. Anyang' Nyong'o, Nairobi, August 22, 2003.

It was resolved that the National Council would be called to confirm Wamalwa as the interim Party Chairman until a National Delegates Conference could be held. Raila claimed that Wamalwa had initially asked him to run for the post of first Vice-Chairman of FORD-Kenya because Jaramogi had expressed a private wish before he died that he and Raila should lead the party.[37] However, before Raila came forward, Wamalwa was persuaded that it would be politically unwise for him to have Raila as his number two as Raila would overshadow him. Instead, he was urged to support Orengo, Wamalwa's former student, and with whom he had a closer relationship.

Wamalwa wanted the position of first Vice-Chairman filled at the National Council meeting which would also confirm him as Chairman in spite of Anyang' Nyong'o's position that the National Council should not wield such authority. Oburu, sensing tension over the post, between Raila and Orengo, did not want the Vice-Chairman appointed at the meeting. He tried to persuade Wamalwa not to fill the position of Vice-Chairman at the meeting, arguing the need for a cooling-off period. But Wamalwa told Oburu that he would be a weak Chairman if he avoided the issue for fear of the tension degenerating into conflict.[38]

The confirmation of Wamalwa as the Chairman of FORD-Kenya by the National Council on March 19, 1994, pending a National Delegates Conference was uneventful. But the contest for his deputy, pitted Raila against Orengo. Oburu claimed that Wamalwa, who was supporting his former student, had his bodyguard and Personal Assistant to vote when they should not. Raila claimed that twelve delegates from Kajiado, Turkana and Pokot were also switched.[39] Orengo defeated Raila narrowly by 61-59 votes. Raila congratulated Orengo on his success. But this development marked the beginning of the irreparable split in the party. According to Anyang', Raila justifiably, felt short-changed.[40] The event created bitterness, marked a false start for Wamalwa's leadership, and began what was to become clearer much later: that Raila had inherited the constituency of his father as a springboard to consolidate his position in Kenyan politics.

---

[37] Interview with Raila, Nairobi, October 10, 2003.
[38] Interview with Oburu Oginga, September 2, 2003.
[39] Interview with Raila Odinga, October 10, 2003.
[40] Interview, *ibid.*

The Goldenberg Scandal and the FORD-Kenya Split

For Raila, the Goldenberg issue, and not personal rivalry, was the fundamental problem that caused the split in FORD-Kenya. In 1993, a Central Bank of Kenya staff approached the leadership of FORD-Kenya with documents as evidence of a huge financial scam. Raila claimed that the documents were given to Muite and Robert Shaw, who examined them and returned them when they could not make much out of them. Raila gave the documents to Sarah Elderkin, a Briton whose husband taught at the University of Nairobi, and who, before taking charge of the media at the FORD-Kenya Secretariat, was a journalist at the *Weekly Review*. She produced a ten-page report for Jaramogi, then the Chairman of the Parliamentary Public Accounts Committee (PAC). Raila encouraged Elderkin to publish an account on the scam. This she did with the *Daily Nation*.

At the same time, FORD-Kenya entered the contest for two by-elections to be held in Bonchari and Migori constituencies on May 22, 1993. Dr. Protas Momanyi Kebati of the DP and Charles O. Owino of the FORD-Kenya who had won their seats in the 1992 General Elections had defected, hence the need for the by-elections. Raila claimed that Orengo introduced an Asian who wanted to contribute to the party's effort, to Jaramogi who received a two million shillings "gift" without asking about who the giver was.

However, as soon as Jaramogi realized that Pattni was the benefactor, he sent for him and told him that his contribution would not insulate him or his company from examination by the PAC. True to his word, the Jaramogi-led PAC decided that Pattni's Goldenberg International, had perpetrated a fraud against Kenya, and recommended that the culprits should be prosecuted and the money recovered.

A leak to the press that Jaramogi had been bribed by Pattni became a national issue. Jaramogi admitted that he had received money from Pattni for the party and that it had been used to fight the by-elections in Bonchari and Migori. Apparently, Jaramogi passed the money to the two candidates through Raila.[41] Muite and some others who had become disenchanted with the party, seized on this development. Muite stated that he could not reconcile his conscience with being in FORD-Kenya whose image had been tainted by such a despicable act.

---

[41] Interview with Raila Odinga, September 28, 2003.

Raila's reaction that Muite was merely being hypocritical, resulted in an unresolved civil suit against Raila by Muite.

There were major changes in the PAC following Jaramogi's death. Wamalwa succeeded Jaramogi as Chairman and Raila took the second Ford-Kenya place. Wamalwa, according to Raila, was invited to the Speaker's office to meet George Saitoti, then Kenya's Vice-President, and Nicholas Biwott, President Moi's closest confidante.[42] They persuaded Wamalwa to revisit the PAC's recommendations on Goldenberg.

Wamalwa returned to AGIP House, the FORD-Kenya office and sought Raila's advice on what to do. Raila advised him that the PAC should not reconvene since the report had been completed and sent for printing under Jaramogi's chairmanship. But Wamalwa had already agreed to reconvene the PAC and that night, he used the media to summon members to a meeting.

The PAC members divided down the middle, four against four, and the Chairman's casting vote resulted in a recommendation that nothing was wrong with the Goldenberg deal. Thereafter, Wamalwa was attacked for being soft on Pattni and he faced calls to resign from the PAC and the FORD-Kenya chairmanship.

The Goldenberg issue further divided FORD-Kenya between those who stood by Wamalwa on his action, and those who felt betrayed by the fresh PAC report to Parliament. The latter group, to which Raila belonged, pushed for a National Delegates Conference, to hold new elections for party leadership as set out in the Party Constitution. Initially, this was resisted by the Wamalwa party leadership. But finally, a National Delegates Conference took place at Thika stadium. It was to have been supervised by Archbishop Manasses Kuria. Raila had preferred an election at the Nairobi Stadium and although the venue was settled late, he agreed to use Thika stadium. Delegates who had arrived in Nairobi were ferried to Thika. Raila believed that delegates loyal to him outnumbered those of Wamalwa by a margin of 3:1.

Archbishop Kuria arrived late to face a restive crowd. Wamalwa's faction wanted the election postponed, but Raila's group pushed for it to go ahead. All hell broke

---

[42] This account depended on *ibid*. Wamalwa had died and the author did not have the opportunity of an interview with him.

loose at the Stadium and Archbishop Kuria and Wamalwa's group left. The Raila group saw postponement as cheating. They carried on with the election, made Raila the party Chairman and filled five other posts of a total of thirty-six. They called an election in Kiambu two weeks later and filled the remaining posts. But the Wamalwa group returned to Thika Stadium the day after the fracas and he was elected Chairman. This situation led to suits and counter-suits in court on what became a long war of attrition. Wamalwa was successful in court which ruled that he should continue as the Chairman but instructed him to call fresh elections. According to Bob Wekesa, Wamalwa and his supporters were not keen in calling an election.[43]

---

[43] See, Bob Wekesa, *The Road Not Taken: A Biography of Michael Wamalwa Kijana*, (Nairobi: Oakland Books, 2004), pp. 131-138.

Chapter 13
The Tractor

The Raila-Wamalwa struggle was eventually seen as a Luo-Luhya fight. Friends of Raila like Mukhisa Kituyi, whatever their private feelings, followed ethnic lines and backed Wamalwa. Most of the Luos, with a few exceptions like Achieng' Oneko[1] and Joe Donde, stood steadfastly behind Raila. As a series of court cases continued on different aspects of the problem in FORD-Kenya, it was impossible to convene party elections acceptable to both sides.

The Social Democratic Party

In a response to the protracted struggle, Anyang' Nyong'o took over the moribund Social Democratic Party (SDP) and never returned to FORD-K. Anyang's explanation was that he became tired of what he saw as a personality cult crisis and decided to form the SDP as an ideological party. His plan for the 1997 election was to have a presidential candidate from Eastern Province, to deny President Moi success there and by so doing, make it impossible for Moi to secure overall victory.[2]

Oburu saw Anyang's move differently. For him, Anyang' thought that his chances would be better if he supported Charity Ngilu, then a Democratic Party MP, in the 1997 elections on an SDP platform, knowing fully well that she would lose. In return for such support, he calculated that he would be able to count on the support of Ngilu's Akamba ethnic community as well as his own Luo community in the 2002 Presidential race.[3]

---

[1] Raila, in an interview suggested that he started life by revering Achieng' Oneko and looked on him and Wesonga Sijeyo with a lot of respect. For Raila, however, his position that KANU and the Moi regime should be confronted in 1981 was opposed by his two icons. His statement suggesting that the fact that both had put in a joint 30 years in jail in the struggle could have softened them up and should step aside for younger ones who were ready to continue with the struggle did not go down well with either elderly men. This, for Raila, marked the beginning of a sour relationship that never healed in spite of the efforts of Jaramogi.

[2] Interview with Prof. Anyang' Nyong'o, Nairobi, August 22, 2003.

[3] Interview with Oburu Oginga, September 2, 2003.

Anyang' made the same mistake as many before him. He thought Luos would accept him as an alternative leader who could fulfil their dream once he offered development. But the General Elections of 1997 told a different story.

Formation of the National Development Party

Aware that the General Elections of 1997 were not far away, Raila could not be sure that he would have a political platform for his teeming supporters, and for himself to contest the Presidency. In taking stock of the predicament he was in, he asked himself three questions:

The first was whether he could win an election in FORD-K. Two if he won, whether the results would be acceptable to his adversaries. Obviously the answer to the latter question was no. The third was whether after such an election, if he were to go to court, the court would rule in his favour. Raila could not be sure.

He concluded that it was a waste of his time to cling to FORD-Kenya. He realized that it was an exercise in futility to seek democratic rights in an undemocratic environment. He decided to leave the party he had played a major role in forming and seek a different party to advance the interests of himself and his colleagues.

Knowing that the vetting process by the Registrar of Societies could take a year, and could end with rejection, Raila decided against trying to register a new party. Instead, he went in search of moribund parties. He considered the Labour Party and then settled for Steven Omondi Oludhe's National Development Party (NDP), in exchange for half a million shillings and his used Mercedes. This was the answer to a possible bureaucratic impediment over the registration of a new party by the KANU government. According to Raila, Oludhe, also wanted automatic nomination as the Party's candidate for election to parliament. For Raila, he never promised nomination, arguing that the democratic way was for the party to support Oludhe if he secured nomination, which he did not.

Raila kept the acquisition of the NDP close to his chest and told only Joab Omino and George Odeny Ngure. He showed interest in KENDA (another small moribund party) and the Labour Party, to distract the Registrar of Societies until on December 31, 1996, he announced at a press conference in Chester House, Nairobi that NDP would be his platform for the 1997 General elections. He also announced his resignation from FORD-Kenya and parliament stating that he would fight a by-election under NDP. At the same time, the party was re-launched in many other parts of Kenya.

The NDP adopted a tractor as its symbol, so giving Raila the nickname:*tinga tinga* (*tinga is the* Kiswahili word for tractor). The post of the first among equals was changed from Chairman to Party leader. Oludhe stepped down from the party's leadership position in favour of Raila who was formally elected to the post of Party Leader at the first delegates' conference on January 8, 1997. Geoffrey Ole Malloiy, an academic who had run into problems, for his opposition in Maasailand to Vice-President George Saitoti and had lost his University job, was elected Deputy Leader. The inclusion of an untested politician was aimed at a national spread.[4] Dr. Chris Bichage who had been the Secretary-General of the Raila Odinga faction in FORD-Kenya, was elected to the same post in NDP.[5]

Putting his money where his mouth was, Raila showed leadership by defecting to the unknown NDP. His supporters did not take the same risk and held on to their parliamentary seats on the platform of FORD-Kenya till the end of the seventh parliament. On the basis of the Tom Mboya-sponsored bill which, in 1966, had reduced his father's support in Parliament, Raila's move caused a by-election in his Lang'ata parliamentary constituency.

With his unknown party, Raila won the by-election in March 1997. The turnout was low as is usual in by-elections. Out of the 7,050 votes, Raila got 4,798 (68.7 per cent) against a younger Luo, Fred Amayo of KANU, who received 1,874 votes (26.8 per cent). The runner-up in the previous General Election, Kimani Rugendo of FORD-Asili, got a miniscule 279 votes (4.0 per cent).

NDP in the 1997 General Elections

The NDP sponsored presidential, parliamentary and civic candidates in the 1997 General Elections. In the NDP manifesto, Raila wrote an introductory note calling for change.[6]

---

[4] Interview with Raila Odinga, October 10, 2003.
[5] Dr. Bichage was subsequently replaced by Dr. Charles Maranga.

The manifesto, set out the problems faced by Kenya and how the NDP would address them. For example, unemployment was identified as the number one national enemy. It was claimed that Kenya had been held back by corruption in economic management, and chronic under-investment. The manifesto committed NDP to removing the bureaucracy hampering business growth and, with the development of infrastructure and promotion of small and medium-sized businesses, to create thousands of extra jobs. NDP would foster an overall environment for private business. Emphasis was put on improving agricultural production to provide food for all.

The NDP manifesto also committed the Party to restructure education in Kenya from primary to tertiary level, and promised to bring health services closer to the people by concentrating on preventive health care through public education policies aimed at preventing communicable diseases like HIV/AIDS. Crime, homelessness and insecurity would also be tackled.

The manifesto proposed a sound environment management policy and advocated biological diversity. The NDP promised freedom from hunger and poverty; the provision of adequate shelter; and to free Kenyans from tyranny, corruption, torture, fear, legal injustice, judicial partiality, abuse of power, curtailment of civil liberties and political and personal disempowerment. The NDP would address gender issues and would implement affirmative action. It would also prepare the youth for future leadership and national development. The NDP manifesto focused on KANU in an appendix comparing what it described as KANU's empty promises in 1992 with an analysis of "achievements" on the eve of the 1997 elections.

The NDP manifesto differed from the radical position of the banned KPU which had advocated land to the tiller. Raila had evolved with society. He was no longer the fire-brand of earlier years. His first free attempt to define a structure for the capture of power showed him as a liberal democrat keen to run an efficient version of KANU.

However, Raila, the risk taker demonstrated that he was a grass-roots organizer. Rather than wait for the courts, he had moved out of FORD-Kenya and acquired a totally new party. More importantly, he had the courage to resign his seat in parliament to face a by-election in which he knew that many of the established parties would field candidates against him. Most individuals would have played safe till the General Elections of 1997.

The NDP nominated Raila Amolo Odinga, its Party Leader, as its presidential candidate. Raila also decided to defend his parliamentary seat in Lang'ata. As Kimani Njogu pointed out: "Raila's opposition in Lang'ata before the 1997 elections was such that most political analysts thought he would be better off contesting the polls in Bondo instead of Lang'ata, because the latter was viewed to be a shaky political base due to, among other things, its ethnic diversity and migratory tendencies typical of urban constituencies."[7] His opponents argued that he had failed to initiate any project in the Lang'ata constituency during his stay in the seventh parliament. And the ruling party, KANU, was determined to see the end of Raila in Lang'ata.

However, Raila ran a determined and serious campaign to retain his seat, and won more than half of the votes cast: 22,339 (51.8 per cent) to KANU's Perez Malande Olindo's 11,883 (27.6 percent) and DP's George Njage Ngentu's 4,667 (10.8 per cent).[8]

In the 1997 General Elections, Raila showed that he had a following when most Nyanza parliamentarians and politicians from other parts of Kenya followed him into his new party. Almost all those who resisted the change he had put in place, were wiped out at the polls in Nyanza. These included Nyong'o and surprisingly Ramogi Achieng' Oneko, his father's colleague who failed to capture the Rarieda parliamentary seat in Nyanza.

---

[7] Kimani Njogu, *op cit.* p. 400.
[8] *Ibid.*

Chapter 14
Cockerel Swallowed Tractor

"Immediately after the 1997 General Election, we saw President Moi's tactics in rigging through the use of state machinery, cash and state intelligence network to block the opposition. We thought the best way to unseat KANU was to work closer with them. From the time of the late President Jomo Kenyatta, Luos have been frustrated on development. We thought that by talking to KANU we would get breathing space and get some little resources for the people who have been suffering. We did not get much. But we got into the system to learn their soft spot and gave courage to people who had been frustrated inside KANU but would not move out."

Oburu Oginga, MP for Bondo constituency, in an interview on September 2, 2003.

Raila shocked many of his admirers and family members when he entered into a working relationship with President Moi's KANU. It was a surprise that a dogged member of the opposition for so long, would easily give up his opposition garb and enter into a co-operation, partnership and then a merger with the party which had repressed his family for over two decades. But he had thought through his strategy, and was again borrowing from the script his father had written.

Oginga Odinga's Precedent

Towards the end of his life, Jaramogi Oginga Odinga adopted a policy of cooperation with the Moi regime. He shocked many of his admirers when he led some colleagues to the June 1, 1993 Madaraka Day celebrations. This was followed by a visit by President Moi to Bondo, Jaramogi's constituency, with Jaramogi as Chief Host.

In Sarah Elderkin's compilation of tributes on Jaramogi's death, entitled: *The Passing of a Hero,* Jaramogi, in a written response to questions by *Time* Magazine about the criticism from a section of the opposition, including his own party FORD-Kenya offered no apologies for his cooperation with KANU. As he wrote: "Perhaps because the majority of us in Kenya have never lived as adults under multi-party rule, many of us have not yet fully grasped the idea that the role of the opposition is not to engage in confrontational stand-offs with the government every day of the week."[1] He said that he was co-operating with the government as leader of the opposition, (as he felt it should be), and not with KANU. He dispelled any idea that such cooperation could be seen as a sell-out and questioned why he would sell out after 25 years of being in limbo.

The colonial administration had shown the way by skewing policies to favour accumulation by the White settlers. It is generally accepted in Kenya that the Kenyatta Presidency followed that pattern and disproportionately benefited Kikuyu elites as Moi benefited those well connected in the Kalenjin community. It may be a different debate when the relative developments of territories occupied by, say the Kalenjins, are considered. Luo Nyanza, like many parts of Kenya, remained very poor as it was in opposition to the Kenyatta and Moi Presidencies.

President Moi did not hide the fact that his Administration would starve communities opposing KANU. At a rally on July 6, 1994, Moi reportedly stated that FORD-Kenya MP, Henry Obwocha's contributions in parliament would come to nothing and there would be no development in his constituency until he defected to KANU. The message was clear: 'be in KANU or find a way of contracting with it, or you are out in the cold.'[2]

Lazarus Amayo while contesting the Karachuonyo constituency seat for KANU in the 1997 General Election, made a similar plea to Luos. He urged them to elect, at least, a few KANU MPs to benefit from President Moi's Administration. He argued:

> Luos should give President Moi a couple of MPs to work with, because this will be to our advantage....political arithmetic requires that Luos, like Luhyas, Kisiis and Kambas spread their leaders among the main political parties...Vote like

---

[1] Sarah Elderkin, *The Passing of a Hero: Jaramogi Oginga Odinga*, (Nairobi: Jaramogi Oginga Odinga Foundation), p. 50.

[2] See, *Daily Nation* November 20, 1994 as recounted in Wambui Kimathi, "A Strategic Seclusion – Yet Again! The 1997 General Elections in Luo Nyanza," in Marcel Rutten, Al-Amin Mazrui & Francois Grignon, *Out for the Count: The 1997 General Elections and Prospects for Democracy in Kenya,* (Kampala: Fountain Publishers, 2001), p. 501.

Luhyas who in 1992 made sure that they had MPs in KANU, FORD Asili, and FORD-Kenya...Tribes like Luhyas "eat" from each side.[3]

This economistic approach to politics in Kenya was what Kiraitu Murungi illustrated with a local saying to the effect that when the elephant dies, it is the grass near it that grows tallest. This reality has been dominant in Kenyan politics. After elections, the winning party rewarded those who supported them and excluded those who supported the opposition when sharing out state resources. So, it was no surprise that Luo elites and their communities were kept out in the cold when it came to the distribution of resources by the Kenyatta and Moi Presidencies. The Luo elites had limited access to wealth through their professional efforts achieved by their commitment to getting Western education.

This reality was visible to all, including Jaramogi who, as a result, decided that it was right to consort with KANU. Immediately after the opposition failed to remove President Moi from power in the 1992 General Elections, the three major opposition leaders (Matiba, Jaramogi and Kibaki), united to challenge the election results. This "unity in defeat" was short-lived. The first contention was over who should chair the meetings. Although chairmanship by rotation was agreed, Matiba's group demanded later that he should be the leader as he had received the most presidential votes after Moi. The meetings ended abruptly.[4]

Thereafter, Jaramogi began his policy of co-operation with KANU. He explained his position to many of his close lieutenants. Raila remembered a one-on-one meeting with his father about co-operation with KANU when Jaramogi argued that it was no longer possible to alter the election results, without causing chaos in Kenya. In his view, the absence of opposition unity had allowed the KANU regime to rig successfully and the opposition must accept its share of the blame. In effect, although Moi had re-entered State House by rigging, he was now there and removing him would be impossible.

Therefore, Jaramogi argued, the following five years must be used constructively. It would be impossible to keep people on the streets in civil disobedience for five years. It was thus important for him to co-operate with the ruling party, to realize

---

[3] *Daily Nation,* October 9, 1997, p. 5.
[4] Interview with Raila Odinga, October 26, 2003.

reforms that would create a level playing field at the next elections. By cooperating, the Government would allow the opposition to campaign without molestation countrywide, including in the KANU safe zones of the Rift Valley, North-Eastern, parts of Eastern and most of the Coast Provinces. Jaramogi also saw co-operation with Government as providing opportunities for opposition leaders and supporters, to do business and realize some resources to face the next elections. Finally, Jaramogi, saw Government projects to alleviate poverty as necessary to reduce rigging through the bribing of poor people who had no alternatives.[5]

President Moi welcomed the overture from Jaramogi. He calculated that a relationship with Jaramogi's FORD-Kenya would further undermine prospects for opposition unity.

Raila, Orengo and a number of Luo MPs would have nothing to do with KANU. Raila opposed his father on this issue, at numerous FORD-Kenya national executive committee meetings. He saw co-operation with KANU as self-serving and he wanted a position that accommodated all members of the party. Raila also wanted to cut the image of a cosmopolitan nationalist.[6] But Raila did not criticise Jaramogi publicly.

By the time of Jaramogi's death, there was weariness in KANU over co-operation with FORD-Kenya. This arose from the keen contests in which FORD-Kenya engaged KANU in by-elections in Migori, Bonchari and Kisauni Constituencies. FORD-Kenya won Kisauni, where Professor Rashid Mzee of FORD-Kenya defeated KANU's Karisa Maitha. Though KANU won Bonchari, President Moi was not pleased. Raila claimed that Moi had issued a statement terminating the co-operation, by coincidence, a couple of hours before the death of Jaramogi. But he asserted that the statement was withdrawn when Jaramogi's death was announced.[7] But Moi did not wait for long to end the cooperation. Probably in reaction to the names he had been called by Orengo to his face at the funeral of Jaramogi, he said at Kericho: "I will not accept to be abused, and, therefore, I will

5   *Ibid.*
6   See, *Weekly Review*, December 3, 1993 and David W. Throup & Charles Hornsby, *Multi-Party Politics in Kenya: The Kenyatta & Moi States & the Triumph of the System in the 1992 Election*, (Oxford: James Currey, 1998), p. 548.
7   Interview with Raila Odinga, October 26, 2003.

not cooperate with them."[8] He asked people in neighbouring districts to ostracise the Luos.

Prelude to the KANU-NDP Merger

On the death of Oginga Odinga, Raila, did not immediately follow the path his father was building, although he claimed he understood the reasoning of his father fairly well. He sought leadership in FORD-Kenya, first with Orengo, over the First Vice-Chairmanship, and subsequently in the struggle with Wamalwa that ended in the split of the party.

But there was the need for a platform to realize the goals that Jaramogi had begun to articulate towards the end of his life. The answer was not to be through personal defections into KANU but through a political party to be used for political bargaining and contracting. That political platform was the NDP. The other side of the equation was a major political organization to work with.

When Raila left FORD-Kenya for the National Development Party, he sacrificed the support of a major bloc of votes from the Luhya within FORD-Kenya. It was obvious to the leadership that a party like NDP could never make an impact at the national level. As Otieno Kajwang' eloquently said: "We recognized that NDP was a small party and its support was largely from Luo Nyanza. We knew that if we went into elections in 2002, we would be number 3 as in 1997 after KANU and the Democratic Party."[9]

NDP's relationship with Matiba's FORD-Asili had gone from bad to worse with Raila's decision to participate in the 1997 General Elections, under protest, instead of boycotting them as Matiba preferred, based on his argument that the elections had been pre-rigged.

After the elections, opposition leaders concluded that they had indeed been rigged and that they would not accept such fraud.[10] Initially, it appeared that foreign diplomats were taking a similar position. Some approached opposition leaders expressing dissatisfaction with the polls and assured them of support if they

---

[8]   See, David W. Throup & Charles Hornsby, *op. cit.,* p. 566.
[9]   Interview, Nairobi, April 11, 2003
[10] See, *Daily Nation* and *East African Standard,* January 2 and 3 1998.

could mobilize the people to demonstrate on three consecutive days against the results.[11] However, European Union countries' embassy officials agreed to alter the report of the European Union observers. The British High Commissioner, in a letter to his Canadian counterpart Bernard Dussault justified this approach when he remarked: "What we attempted to do in re-writing this paper was to turn it into more of government to government document... We have to be extremely careful what we say, or to be more accurate, what we allege."[12]

Raila joined Mwai Kibaki at two press conferences in making statements denouncing the election results. On the eve of Moi's swearing-in they organized a meeting of all Presidential candidates and key advisers at the Nairobi Club . Mwai Kibaki was accompanied by Njenga Karume, George Muhoho and Joe Wanjuhi; Charity Ngilu by Nginyo Kariuki; and Raila by Joab Omino. Wamalwa could not be reached, as his phone was not being picked-up. The reason became clear later when Wamalwa, who was fourth in the election after Raila, was the first major opposition leader to accept the results of the Elections.[13]

At the Nairobi club meeting, it was suggested that the opposition should mobilize its supporters to disrupt the swearing-in ceremony in Uhuru Park on the following day January 5, 1998.

Raila was hesitant and Ngilu wondered out loud if the courageous Raila she knew, had become a coward. She expressed her readiness to lead the people and if necessary to pay the ultimate price. Similar sentiments were expressed by all including Kibaki who said leaders must lead a struggle they believed in. Raila acquiesced.

They agreed to mobilize their respective supporters at the General Post Office (GPO) by 7 am on the following day. The leaders would gather at the Norfolk hotel at 8 am and join their supporters at 9 am to march on Uhuru Park and disrupt the swearing-in at 11 am.

---

[11] Raila in an interview on October 26, 2003, told the author the name of the diplomat who met with him at the Muthaiga Club on this issue.

[12] Macharia Munene, *The Politics of Transition in Kenya: 1995-1998,* (Nairobi: Quest & Insight, 2001), p. 84.

[13] Raila as would be seen later became the second as reported. See, *Daily Nation,* January 7, 1998, p. 1.

Raila got word round to NDP supporters. The crowd started arriving at the GPO, a stone's throw from Uhuru Park, as early as 6 am. Raila arrived at the Norfolk Hotel at 8 am and saw Mark Kiptarbei arap Too arrive for breakfast at 8:30 am. Though Mark, then a pleasant, blue-eyed boy of Moi, was on the other side, they exchanged pleasantries. It was not until 10 am that Nginyo Kariuki showed up and announced that he had come to represent Ngilu who was otherwise engaged. At 10:30 am, Njenga Karume arrived and apologized that he had to take care of some engagements as his business interests had suffered during the campaign. He had no information on what had become of Kibaki.[14]

The event was being screened live on television. Raila was kept abreast of developments at the GPO and at the Uhuru Park. His supporters were restless as they saw buses moving people into Uhuru Park for the ceremony. Mark Too finished his breakfast and asked what the agitated Raila was up to. Raila said that he was to meet other leaders who were yet to show up.

Raila drove towards the crowd at the General Post Office. He saw his supporters standing bewildered not knowing what to do. He felt betrayed by people who had called him a coward only the day before. For him, this was a strong political statement from the people who wanted opposition unity. But as in 1992, he doubted the possibility of "unity in defeat."

The swearing-in ceremony was a big success and a boost for President Moi. Presidents Yoweri Museveni of Uganda and Benjamin Mpaka of Tanzania attended. Museveni warned against chaos and ridiculed Kibaki's claim that the election had been rigged.[15] The American Embassy made its support for Moi public, a day after the swearing-in.

Though Kibaki continued to swear that he would never accept the election result, Raila refused to be part of the empty threats that accompanied demands for a rerun of the elections. On January 6, 1998, he decided to accept the results "under protest" and not to contest them, but to focus on constitutional review. He wrote to President Moi: "We extend the hand of cooperation to all parties committed

---

[14] This detail was from interview with Raila on November 26, 2003.
[15] See, Munene, *op. cit.,* p. 85.

to reforms in the belief that the artificial divide which has caused untold suffering to ordinary Kenyans shall be bridged in the interest of peace, stability, progress and national development."[16]

Raila's next move was to summon all 118 NDP candidates and party officials country-wide, to a review meeting. The candidates gave what Raila saw as overwhelming proof of rigging in various parts of the country. But the party members agreed his position that there could be no guarantee that fresh elections would not be equally rigged. After all, fresh elections would be based on the same defective voters register, and supervised by the same set of electoral officials with the effective backing of the Provincial Administration and security officials. Basically, NDP, as a new party lacked the resources to gamble money it did not have for the same results or even worse.

On a positive note, the meeting, agreed to take a long term look at the situation and design a strategy that would achieve a win in 2002. Fundamental to this, would be a level playing field through the introduction of constitutional reforms. The party leadership was mandated to design a five-year strategy for the party. This would involve consultation with all parties, including KANU, since the delegates realized that KANU support would be essential for constitutional change.

The strategy paper embodying the expectations of the NDP from co-operation with KANU, was articulated in a paper that Raila, as party leader, signed on behalf of the National Executive Council (NEC) and released in January 1998. The paper entitled: "NDP's Position On Co-operation Among Political Parties and Reforms," read as follows:

A. Co-operation

1. Having witnessed the last 5 years of multi-partyism, largely characterized by highly ethnicised and polarised dispensation; opportunistic vacillation in opposition circles, and reinforced by hawkish obstinacy and intransigence of certain cliques within KANU, the NDP, being the youngest major party in Kenya's political arena, has decided to steer clear of this culture of political rigmarole and opportunism. Instead, NDP has taken some bold initiative to

---

[16] *Daily Nation,* January 7, 1998.

break this *impasse* so as to bring pressing national issues such as constitutional reform, corruption, poverty and economic management into sharper focus.

2. Despite its shortcomings, KANU is still a party of choice for millions of Kenyans whose stake in Kenya cannot simply be ignored or underestimated by any other political player.

3. The NDP disposition toward KANU is one of opening channels for dialogue and identifying possible areas of co-operation, and not an endorsement of KANU's predatory policies of the past, present or the future.

4. Being a party with a clear vision for the future, the NDP intends to utilise this disposition, not for any benefits or desserts from KANU, but rather to try to reason with – and hopefully – influence KANU's approach to national issues such as the current question of the constitutional reforms and other pressing socio-economic issues.

5. The NDP is determined to chart a new path for Kenya's fledgling multi-partyism based on constructive dialogue with any political party in the search for enduring solution to our national problems, especially problems faced by the impoverished masses including the perennial ethnic clashes.

6. The Party's surname is Development; and having bound ourselves to the principle that Kenya is a society culturally diverse, but politically equal ethnic nationalities, the NDP will seek equal rights and development for all. It is on this basis that we shall continue to solicit the people's popular mandate and engage in constructive dialogue or cooperation with any other parties or political organisations.

B. Reforms

7. The Constitution of Kenya is the embodiment of the collective sovereignty of the entire people of Kenya. The Constitution is the covenant that binds the people of Kenya to a common and collective destiny based on democracy, equality, freedom, justice and unity. The NDP believes that the constitutional reform process is a collective responsibility of the people of Kenya in their diverse national character.

8. It is NDP's view that whichever modality is used, be it by a convention, a conference or a commission – is irrelevant: the real issue is – which modality will achieve the people's maximum participation? Different modalities have been used in other countries with considerable degree of success and there is no reason why Kenyans should be unable to agree on a compromise, a situation that would necessitate a national referendum.

9. This crucial matter should be discussed in an atmosphere devoid of tension, blackmail, jingoism or brinkmanship i.e., "we will go to the bush unless our demands are met," or "there will be civil disobedience if, Ö." etc., if we are to save this country from civil war and attendant chaos.

10. In this regard, the NDP would like to propose amendment to the Constitution of Kenya Review Commission Act 1997. Section 4(3) and (4) of the said Act, provides and states as follows:

4(3) The President shall, in consultation with –

    a. parliamentary political parties,
    b. religious organizations,
    c. the Association of Professional Societies in East Africa,
    d. the Kenya Women Political Caucus,
    e. the Non-Governmental Organisations Council established under the Non-Governmental Organisation Co-ordination Act, appoint Commissioners from nominations submitted to the President by registered political parties, religious organisations, institutional organisations or associations, trade unions, the business community, the farming community, women and youth organisations, association of disabled persons and non-governmental organisations.

    (4) The Nominations and appointments under this Act shall take into account Kenya's ethnic, regional, cultural, political, social and economic diversity and reflect the national character of Kenya.

We would like the Act amended to make the following provisions:

a. membership of commission to be increased from 29 to 50 in order to provide for more representation:

b.   interested parties to nominate their representatives directly without further vetting by the Attorney-General;

c.   at least 30% of members to be female;

d.   the commissioners to elect their own Chairman;

e.   a National Constitutional Consultative Council (NCCC) be established to review the recommendations before they are presented to the Parliament.

11.   The need for quick resolution of the current stalemate cannot be over-emphasised hence the need for constructive suggestions for the way forward.

It was clear that the NDP, like all parties, wanted power to have its programmes adopted and implemented. To enter the 2002 elections alone, would be to accept third place in the Presidential race. Given the ethnic nature of Kenyan politics, re-alignment of forces across the political divide was needed ahead of these elections. The NDP's strategy aimed to facilitate dialogue and at the same time to attract support in KANU zones.

KANU's Move

However, even before NDP could move, KANU sought them out. President Moi was impressed with Raila's decision not to contest the election results. As a result, Raila received an invitation to meet Moi, from Reuben Chesire, a successful farmer and a relative of Moi, who had represented Eldoret North in Parliament under KANU. He decided to honour the invitation and agreed to meet the President at Kabarak, in the company of Joab Omino as a witness from his side, to whatever transpired.

Chesire also attended the meeting. Raila briefed the President on the decision of his party to cooperate with all political parties in the country. They discussed the state of the country. As Raila and Omino were about to leave, Moi asked Chesire to step aside as he had a private talk with Raila and Joab. He then suggested that in future Raila should deal with Mark Kiptarbei arap Too, rather than Chesire.

Raila thought this strange. He was not impressed with Moi putting his lieutenant down after Chesire had delivered.[17] But he knew Too fairly well, he having visited

---

[17] This account is from interview with Raila on November 23, 2003.

Jaramogi at East Africa Spectre, in those dark days that people feared to come near. When Too had a major accident in 1994, Raila had visited him as he received medical care.

So, Too, an astute Kenyan politician of Kalenjin extraction, became the point man on the KANU side for a relationship that would change the face of Kenyan politics. Too was generally dubbed *"Bwana Dawa"* or literally "Mr. Fix it," given his political ability to accomplish tasks whether at local or international levels. He normally worked quietly as an ambassador-at-large on missions that accredited and accomplished diplomats would be cautious to undertake.[18]

In the aftermath of the 1997 elections, Mark arap Too was nominated by KANU as an MP and Assistant Minister in the Office of the President. It was obvious that KANU had a slim majority in parliament. KANU had a total of 107 seats compared to the combined opposition of 103. However, that slim majority could not be counted on at all times as some MPs like Kipruto arap Kirwa; Jimmy Angwenyi; John Sambu; Wycliffe Osundwa and Cyrus Jirongo, were being dubbed as KANU rebels.[19] Too realised that KANU rebels, with the combined opposition, could easily defeat government bills in parliament. This bothered him.

Rather than negotiate with a few KANU rebels, Too claimed he proposed to Moi that it would be better to build working relationships with some of the opposition parties. He invited FORD-Kenya's Wamalwa to meet President Moi, [20] as Chesire had invited Raila.

Joe Donde, (a relatively new politician who won the Gem parliamentary seat and became the main Luo in FORD-Kenya and its Vice-Chairman), accompanied Wamalwa to one of the meetings with President Moi.[21] Wamalwa and Donde were convinced that an alliance with KANU was the only way for a cash-strapped

---

[18] On accounts about his exploits both internationally and locally and with respect to the KANU-NDP relationship as well as his removal from office, see, *Sunday Standard,* September 23, 2001, pp. 10-11 and *Daily Nation,* August 12, 2002, pp. 1-2.

[19] Much of the information here comes from extensive interviews with Mark Too, Nairobi, April 10 and 14, 2003.

[20] Wamalwa's biographer actually stated that Wamalwa's effort to have a relationship with KANU started immediately after the 1997 General Elections when he was the first opposition leader to concede defeat to President Moi. See, Bob Wekesa, op.cit., pp. 144-145.

[21] Interview with Joe Donde, Nairobi, August 25, 2003

party which had lost many members. But progress towards cooperation far less a merger, failed as grassroots party members opposed any relationship with KANU. According to Donde, Wamalwa was constantly insulted by party members and it became clear that an alliance with KANU was not the way out.

But Raila received the support of his party members. This was not easy. Many, including members of his family, were against an alliance with KANU. Both Ida and Rosemary Odinga remember that the entire family was against it. Rosemary, arranged a conference call involving her two brothers and their father, in which all the children differed with Raila on trying to work with KANU.[22] But Raila insisted that in time, they would see that his position was the right one.

Opposition party members were livid. They called Raila all sorts of names. He was accused of betrayal. But Raila remained undaunted. He was convinced that KANU, as a parliamentary party, was much weakened in comparison to its position in 1993. He decided that the opposition should take advantage of a weakened KANU by exerting pressure through constructive engagement to receive maximum concessions. The main concession was clear to Raila: a constitutional review.

Thus, Raila began to work with KANU, ostensibly in the interest of Kenya. This involved consultations on government and private members' bills even before they were brought to the floor of the Parliament. To some extent there was cooperation. But, as Mark Too noted, sometimes, "KANU brought motions that were not satisfactory to the NDP. In those instances, Raila asked the NDP parliamentary members to vote with their consciences."[23] For Raila, getting KANU to accept fundamental change was more important than working out Government bills.[24]

---

[22] Interview with Rosemary Odinga, July 20, 2003. Strong party members like Oloo Aringo and Shem Ochuodho remained in the party but were critical. The Deputy Chairman, Geoffrey Ole Maloiy, claimed that he could not accept cooperation with KANU and he resigned. However Raila, in an interview informed the author that the Deputy Chairman's reason for leaving had to do with what he termed the inability of the party to pamper to his desires. Raila pointed out several subsequent appearances at the State House by Prof. Geoffrey ole Maloiy and his subsequent appointment as Chairman of Museums by the same KANU government he had indicated he would not cooperate with.

[23] Interview with Too, *op. cit.*.

[24] This is indicative from Raila's speech in Reru, Kisumu Rural constituency as reported in *The Standard,* October 20, 1998, pp. 1-2.

On their part, the NDP leadership, assumed that President Moi had no chance of running for the Presidency in 2002. They concluded that joining the large party, KANU would make it possible for the NDP leader to have a good chance of standing for President. It was obvious that no single ethnic community could win. So better to have the support of the large coalition of smaller ethnic groups in Moi's camp.[25]

Aside from the benefits that Mark Too and Moi could see from NDP/KANU co-operation, other KANU leaders supported what was seen as an attempt by the President to bring all the major ethnic groups into KANU and so reduce the politicisation of ethnicity in Kenya.[26] The question, however, was whether this was a new phenomenon in Kenyan politics. After all, KANU when it joined KADU in 1964 contained all the ethnic groups. That de facto one party system did not preclude other parties from being formed. Indeed the KPU, as noted earlier, operated for three years as the politicisation of ethnicity continued.

The numbers game was also clear. Jonah Bett summarized the thinking in the higher echelons of KANU thus: "KANU at that time was bigger than all other parties. But if the others came together, the chances of KANU winning would be very slim. It was a question of reaching out to other parties to ensure a landslide victory."[27] Winning the 2002 General Elections was in KANU minds as much as in Raila's NDP.

The relationship between KANU and the NDP deepened with Orengo's attempt to constitutionally remove President Moi from office. Early in the eighth Parliament, in October 1998, Orengo sponsored a motion of no confidence in the Moi Administration. The entire opposition and 4 KANU MPs backed the Orengo motion as NDP, with the exception of Oloo Aringo and Shem Ochuodho, voted with the rest of KANU to defeat it.

---

[25] Interview with Otieno Kajwang', Nairobi, April 11, 2003

[26] April 16, 2003 interview in Nairobi with Mohamed Abdi Affey, former MP for Wajir South and former Assistant Minister for Foreign Affairs who served as Joint Secretary (with Sospeter Ojamong) for the 17-man Merger Committee that was made up of politicians and chaired by Dr. Njoroge Mungai.

[27] Interview with Jonah Bett, Nairobi, 18 June 2003.

The rest of the opposition saw the NDP's act as a sell-out by Raila. Raila rationalized the NDP action by arguing that it was ironic that the Democratic Party which had refused to support an NDP candidate for the post of Deputy Speaker in the 8th Parliament could be crying foul. It was insincere for the DP, already holding leadership of the Official Opposition and its Chief Whip, to field a candidate against the NDP's. He questioned how the DP could now speak of opposition unity in a gang up against KANU.

He also suggested that Orengo's motion was actually directed against the NDP, claiming that some forces intent on blocking NDP from power, wanted to force early fresh elections, knowing that NDP did not have the resources for this. Their idea was to reverse NDP's relative success in the 1997 General Elections. Raila opined: "They knew that they have the resources to finance their campaigns had Parliament been dissolved."[28] He continued to maintain that "the move would have been suicidal for the NDP."[29]

Raila denied the suggestion by Orengo that NDP MPs had been bribed by KANU. He argued that NDP and KANU voted the same way although their interests in so voting differed, and that the NDP position was in line with the emphasis on dialogue among political parties in Kenya.

However, whatever the intention of the NDP leadership, according to Too, Moi really appreciated NDP's assistance to defeat a motion which, if it had succeeded, would have seriously embarrassed President Moi. This event sealed the relationship being built by Too, and the cooperation strengthened. As a result, NDP was given a number of ministerial positions in June 2001. Raila was made Minister of Energy; Adhu Awiti became Minister of Planning; Peter Ochieng Odoyo, Assistant Minister for Foreign Affairs; and Joshua Orwa Ojodeh became Assistant Minister for Education.

Beginning of a New Game

The removal of Mark Too from his Assistant Ministerial post, signalled a new game plan in President Moi's strategy. Too claimed he was removed because

---

[28] *The Standard,* October 20, 1998, p. 2.
[29] Interview with Raila, May 9, 2004.

having secured the relationship with the NDP, he was expendable.[30] He felt that some powers within KANU knew that President Moi was not serious about the merger, merely wanting to use and then dump Raila. These forces were worried about Too's close relationship with Raila and suspected that he was bound to reveal private thinking in KANU to Raila.

Too's suspicions began when Raila was asked to see President Moi without him. When Too was asked to bring Uhuru Kenyatta, son of the first President of Kenya and Chairman of the Kenya Tourist Board, to dine with Moi, little did he know that he was sealing his fate. Too and Uhuru accompanied Moi to Siaya without Too knowing that Uhuru had been earmarked to replace Too as a KANU nominated MP. Kenyatta's "sponsors" were William Ruto (whom Too claimed he had helped to bring close to President Moi),[31] Joshua Kulei Moi's closest Presidential aide, Hosea Kiplagat and Gideon Moi. Ceasing being an MP automatically meant removal as Assistant Minister. According to Too, the quartet joined hands to show him the door, arguing that they needed space for Uhuru.[32] He claimed that he was forced to write a resignation letter to the Speaker. Too, well aware of the Nyayo House torture chamber, feared that if he did not resign as instructed, he could find himself in trouble.

It is unnecessary to look for other reasons for Too's removal: the pedigree of his successor and subsequent events prove his case. Uhuru had remained in KANU when the Kikuyu mainstream left the party. He tried and failed to win the Gatundu Parliamentary seat in the 1997 elections. But he remained as Chairman of the Thika branch of KANU.

Moi, having pocketed the Luo, as he thought, now started on a strategy to lure the Kikuyu back to KANU. He calculated that Uhuru Kenyatta would be his best entry point. He believed that the Kikuyu elite would look forward to the good old days of unbridled bleeding of the Kenyan State, but now under the young Kenyatta. The Kikuyu people, (even those who stood to benefit nothing beyond the ethnic satisfaction that one of their own was in State House), would be excited about

---

[30] For this reason that Too gave at the interview with the author and other speculations on why Too was removed, see, *Sunday Standard,* September 23, 2001, pp. 10-11.

[31] See, ibid.

[32] Interview with Mark Too, April 14, 2003

young Uhuru returning them to power in 2002. Moi figured that the inexperienced young man would have to depend on the grand old master of politics, to keep abreast of Kenyan political realities. With overwhelming Kikuyu support and Moi's coalition of smaller ethnic groups, the Luos in their entirety, could be dispensed with if they chose to leave. If they stayed, so much the better for Moi.

A puppet President combined with his party chairman's hold on KANU would give Moi the apparatus to control the Kenyan State for a while. He had seen the late Julius Nyerere play this game in Tanzania. But he appeared to delude himself that he was as popular in Kenya as Nyerere in retirement was in Tanzania.

But perhaps more important in Moi's plans was his expectation that as a *quid pro quo* Uhuru Kenyatta would protect him. Moi had raised no queries over the Kenyatta family's acquisitions when he succeeded Jomo Kenyatta. Kenyatta was born poor but at his death, his family had "vast holdings in farming, ranching, gemstones, hotels, movies, advertising, insurance, pipelines, casinos, commodity trading, timber, ivory, and the export-import business."[33] Moi himself knew well about the acquisition of such vast wealth and would not want an Uhuru Kenyatta presidency investigating the holdings of the Mois and their hangers-on.

To bring Uhuru into the fold, Mark Too's nominated parliamentary seat was needed.[34] The entry of Uhuru into Parliament and Cabinet as Minister for Local Government, was combined with a restructuring of KANU that produced cosmetic changes rather than the fundamental ones hoped for by Raila. But Raila stayed on and bargained for the post of KANU Secretary-General. Uhuru Kenyatta and three others were earmarked to vie for the four posts of Vice-Chairmen. It was still necessary to maintain the idea of four possible choices for the presidency, thus giving hope to other ethnic elites, and through them their constituencies that their kin could become President.

---

[33] Smith Hempstone, *Rogue Ambassador: An African Memoir* (Sewanee: University of the South 1997), p. 34.

[34] There were also rumours of some business fall out between President Moi and Mark Too. It was not possible to interview President Moi in spite of many requests, including in writing.

Merger Negotiation

After several delays, Moi made it clear that he would prefer a full merger between Raila's NDP and KANU. Raila took this opportunity to ask for changes in the structure of KANU, to create a "new KANU." A four-man committee was set up to draft a new manifesto, a flag and a new motto.

This committee comprised: Prof. Henry Mwanzi; Jonah Bett and Joseph Kibati from KANU and Rateng Oginga Ogego from NDP. Although the top leaders of both parties had agreed the rationale for the merger, the committee faced a major problem of choosing a name for the merged parties. KANU wished to retain its name, but NDP, not wanting to be seen as having been "swallowed," wanted a distinctly new name reflecting the merger of two differing entities.

The KANU side argued that a new name would be difficult to sell in an election year. Besides, there was the general worry of registering a new party in Kenya. And even if the new party was registered, KANU argued that some electoral conditions set time limits before such a party could take part in elections. It was unclear whether there was enough time to meet all such conditions. Moreover, as Rateng pointed out, while the NDP as a parliamentary party could be adopted by another party in parliament, KANU as the ruling party would have a different problem. KANU had fought elections in 1997 under its registered name, and its status as the ruling party could raise legal implications which would be best avoided.[35]

The NDP reluctantly accepted the name of KANU and its symbol: *Jogoo* (the Cockerel) but wanted the name KANU modified to read: "New KANU." The argument of the KANU side that this would amount to a change of name was accepted with a compromise proviso that the word "new" would be added to all slogans, the manifesto and fliers of the post-merger party, while KANU would remain the name of the merged parties in every legal document.[36]

---

[35] Discussion with Rateng Oginga Ogego on June 23, 2003.

[36] Though other sources, including Rateng Oginga Ogego, the NDP point man on the merger, were consulted, much of the account in this section depended on an interview with Jonah Bett, Nairobi, June 18, 2003.

The structure of the new KANU was contentious. The higher echelons of the two parties were suspicious of each other, and worried about how they would fare as individuals in a new arrangement. They saw that only Moi and Raila were being briefed by the four-man committee. So, they used KANU's National Executive Committee to protest that non-politicians were designing a political merger. This acrimony led to the setting up of a seventeen-man committee, chaired by Dr. Njoroge Mungai, a former Foreign Minister and a member of KANU, and with a joint secretaryship of KANU's Mohamed Abdi Affey and NDP's Sospeter Ojamong. This also served Raila's purpose since it was now impossible to accuse him of being in a lone Moi-Raila merger. The NDP made Dr. Oburu Oginga point man, for NDP in the committee.

According to Affey, the KANU side, trying to shore up the falling stock of Vice-President Saitoti, sought guidance from Moi on what role he had in mind for Raila. They noted that Raila was poised to become the KANU Vice-Chairman, which could automatically make him Moi's successor. With the merger, they expected Raila to become Vice-Chairman of the new party. President Moi said that he wanted to use Raila to stabilize his government. To address their fears, he asked them to work for abolition of the Vice-Chairman post and replace it with four non-hierarchical Vice-Chairmen.[37]

This position was put to the more effective four-man committee using the argument that all Kenyan provinces would thus have a senior politician in the highest echelon of the new party. The four-man committee agreed that it was essential to the major ethnic groups to see one of their own as a leader and a possible presidential candidate. The posts of Chairman, Secretary, Treasurer and Organizing Secretary were already in existence. The four-man committee, created the four Vice-Chairmen slots. But to accommodate more leaders, the positions of Director of Elections and Secretaries for major activities were borrowed from the NDP constitution. Thus they created Secretaries for: Foreign Affairs; Information; Legal Affairs; Environment; Gender etc.

Moi and Raila considered and commented on the four-man committee's constitutional draft. They then produced an improved version. This was sent to the seventeen-man committee which having failed to produce any document, rubber-stamped it. Committees of the two parties also examined the draft.

---

[37] Discussion with Mohamed Abdi Affey, July 20, 2004.

The four-man committee also produced the manifesto for new KANU. According to Jonah Bett, however, time constraints prevented the manifesto from going through the same thorough approval processes, and it was not presented at what was later dubbed the "Kasarani I" delegates merger meeting. The merger was agreed on March 18, 2002, when the NDP flag was finally lowered and elections into KANU's new offices took place.

At Kasarani I, delegates were to vote for appointments to all the posts created under the new party constitution, with the exception of that of Chairman which everyone knew was Moi's. Raila decided against standing for Vice-Chairman, opting to go for Secretary-General which pitted him against the long time Secretary-General of KANU, John Joseph Kamotho. Kamotho had a simple legalistic argument: "A merger between NDP and KANU had no constitutional or legal backing on the strength of the constitutions of the two parties. If NDP wanted a merger with KANU as a bigger party, then NDP should dissolve and then join KANU."[38]

Although Kamotho knew that the KANU list of delegates for the merger at Kasarani (NDP brought its own delegates) had been manipulated, he put in a last minute pitch. On the morning of March 18, he had breakfast in State House with President Moi and Vice-President Saitoti. At a one-on-one meeting with the President he argued for democracy to the effect that a free and fair election in a secret ballot would be the best approach, despite the other irregularities. The President said that the delegates should decide if they wanted secret balloting. Kamotho claims that he knew he was being deceived and that on the previous night, every move had been choreographed with Joab Omino as Master of Ceremonies, to reject any proposal which could undermine the stage-managed elections of the agreed candidates.[39]

Kamotho was wrong to have thought he could change the veteran's grand plan which was larger than persons. Despite the constant public assertion of the interests of KANU and Kenya, this was the strategy for the survival of President Moi and

---

[38] Interview with JJ Kamotho, December 9, 2003.

[39] *Ibid.* Saitoti, during the referendum campaign seemed to back Kamotho's position. However a scheduled interview with Joab Omino could not take place before he died. However, Raila, in an interview on May 9, 2004, maintained that there was no such choreographed plan of Moi with Joab Omino. He argued that Kamotho threw in the towel when he saw the odds.

202 RAILA ODINGA: An Enigma in Kenyan Politics

his hangers-on. Mohamed Affey stated that Kamotho was a natural casualty of a power game about who would bring more value to KANU.[40] Rather than retreat and claim to have done so "in the interest of the party," to block the NDP group, Kamotho put forward arguments he believed were based on the KANU constitution. But the die was cast. Kamotho appeared not to see the way the wind was blowing, and was swept aside, withdrawing at the last minute, from a bitter contest to retain his seat as Secretary-General.

Vice-President Saitoti a key ally of Kamotho, continued his downward spiral in KANU and was dealt another humiliating blow. For about 15 months after Moi was re-elected in the 1997 General Elections, he refused to name a Vice-President. Saitoti patiently waited on the side until he was re-appointed on April 2, 1999. Three months later, Otieno Kajwang' moved a private member's motion of no confidence in the Vice-President for his alleged role in the Goldenberg fraud. He survived the vote with difficulty, having rallied support from the Kikuyu-dominated DP as well as KANU and NDP.[41]

Saitoti's star was no longer shining bright in the Moi scheme of things. That he would no longer be the undisputed, lone Vice-Chairman of KANU or even first Vice-Chairman in a new configuration, indicated that he was to be cut down to size. All Vice-Chairmen would be equal. As the Kasarani meeting neared, it was clear that Moi did not even want Saitoti as one of the four Vice-Chairmen. This was serious as there was an unwritten understanding that Moi's successor would be one of the four Vice-Chairmen. By the time the elections were to take place, Saitoti knew that his name would not make the ballot. He withdrew from the race at the convention to sulk with his supporters.

Though there were serious campaigns for the posts of Vice-Chairmen and Secretary-General, it was clear that Raila Odinga had been slotted to become Secretary-General. His decision to stand for Secretary-General removed Nyanza province or Luoland from contention for the Vice-Chairmen posts. Each of the

---

[40] Interview with Mohamed Abdi Affey, Nairobi, July 23, 2003.

[41] Raila, in an interview on April 4, 2004 claimed that Kajwang' like Orengo engaged in a one-man show without consultation with the NDP Parliamentary Group. Though Raila himself had sued Saitoti and others over their alleged role in the Goldenberg scandal, he argued that the problem could not be solved by a vote of no confidence in Parliament on only one person when so many were involved.

Central; Eastern; Western and Coast Provinces would provide the Vice-Chairmen. There was no contention over who would represent Central and Coast Provinces: Uhuru Kenyatta and Katana Ngala. Mudavadi and Cyrus Jirongo engaged in a bitter battle over the post of Vice-Chairman for Western Province before Mudavadi emerged un-opposed after negotiations. In the race for the Eastern slot among Harun Mwau, Joseph Nyagah and Kalonzo Musyoka, Musyoka was eventually made Vice-Chairman.[42]

Restructuring the Secretariat and KANU

Raila knew that past party Secretary-Generals had given little attention to developments at the Secretariat beyond occasional visits to sign press statements or attend meetings of the National Executive Council or Governing Council. The Secretariat was bloated with far too many support staff, such as cleaners and security personnel, who had been hired by successive Secretary-Generals and other officials, to reward their respective ethnic groups. There were no staff terms and conditions or proper administrative structures.

Raila presented a new organizational structure and terms and conditions for staff to the next meeting of the National Executive Council for its approval. This put the Secretariat at the centre of authority by requiring other elected officials to answer to it. Biwott, the Organising Secretary of the Party and a dreaded close ally of President Moi for about four decades, led a number of the President's men who rejected this innovation. But Raila had already received Moi's approval. It was too early in the day for Moi to clearly show Raila that he was planned for the dumping ground.

KANU had acquired the imposing Kenyatta International Conference Centre (KICC) during Kenyatta's regime,[43] and each month was collecting about 9 million shillings in rent. From this a 2 million was used each month for staff remuneration without any account for the balance from the President's Office. Raila did not question this and the President's men continued to spend the rent balance as they wished.

---

[42] Kalonzo Musyoka, in an interview with the author on March 13, 2004 thought Raila Odinga was involved in clouding President Moi's perception on backing him from the very beginning, as the undisputed Vice-Chairman for the Eastern Province.

[43] The ownership of KICC was subjudice at the time of writing.

Raila created an Executive Office of the Secretary-General to which he brought his hard-working, self-effacing Secretary of many years, Susan Kibathi; Rateng Oginga Ogego, a former student leader, who had spent years in jail after the 1982 coup and who was at that that time, a die-hard Raila loyalist; John Kiema who was Executive Officer at NDP; and two elected party officials: Sospeter Ojaamong, the Deputy Organizing Secretary and Otieno Kajwang', the Legal Secretary. This group, which had come from NDP, assisted Raila to handle problems from party branches. They also introduced the NDP idea of a Newsletter to inform party branches of party activities and positions on key national issues.

As Minister of Energy, Raila could call at party branches during official visits to remote parts of the country which opposition parties could never have accessed in the past. He opened new branches in some places and used these visits to sell the idea of "New KANU," which he assumed President Moi had agreed to. He produced a brochure for the "new" party setting out its vision, aims and objectives, including abhorrence of corruption and friendliness towards investors.

In furtherance of a new look, Raila pushed for a dinner with the business community, diplomats and professionals for the launching of the "new KANU." This event, took place on Friday June 28, 2002. It was followed on the following day, with a visit to the famous Kamukunji ground that had been a familiar territory for the opposition where the police charged at them during the struggle for multi-party democracy. Raila's idea was to take President Moi to the people on the popular grounds for the first time ever. The public was not too friendly to President Moi but welcomed Raila. However, President Moi used the opportunity to inform the crowd and the media that he would soon tell them the way forward on his successor. This again made it further clear to all that President Moi had no intention of allowing free democratic contest over his successor.

Moi and Raila had guided KANU and the NDP to the merger which included cosmetic changes to the leadership, and saw a delegates conference which ratified the changes and elected new leaders by acclamation. Although Raila would argue that there was provision for secret ballot if needed, this event represented one of the major ironies of Raila as a democrat. He was part of the decision by President Moi and his handlers that the election of Party officials at Kasarani I, would be by acclamation rather than the secret ballot that Joseph Kamotho, Raila's adversary, was pushing for. Acclamation was allowed under KANU's constitution. But it was clear that such a mob could not provide free choice. Raila opposed acclamation for the "Kasarani II" vote for a successor to Moi, when it became clear that Moi planned to impose Uhuru Kenyatta to attract the large Kikuyu vote.

Even when it became clear that he could not keep the Luo, if he continued his Uhuru Kenyatta "project," Moi was adamant that the Kikuyus were more valuable than the Luos whose votes he was ready to sacrifice. He must have reasoned that KANU would keep its coalition of minority ethnic groups and top it up with sizeable Kikuyu votes to ensure that KANU performed much better than 1997. This calculation also rested on the thinking that opposition presidential candidate, supported by their ethnic constituency, would each go their different ways in 2002.

What looked like a formidable alliance between KANU and NDP scared opposition leaders like Kibaki, Ngilu, Wamalwa, Anyang' and Nyachae among others into a frenzied search for opposition unity. As plan to dump Raila and other Vice-Chairmen progressed, a rebel alliance, led by Raila, started to emerge in KANU, and was later to change the face of politics in Kenya.

Chapter 15
The Rainbow Alliance

President Moi underestimated Raila by thinking that the dissolution of the NDP had turned Raila into a Lion in a cage that could roar but not kill.

Mark Kiptarbei arap Too, Interview, Nairobi, April 14, 2003

The political fortunes of KANU took a long time to wane and by the time elections were called in December, 2002, the stage had been set for a defeat, largely because of the party's negative image in the eyes of many Kenyans. The background to this was multifaceted and related to increased poverty and unemployment; endemic corruption; abuse of human rights; relationships with development partners and the media; the infamous 1992 tribal clashes; and finally KANU's self-inflicted damage. Over a long period, these factors tainted KANU's image in the minds of Kenyans. Despite the advent of multiparty democracy in 1992, the party failed to change with the times, and continued with its one party mentality against a background of rapid social and political change.

KANU, "Report of the task force on the Re-Organisation of the Kenya African National Union," 28th February 2003, p. 7.

KANU "decided to disregard its constitution by not conducting grassroots and national elections for many years, in the process endangering internal democracy, which resulted in a botched nomination process that alienated the party's rank and file."

Musalia Mudavadi, during an interview by Fred Oluoch, *The East African*, NO. 454, July 14-20, 2003, p. 8.

The KANU-NDP merger was a formidable bloc on the Kenyan electoral stage. Had they agreed it, Moi could easily have been President for life. But global pressure and in a multi-party Kenya, dictated that he had to leave power as agreed in 1992 when the constitutional amendments provided the President a maximum of two five year terms. The merger produced, was of concern to other opposition leaders.

These opposition leaders were not going to sit back and let Moi change the constitution to stay on in power. While Moi saw that he could not alter the constitution and be comfortable in power, he failed to recognize that a lame duck President does not wield power as he did when he came into office. He played games with his lieutenants and led each of them to feel that he would be the anointed successor. When he named Uhuru, as his successor, Raila went up in arms. Although Moi had reportedly promised Luo Elders that Raila would succeed him,[1] Raila was more interested in being Prime Minister in a restructured system. While he might have accepted other presidential candidates, he thought Uhuru was too inexperienced and a Moi ploy to rule from behind. He opposed the annointment and pulled many other leaders who had suffered in silence out of KANU with him to form what became known as the Rainbow Alliance.

Opposition Attempts to Counter the "new" KANU

Raila's cooperation, collaboration, partnership and eventual merger (names for different stages) with KANU, scared the opposition badly. It was clear that a divided opposition would have no chance against the formidable build-up that Moi's "new KANU" had achieved, by adding the votes of most Luos to his normal support among other Kenyans who were neither Kikuyu nor Luo. The frenzy led to serious discussions among various small parties and pressure groups. In effect, Raila could be said to have inadvertently strengthened the opposition's drive towards unity.

One such move for opposition unity came from Simeon Nyachae. Nyachae, who was born in 1932 to the late Senior Chief Musa Nyandusi, retired from the civil service after a thirty three year career in which he had moved through all the levels of the Provincial Administration system from District Clerk through to Provincial Commissioner before becoming Permanent Secretary and finally Chief Secretary, Head of the Public Service and Secretary to the Cabinet. He became a politician in 1992 when he gave up his powerful position to contest the Nyaribari Chache Constituency in Parliament for KANU. He was a strong Moi loyalist until February 1999 when he resigned from the Cabinet. At the time, it was thought that Nyachae resigned because he felt humiliated by being moved from the higher profile Ministry of Finance to Industry.

---

[1] President Moi insisted he never promised anyone the presidency.

However, Nyachae argued that being moved from one Ministry to another was not an issue.[2] He recollected that in 1992 he had been appointed Minister for Agriculture. This was a very prominent post. Then for a by-election in Kisii (Kitutu Chache), he differed with President Moi on the choice of candidate to represent KANU, and won. Moi was not happy. He redeployed Nyachae from Agriculture to the less important Ministry of Water Development. Nyachae took his new post in his stride.

But a similar cabinet reshuffle in 1999 did not get the same reaction from Nyachae, who by then was having fundamental differences with the Moi Administration. These, according to Nyachae, included:

1.   Doubtful pending bills that Nyachae felt should be investigated. The President was unhappy with Nyachae's stance.
2.   Some cloudy issues of procurement.
3.   The negative reaction of colleagues to his decision to implement the terms of the budget which would include reducing the number of ministerial cars, and limiting their engine capacity to no more than 2000 cc.

The last issue, for Nyachae, was aimed at reducing the level of domestic debt to balance the budget. But pressure grew on Moi to remove Nyachae who also felt the President was unhappy with his avowed intention to deal with corrupt contractors.[3]

President Moi's moving Nyachae from the Ministry of Finance, could be interpreted in two ways. Either he wanted a more agreeable person in the crucial Ministry, or he wanted Nyachae in a different Ministry because he had picked up the rancour at the Ministry of Finance which was pushing Nyachae to resign. Moi, by making this move thought that Nyachae, whom he knew KANU needed for the next election, would not resign.[4] But Nyachae could not stay on, feeling he had lost cooperation from colleagues and the President. He left the cabinet, moved to the KANU back bench in Parliament, and became lukewarm about the party itself.

---

[2]   Interview with Simeon Nyachae, Nairobi, September 1, 2003.
[3]   These accounts were based on interview with Simeon Nyachae, *ibid.*
[4]   Simeon Nyachae in *ibid.*, proffered the latter explanation.

As the 2002 elections approached, Nyachae decided to play an active role with the aim of leading Kenya. He prepared a paper titled: "Government of National Unity," which he shared with other politicians as the way forward. At the time, the move was underway to bring together those opposed to KANU.

Charity Ngilu, leader of the National Party of Kenya, who was a friend of Nyachae's wife, used to visit the couple's home and sought advice, as she was having problems in SDP before setting up her own party. In Parliament, she invited Nyachae to a meeting over tea with Kibaki, Wamalwa and herself. Nyachae insisted on knowing what would be discussed so that he could brief his colleagues.

After consulting his colleagues, Nyachae decided to meet the trio individually. At Nyachae's house Ngilu briefed him on the need for opposition unity, and suggested that Nyachae should meet Kibaki who knew more. Nyachae invited Kibaki to lunch and after two hours of intensive discussion, they agreed to pursue how to work together.

Two weeks later, Wamalwa asked to visit Nyachae for breakfast. At the meeting, Nyachae put the idea of working together to Wamalwa, who said he would first need to consult Luhya Elders.

According to Nyachae, without further discussions from any of Ngilu, Kibaki or Wamalwa, he was invited to a breakfast meeting at a Nairobi hotel. Concerned that he had reached individual accords for further discussions and none had taken place, he asked for the agenda of the meeting, and received none. So he stayed away.

As his relationship with KANU continued to deteriorate, Nyachae decided not to resign his party membership until just before the 2002 elections when he joined FORD-People. Apart from losing his parliamentary seat if resigned from KANU, Nyachae had decided not to rush but to plan carefully what needed to be done to bring an end to corruption; and ensure transparency and delivery of services to the people. To execute such a plan required a political forum. During consultations with friends and colleagues about finding answers to KANU's problems, they decided to take over a moribund FORD-People, then in the hands of Nyoike wa Kimani.

National Alliance Party of Kenya

What started with breakfast meetings of Mwai Kibaki, Charity Ngilu and Michael Wamalwa, was initially called the National Alliance for Change (NAC).[5] According to Willy Mutunga, one of the memoranda of understanding signed by the NAC stipulated an "undertaking by the leadership and the member organizations that they will be bound by the electoral pacts, the nominations, the sharing of power and the programmes of recovery once democratically agreed upon by the NAC Council."[6] The Council was made up of the leadership plus four representatives from each member organization. Over time, the NAC attracted several others. Very quickly, the number of groups and/or parties interested in forming a single party to contest the 2002 Elections grew to fourteen. They were: Democratic Party; National Party of Kenya; FORD-Kenya; Social Democratic Party; FORD-Asili; United Democratic Movement; Social Party for the Advancement of Reforms in Kenya; Saba Saba Asili, Mass Party of Kenya; National Convention Executive Council; Federal Party; Kenda; PPF; Mazingira Green Party of Kenya.

Over a year, the consultations among the fourteen parties went beyond breakfast meetings at Nairobi hotels as the NAC changed its name into a derivative from the manipulation of Charity Ngilu's NPK, to the National Alliance Party of Kenya (NAK).[7] KANU had thought that opposition unity would collapse under the individual ambitions of the main players in NAK. But after further deliberations and behind the scene consultations, a nomination panel was set up to vet candidates applying for the main posts in NAK and come up with a short list. The panel of eight had businessman Wanjala Welime as its chairman and Ms. Wambui Kimathi of the United Democratic Movement as his deputy. Others were: Osingo Migure of the Social Party for the Advancement of Reforms in Kenya (SPARK); David Mutiso, a member of the National Party of Kenya; Alex Muriithi of the Democratic Party; Ms. Mercy Kanyara of the FORD Asili; Peter Kubebea of the Labour Party of Kenya and Ms. Njoki Ndung'u of the Social Democratic Party.

---

[5] For an account on this and formation of alliances in general, see, Willy Mutunga, "The Unfolding Political Alliances and their Implications for Kenya's Transition," in Mute, Kioka and Akivaga, eds., *Building on Open Society: The Politics of Transition in Kenya* (Nairobi: Claripress, 2002), pp. 60-97.

[6] *Ibid.,* p. 93.

[7] Apparently there was a concern as the name National Alliance for Change had been used and there was the risk that NAC may, as a result, not be registered.

On September 18, 2002, at Ufungamano Hall, the result of the nomination process on the major posts, was announced. Mwai Kibaki, the leader of the Democratic Party who had been rumoured as the main candidate for the presidential race, was announced as the flag bearer for NAK. Michael Kijana Wamalwa, the leader of FORD-Kenya was named as his running mate and Mrs. Charity Ngilu, leader of the National Party of Kenya was offered the non-existent post of Prime Minister to be created under a new constitution.

KANU's Failed Nomination Process and Raila's Creation of Rainbow Alliance

As the NAK group worried about how to respond to what appeared to be a formidable new KANU, the drama between President Moi and Raila in KANU began. The main plot centred on the question of who would be KANU's presidential candidate and hence the almost certain successor to Moi as President.

From day one, Raila doubted Moi's sincerity in their new relationship, ostensibly for the betterment of Kenya. He had his own plan, should Moi start to play his usual "use and dump" game. According to Raila:

> Only a fool will go into this kind of arrangement without a plan B aimed at preventing being "used and dumped." To allow oneself to be uprooted from one's roots and popular support as well as compromise on one's principles is to be hanging in the air. Anyone hanging in the air could be easily used and dumped.[8]

Two incidents within two days of the merger between the NDP and KANU put Raila on his guard. Raila had wanted to make a speech at the March 18, 2002 merger. He knew that his supporters were emotionally distressed about losing their party, and wanted to assuage their feelings. He prepared an elaborate speech that traced the historical achievements of the NDP and why the merger at the Kasarani stadium was necessary for a brighter future for Kenya. He wanted to convince them that the merger was not an end but a means to a greater end for Kenya.

---

[8] Interview with Raila, November 26, 2003.

Raila sought Moi's permission to make the speech just before the dissolution of NDP. But the President refused, saying that he would be the only speaker.

Joab Omino and Kalonzo Musyoka, the Masters of Ceremonies, knew that they were not to call Raila to speak. The NDP flag was lowered and elections into KANU offices followed. Resolutions were passed, Raila as the new Secretary-General of KANU was called to read them, and by default, got his chance to defy Moi. He read his speech. But this incident confirmed his worst fears that Moi would stop consulting him and would dictate terms as soon as he got control.

The second incident was on the same day. He left Kasarani stadium and went straight to the Kenyatta International Conference Centre (KICC, then KANU's party Headquarters). He looked around without touching anything. He decided he must start to heal the wounds and acrimony with John Joseph Kamotho, the former Secretary-General who had opposed his appointment. He went to Kamotho's Ministerial Office, shook hands and suggested that Kamotho formally handed over to him. Kamotho appreciated this gesture and agreed.[9] Kamotho had decided to cut his losses and put power struggle in KANU behind him to prevent their respective supporters from reading the problem as ethnic.[10]

On March 19, Kamotho took Raila through the KANU offices and formally handed over the office of the Secretary-General. As Raila settled down to work, he learnt from Peter Gichumbi, KANU's Executive Director who had been at the party Secretariat since the time of Jaramogi, that William Samoei Ruto, had preceded him to the party Headquarters.

Ruto an ambitious young Kalenjin had received a Bachelors of Science degree from the University of Nairobi in 1990. He came into the limelight under the Youth for KANU'92 lobby group in the 1992 election when he was executive officer/operations manager with Cyrus Jirongo as chairman. They both reportedly acquired a lot of wealth along the way and defeated seasoned politicians in the 1997 General Elections. William Ruto became the MP for Eldoret North and Jirongo captured Lugari. William Ruto became close to Moi and became one of his blue-eyed boys. He was made Director of Elections at the KANU-NDP merger.

---

[9] Interview with J.J. Kamotho, December 9, 2003.
[10] Kamotho's personal explanation during the interview of December 9, on why he willingly agreed to Raila's request.

Ruto went from Kasarani to party Headquarters and directed Gichumbi where the offices of all KANU leaders would be. He instructed him that two offices should be merged for Ruto's use and carelessly told Gichumbi that he and Uhuru would call the shots at Party Headquarters. Gichumbi dutifully reported Ruto's every move to Raila, the new Secretary-General, whose father had sent Gichumbi to Moscow for training in Party Organisation many decades earlier.[11]

Ruto, in his youthful exuberance, had inadvertently spilt the beans. Thus Raila was on his guard from day one in the emerging power game that ended with President Moi putting Uhuru Kenyatta forward as his successor and presidential candidate.

Undaunted, Raila decided to make best use of his position as Secretary-General to instil new ideas into the party and change it from within. He would not lose any opportunity to popularise himself with Kenyans in remote parts of the country, normally referred to as KANU zones since they were not easily accessible by opposition parties.

Raila's goal in pushing for a merger between the NDP and KANU was to get fundamental constitutional changes which would deconcentrate power at many levels in the furtherance of democracy. The NDP's push for a "new KANU" was meant to signify that the new-look party would be democratic in its decision-making. "We were alive to the realization that to make politics in Kenya worth the salt, we had to move into KANU to make it an instrument of change or move in and destroy it from within."[12]

Uhuru Kenyatta as Moi's Choice of Successor

Prior to the Kamukunji KANU rally of June 29, 2002, Ruto, and Julius Sunkuli, the Assistant Secretary-General of KANU, a Maasai and MP for Kilgoris constituency, had voiced their support for the Uhuru Kenyatta candidacy for president in 2002. They criss-crossed the Rift Valley and Central provinces and used every week-end *Harambee* (a Swahili concept that implied pulling efforts

---

[11] This account is from interview with Raila on November 26, 2003.

[12] *East African Standard,* Thursday, July 17, 2003, p. 2. See also, *Daily Nation,* November 11, 2002.

together for the execution of community projects or support for individual efforts) to express support for Uhuru.

Where Moi stood on this early campaign for Uhuru was not clear. Raila and others assumed that President Moi would make his stand clear at Kamukunji. But he did not.[13]

It was claimed that Moi invited all Vice-Chairmen and the Secretary-General to State House on July 5, 2002 and urged them all to support Uhuru Kenyatta as the KANU presidential candidate.[14] Raila and Musyoka categorically deny that there such a formal meeting.[15] But the clamour by Ruto and Sunkuli grew louder by the day. Their closeness to Moi, led to a sense that they could be more than testing the waters. In a reaction, a group of 32 KANU MPs, led by Peter Oloo Aringo, veteran politician and MP for Alego constituency in Nyanza province, at a press conference at Parliament buildings on July 9, 2002, denounced any undemocratic imposition of a presidential candidate on the party. They argued for a nomination process conforming to the party constitution[16]

However, Moi took the bull by the horns on July 28, 2002 when he made a statement to the effect that Uhuru Kenyatta would be his successor. He made his position clear when Cyrus Jirongo, the Minister for Rural Development, led a Western Province delegation to meet Moi at Eldoret State Lodge. Before the meeting, Jirongo had informed the delegation that President Moi had told him that Uhuru Kenyatta was his personal choice as successor. Confirming the Jirongo story, Moi reportedly told the delegation that Uhuru's nomination was sealed during the March 18 merger between KANU and the National Development Party. He said:

---

[13] Raila, in an interview on November 26, 2003 claimed that President Moi decided in favour of a later occasion for his announcement, when he saw that the crowd was visibly pro Raila. While President Moi failed to control the unruly crowd, they easily followed the pleas of Raila.

[14] See for instance, C. Odhiambo-Mbai, "The Rise and Fall of the Autocratic State in Kenya," in Walter Oyugi, Peter Wanyande and C. Odhiambo-Mbai, eds., *The Politics of Transition in Kenya: From KANU to NARC* (Nairobi: Heinrich Boll Foundation, 2003), p. 74. See also *East African Standard,* Saturday, January 24, 2004 where the same claim was made without crediting the story to any source but passing it off as if it was from Uhuru Kenyatta.

[15] Interview with Raila on November 26, 2003 and with Kalonzo Musyoka on March 13, 2004.

[16] See, *Daily Nation* and *East African Standard,* Wednesday, July 10, 2002.

I have chosen Uhuru to take over leadership when I leave. This young man Uhuru has been consulting me on leadership matters. I have seen that he is a person who can be guided. If there are others who are chosen, then it will depend on the people.[17]

The Announcement of Rainbow Alliance

Mudavadi who had previously been rumoured as the Presidential front-runner, announced his candidacy on July 27, and was followed on the next day by Raila, during a fund-raising for Changamwe Secondary School in Mombasa. Katana Ngala followed suit in Mombasa on July 30. Kalonzo Musyoka chose the same day as Ngala to put his name forward. George Saitoti did not declare his candidacy until August 14.

Raila, sensing wavering by Saitoti, when he refused to announce his candidacy at Narok on August 4, phoned Saitoti to find out what was going on. They agreed to meet for coffee at the Norfolk Hotel on August 5.

On that day, JJ Kamotho, (who was sacked as Minister of Environment together with Fred Gumo, an Assistant Minister in the Office of the President, for daring to challenge Moi's right to name Uhuru) had visited a besieged Saitoti who was Vice-President in name only, and was soon to join Kamotho on the unemployment list. Kamotho was invited to join the meeting with Raila at the Norfolk.[18]

Raila had decided it was time to pull Saitoti into the open. He asked Herbert O. Ojwang', his Personal Assistant, to alert the press to a major meeting he would be having with Saitoti. Saitoti and Kamotho were shocked to find a battery of pressmen at the Norfolk.

At the closed-door meeting, Saitoti explained that he was not wavering. He expected to be fired as Vice-President when he announced his candidature and to have his passport seized. While he was not worried about being sacked as Vice-President, he needed to travel out of Kenya that evening to be at the bed-side of

---

[17] See, *Daily Nation*, Monday July 29, 2002, p. 3.
[18] Interview with Kamotho, Nairobi, December 9, 2003.

an American who had supported him in going to school and was dying from terminal cancer. This benefactor had asked Saitoti to visit him before he died, and Saitoti did not want to jeopardize this important journey. He promised to announce his candidature as soon as he returned from the trip.

Raila who had expected to make Saitoti declare his candidacy to the press, was persuaded by the human angle of the story. He agreed to the time frame for Saitoti's announcement. However, he now had the problem of what to tell the pressmen who had gathered.

Raila's pressure on his ambitious colleagues to declare their candidacies, was meant to make Moi see the difficulty in insisting on Uhuru as the KANU candidate. Given the experience of earlier elections, especially that in 1997, he had figured out that ethnic groups normally supported one of their own. He thought that each candidate's ethnic bloc could persuade Moi not to risk a KANU election loss. Although Saitoti had good reason not to announce, Raila, without clearing with the others, decided to inform the press of a tendency towards a like-minded alliance in KANU. He borrowed from the Reverend Jesse Jackson of the United States, who had floated the idea of a Rainbow coalition. But as a starter, he chose alliance instead of coalition. He guessed that the idea of coalition would imply different parties in the relationship. But as an alliance, the entity he was proposing, would be a faction within KANU.

The Rainbow Alliance was to be announced after Saitoti's declaration after consultations. But he needed something important to tell the press. He suggested that all three of them should address the press. Saitoti, not wanting to take questions about his possible candidacy, declined and asked Kamotho to represent him.

Raila spoke about the need to strengthen KANU by closing ranks and working under the party constitution. He went further to state that agreement had been reached to form a Rainbow Alliance of all candidates (with the exception of Uhuru) in KANU's run for the presidency. Kamotho was taken aback. But as a shrewd politician, he supported Raila.

The cat was out of the bag. Although Raila had been nursing the idea of an alliance within KANU, he did not know how it would work. He had not consulted, on the spur of the moment he took the initiative. Though the press announced the formation of a Rainbow Alliance within KANU with a bang, Musyoka and

Ngala issued press statements that they knew nothing about the existence of such an alliance.

Raila now needed to rush to explain what had happened in order to prevent the idea of Rainbow Alliance being still-born. He reached Musyoka through Johnstone Muthama, a wealthy business man from Musyoka's ethnic group, who had been the benefactor of Ngilu in the 1997 General Elections. Muthama had left the opposition and joined KANU. Raila explained how he saw the transition process and why Musyoka's support was essential. At a meeting with Musyoka in Muthama's, Raila convinced Musyoka that their survival depended on their working together.

Fred Gumo and a relatively young George Munyasa Khaniri, MP for Hamisi constituency of Vihiga District, persuaded Mudavadi of the need join the Rainbow Alliance. Though Mudavadi was initially reluctant, he agreed.

Muthama hosted the first meeting of the Rainbow Alliance at his house in Nairobi's Spring Valley. A select few were invited. Saitoti who on his return to Kenya, had announced his candidacy at the Jomo Kenyatta International Airport, like other candidates, did not attend the meeting, but was represented by his supporters: Kamotho; William ole Ntimama; and Adams Karauri. Musyoka attended with David Musila and Mutinda Mutiso, while Mudavadi was represented by Moody Awori, Fred Gumo and George Khaniri. Raila took his brother Oburu and Joab Omino.

Katana Ngala had been avoiding Raila as he considered whether he should continue to be associated with the KANU rebels. He eventually told Raila that he did not want a confrontation with Moi who was like a father to him. So, he was conspicuously absent.

After a long deliberation, Raila posed the problem. He asked if it was possible for them to attend the Kasarani II delegates' conference and experience a democratic process that would be acceptable to President Moi if any of the candidates at the meeting was the popular choice. The answer was an obvious no. President Moi had put so much into campaigning for Uhuru Kenyatta. He had advised Mudavadi to look for any post other than the presidency and told Saitoti that he was not presidential material.

Raila summed up that the only choice left was to use all the resources available to popularise the Rainbow Alliance with the aim of moving out of KANU at the appropriate time. Raila had a lot of experience in building movements and parties. They would have to look for a party as they could not expect to be registered before the elections. In the meantime, he suggested a launch on the following day at the Intercontinental Hotel. All the Presidential candidates would announce to the press at the launch that they belonged to the Rainbow Alliance inside KANU, and give assurances that they were ready to back whoever emerged as the candidate of KANU after a transparent and democratic process.

The launch was highly successful. The idea of a Rainbow Alliance took Kenya by storm. Thereafter, a series of countrywide rallies was planned, as President Moi did the same by taking Uhuru Kenyatta round.

At a function at Modogashe in Lagdera constituency, Raila got the North-Eastern MPs to assure him of support for the Rainbow Alliance. However, President Moi upon his return from a visit to South Africa, called all the North-Eastern MPs to State House, Nairobi. He reminded them about how he had stood by them from his early days in politics and threatened to put up candidates against any of them who stood against his decision on Uhuru Kenyatta. A prepared joint statement was issued by the MPs affirming their support for Uhuru Kenyatta.

In Mandera and Wajir Moi introduced Uhuru Kenyatta as the candidate, most qualified to succeed him. Raila decided to challenge Moi head-on. He issued a statement in which he called President Moi the campaign manager for Uhuru Kenyatta, and asked him to disqualify himself from presiding over party functions in the interest of fair-play and party unity. This was daring and many expected him to be fired like Gumo, Kamotho, Khaniri, Odoyo, Saitoti etc. before him.

But the die was cast for Raila who did not care about being sacked, knowing that he could count on his NDP constituency in KANU. After all, Raila and the ex-NDP MPs knew that their return to Parliament depended totally on Raila's hold on the Luo people and not on Moi. Besides, the die was also cast for a number of other politicians who had been subservient in KANU and were suffering in silence.

But Mudavadi, who was in that category, did not show up at the Rainbow Alliance rally at Kapsabet. This raised the suspicions of fellow Rainbow Alliance members. The next rally was to be in Eldoret after the burial of Mzee Adagala in Mudavadi's constituency. But he arrived very late for the burial and avoided the rally. As President Moi was leaving for South Africa the following day for the World Summit on Sustainable Development from 2-4 September, it was no surprise when Mudavadi went to the airport to bid him farewell. His colleagues in Rainbow Alliance were convinced that they had lost him to KANU.

Mudavadi could not withstand the pressure. Moi had had a long cordial relationship with the late Moses Mudavadi, Musalia's father whom young Mudavadi had been handpicked to succeed. He owed his growth in politics to Moi who reminded him of all he had done for him and suggested that his action betrayed the spirit of his father. Pressure from his mother and peers followed as Chahonyo, his friend and financier in previous elections stood against him.

Before publicly returning to mainstream KANU, Mudavadi phoned Raila and told him he was throwing in the towel. He claimed that he would like to use the opportunity to create a middle ground for dialogue in KANU.[19]

Mudavadi's departure had to be addressed if support for the Rainbow Alliance was to be ensured in Western Province. Raila convinced Moody Awori (who had remained an Assistant Minister throughout his service in the Moi administration) to step into Mudavadi's shoes. At the Kakamega rally, Awori declared his candidacy to sustain Luhya interests in the alliance.

The first Rainbow Alliance rally was at Uhuru Park on September 23, 2002. Mungiki, a violent Kikuyu sect that had been declared an illegal organization, had threatened to harm Raila and the Rainbow Alliance if they dared to campaign at Uhuru Park. This sect, appeared to be favoured by the Government. Aside from Raila's own security, William ole Ntimama, a Maasai chieftain and MP, provided Maasai escorts from Narok.

So, Raila, in a counter move to Moi's, wooed other leaders disappointed by Moi's action, to form an alliance initially to pressure the old man of Kenyan politics to retrace his steps and agree to a popular choice of KANU Presidential candidate. But Moi, rather than relent, went on the offensive by firing Kamotho, Gumo, Khaniri and Odoyo from the Cabinet and Saitoti from the Vice-Presidency. These

---

[19] Interview with Raila, December 7, 2003.

leaders, with nothing to lose, had no choice but to work harder with Raila to consolidate the opposition to Moi in KANU.

Katana Ngala and Mudavadi, like prodigal sons, returned to the Moi fold as the rest stuck with Raila. Raila rallied popular support for the Rainbow Alliance by presenting each member in his ethnic backyard as a potential presidential candidate. This style made it impossible to have a candidate in the Rainbow Alliance that all others would have followed with their respective ethnic constituencies.

Chapter 16

The Rainbow Coalition

Raila handed power to Kibaki because he wanted wounds of the past healed for the future. He told us in confidence that we must bring the Luo and Kikuyu as well as other ethnic groups together for a brighter future for Kenya. Without this spirit, the Raila led LDP would have carried the day in the 2002 General Elections. With NAK on its own under the leadership of Kibaki and Uhuru leading KANU, Kikuyus would have had to vote for themselves. LDP would have won with a slim majority in Parliament but this would have been bad for Kenya. If Mudavadi had stayed on with the Rainbow Alliance, he would have been President today.

Phoebe Asiyo, Interview, July 2, 2003

They claim Raila gave power to Kibaki. Who is Raila to give power? Nobody gives power to anybody. The truth was that he did not give but was forced to hand over. His options were bad. He was a jilted lover that broke all the pots before leaving.

Dalmas Otieno, Interview, February 21, 2003

The Rainbow Alliance was a formidable force in the electoral politics leading up to the 2002 Elections. But it was difficult to be certain that KANU would be beaten if the Rainbow Alliance entered the elections without joining hands with Kibaki's NAK.

Compounding the problem of a possible three-way run for the presidency was the fact that both Musyoka and Saitoti would not give up their canditures for the Rainbow Alliance. Even if both resolved the problem and agreed on one of them as the candidate, it was difficult to predict how their personal supporters would react. All the leaders had persuaded their supporters that they would be the Alliance's Presidential candidate.

Given such an uncertain situation, and with the desire to see KANU out of power, the Rainbow Alliance had no choice but to seek additional clout by working for opposition unity. The options were to build a relationship with either Nyachae's FORD-People or the Kibaki's NAK, or build a grand coalition of all three anti-Moi tendencies.

FORD-People's Flirtation with the Rainbow Alliance

Nyachae saw the divisions in KANU over the nomination of Uhuru, as a good opportunity for opposition unity. His wife, Grace contacted Ida (they had been very close friends, Grace having been one of the very few who stood by Ida during her tribulations) and told her that Nyachae would like to meet Raila. At the same time, Chris Bichage a Kisii like Nyachae, who had been with Raila in NDP, told Raila that Nyachae wanted to meet. Nyachae was convinced that the Raila group (now called Rainbow Alliance) was serious about leaving KANU.

He met Raila and Joab Omino at his house. After a general discussion on the political situation, they agreed to appoint two technical persons each, to look into the modalities of working together. This committee was chaired by Joab Omino.

In the meantime, the Rainbow Alliance, the National Alliance Party of Kenya and Nyachae's FORD-People were running separate campaigns. However, they agreed to send representatives to each other's rallies. As the Rainbow Alliance held its Kisumu rally, the National Alliance Party of Kenya had one at Kakamega. Ochieng Mbeo, the East African Parliament legislator, with George Khaniri and Ochillo Ayacko represented Rainbow Alliance in Kakamega, as G.G. Kariuki, Noah Wekesa, Wanguhu Ng'ang'a, Joshua Toro and Joseph Munyao represented the National Alliance Party of Kenya in Kisumu. Nyachae also attended the Kisumu rally to show solidarity with the Rainbow Alliance. This was the first time that the three opposition groups were at the same event.

At the Kisumu rally, Nyachae made a scathing attack on the Moi Government, fuelling the cries of the KANU hawks claiming that the Rainbow Alliance had left KANU. An emergency National Executive Committee meeting was announced by radio and was scheduled for the KICC headquarters on the following day.

Raila suspected that they planned to remove Alliance members from the party on disciplinary grounds. With the meeting scheduled for 9 a.m., Raila went to State House at 6:30 a.m. and met the President whom he asked for the meeting agenda.

Moi replied that it would be on Party Unity and Preparation for Kasarani II. Raila rushed to the KICC to prepare the agenda as stated.

The meeting having been announced on radio, Kenyans suspected that a big event was about to happen. So, many people were milling around KICC as Cabinet Ministers who had gone to State House were going there in a convoy. The crowd jeered and booed the cabinet. Shouts of "Traitors" were heard as Uhuru, Sharrif Nassir, Mudavadi, Ngala and Biwott, entered the building. They were disturbed. The Presidential motorcade was diverted to the Office of the President, next to KICC, and the President walked to KICC unnoticed by the crowd.

At the start, party discipline was raised from the floor, as the issue to be discussed. Raila insisted on following the agenda. But with the approval of President Moi as Chairman, the prepared agenda was set aside. The KANU Secretary-General and his Rainbow Alliance colleagues found themselves before a kangaroo court. The charges were treachery and undermining the party, evidenced by the participation and statements of opposition leaders, especially Nyachae at the Kisumu Rainbow Alliance rally. President Moi said that Rainbow Alliance was now a party and not a KANU faction.

These sentiments were echoed by most of the speakers. Mohamed Abdi Mahamud, MP for Wajir East decided to out-do all others. He drew parallels between 1966, when Jaramogi organized a rebellion against the KANU Government, and what Raila and others were now doing. He said that Raila, like his father, would fail miserably.

Raila stood his ground. He explained in detail why the situation had come to what it was and described the sentiments being expressed as unhelpful to party unity. He was backed by Musyoka, Gumo, Omino and Awori.

The meeting was briefly interrupted when Security officers told the President that the crowd outside was becoming unmanageable. They had begun stoning the police who were firing tear-gas in return. Raila was convinced that this crowd prevented the hawks from passing a vote of no confidence on him and his Rainbow Alliance colleagues.[1]

---

[1] Interview with Raila Odinga, December 7, 2003.

Having survived, Nyachae invited Raila to another meeting at his residence, but without aides on either side. Nyachae said that his FORD-People alliance with Muite's Safina Party and Orengo's SDP, wereto form Kenya People's Coalition which was a fluid relationship and that he wanted to work with the Rainbow Alliance when they quit KANU. He suggested that they should decide which of the two would run for the presidency, with the other as running-mate. If they could not agree, a meeting of Elders from their respective communities, could work it out. Raila agreed in principle to continue to work together, but said that he must consult his colleagues on the details.

Meanwhile, Joab Omino's Committee had drafted a Memorandum of Understanding (MoU) and cleared it with their lawyers. Even an organizational structure for the coalition was specified. Since Rainbow Alliance leaders had begun to discuss acquiring the Liberal Democratic Party they had no hesitation over using the name in the draft MoU.

This MoU was signed at the Serena Hotel on October 14. The media had been invited to politicise the new working accord. An hour later, Nyachae, not knowing that Raila had been consulting the Kibaki group, saw Kibaki arrive with his NAK group at the Serena Hotel. Raila suggested that he and Nyachae should join the new arrivals. Nyachae thought this good for opposition unity and joined. At this meeting, it was clear that another MoU was being negotiated between the Rainbow Alliance (now LDP) and NAK.

Initial contacts with the National Alliance Party of Kenya

Before the Kisumu rally, consultations had started between the Rainbow Alliance and the National Alliance Party of Kenya. This was announced publicly for the first time by Ntimama, on September 7 at a rally in Ngong, Kajiado District. A week later, Wekesa from NAK went further to dub the developing political reality, a super anti-Moi alliance.

In this spirit, Raila and Saitoti lunched with Wamalwa at a restaurant in Valley Arcade on the day before NAK announced its line-up of candidates for the major posts at the Elections. According to Raila, Wamalwa took the position that NAK should delay agreement until the Rainbow Alliance had severed its relationship with KANU.[2]

However, Wamalwa lost the argument, and NAK's line up for the major posts (including those anticipated in a constitutional change) was announced.

Apparently, Mukhisa Kituyi[3] and others in NAK, wanted to accommodate Raila as an individual, because he, unlike others could deliver a formidable number of votes. Although willing to dialogue, Raila knew he would be short-changing himself if he were to sacrifice a major political movement resulting from his acquiring more support from KANU than he had taken to it in the merger. He needed to get beyond the narrow ethnic issue of delivering Luo votes, if he was to make an impact on Kenyan politics. Rather than be courted for a post, Raila supported the efforts of the Rainbow negotiators in dialogue with Nyachae's FORD-People and separately with NAK.

One such negotiation with NAK, took place at the Intercontinental Hotel in Nairobi on Sunday, October 13. Ngilu, G.G. Kariuki, Wekesa and Anyang' represented NAK. Kibaki and Wamalwa were supposed to join later. The Rainbow Alliance wanted to complete all negotiations before their rally at Uhuru Park the next day.

Ngilu was agitated when Kibaki and Wamalwa did not show up. She was convinced that every effort should be made to realize the idea of a super-alliance, if Moi was to be unseated. The meeting was adjourned and reconvened at Joab Omino's residence in the evening, eventually ending at 1 am without the attendance of either Kibaki or Wamalwa.

Though Raila sensed foot dragging by Kibaki and Wamalwa, he agreed that the meeting should continue with Kibaki and Wamalwa at 7 am on 14 October, at the Nairobi Club. It was fixed at that time to ensure an interval before the Rainbow Alliance rally at 11 am.

---

[2] *Ibid.*

[3] This is deduced from interviews with Ling Kituyi and Raila Odinga who remembered the visits of Mukhisa Kituyi to his office in the Ministry of Energy. It was at one of such meetings that the name National Rainbow Coalition was coined as Mukhisa added "National" to Raila's original idea of "Rainbow Coalition."

That morning, Raila was the only one to show up at the Nairobi Club. At the Serena Hotel he learned that Wamalwa had another engagement and would not be available until after the rally. Kibaki too would only be available after a 10 a.m. meeting.

Raila felt that neither Kibaki nor Wamalwa, wanted to reach agreement, and decided to go ahead with his Rainbow Alliance colleagues, and sign the MoU that had been prepared for signature at the Serena Hotel with Simeon Nyachae.

In the MoU with Nyachae, the Rainbow Alliance used their newly acquired party's name, the Liberal Democratic Party (LDP). As noted above, the Alliance had agreed to find a political party as a vehicle for participation in the 2002 Elections. The search led by Ali Mwakwere, produced the inactive Liberal Democratic Party with Dennis Kodhe as its Secretary-General, and his father-in-law as Chairman. LDP also had some Asian members. Ali Mwakwere, a retired diplomat turned politician, was charged by Kalonzo Musyoka to negotiate with the LDP leaders. An unpublished sum was paid and the party changed hands. J.J. Kamotho became the interim Secretary-General. In a departure from the norm in Kenyan parties, the post of party chairman was separated from the presidential candidate. Indeed, presidential candidates were not to hold any party office. Thus, Joab Omino who was not a presidential candidate, became the LDP Chairman. Other officials were: Musila as Vice-Chairman; Ntimama as Treasurer; former flamboyant Mombasa Mayor, Najib Balala, as Secretary for Publicity and Westlands Nairobi MP, Fred Gumo as Organizing Secretary. The October 14 rally at Uhuru Park would mark the public unveiling of the LDP.

Overnight, an LDP Mission Statement was drafted, and a rainbow was chosen as thir logo. The flag and colour were also agreed, and a raised thumb was chosen as the party symbol.

As time was running out, and with KANU planning its delegates' conference, the Rainbow Alliance had to redouble its efforts. The Alliance's leaders had to leave KANU to become part of a formidable alliance. After much prevarication, the Rainbow Alliance leaders announced on October 11, that instead of attending the KANU meeting at Kasarani, they would hold a party rally at Uhuru Park. The circumstances leading to this were interesting.

Uhuru Park instead of Kasarani II

The KANU delegates conference to elect the presidential candidate, was twice postponed, mainly because there was no agreement on the list of delegates.[4] Raila, the KANU Secretary-General had the list used at Kasarani I on March 18. For him, this was the authentic list.

But at party headquarters, Abdi Rotich, (a Kalenjin who had studied in India and was working for President Moi), was said to be working with the Director of Elections to produce a computerised list of delegates, said to be from KANU branches. Raila saw this as an attempt to substitute genuine delegates with branch level cronies who Moi's supporters could be sure would vote for them.

The thought of two lists, reminded Raila of his father's fate at the 1966 Limuru conference, when Jaramogi was voted out of power by delegates believed to have replaced genuine ones. Raila was determined not to have a repeat of the same historical mistake. He knew he must stay away from Kasarani II.

The delegates' conference was set first for October 8, then for October 12th and finally for Monday, October 14. As these changes were taking place, Moi made a last minute effort to woo the Rainbow Alliance leaders back. He summoned them to State House, Nairobi on Thursday October 10. Moi was accompanied by Uhuru Kenyatta; Biwott, KANU's Organising Secretary; and Yusuf Haji the Treasurer. From the Rainbow side were presidential hopefuls Saitoti, who was meeting the President for the first time since being sacked as Vice-President; Raila Odinga; Kalonzo Musyoka; and Moody Awori.

This meeting failed to achieve the President's objective, as the Rainbow Alliance leaders stuck to their guns and argued that a free and fair poll to select the presidential candidate of KANU was a *sine qua non*.

They wanted party hierarchy respected, and deplored a situation where the Secretary-General did not know what was happening at the party Secretariat. They also wanted the list of delegates to the conference, published. Moi made it clear that he would not relent on his choice of Uhuru as the KANU candidate, having reached his decision after serious deliberations.[5]

---
4   Interview with Raila Odinga, December 7, 2003.
5   See, *East African Standard,* Friday, October 11, 2002, pp. 1-2.

The day after meeting Moi, the Rainbow Alliance met in Parliament and decided against going to Kasarani II. They announced this at a press conference at KICC the same day. The Rainbow Alliance opted to meet Kenyans at Uhuru Park on October 14, the day of the KANU delegates' conference.

On October 13, before the Uhuru Park rally, either to show commitment or to move ahead of the rumour that President Moi would dismiss all KANU cabinet rebels before the Kasarani meeting, Raila led three other cabinet ministers out of their offices. However, they promised to hold on to party offices until the Alliance rally at Uhuru Park. Those at the press conference to announce relinquishment of their posts, were: Raila (Energy); Ntimama (Office of the President); Awiti (National Planning); and Awori, (Education Assistant Minister). On this occasion, Raila lashed out:

> We cannot work with an authoritative [sic] and undemocratic government...We
> have decided to resign because, in spite of our efforts to compromise and
> reconcile with the President on how the KANU presidential nominee should be
> elected, this has fallen on deaf ears....We, the three undersigned ministers and
> assistant minister, having been appointed by President Moi, to serve in the
> Government of Kenya, in different portfolios, do hereby tender our resignation
> from the government with immediate effect.[6]

Conspicuously absent were: Musyoka, Minister for Information and Tourism; and Orwa Ojodeh, MP for Ndhiwa and former NDP member in the pre-merger days. For the latter, Raila explained that he had travelled to the countryside and would relinquish his Assistant Education Ministerial post, as soon as he arrived in Nairobi. On Musyoka, Raila explained that he would resign in due course and had missed the press conference as a result of some personal commitments.[7] Musyoka's dilly-dallying was causing concern. Raila knew Musyoka was under pressure from Moi, and was being promised the vice-presidential slot or even the dumping of Uhuru for him.

---

[6] See, *Daily Nation,* Monday, October 14, 2002, pp. 1-2.
[7] *Ibid.,* p. 2.

By explanation, Musyoka said that he had been working to win a contest against Saitoti, for LDP chairmanship.[8] They both thought that whoever had the chairmanship would be the LDP presidential candidate. Saitoti having been fired, could not resign. But by holding out, Musyoka had thought he would receive support for his candidacy, in exchange for his resignation. Whatever might have been the real reason, on the following day he announced his resignation.

By boycotting Kasarani II, the leaders of the Rainbow Alliance were in limbo. They had the choice of transforming themselves into a political party to fight the elections alone, or of entering an alliance with either Nyachae's FORD People or the Kibaki led National Alliance Party of Kenya.

It was a painful choice. Raila was convinced that the Rainbow Alliance could win on its own. But he was realistic enough to recognise that this would be a gamble. Each of the leaders of the Rainbow Alliance was personally confident about his emergence as the Alliance's presidential candidate.[9] In particular, Saitoti, who felt cheated by President Moi in KANU would accept nothing less than being the flag bearer of the Rainbow Alliance. Musyoka who had surprised most Kenyans by not looking back as President Moi used all sorts of tricks to bring him back into the fold felt that his sacrifice and stature in the country was enough to make him the Alliance's presidential candidate. Raila, who had used the relative independence of his old party network in "new KANU" to challenge Moi's plan to impose a candidate on Kenyans, knew that his supporters would be upset if he handed the leadership to one of the Rainbow Alliance leaders, even if he wanted to do so. Even Awori, who had steadfastly supported Mudavadi before he became a turn-coat, also declared an interest in being the flag bearer if only to show the Luhyas that they were not being left out.

By putting the presidential candidacy on the back burner, the Rainbow leaders made a successful tour of Kenya which demonstrated solidarity and unity of purpose everywhere in each ethnic base of the Alliance. The strategy was for each leader to handle issues and events at his constituency or home base. Thus, the Luos, seeing Raila's pre-eminent position at the Kisumu rally, automatically

---

[8] Interview with Kalonzo Musyoka, March13, 2004.
[9] This was the sense of a dialogue on this issue with Raila early December 2002.

assumed that he would be the presidential candidate. The Kamba felt the same when the Alliance train stopped at Machakos and Kitui and Musyoka took charge.

The problem was if a presidential candidate was to be named against a background of acrimony among the leaders; would the ethnic supporters accept a nominee who was not their son? The question was germane to a situation where there was little time left to consult and solidify around a single Alliance candidate.

The Uhuru Park Rally

The park was full by 7 am. It was the biggest crowd that had been seen in years. People had come from all over the country. Even some who had been ferried to Nairobi by KANU, joined the rally.

When Kibaki and Wamalwa could still not be found, Ngilu and G.G. Kariuki, impressed by the crowd, found them and took them to a meeting at the Serena Hotel with Ngilu, Nyachae, Musyoka, Saitoti, Awori and Raila, where the LDP group, announced that they had formed a Rainbow Coalition with FORD-People.

Realizing that it was too late to finalize a deal with NAK, Raila suggested that they should all attend the rally and announce:

1) The transformation of Rainbow Alliance into a formal party and concurrently launch the LDP.
2) The coalition of LDP and FORD-People to be known as the Rainbow Coalition.
3) The intention of Rainbow Coalition to join with NAK to form a super alliance to be known as the National Rainbow Coalition (NARC).[10]

Raila's proposal was agreed. The understanding was that they would all meet again to agree on a single presidential candidate. Nyachae had argued in favour of a clear formula for identifying the candidate. But they were all aware of how the crucial issue of finding an acceptable single opposition candidate, had ruined past opportunities to remove KANU from power.

---

[10] This was a name that Raila had agreed upon with Mukhisa Kituyi a long while earlier. Raila had suggested Rainbow Coalition and Kituyi had added National.

At Uhuru Park, Gumo, as Master of Ceremonies, started the meeting. They launched the LDP and raised its flag. Thereafter, the Rainbow leaders threw their KANU caps into the crowd as their resignations from KANU were announced.

Joab Omino, Chairman of the LDP, spoke and Dennis Kodhe, the out-going Secretary-General of the LDP made a statement and handed the party and the microphone over to Raila who announced that the LDP had reached a coalition arrangement with Nyachae's FORD-People to form Rainbow Coalition. Raila invited Nyachae to address the crowd. Many other speakers from the Rainbow Alliance, including Saitoti, Musyoka and Awori also made speeches. Raila then announced that Rainbow Coalition would work with NAK and invited Wamalwa, Ngilu and Kibaki to address the crowd.[11]

Raila was convinced that it would be an uphill task to find a single presidential candidate at the rally. Some of the speakers told the rally that another rally would be held to introduce a single opposition candidate. Raila was concerned by a statement credited to Shariff Nassir, Minister in the Office of the President, to the effect that Parliament would soon be dissolved, thus lowering the political temperature in the country.[12]

Raila knew that dissolution of parliament, would drive most politicians back to their constituencies to canvas for re-election. He could not envisage a bigger rally than the one they were at, suitable for announcing a presidential candidate. He also knew that it would be impossible to agree a single candidate behind closed doors.

Raila had weighed up the possible candidates, including himself. He knew that Kibaki would split the ethnic Central province votes with Uhuru Kenyatta as the KANU candidate. An International Republican Institute poll immediately before the rally had claimed that in a three way run, Rainbow Alliance would lead the pack with 39%, followed by NAK with 31%, KANU with 21% and FORD-People with 4%. However, Raila expected that as the campaign developed, given the national resources behind KANU, the situation could change and KANU

---

[11] James Orengo also spoke as a result of the popular demands from the crowd for him to address them.

[12] See, *East African Standard,* Monday October 14, 2002, p. 4 , for a statement credited to Shariff Nassir.

would reach 30% at the expense of the other two parties. This would make it easier for KANU to rig the election.[13]

He reasoned that if Kibaki could split the Kikuyu votes and win the support of other Rainbow Alliance leaders and their ethnic communities, it would be possible to defeat KANU overwhelmingly. It would be foolish for KANU to try to rig out such a crushing defeat. Acting against Musyoka, Saitoti and Nyachae, who all wanted further negotiations on the issue, Raila threw down the gauntlet: He asked the crowd if Kibaki was not good enough as the presidential candidate (in Kiswahili, Kibaki *Tosha?*) The crowd reacted with overwhelming approval (*Anatosha!*) That ended the rally.

Mwenda Njoka aptly grasped the events leading to Kibaki's candidacy and the role of Raila in them, when he wrote:

> When Raila realised what Moi's game plan was, he moved quickly to forestall its success. Meaningful opposition unity, hitherto a most elusive political commodity, was born out of Raila's disenchantment with the KANU chairman. You could call it Raila's revenge against what he saw as Moi's betrayal of the spirit of the KANU-NDP marriage by imposing Uhuru as KANU's (and by extension NDP's) presidential candidate, or you could call it a case of Raila being hit by a bout of political realism. Whatever label one gives it, the simple fact is that Raila's withdrawal from KANU just weeks before a most crucial General Election left the party that had ruled Kenya for almost four decades mortally wounded. Similarly, Raila's personal commitment to supporting Mwai Kibaki's presidential candidature firmly galvanized the opposition in a manner that had never happened before.[14]

Nyachae's Displeasure

Nyachae was not amused by Raila's intervention at the end of the Uhuru Park rally. Before Raila arrived home, Nyachae's wife Grace, had called Ida three times to relay her husband's displeasure at Raila's remark. He felt duped and betrayed by Raila.[15]

---

[13] Raila's brief at a private dinner on March 29, 2003.
[14] Mwenda Njoka, *Sunday Standard,* April 20, 2003, p. 12.
[15] Interview with Simeon Nyachae, September 1, 2003.

However, Oburu, who was an LDP member of the committee that drafted the MoU between Rainbow Alliance and FORD-People, insisted that there was no treachery as the Rainbow Alliance had lived up to the agreement they signed.[16] That agreement was clear. One of its clauses said explicitly that, consultations with other parties could still take place, and that the Rainbow Coalition was not necessarily the final formula for winning the Election.[17] Oburu insisted that the cards were still on the table and that Adams Karauri and Kipkalya Kones, who represented Nyachae, knew the details. For him, the LDP side was very clear that a relationship with NAK was needed to win overwhelmingly. He also noted that Nyachae's son Charles, a lawyer, drafted the MoU. Oburu felt that Nyachae was too conceited and had believed that FORD-People would win if Raila had joined him. He was not really interested in LDP.

Nyachae believed he could still turn the tables, by implementing the MoU with the LDP, and finding a formula defining the relationship with NAK which would include a plan of post-election victory action, including leadership selection rules.

At a meeting in Awori's residence on October 19, Nyachae pressed for a focus beyond power-sharing, and for an agreement on how to serve Kenyans. To select the single opposition candidate, he proposed an electoral college of a fixed number (300 or 500) to be selected by each of the constituent parties: FORD-People; FORD-Kenya; Democratic Party; Liberal Democratic Party and National Alliance Party of Kenya.[18]

Nyachae's position was endorsed in an *East African Standard* editorial. Summing up the argument, the newspaper wrote:

> If it was not right for one man to impose a candidate on KANU as was argued, it is not right for the National Rainbow Coalition to impose a nominee on the people without exhausting all democratic options. The shortage of time is an excuse rather than the explanation for the avoidance of democratic principles.

---

[16] Interview with Oburu Oginga, Nairobi, September 2, 2003.

[17] *Ibid.* This position was shared by LDP leaders in general. See *Daily Nation,* Monday, November 4, 2003, pp. 1-2

[18] Interview with Simeon Nyachae. See also, *Sunday Standard,* October 20, 2002, pp. 1-2 and "Nyachae: Why I resigned from Super Alliance," *East African Standard,* Monday October 21, 2002, pp 1-2.

If the advocates of a Super Alliance cannot listen to the logical and alternative view presented by Mr. Simeon Nyachae, and members of the Kenya People's Coalition, then they better say they do not want to be truly and sincerely democratic, rather than accusing those with an alternative view of being stumbling blocks to opposition unity.[19]

Raila was among those who disagreed with this strategy. He argued that equal representation in an electoral college assumed that each party was equal in strength. To quantify party strength, Raila argued that past election performance could be a yardstick. While LDP could muster many parliamentary candidates beyond the solid block of NDP, FORD-People (without those who had defected) could only muster 4 MPs. Raila suggested that in the absence of assessing strength, consensus could be the way out.

The others insisted on power-sharing, based on the argument that there was insufficient time, and that other issues should be delayed till after the election. Nyachae argued that he needed a working formula as he would want to know the promises he would be making to the people. When he failed to get agreement, Nyachae decided with the FORD-People National Executive Committee, to go for the presidency alone.

When asked why he thought the LDP walked out on the MoU with FORD-People, Nyachae said that, Raila, who he claimed, had made clear that he wanted to be an Executive Prime Minister to Nyachae's presidency, must have had a change of mind. Nyachae argued that Raila must have felt that Kenyans would object to such a team, since they were both from Nyanza province. He argued that it was in Raila's interests to join Kibaki who was from a larger ethnic group and a different province.[20] With the FORD-People and LDP relationship stillborn, the options for LDP were to go it alone or join hands with NAK. The earlier negotiations with NAK continued and on October 22, resulted in a MoU. The leadership line-up was announced at the Nairobi Hilton.[21]

---

[19] *East African Standard,* "Listen to alternative view of democracy," p. 6.

[20] Interview with Nyachae, *op. cit.*

[21] At the time of writing this book, the signed copies of the MoU remained hidden. It was said to be with Lawyer Ambrose Rachier. However, Raila's unsigned copy, is reproduced as appendix. Newspapers in Nairobi have also published identical texts to the one in the appendix.

Election campaign and results

Immediately after power-sharing had been agreed, Raila was one of the few leaders to consistently follow candidate Kibaki on the campaign trail. Raila was confident he would retain his Langata seat and so, spent his time assisting Kibaki. On December 2, the Kibaki team including Raila, campaigned in Mwingi, where they spent the night. The following day, they drove to Kabati market in Kitui West constituency and addressed a rally in the morning. They made stops at Matinyani and Zombe markets before returning to Kitui town for the main rally, which ended at 5:30 p.m. The campaign team were returning to Nairobi, when, at the Machakos junction on the Nairobi-Mombasa Highway, Kibaki's driver in trying to avoid an earlier accident, crashed 5 feet into a ditch.

The air-bags in the car protected Kibaki. He was removed from the wreck of his Range-Rover, and rushed to Nairobi Hospital in David Musila's vehicle. Dr. Dan Gikonyo, Kibaki's personal physician, re-assured the nation that Kibaki's situation was not life-threatening. He had suffered a fracture to the upper right arm and a dislocated right ankle. He then said: "Mr. Kibaki has not suffered any major injury. He is fully conscious. These are significant injuries but not major. They are fixable injuries that we will still work on tonight."[22]

Characteristically, Raila decided to deal with the distraught state in which Kenyans had found themselves. He told the press that the accident would not affect the campaign to make Kibaki President: "Our campaign will proceed as usual. This is a temporary setback but it won't stop us. We will proceed with our programme as arranged."[23] Adding with his usual football allegory: "The captain is injured but the match will continue to the end."

Kibaki's accident gave Raila the opportunity to show his leadership skills in coordinating a team. He took over the campaign and criss-crossed the country paying little attention to his own Langata constituency. Professor Wanjiku Kabira, then a Commissioner of the Constitution of Kenya Review Commission, appreciated the leadership role played by Raila thus:

---

[22] For additional details, see, Daily Nation, Wednesday, December 4, 2002, pp. 1 & 3.

[23] *Ibid.,* p. 1.

During the last general election, his [Raila] national image blew to a higher level as he led people like George Saitoti, Kalonzo Musyoka into NARC and then took over leadership as Kibaki went into hospital until victory. The last election confirmed his national appeal as the Luhya and Kikuyu as well as other Kenyans relied on his leadership capabilities as Kibaki and Wamalwa were in hospital in England. He was confirmed as a nationalist.[24]

The two main parties, NARC and KANU, decided on primary elections to choose candidates for the General Elections. But NARC started off undemocratically, by declaring that none of its Summit members would face the primaries as their seats were automatically assured. Raila defended this position by arguing that leaders of British parties did not spend time fighting primary elections.

The primaries of the two parties were nightmares. People who lost still obtained accreditation papers enabling them to file their papers with the Electoral Commission of Kenya (ECK). In some cases, two competing candidates had such papers and it became a question of who got to ECK first. Losers from one party went to the other to obtain accreditation papers and in many instances, displaced less popular but loyal party members who had won. At other times, changes in nominations were sought by the parties against the ECK rules.

Mr. Samuel Kivuitu, the ECK chairman was not amused by the rowdy process in the parties. He noted that last minute changes to the names of validly elected candidates, were unfair and disruptive. He told the press that: "The procedure is very chaotic and unpredictable; something has to be done. There should be a definite date for the nominations to be handed in. On or from a certain day in the process, there should be no room for changes."[25]

After a vigorous campaign, in elections on December 27, 2002, Kibaki received 3,646,227 votes of a total 5,861,844 votes cast. He took 62.2% to Uhuru's 31.3% (1,835,890 votes). Nyachae in third place got 345,141 votes or 5.9%, and Orengo and Waweru Ngethe had 0.4% and 0.2% respectively.

NARC also swept the parliamentary polls with 125 seats, and had the right to nominate another 7 MPs. KANU took 65 seats plus 4 nominated MPs. Nyachae's

---

[24] Interview with Wanjiku Kabira, Nairobi Serena Hotel, April 12, 2003.
[25] *Saturday Nation,* January 4, 2003, p. 28.

FORD-People took 14 seats plus one nominated MP. Small parties like Safina and Sisi Kwa Sisi won two parliamentary seats each, and FORD-Asili and Shrikisho party each won a seat.

The election proved that Moi was, after all, fallible. Though reputed to be a "Professor of politics" with a shrewd ability to use and dump people to advance his interests, on this occasion, he met his match in Raila.

In addition, Moi did not factor into his calculations, the extent of Moi fatigue in Kenya. He thought he could continue to rule by controlling the party apparatus, as Nyerere did in Tanzania. But he failed to see the difference between him and Nyerere. In Tanzania, Nyerere was loved by most of his compatriots until he died. He did not acquire earthly possessions but dedicated himself, in spite of his policy shortcomings, to the improvement of the quality of Tanzanians' lives. As a result, Tanzanians savoured what was seen as his fatherly advice on the country's leadership. Kenyans, however, would not accept Moi's hand-picked successor. It appeared that his choice was made to ensure Moi's protection by Uhuru, whose family he had protected when he succeeded Jomo Kenyatta. Moi's choice was met with the displeasure of many Kenyans. The electoral avalanche also swept away many of Moi's hitherto docile lieutenants, who had resisted Raila's challenge to leave KANU. For the first time in the history of post-independence Kenya, the lot of KANU, as a parliamentary party, changed. The end of the KANU order in Kenya gave birth to another order. But this new coalition very quickly became discordant.

Chapter 17
The Discordant Coalition

Technically, President Moi remained in office until a new President was sworn in. He was to fix a date to hand over in consultation with the incoming President. But there were fears that some of Moi's lieutenants were trying to persuade him to challenge the election in court as the basis for a delay in the handing over and probably to achieve an extension of power for the doyen of Kenyan politics. Moi to his credit, would have nothing to do with such scheming. But Raila, not knowing this, thought it best to seize the initiative. On December 29, he announced that Kibaki would be sworn-in on the following day and set in motion invitations to other African leaders to the swearing-in ceremony. The fear of resistance by the KANU government fizzled out as Uhuru Kenyatta graciously conceded defeat in a speech at the Serena Hotel on the same evening.

The mood of Kenyans at President Kibaki's swearing-in, was that of a carnival. But the carnival was visibly anti-Moi. All hopes were placed on expectations of a new life under a new President. On his arrival, the outgoing President Moi, was booed by an energised crowd chanting the NARC campaign anthem: "Everything is possible without Moi." Some even threw mud at the outgoing President.[1]

However, like a statesman, Moi took the situation in full stride. In his speech, he paid glowing tributes to his successor, describing him as a man of integrity and courage.[2] President Kibaki's maiden speech was less conciliatory, as he avoided acknowledging anything positive in Moi's 24-year rule. In clear terms, he indicated that his government would not be run on the whims of an individual. In a direct critique of the Moi era, he stated: "The era of roadside policy declarations is gone. My government's decisions will be guided by teamwork and consultations."[3] He made it clear that he was "inheriting a country which has been badly ravaged by years of misrule and ineptitude."[4] He described the situation further:

---

[1] For more details, see, *Daily Nation,* Tuesday, December 31, 2002, p. 1.
[2] See, Moi's speech in *ibid.,* p. 4.
[3] For the full speech, see, *ibid.,* p. 4.
[4] Ibid.

My government will adhere to the principles and practice of the rule of law in a modern society .... Corruption will now cease to be a way of life in Kenya .... there will be no sacred cows under my government. The economy, which you all know has been under-performing since the last decade, is going to be my first priority. There is deepening poverty in the country. Millions of our people have no jobs. School enrolment has been declining. In fact, the agricultural sector, like all other sectors, is steadily deteriorating. Majority of our people do not have access to basic and affordable health services. Our roads and other infrastructures are dilapidated. Most of our institutions are failing and basic road services are crumbling. There is growing insecurity in our cities and towns. The list is endless.[5]

President Kibaki raised a lot of hopes. But, as soon as his government took power, discord in the constituent parts of NARC pushed delivery of promises made to the back stage. The origin of this paralysing discord was in the MoU that brought NARC into being.

Appointments without consultations

As soon as Kibaki was sworn-in as the third President of Kenya on December 30, 2002, he put behind him the agreement he had signed before the election, and did not call a meeting of the Summit chaired by Awori. While the President may have consulted individuals, he did not consult the Summit on his Cabinet appointments as envisaged in the MoU.

The MoU had specified a 50/50 power-sharing of cabinet posts. Each party was also to nominate their representatives. President Kibaki directed that the Summit, under Awori, should meet to consider the cabinet lists. The final list from the Summit was handed to Kibaki by Awori on January 1, 2003. Two days later, the President announced his cabinet. Of the 23 posts, he gave LDP 8 and NAK 15. But more significantly, he disregarded the list suggested by LDP, and appointed other LDP members, including some who claimed LDP adherence, for convenience. Kibaki's aides, sought to drive a wedge into LDP, by informing such appointees that LDP had not recommended them, and they had been appointed by the grace of the President.[6]

---

[5] *Ibid.*
[6] Raila Odinga's comments at a private dinner on March 29, 2004.

The Cabinet appointments marked the first open discord in NARC. The day after the announcement, a number of LDP Members of Parliament-elect stated that their wing of NARC had been badly treated by President Kibaki. Oburu stated at a press conference to announce the convening of an LDP Parliamentary Group meeting on January 5: "This is a raw deal. We are not happy."[7] The first salvo challenging the concept of a single party to replace the NARC coalition, which had been promised in Kibaki's swearing-in speech, was fired at this press conference by Gor Sunguh, the Kisumu East MP, and one of Raila's close colleagues. He said: "We will not be dictated to by anybody. What we are asking is justice. To form a single party or not is our party's decision, we have to discuss it ourselves as a party. Such a decision cannot be arrived at by one person."[8]

About 25 LDP MPs-elect met for four hours on January 5, and afterwards addressed a press conference. Otieno Kajwang', the Mbita MP-elect, spoke for all and called on Kibaki to change the cabinet list. He said: "The MOU is not portrayed in the Cabinet announced last Friday. Unless the President follows the MOU on appointments, the tenets on which NARC was founded will be betrayed."[9]

However, two cabinet Ministers and the new Vice-President, Michael Kijana Wamalwa came out in favour of the President's list. Surprisingly, Raila expressed satisfaction with the cabinet line up, noting that the Government needed talents to help realize economic growth. He gave assurance that the government would respect its election pledges.[10] He continued along the same line at the ministerial swearing-in ceremony on January 6, when he said: "This is a storm in a tea cup. These are minor problems, which are surmountable. I have confidence in the Cabinet as constituted. It is inclusive and representative."[11] He called on his LDP colleagues to wait for a meeting of the NARC Summit, and expressed the wish that NARC would unite as one single party.

Chris Murungaru, the new Minister of State for Internal Security, sang a similar but different tune from that of Raila. He stated that the LDP could not feel

---

[7] *Sunday Standard,* January, 5, 2003, p. 1.
[8] *Sunday Nation,* January 5, 2003, p. 1.
[9] For more details, see, *Daily Nation,* Monday, January 6, 2003, pp. 1 & 3.
[10] *Sunday Standard,* January 5, 2003, p. 1.
[11] *Daily Nation,* Tuesday, January 7, 2003, pp 1-2.

short-changed, because NARC had participated in the Elections as a single party rather than separate ones. He said that the MoU spoke about equity in distribution of posts, not equality. He added that the appointment of ministers was the constitutional prerogative of the Head of State.[12] By implication, Murungaru blazed the trail in suggesting that the MoU which was clearly based on the principle of a coalition of parties, was dead. He also found it convenient to mis-read or not to read the part of the MoU that explicitly referred to equal partnership between NAK and LDP. And he ignored the provision that a post-election government of national unity was to be based on 50/50 cabinet appointments arrived at through a consultative process.

Wamalwa also dismissed the concerns of the LDP members in NARC. He argued that the complainants were remnants of KANU who were used to having power, were now upset at being left out, and were trying to sow seeds of discord. He saw this as a teething problem which would fizzle out.[13]

The strong good-will the Kibaki government enjoyed, led to public condemnation of the pressure for equality in cabinet appointments. The Maseno West Anglican diocese head, the Right Reverend Joseph Wesonga; the Bishop of the Nairobi Diocese, Right Reverend Peter Njoka; and the Presbyterian Minister, Timothy Njoya, all dismissed the LDP complainants and urged all parties to work towards revamping the Kenyan economy.[14] Gibson Kamau Kuria, former chairman of the Law Society of Kenya, reacted strongly, describing the demands of the LDP MPs as: "Arrogant, unfair, ahistorical, uninformed and telling as it is premature. It is designed to perpetuate in Kenya the kind of politics which has ruined post-colonial Africa in general and Kenya in particular."[15]

Encouraged by such popular endorsement of his style, President Kibaki adopted the same approach to appointing Permanent Secretaries. Again the Summit was sidelined. Kibaki left hospital on 28 January, and announced his Permanent Secretaries on 31 January.

---

[12] *Sunday Standard,* January 5, 2003, p. 1.

[13] *Daily Nation,* Monday January 6, 2003, p. 3.

[14] For details, see, *ibid., and East African Standard,* Monday, January 6, 2003.

[15] *Daily Nation,* Monday January 6, 2003, p. 3.

Concern about the preponderance Cabinet Ministers or Permanent Secretaries from the Mount Kenya area, led to talk of a so-called "Mount Kenya Mafia" having taken over State House. Further ethnic dis-aggregation, gave emphasis to the over-representation of people from Meru district or, in fact, the Imenti area of greater Meru. These senior officials included: David Mwiraria, the Finance Minister and Kiraitu Murungi, the Justice and Constitutional Affairs Minister. The Head of the Civil Service, Francis Muthaura and three Permanent Secretaries (Erastus Mwongera, Roads and Public Works; Julius Meme, Health and Kiriinya Mukira, Local Government), were also from the Imenti area. Julius Meme was removed from Office later, not to address the political imbalance but over problems associated with deposits allegedly made by the Kenyatta National Hospital in the Euro Bank that went into liquidation. Gerishon Ikihara was brought in and took charge in the Transport Ministry as Permanent Secretary. Other changes to this line up of powerful men from the same district, saw swapping of Ministries by Permanent Secretaries. Mukira to Roads and Public Works and Mwongera to Lands. To cap it all, a Judge of the Court of Appeal, with eminent qualifications but from the same area, Aaron Ringera, became Chairman of the Kenya Anti-Corruption Commission after a rancorous parliamentary struggle between the Government and LDP MPs, in which the Government championed the appointment.[16]

The struggles inside NARC

On March 13, 2003, a hitherto unheard of group met at Mwenge House (the headquarters of NARC). The group, it was claimed, was chaired by Titus Mbathi, a former Cabinet Minister. Through Wang'uhu Ng'ang'a, who claimed to be its spokesman, the group referred to itself as the NARC National Council. They discussed the possible contents of a draft NARC constitution, and argued for the dissolution of all NARC parties in favour of a single party. They stated that the NARC Summit was an extra-legal arrangement that has no place in their constitution. The highest organ of NARC should be the National Council. Article 8 (b) of their proposed draft constitution was explicit: "The NARC Council shall be the highest authority of the party and shall determine the party's policies."

---

[16] For a newspaper account and additional details on these men of power in President Kibaki's set up, see, "The Power Zone," pages 5-7 in a Supplement in the *Sunday Standard,* March 27, 2005.

This Council would be made up of 60 persons: 5 from each of the 12 parties they claimed made up NARC.[17]

The group then questioned the validity of the MoU between NAK and LDP, claiming that it was no more than an "arrangement meant to enable NARC go through the elections."[18] However, on the following day, Titus Mbathi denied attending any meeting at which the dissolution of the Summit had been discussed, and argued that the NARC coalition owed its origin to the Summit. He said that this "NARC Council" had no authority to initiate debate on the Summit.[19]

Awori, the Chairman of the NARC Summit, argued that Wang'uhu Ng'ang'a was expressing a personal view, and Raila dismissed him as inconsequential and not worth a reply. But other more credible politicians came out in support of Ng'ang'a. John Michuki, the Transport and Communications Minister was said to have argued for the dissolution of the NARC Summit which he claimed existed for the purpose of bringing 14 parties together for the elections. For him, the Summit's 6 key members were already in the cabinet, and its continued existence would undermine the Presidency: "If a NARC Summit meeting is allowed to take place, won't the President be out of the picture if a Cabinet appointee is allowed to chair the group"?[20]

On the argument that President Kibaki was not operating in the spirit of the power-sharing arrangement agreed in the MoU, Koigi wa Wamwere, the MP for Subukia constituency saw the NARC's LDP members' demands for power-sharing as: "an illegitimate weapon of blackmail whose spirit is impractical. The MoU is wrong because it is founded upon the spirit of blackmail. It is quite clear the LDP extracted the agreement to share power equally because they knew then that NAK and the whole country were desperate for unity."[21]

This debate did not help ethnic relations in the country. Ethnic groups who had supported NARC in the elections, began to suggest that a cabal had taken over at State House with the sole aim of furthering the parochial interest of the GEMA

---

[17] For more details, see, *East African Standard* and *Daily Nation* of March 14, 2003
[18] *Ibid.*
[19] See, *Saturday Nation,* March 15, 2003
[20] *Daily Nation,* March 31, 2003, p.2.
[21] Koigi wa Wamwere as quoted in *Sunday Nation,* March 16, 2003, p.2

group now referred to as the "Mount Kenya Mafia." Phoebe Asiyo reviewing Kibaki's administration first six months, noted:

> "Six months later, appointments have been made that were totally unexpected. The bulk of the positions had gone to Kikuyus that were mainly DP. These things happened when Kibaki was not well. Luos would like to believe that people took advantage of such a situation. If Kibaki was in control, he would have known that the Kikuyu would be isolated. Moi tried to isolate Kikuyus for 24 years and failed. The NARC Government has succeeded in doing that within six months."[22]

LDP back-benchers in Parliament reacted to Kibaki's silence on calling a Summit meeting to discuss LDP's concerns, by dealing the Government two quick blows. Peter Oloo Aringo, nominated NARC MP tabled a bill to create a Parliamentary Budget Office. David Mwiraria, the Finance Minister, who had supported a similar bill when in the opposition, changed his position and argued that such an institution, would usurp Treasury functions. But on 12 March 2003, NARC's LDP back-benchers supported by KANU, passed the bill to the dismay of the Government.

The following day, Justice and Constitutional Affairs Minister, Murungi was forced to withdraw an anti-corruption bill that was a pre-requisite for the donors' resumption of financial support to Kenya, when it became clear that the Government could not be sure of its MPs support. Murungi needed a two-thirds majority to pass what would be a constitutional amendment. But KANU MPs argued for a thorough overhaul of the constitution, unlike the piece-meal approach that the NARC Government now seemed to prefer. Uncertain about the position of the 57 LDP MPs (out of the 132 NARC) the Government decided that it could not win, and withdrew the bill.

Late Joab Omino, then LDP Chairman, chaired a five-hour closed-door meeting of LDP MPs at the United Kenya Club on March 26. Omino reportedly expressed dissatisfaction with the non-consultative and unprofessional appointments of heads of state corporations. The meeting also expressed concern about appointments of people over age 65. Moody Awori, Home Affairs Minister and

---

[22] Interview, July 2, 2003.

Chairman of the Summit, attended part of the meeting, ostensibly to listen to the complaints of the LDP MPs.[23]

Though Raila downplayed the differences in NARC at every opportunity, Mbita MP, Otieno Kajwang' was much more vociferous, and some saw him as setting out a position Raila could not articulate publicly. So on March 19, when Raila sought to be reappointed as Chairman of the Parliamentary Select Committee (PSC) on the constitutional review process, it was no surprise that Murungi, the Justice and Constitutional Affairs Minister, a Cabinet colleague of Raila and a fellow NARC member seconded Ford People's, Kipkalya Kones' nomination of Safina's Muite, as the Chairman. Vice-President Wamalwa, nine other NARC MPs and KANU MPs (who continued to see Raila as the reason for their election loss), voted to defeat Raila.

According to the *Sunday Standard* in its April 20, 2003 edition, the "Mount Kenya Mafia" had, two weeks before the elections, resorted to their age-old style of *ndundu* (secret group meetings) and *muma* (oath taking) to ensure that participants were silent on what was discussed. So, Raila was unaware that a deal had been reached by some NARC MPs led by his cabinet colleague, Murungi, to deny him Parliament's Constitutional Select Committee chair and give it to Muite, who though competent, was an opposition MP.

On Kenya Television Network Oburu described the Vice-President's and other ministers'decision to ditch Raila, as symptomatic of a general fear of him. He said that since Raila had been suggested as the Prime Minister in the MoU, some of his colleagues were worried that as Chair of the Constitutional Select Committee, he would manipulate the process to favour an executive Prime Minister so cutting the powers of the President.

Oburu's view was confirmed when the late Karisa Maitha's Local Government Ministry, in a submission to the Constitutional Review Commission, called for the removal of the Prime Minister's post from the draft constitution.[24] Two State counsels argued for the ministry, that the then draft constitution did not give the President enough power, but put him at the mercy of Parliament and the Prime

---

[23] *East African Standard,* Friday, March 28, 2003, pp. 1 and 5.
[24] *Daily Nation,* Wednesday, April 2, 2003, pp. 1 and 3.

Minister. They suggested that President was popularly and directly elected and his powers should not be usurped by aPrime Minister that was not popularly elected. However, Kajwang', Oburu, and others, reacted fiercely, that the issue was not about Raila being Prime Minister, but about devolution of power in this unique opportunity to re-construct the Kenyan polity.

Raila, again downplayed the significance of his loss at the chairmanship election. On March 29th at a press conference in London during an official visit to familiarise himself with infrastructure developments in the United Kingdom, he said he was not keen to be either President or Prime Minister. He simply wanted changes that would liberate and empower Kenyans. He maintained that he had a good working relationship with President Kibaki, denied knowledge of any Mount Kenya Mafia, and dismissed speculation that he was being sidelined. He was happy to be a NARC member.

On the issue of rejection by Cabinet colleagues of his nomination as Chair of the Parliamentary Select Committee on the constitution, he said: "I lost to Hon. Muite in a secret ballot, and as far as I'm concerned, the vote was fair."[25] But later comments by Raila and his aides, confirm that he was badly hurt by his rejection by those he trusted. In an interview with the *Sunday Standard*, Raila claimed he was not desperate to be Chairman of the PSC, but he had expected to follow the parliamentary tradition that the mover of a motion for a select committee automatically became the chairman and had the committee named after him: "It (PSC) was the Raila committee, which I had chaired for the last three sessions, and I assumed the tradition would apply. I sought the chairmanship for the sake of continuity, but I did not know that some people went (behind my back) to campaign (against me). I did not talk to anybody about it. I did not campaign, which I could have done if I wanted."

However, in an interview, an LDP MP made it clear that Raila was devastated by what his cabinet colleagues had done: "what injured Raila most, was the likelihood that the President could actually break faith in him. Some of us were selling the idea that Kibaki must have known of the 'coup' and that Kiraitu could not have conspired to do him in without the nod from his boss. And for Raila it was not so much the defeat, but what he perceived as betrayal."[26]

---

[25] *Sunday Nation,* March 30, 2003, p. 3.
[26] *Sunday Standard,* April 20, 2003, p. 11.

If Raila felt betrayed, he did his best to hide it. At every public opportunity, he downplayed any sense of betrayal. But this did not improve the political situation. With assistance from Frederich Ebert Stiftung, on April 3-5, NARC MPs attended a retreat at the Mount Kenya Safari club in Nanyuki to discuss the differences in the coalition, which had paralysed the work of government.

At the retreat, Murungi, the Justice and Constitutional Affairs Minister, in a spirit of reconciliation, said that he had decided not to back Raila for the chair of the Select Committee, because he was under the (false) impression that Raila led the group working against crucial bills the Government had brought before the House.[27]

Raila showed that he bore no grudges against Murungi since, according to Raila, the actions of Kiraitu "arose out of a misunderstanding." Raila said he was used to people fighting him for reasons he did not know. He urged his colleagues to put the country first and pleaded to avoid deciding constitutional change based on the position or aspirations of an individual. The constitution should be reviewed for posterity: "We must review the constitution with open minds. Let us not think of who is supposed to be what. Let us have a Constitution for Kenya and for the generations to come."[28]

At the retreat's end, Vice-President Wamalwa with several MPs showered praise on Raila for saving the talks. The statesman Raila had delivered a speech which cooled tempers and made the meeting a success. He said: "My brother Raila excites such passions as those who love him love him unto death and those who don't are always suspicious of his intentionsÖToday, he has reassured those who love him and allayed the fears of those who doubt him. He has proved his true statesmanship. Today is a historic day."[29]

Chris Murungaru, the Minister of State in the Office of the President reminded all, that Raila had united all Kenyans under NARC, resulting in the landslide coalition win.[30]

---

[27] Detailed accounts on the retreat can be found in the major Kenyan newspapers from 4-7 April 2003.

[28] *Sunday Standard,* April 6, 2003, p. 3.

[29] As quoted in Sunday Nation, April 6, 2003, p. 2. See also, *East African Standard,* Monday, April 7, 2003.

[30] *East African Standard,* Monday, April 7, 2003.

In an 11 point resolution, the major recommendation was that the new Constitution for Kenya should be ready by the end of June 2003. Re-affirming NARC's commitment to wipe out corruption, the Parliamentary Group undertook to support the government's anti-corruption legislation in Parliament, and recommended drastic action against any government officials, parastatal Chief Executive Officers, Ministers or MPs involved in corrupt practices. Other recommendations included affirmation of collective responsibility and unity of Cabinet members; completion of a decade-old Civil Service Reform within a year; a call on civil servants to be loyal to the government of the day by implementing the NARC manifesto; and the dissemination of the NARC manifesto to all the service commissions. It was also recommended that civil service salaries would be reviewed; future appointments must be merit based; the NARC Summit would be retained as the highest organ of the party, expanded from 8 to 15, and strengthened as a leading party organ. Commitment towards the transformation of the coalition into a single strong and unified party, and the MoU were to be discussed at the Summit, with a view to its implementation as part of the constitutional review.[31]

Dissolution of the constituent parties in NARC

NAK had agreed to dissolve all its constituent parties after the elections. But NAK and the LDP had not reached a similar agreement. As noted above, a commitment of the NARC retreat was to transform the NARC coalition parties into a strong unified mass party. Many of the NARC leaders from NAK, like Kipruto arap Kirwa and Joseph Munyao, had informed the press that NARC's constituent parties would soon be dissolved. This was vehemently denounced by LDP leaders like Joe Khamisi, the MP for Bahari and Kamotho, the MP for Mathioya , and LDP Secretary-General.

In an address to the students of the University of Nairobi, on the theme: "The Politics of Coalition Building," Raila said that the parties forming NARC were discussing a merger. He said: "But this (merger process) will be gradual. It will not be drastic, there are pertinent issues to be discussed...a stage is coming when it will be possible to merge the political parties.."[32] For the first time, he asserted

[31] *Sunday Standard* April 6, 2003, p. 2 and *Sunday Nation,* April 6, 2003.
[32] See, *East African Standard,* Thursday, July 17, 2003, p. 1

that the NARC constituent parties were four and not fourteen as others had claimed. The National Alliance Party of Kenya was mainly three parties: Democratic Party; FORD-Kenya and National Party of Kenya. The fourth member of NARC was the Liberal Democratic Party. All the others, claiming to be parties, were social movements with no ideology to qualify them as political parties. Some were created to source funds, and others as man-and-wife parties.[33]

Events after the death in London on August 23, 2003, of Vice-President Wamalwa after a long illness, showed that not only Raila and the LDP, were against dissolution of NARC's parties. When Kibaki appointed Awori Vice-President on September 25, a debate arose over whether Wamalwa should be succeeded as FORD-Kenya Chairman. Dr. Newton Kulundu, the Minister of Environment, and a Luhya like Wamalwa and Awori, was condemned by most Luhya leaders for suggesting that FORD-Kenya should be dissolved. Musikari Kombo (who was given a full ministerial position in the cabinet reshuffle after Wamalwa's death); Mukhisa Kituyi, the Minister for Trade and Industry; and Noah Wekesa, a Luhya MP, campaigned to keep FORD-Kenya going. Kombo won the Chairmanship election on October 26 and was embraced by an LDP delegation led by Foreign Minister Kalonzo Musyoka, who made clear the LDP (and not NARC) would undertake similar elections in January 2004.

But at the Kenyan coast on the first anniversary of the elections that brought him to power, President Kibaki announced that all the NARC parties were obsolete. The LDP Secretary-General, Kamotho, responded that the President might be speaking illegally as the NARC constitution was clear that membership was through existing political parties.

Nonetheless, discord had been reactivated. Justice Minister, Murungi; Health Minister, Ngilu; Local Government Minister, Karisa Maitha; Labour Minister, Chirau Ali Mwakwere, who replaced Ahmed Mohamed Khalif killed in a plane crash in Busia on January 2003; Assistant Ministers Kivutha Kibwana, Mwangi Kianjuri, Danson Mungatana; and others, demanded a NARC membership drive.

They met determined resistance from the Raila-led side that included Energy Minister, Ochillo Ayacko; Minister for Culture, Youth, Sports and Gender, Najib

---

[33] See, *ibid.*

Balala; LDP Secretary-General Kamotho; Oburu, MP for Bondo; Khamisi, MP for Bahari; Otieno Kajwang', MP for Mbita; and others. They argued that the basis for NARC was clearly stipulated as corporate membership. This position was supported by Musikari Kombo's FORD-Kenya members who were not named in the MoU sanctioning corporate membership having already agreed to dissolve into NAK.

The issue was discussed at another "Nanyuki II" retreat on February 5-6, 2004. where Raila reportedly led the rebellion against dissolution of parties. He also insisted on individual membership through the coalition partners. LDP would not accept direct membership or even dual membership, but insisted on NARC corporate membership. Raila was challenged by Murungi, his nemesis in NARC, who asked delegates either to kill the baby NARC or let it live. He said: "The MoU was written by a few people at Nairobi Club. The Summit was created the same way. Rank and file were only informed later."[34]

Vice-President Awori who chaired the meeting, could not break the stalemate. He set up another Committee to consider how to harmonize the differing positions of NARC's constituent units. The eight person committee, co-chaired by Assistant Minister for Foreign Affairs, Moses Wetangula, and Mrs. Nyiva Mwendwa, MP for Matinyani, included: JJ Kamotho, Otieno Kajwang'; Joe Khamisi; Assistant Ministers Danson Mungatana and Kivutha Kibwana, and Bonny Khalwale, MP for Ikolomani.[35]

But on 21 February, before the Committee could report, Ministers Maitha and Mwakwere lured a crowd with the offer of food for a NARC recruitment[36] drive in Kwale District. They accused Raila of trying to derail NARC's leadership. Maitha stated: "As happened between President Kenyatta and Jaramogi Oginga Odinga in the 1960s, I can see a fallout between President Kibaki and Mr. Raila Odinga in the offing."[37]

Raila decided to carry the battle to the Coast hoping to prove the LDP's strength in Maitha's home base. But the rally scheduled for March 13, was cancelled as

---

[34] *East African Standard,* Saturday, February 7, 2004, p. 2.
[35] For details on this meeting, see, ibid., pp. 1-3
[36] On "food for recruitment," see, *Saturday Nation,* February 21, 2004, pp. 1-2.
[37] *Sunday Nation,* February 22, 2004, p. 1.

they could not find a vacant space. A follow-up rally was also cancelled as it would have clashed with a NAK rally.

However, the tension over membership was clear. Hope that the report of the 8-person Committee would bring a let-up, was unfounded. The Committee recommended corporate membership thus continuing in the spirit of the MoU.[38] Apparently, the LDP and FORD-Kenya would have nothing to do with the individual membership supported by the Democratic Party and other NARC groups. The recommendation was immediately challenged by Kibwana who had walked out of the Committee with Mungatana, the MP for Garsen. Kibwana asserted that: "The committee's purported decision and recommendation is null and void since it is a usurpation of the democratic process."[39]

Raila continued to argue that the dissolution of the constituent parties in NARC would be turn back the clock by returning Kenya to the unacceptable one-party era: "coalition governments have succeeded in Japan, India, Israel and many other countries and Kenya should not be an exception."[40] At a workshop in Nairobi on April 21, Raila also argued that dissolution of coalition parties could ignite tribal animosity. He suggested that the NARC parties represented regional interests which would be compromised if they were dissolved. Using the example of Malaysia where the ruling coalition comprised 13 parties each representing a region and its people, Raila claimed: "coalitions are an idea whose time has come in Africa. The creation of a monolith is not a guarantee of unity."[41] For him, coalition governments are essential to democracy.

Government of National Unity

As the situation heated over the calls for dissolution of NARC parties and the struggle for a new constitution, President Kibaki, opening the third session of the 9th Parliament on March 30, defused tension by promising that a new constitution would be in place by June 30, 2004.[42] As it became clear that this

---

[38] See, *East African Standard*, Monday April 5, 2004, pp. 1 & 4.

[39] See, *Saturday Nation*, April 10, 2004, p. 2.

[40] See, East African Standard, Wednesday February 18, 2004, p. 1.

[41] *East African Standard*, Thursday, April 22, 2004, p. 10.

[42] A chapter will shortly be devoted to the struggle for a new constitution in Kenya.

deadline would not be met, Kibaki in his Madaraka day address on June 1, announced that the challenge of putting a new constitution in place, rested with parliament which he called on to reach consensus to enable enactment of the constitution.[43]

On June 30, instead announcing a new constitution, Kibaki announced a cabinet reshuffle to create a "Government of National Unity." He retained the 'rebel' LDP members in Government but shifted some of them to less strategic ministries. Kalonzo Musyoka, the Foreign Minister, touted as a Presidential challenger to Kibaki in 2007, was moved to Environment, despite his effectiveness on the Kenya-led Somalia and Sudan peace processes. He was allowed to continue working on the peace processes as a result of Kofi Annan's personal intervention with President Kibaki on July 8. But he was removed from the position of lead negotiator on August 20, on the eve of the swearing-in of the Somali Parliament at the UN.

Ochillo Ayacko, (who had joined with Raila and Balala to vote against what was wrongly defined as the Government position, at the constitutional gathering three months earlier), vacated the Ministry of Energy and took Balala's position at the Ministry of Youths, Sports and Gender. Balala was moved to National Heritage in the Office of the Vice-President. Ntimama, one of the strong voices in support of respect for the MoU, was placated and made Public Service Minister of State in the Office of the President.

FORD-Kenya MPs who had been allied with the LDP on the issue of dissolution of constituent parties, were rewarded with four Assistant Ministerial positions. A major beneficiary was Soita Shitanda, FORD-Kenya's vociferous spokesman, who became Public Service Assistant Minister in the Office of the President.

More significant, however, was that President Kibaki poached from the ranks of the opposition. Important catches included Nyachae, the FORD-People leader, who became the Minister for Energy; and Njenga Karume, a long time ally and personal friend of Kibaki who had ditched him and the Democratic Party, at the last minute in the 2002 Elections and joined KANU to shore up Uhuru Kenyatta's campaign, was made a Minister of State, Special Programmes in the Office of the President. The KANU MP, John Koech, who had been leading a group trying to

---

[43] See, *East African Standard,* Wednesday, June 2, 2004, pp. 1-5.

build consensus on a new constitution, was made Minister for East African and Regional Cooperation. Abdi M. Mohamed, an ethnic Somali from North-Eastern and member of KANU was made Minister, Regional Development. Other members of KANU and FORD-People, like Kipkalya Kones, received Assistant Ministerial positions.

This development marked the end of the NARC idea of a multi-party coalition government. With new strength from other parties, the Government reduced LDP's ability to join KANU to defeat Government bills such as one on the environment. Despite the LDP-KANU alliance against the appointment of Justice Ringera as head of the Kenya Anti-Corruption Commission, the strong Government campaign paid off on August 4, when Ringera was appointed by an overwhelming 114 votes to 74. Raila who was out of Kenya, told the BBC that he was returning to participate in that vote. But he and most of the LDP Ministers "ran away" and Ayacko who was in Parliament, abstained.[44]

Discord in the NARC coalition, was not limited to the issues of dissolution of parties and support of Government bills. There was also disagreement over the structure of government and constitutional devolution of power. This pitted Raila's side against President Kibaki's. This development is significant, given that the struggle for constitutional change, was one of the major areas of agreement between Raila and Kibaki before the 2002 Elections. It is essential to examine the struggle for a constitution in Kenya and Raila's role in it.

---

[44] See. East African Standard, Thursday August 5, 2004, pp. 1-3.

Chapter 18
Restructuring Kenya's Polity

Constitution-making reflects class struggles in society, and the national consensus that is reached in the constitution-making process is a reflection of the interests of some dominant social groups and the concession they have made to the other dominated social groups in society. That this political consensus is called "people's constitution" does not make it so. Constitutional practice, therefore, becomes crucial in the implementation of this consensus.

Willy Mutunga, *Constitution-Making from the Middle: Civil Society and Transition Politics in Kenya, 1992-1997*, (Harare and Nairobi: MWENGO and SAREAT, 1999), p. 20.

Kenyans, however, must look to the future. What kind of constitution do we want, how do we want to devolve power, how much power do we want to give to local assemblies, how much power do you want to give to the Presidency and the Premiership and so on. This should be discussed without taking the current situation into consideration.

Raila Odinga *Sunday Standard*, April 20, 2003, p. 10.

Though Raila Odinga has served Kenya as Minister in different ministries under two regimes, nothing reflects his role in the movement for a new Kenya, more than his insistence that the problems of Kenya could be best dealt with by focusing on structural changes beyond personalities. This position was paramount to the NDP membership in the aftermath of the 1997 Elections. But the struggle for constitutional reform did not start with the NDP. Various groups had coalesced around achieving a new constitutional order when political parties were making multi-partyism their focus.

The Independence Constitution which Kenya inherited from the de-colonisation process and which came into force on December 12, 1963 went through 38 amendments. The Constitution of Kenya Review Commission categorized these amendments into three types: The first category concentrated power in the hands of the central government at the expense of the regions by doing away with *majimbo* (federalism). These amendments produced a strong Provincial

Administration, which became an instrument of central control. The second set of amendments produced a hybrid Constitution in which the inherited Parliamentary system of governance was replaced with a strong Executive Presidency without the checks and balances expected from separation of powers. The pressures from various Kenyan groups and international partners against the oppressive order that these amendments had put in place, resulted in some minimal amendments aimed at defusing the tension that arose from demands for a new constitution.[1] But the attempt in these amendments, to respond to tension from below did not satisfy those clamouring for change.

In October 1968, Joseph Theuri, the Nyeri Town MP moved a constitutional amendment to remove the fundamental change in 1964 that had made Jomo Kenyatta an Executive President. Seconding the motion, JN Kibuga, MP for Kirinyaga West said: "We need a prime minister who is directly answerable to the House, a person who can be heckled and shouted at by members."[2] The motion, which received the strong support of Oginga Odinga and was opposed by Vice-President Daniel arap Moi, was roundly defeated. Moi argued that any attempt to remove any of Kenyatta's powers, would result in trouble with the people of Kenya.[3]

Two decades later, segments of the Kenyan people again began to articulate a strong desire for a new constitutional order. As will be shown later, Raila made the first recorded call for constitutional change in Kenya in Oslo in November 1991. FORD and Bishop Okullu and Muge, amongst others followed suit. Willy Mutunga detailed some of these popular struggles.[4] The National Council of Churches of Kenya (NCCK) had been involved in the struggle for the repeal of Section 2A. With repeal achieved, NCCK wanted a peaceful transition to multipartyism and free and fair elections in December 1992. To this end, NCCK organized two symposia in May and June of 1992.

---

[1] Constitution of Kenya Review Commission, *The People's Choice: The Main Report of the Constitution of Kenya Review Commission*, (Nairobi: C.K.R.C, 18th September 2002), pp. 20-25.
[2] See, *Daily Nation*, August 14, 2003, "Keny@40" Supplement, p. 3.
[3] See, *ibid.*
[4] See, Willy Mutunga, *Constitution-Making from the Middle: Civil Society and Transition Politics in Kenya, 1992-1997*, (Harare and Nairobi: MWENGO and SAREAT, 1999). Much of the following account on the non-party pressure for a new constitution depended heavily on this volume.

The first symposium centred on the restricted aim above and on the release of political prisoners. The Release Political Prisoners (RPP) pressure group had produced a list of 52 political detainees including Koigi wa Wamwere and George Anyona. By the second symposium, however, the various groups including: Students Unions, trade associations and other pressure groups, joined by two registered political parties (Kenya Social Congress and Labour Party Democracy) as well as four unregistered parties (Green Party of Kenya, the Islamic Party of Kenya, the Democratic Movement and the Peoples Party of Kenya), had realized the need for a new Constitution.[5] It was no surprise when:

> In the second symposium held on June 11-12, 1992, it was agreed that a national convention to debate a new constitution be convened on July 20, 1992. Meanwhile, it was also agreed upon that the process of the registration of voters that was about to begin be boycotted.[6]

On June 17, 1992, the groups involved in this enterprise formed the Coalition for National Convention (CNC). But this national convention never met although an agenda for its first meeting was prepared. The agenda of CNC was too radical. The CNC wanted a mood for national reconciliation; dissolution of parliament; adoption of the 1962 Independence Constitution; and formation of a national convention-appointed transitional government for 2-3 years. KANU was to transfer power by the end of March 1993. But the CNC lacked funds and foreign partners, hopeful of change via political parties, did not want to invest in the process. Religious groups and mainstream political parties were also not interested in the CNC. Political parties' rallies attracted huge crowds of Kenyans. The parties were myopically focused on power through the electoral process and were not interested in structural changes.

In the circumstances, the CNC did not survive. But its goal was adopted by the Kenya Human Rights Commission (KHRC), whose origins were in the United States. Makau wa Mutua had been expelled as a student leader in May 1981 for demonstrating, and went from the University of Dar es Salaam to the Harvard Law School for his Masters, and became a staunch anti-Moi campaigner. Mutua, with Maina Kiai, a US-based organizer against Moi and KANU; Kiraitu Murungi,

---

[5] For a listing of all the social groups involved, see, *ibid*, pp. 27-30.
[6] *Ibid.*, p. 27.

hen a former law teacher in exile and reading his Masters at Harvard Law School, nd Wily Mutunga, a Kenyan activist in the pursuit of a doctorate at Osgoode Iall Law School, Toronto, Canada, agreed to form the KHRC. The KHRC elocated to Kenya with Kiai in 1992, and began operating from the Chambers f Kamau Kuria and Kiraitu Advocates. It was registered in March 1994.

ccording to Willy Mutunga, the KHRC played a crucial role in the formation nd the activities of the CNC. In pursuit of the CNC goal, the KHRC set about rafting a constitution to galvanize and focus debate on a new constitutional rder. The KHRC, seeking to broaden the ownership of the draft, sought partners nd was joined by the Law Society of Kenya (LSK) and the International Commission of Jurists (Kenya Section).

heir efforts received a fillip in March 1994 when Catholic Bishops issued a astoral letter stressing the need for a new constitution based on multipartyism. his was followed in May 1994 by a workshop of the three organizations to efine the draft constitution. A June 1994 workshop received the report of the apporteurs, which drew together the various plenary and group discussions, with preamble by Kivutha Kibwana and Gibson Kamau Kuria, and a gender document repared by Maria Nzomo and Jane Michuki. In July 1994, a Core Committee approved a *Proposal for a Model Constitution*.

he *Proposal for a Model Constitution* was launched at *Ufungamano* (Solidarity) House Nairobi on November 3, 1994. This was followed on December 9 by a onstitutional Caucus attended by 217 participants from all over Kenya. Bishop hn Njue, a member of the Episcopal Conference of Catholic Bishops and at at time, Vice-Chairman of the Catholic Peace and Justice Commission, made a markable intervention. He stressed that "making, revising and even amending e constitution was the responsibility of the peopleÖIt is the people who make e constitution and hand it over to the governors."[7]

he building of popular pressure for a new constitution did not go unnoticed by e KANU government. In his 1995 new-year message, President Moi knowledged that a new constitution was needed. He said that he would invite reign experts to come to Kenya, canvass the views of Kenyans and submit a

---

bid., p. 60.

draft to Parliament for debate and enactment. This was one of Moi's attempts t
diffuse tension before the precipice was reached. While those clamouring for
new constitution welcomed the Presidential admission of the need for a ne'
constitution, they reacted furiously to the idea of foreign experts.[8] But by Jun
1995, the Moi Government had changed gear. It was no longer talking (
expatriates but minor changes to be debated in parliament. By August 1995, Moi
position became clearer when he said that Kenya had no constitutional crisis.[9]

Despite this see-saw, the groups seeking a new constitution, remained undaunte
and continued their pressure. On January 6, 1995, the Steering Committee of th
Proposal for a Model Constitution that had been set up at the end of the December
1994 Constitutional Caucus had been renamed Citizens Coalition for Constitution
Change (4Cs). The 4Cs embarked on efforts to broaden the base for the clamo'
on constitutional change by educating its members on a common purpose f(
their demands, and by proselytizing in many segments of society. The 4Cs als
tried to make opposition political parties support democratisation, decentralizatic
and deconcentration of executive power. Some of their activities were disrupt
by police.

With support from the Centre for Governance and Development (CGD), :
NGO partner of the International Centre for Human Rights and Democra'
Development based in Montreal, Canada, seventy-three MPs had signed a pact
work for opposition unity.[10] In March 1996, 43 of these MPs met Willy Mutun
and Chris Mulei of the 4Cs. Mutunga claimed that at this meeting the idea of
national convention was first mooted.

Subsequently, the 4Cs had a formal meeting with the Inter-Parties Committ
(IPC), the executive arm of the Inter-Parliamentary Group (IPG), which broug
all opposition parties together in Parliament. Details for a national conventi
were refined. The IPC invited others including the National Council of NG(
the Episcopal Conference of the Catholic Bishops, the National Council
Churches of Kenya (NCCK) and the Supreme Council of Kenya Musli
(SUPKEM), to nominate representatives on the Planning Committee of '

---

[8] For all the details, see, *ibid.* pp. 61-62.
[9] *Ibid.,* p. 62.
[10] For details, see, *ibid.,* p. 110-111.

ational convention scheduled for May 29, 1996 at the Limuru Conference
Centre.[11]

Differences between politicians and civil society on arrangements for the
convention saw the 4Cs delinking from the IPC and getting Bishop Professor
Zablon Nthamburi, the Presiding Bishop of the Methodist Church, to be interim
convener of the National Convention Planning Committee (NCPC) meeting on
May 31, 1996. All stake-holders, including MPs, and registered and unregistered
political parties, were invited.[12]

Many party leaders attended the meeting and expressed solidarity. Raila attended
, leader of a FORD-Kenya faction, and made a major pro-constitutional reform
speech.[13]

Meanwhile, although in August 1995, Moi had asserted there was no constitutional
crisis, the popular demand could not be ignored. He used the occasion of the
October 1996 Moi Day (a public holiday until it was removed by the Kibaki
administration), to admit that fundamental constitutional review was necessary.
However, he argued that the year before General Elections would be too short
for the task. Moi had again sought to defuse tension and buy time.

However, there was no relenting on the demands for constitutional review. The
popular push of the NCPC, resulted in a list of minimum constitutional,
administrative and legal reforms necessary for free and fair elections. This list
was to be considered by the first plenary session of the National Convention in
April 1997. The minimum constitutional changes that was recommended by this
meeting of all interested religious organizations, other civil society groups and
political parties were:

- The presidential candidate to receive at least 50 per cent of the votes
  cast, in addition to 25 per cent in five provinces;
- A provision for a coalition government be made;
- A truly independent and non-partisan electoral commission be
  established;

---

n all the details, see *ibid.,* on which the author has depended.
e, *ibid.,* pp. 115-116.
id., p. 144.

- To amend the way the president nominates 12 members of parliamen
- To have a fixed date of elections;
- To allow independent candidates to vie for elective offices.[14]

As a minimum legal reform, there was pressure for repeal of the Public Ord
Act, the Preservation of Public Security Act, the Societies Act, the Chief
Authority Act, the Penal Code and the Public Collection Act. On administrati
reforms, they called for the release of all political prisoners, resettlement
Kenyans displaced by what was described as "ethnic cleansing," registration
all political parties, removal of police and the provincial administration syste
from the electoral process, prohibition of illegal presidential decrees on electior
immediate licensing of private radio and television stations, and the prohibiti
of the gagging of the press and religious organizations.[15]

The first plenary session of the National Convention was held as scheduled
Limuru. The National Convention converted itself into a National Constitue
Assembly (NCA) and resolutions were passed to the effect that mass action wou
be employed to force the Government to accept constitutional change. And th
would hold nation-wide rallies to popularise the need for constitutional refor
The first of the mass rallies was fixed for May 3, 1997 with provincial rallies
begin three weeks later. The assembly put in place a successor arrangement to t
NCPC, known as the National Convention Executive Council (NCEC). Gibs
Kamau Kuria;, Kivutha Kibwana, a former dean of the Law Faculty at
University of Nairobi; Davinder Lamba, a Kenyan of Asian origin and an acti
member of the NGOs Coordinating Council; Rev. Timothy Njoya of
Presbyterian Church of East Africa, and others, led the NCEC. Professor Kivu
Kibwana was the NCEC spokesperson.

The first rally at Kamukunji grounds was disrupted by anti-riot police, reporte
assisted by a group of thugs calling itself *Jeshi la Mzee* (Mzee's army). The bruta
meted out on the participants in the rally was captured by the media. The press
for constitutional reform became more popular. Another pro-reform rally
May 31, 1997 was given the same treatment by the security forces.[16]

---

[14] Macharia Munene, *The Politics of Transition in Kenya, 1995-1998* (Nairobi: Quest and Ins
Publishers, 2001), p. 47.

[15] *Ibid.,* p. 48.

[16] For details on mass action, see *ibid.,* and Willy Mutunga, *op. cit.,* pp. 149-190

o prevent any disruption of Madaraka Day (self-government national holiday) estivities, politicians like Orengo, Raila, Matiba and Muite, were put under house rrest. These events only popularised the push for constitutional reform.

'resident Moi used his Madaraka Day speech to promise changes in the Public Order Act and to appoint a Commission to review the constitution after the 1997 :lections. However, these new delaying tactics did not fool the NCEC. They isrupted Budget Day, June 19, 1997, at Parliament. The Government had expected :reet attempts to disrupt the parliament and security forces as well as *Jeshi la Mzee* 'ere prepared. But the NCEC strategy was different. Sympathizers in parliament :d by Orengo had smuggled placards into parliament and were shown live on V with placards essentially saying: "no reforms, no budget." Moi sat helpless in 1e full media glare as fracas broke out. Muite, Ochieng Mbeo and Kamuiru ʒitau tried to remove the mace, the symbol of parliamentary authority.[17] Jimmy ngwenyi of KANU, came forward to stop them.

fter this success, the NCEC decided to use the 7th anniversary of the *saba saba* 'th of the 7th month, i.e., July) rally of 1990, to push for constitutional reform. A ublic rally was planned for the Kamukunji grounds on 7/7/1997. The overnment declared the rally illegal. But the public showed up in large numbers. he security forces and supporting private militia were brutal. The merciless hipping and kicking of a bleeding Reverend Timothy Njoya in media flashes round the world, put the Moi administration in bad light. The police and residential guards chased people all over Nairobi and even beat up people praying the All Saints Cathedral. Parliamentarians like Mwai Kibaki; Njoka Mutani; the :e George Kapten and Kamau Icharia were beaten up. Matiba was rescued by aila's guards from a fatal blow by a security officer. Kepta Ombati, an NCEC uth leader was maimed, and fourteen people were reported killed.[18]

1e global images of this event contradicted Moi's image as an international ler statesman, trying to host Inter-Governmental Authority on Development ʒAD) leaders in Nairobi for a discussion on progress, or lack of it, in peace .tiatives for Somalia and Southern Sudan. *The London Times* wrote:

---

ee the two authorities cited above.
'or details, see, Mutunga; *op. cit.,* p. 173.

This was no riot until the government made it one. It was a case of unprovoked and unconscionable brutality, ordered by the state, against people assembled to pray for such elementary things as free speech and accountable government.[19]

There was condemnation by many religious organizations. The NCCK demanded minimum reforms before the 1997 General Elections. The Catholic Bishops argued for the immediate appointment of a constitutional review commission. They further posed questions to President Moi and wondered: "How many Kenyans must die that we may have the desperately needed reforms? What other sign must we look for in order to act to avert an immediate crisis?"[20] International reactions also put the Moi Administration on the spot. Diplomats from 2? countries expressed concern and called on the government to dialogue with those pressing for reforms.[21]

The NCEC had made itself relevant. The backlash which followed the NCEC championed rallies, could not be ignored by Moi and KANU. Even attacks on the NCEC by Kipruto arap Kirwa's (Kalenjin MP for Cherangani who made his name by being disrespectful to Moi, and later apologized) Movement for Dialogue and Non-Violence (MODAN), could not change the tide of popular pressure in support of the NCEC.

The NCEC continued its mass action with a rally in Mombasa on July 26, 1997 The Kisumu rally on August 6, 1997 was leaderless as NCEC leaders were held the airport and forced back to Nairobi. The NCEC called for a general strike of *nane nane* (8th day of 8th month). The strike was a resounding success in Nairobi with public and private business virtually closed down. Raila, James Orengo and Paul Muite led an unplanned rally at which an undercover policeman was killed.

Reacting to this death, the Moi Administration arrested many youths, most of whom were members of Raila's NDP. Maurice Genga Nyagol, one of the youths charged with the murder, died in prison.[22] Thirty-nine NDP members, charged with the murder of the police officer, spent nearly one year in Kamiti remand prison.

---

[19] As quoted in Munene, *op. cit.,* p. 53.

[20] *Ibid.,* p. 53.

[21] *Ibid.*

[22] See, Mutunga, *op. cit.,* p. 177.

Ethnic violence broke out on August 13, 1997 at the Likoni-Kwale area of Mombasa, resulting in over 40 deaths on the Coast. The security forces failed to bring the culprits to justice. Ethnic violence was no longer new in Kenya. Inter-ethnic conflicts had accompanied the 1992 General Elections and the initial thinking on the Likoni-Kwale event was that it was engineered to drive out people from communities likely to vote against KANU. However, although an investigation by Prof. Al-Amin Mazrui for KHRC suggested that the violence was politically motivated, the reason was that KANU had panicked over their apparent loss of the political initiative to the NCEC. As he reported:

> Intelligence sources have suggested that the Likoni-Kwale violence had a much grander agenda than the apparent transformation of the demographic equation in the area for the benefit of KANU candidates. This agenda is related to the "rise and fall" of the NCA/NCEC project. As the evidence presented earlier demonstrates, the organization of the violence began within a month or so of the Limuru 1, a dramatic national event which sent strong shivers down the Moi-KANU spine and made the regime feel it had lost the political initiative to the NCA/NCEC.[23]

Basking in glory, the NCEC called its second plenary session at *Ufungamano* House from August 26-28, 1997. This meeting that was tagged Limuru-Ufungamano II, reviewed the way forward. The National Youth Movement presented some politicians as "anti-reformists" for violating the NCA vision that there could be no elections without minimal reforms. These included Kibaki, Matiba, Wamalwa, Nyikuku and Charity Ngilu.[24]

Raila's NDP, in an "anonymous"[25] memorandum, set out the case for a "parallel government" with revolving presidents. The memorandum argued that the Moi-KANU government was not legitimate as it had shown that it could not protect the lives of Kenyans and would not make minimal reforms. This challenge, which Kamotho, then KANU's Secretary-General called treason, was modified into a

---

As quoted in *ibid.,* p. 179.
Ibid., p. 201-202.
Willy Mutunga had called the memorandum anonymous and at the same time stated that it was an open secret that this memorandum was by Raila's National Development Party. See, ibid., pp. 202 and 207.

demand for a "parallel parliament" lest parliament was dissolved before minima reforms were enacted.[26] Though the idea of what could have caused chaos or successful civilian coup was never implemented, it put serious pressure on th Moi Administration.

Before Limuru-Ufungamano II, Moi had invited religious leaders to facilitat dialogue with the agitators; a role, the religious leaders eagerly accepted. The were immediately separated from the NCEC movement. But they found that th Moi regime would not meet the NCEC's demands for minimal reforms. Finall the government refused to dialogue with the NCEC, arguing that it would onl dialogue with popularly elected representatives. The government boycotted meeting the religious leaders had arranged with the NCEC for August 25, 199°

The Moi Government seized the initiative. A memorandum circulated in parliamer called for an inter-party meeting of MPs. This first meeting on August 26, 199 gave birth to the Inter-Parties Parliamentary Group (IPPG) that eventually led t minimal constitutional reforms before the General Elections of 1997.

The NCEC's influence waned as the IPPG came into being. Many like Kirai Murungi, Martha Karua, MP for Gichugu, and George Anyona, all previous critics of the Moi government joined the IPPG. Anyona became its Secretar General.

The NCEC was undaunted and maintained the pressure with more mass ralli One was planned for Moi Day on October 10, 1997 or *kumi kumi* (*kumi* is ten Kiswahili). The NCEC asked Kenyans, to boycott the Moi Day events and ho mourning rallies at alternative sites. The NCEC planned a rally for the popu Kamukunji grounds. The police tried to stop the rally, and Muite, was arreste assaulted and had his ribs broken.

Raila, like other politicians sympathetic to the NCEC position, had boycotted t IPPG but agreed to fight in the General Elections, "under protest." This decisi to participate in the Elections, finally set Raila apart from Matiba with whom had worked. Matiba boycotted the Elections. But Raila's dedication to constitutio reform received a strong boost after these elections.

---

[26] See, ibid., p. 202.

The IPPG process resulted in a number of minimal reforms before the 1997 Elections. These included ensuring the independence of the Electoral Commission and an increase in its membership by 10 to be nominated by opposition parties. It was also agreed that the 12 nominated MPs would be allotted to political parties in proportion to parliamentary seats won in an election. Sedition was abrogated to enable freedom of expression, and the powers of Chiefs were reduced by an amendment to the Chief's Act. Administrative reforms like the registration of applicants for the status of political parties, processing of private broadcasting licences, were also made. More importantly, the IPPG saw to the enactment of the Constitution of Kenya Review Act (1997).

Raila Odinga and the clamour for a new Constitution

Raila's pressure for constitutional change in Kenya dates from his exile in Norway. In a press statement in Oslo on November 1991 titled: "Our Cause is a Just one," he called attention to the repression faced by FORD under the Moi regime. As part of FORD's demands, he called for "the immediate convocation of a National Constitutional Conference."[27] However, despite Raila's trail-blazing, it is probably correct to say that during most of the period when the "people-driven" clamour for constitutional changes began, Raila was more involved in party building, first at FORD, then FORD-Kenya before the struggle for the control of that party. By leaving FORD-Kenya to start a new unknown party a year before the 1997 General Elections, he had his work cut out.

Raila became very active in the fight for a new constitution after the 1997 Elections. The NCEC and IPPG developments had caused a lot of distrust among political leaders. Raila concluded that the wounds must be healed before there could be progress on a new constitution. Remember that the NDP had concluded that constitutional reforms were crucial for democratic elections.

Raila believed healing of political wounds could be helped by foreign diplomats in Kenya, and approached the German Ambassador Michael Gerdts. Knowing that Bernd Mutzelburg, the previous Ambassador, had played a significant role in

---

[27] See, "Our Cause is a Just one," A Press Statement by Raila Amolo Odinga, Oslo, 21 November 1991, p. 4.

the struggle for multi-party elections in the early 1990s, Raila asked Gerdts to hold functions at his residence to bring politicians together.

Gerdts hosted three separate functions. The first in February 1998, was a dinner for key opposition players, which coincided with the visit to Kenya by the German Deputy Foreign Minister. In attendance were Kibaki, Murungi, Ngilu, Anyang', Anyona and of course, Raila.[28] The visiting Minister expressed his disappointment at the lack of dialogue between opposition leaders and the Government following the elections. He noted that Germany had been at the forefront of support for reforms in Kenya, but would no longer be so if opposition leaders rejected dialogue. The way forward on constitutional review was discussed. The dinner drove home the need for dialogue with the ruling party to realize constitutional reform.[29]

The second dinner was arranged so that Raila could talk to key KANU leaders. The attendees included: Attorney-General Wako, Kipkalya Kones, Bonaya Godana, Mudavadi, Biwott, and Julius Sunkuli, all KANU Cabinet Ministers; and Too, an Assistant Minister. At this time, Raila was already warming to Moi and KANU. Again, the occasion was used to emphasize the need for dialogue among Kenyan politicians and especially, between the ruling party and opposition leaders.

Gerdts' third dinner brought together past opposition party leaders and KANU leaders, who agreed regular formal meetings chaired by the Attorney General at his Chambers. These formal meetings, aimed at jump-starting the review process, became known as the Inter-Parties Parliamentary Committee (IPPC).

The IPPC invited Kenyans to propose how to go about constitutional review. Advertisements were placed in the newspapers and on radio, inviting views on

---

[28] Kiraitu Murungi, *In the Mud of Politics* (Nairobi: Acacia Stantex Publishers, 2000), p. 83, recalls this event except that he conveniently left out Raila Odinga, the prime mover, in the list of attendees. This is not unusual as he also claimed to be one of the FORD "Young Turks" and though he was a latter day entrant, he conspicuously left out Raila's name from his list. See, *In the Mud of Politics,* p. 39. More importantly, however, Kiraitu Murungi seems to have mixed up the sequence of events as the IPPC meetings followed the third dinner (actually second dinner for Kiraitu) and not the first. This is important because of the systematic manner in which Raila Odinga organized the discussions to reduce resistance.

[29] The accounts here were based on Raila's recollection in an interview on November 23, 2003.

the review process. The Constitutional Review Act was published for comments within a month, and a secretariat was set up at the Attorney-General's Chambers to handle the responses.

When they were collated, it was realized that responses had been received from Political Parties, Religious Groups, Women Groups, and Civil Society, who became referred to as the stake-holders. Collation was followed by a two-day consultative meeting at Bomas of Kenya (a cultural centre normally used for the display of various dances from different areas of Kenya as a tourist attraction). At Bomas, all those who had submitted written presentations were invited to present their ideas orally.[30] From the report of this meeting came a discussion document for a smaller stake-holder meeting at Safari Park Hotel.[31]

The main issue at the Safari Park meeting was representation on the Review Commission when one was eventually set up. KANU preferred a Commission of experts who would produce a draft for discussion by a representative forum. But most opposition parties disagreed. They had no problem with experts if the experts represented the stake-holders.

Safari Park I agreed to form a smaller committee to draft an amendment to the Act and submit this to Safari Park II for discussion. This Committee of twelve, was chaired by Bishop Philip Sulumeti, and included Anyona, Raila, Wanjiku Kabira, Martha Karua, Pheobe Asiyo and Kivutha Kibwana. Its proposal of a 25 member Review Commission with 13 from political parties; 5 from women groups; 3 from Religious Groups; and 4 from Civil Society, was agreed, and subsequently endorsed by Bomas II and Parliament.

The next hurdle was political party agreement on sharing their quota and putting names against posts. KANU wanted the places shared based on the number of parliamentary seats held by each party. But the opposition parties wanted to use numbers of votes in the Elections. As the Opposition as a whole, had many more

---

[30] Both Bomas and Safari Park meetings were divided into Bomas I and Bomas II as well as Safari Park I and Safari Park II. These divisions normally represented protracted breaks in the process.

[31] The accounts here and below benefited from interviews with Raila, Mrs. Phoebe Asiyo, who was a member of the Committee that drafted the bill as well as member of the Constitution of Kenya Review Commission and Prof. Wanjiku Kabira, also a member of the Constitution of Kenya Review Commission.

votes than KANU, they wanted the same proportion of Commission places. The Women Groups, Religious and Civil Society Groups also could not agree on how to distribute their allocations.

A stalemate resulted and President Moi, expressing his frustration during a visit to Kiambu, made what became a popular remark, in wondering what "Wanjiku" knew about constitutions to want to make contributions.[32] He argued that experts had drafted Kenya's first Lancaster House Constitution, with politicians only invited to debate the draft. But he was countered vociferously by the people-driven "Ufungamano" Group, who quipped that: "Wanjiku" knew what she wanted and must be in the driver's seat.

In a brainstorming session with his colleagues in a Think-Tank he had set up, Raila concluded that the stalemate must be broken by Parliament. He tabled a motion urging Parliament to resuscitate the review process.

Anyona moved an amendment to Raila's motion, urging Parliament to set up a Select Committee to jump-start the process. Although Raila saw this amendment as complementary, the opposition refused to see things the same. They argued Anyona's amendment defeated the original spirit of the motion. Without further explanation, the opposition parties walked out of Parliament as Raila moved his motion. They went to embrace the Ufungamano group in a collaborative spirit. The exceptions were Munyasia of FORD-Kenya and Martha Karua of the Democratic Party, the latter staying to provide the only dissenting voice during the debate. The motion was passed as amended.

The Parliamentary Select Committee (PSC) was set-up and as usual, Raila as the mover of the motion was elected its Chair-person. Raila realized that his task was more than the mere drafting of a bill. He knew he had to recover the public's confidence in Parliament. The Ufungamano group had captured public imagination, and people had become wary of KANU's governance, seeing any KANU support as aimed at manipulating and hijacking the process.[33]

---

[32] "Wanjiku" in this sense was used as a generic name to represent the ordinary Kenyan as Americans use John Doe in the same sense.

[33] Raila's assessment in an interview on November 23, 2003.

Raila decided that public hearings would give people a sense of involvement and increase support for the process. He also decided that inviting experts to Kenya to talk about their experience and involvement in other countries' constitutional reviews would be very helpful. He got two experts to come and share their knowledge. One was Justice Benjamin Odoki, the Chief Justice of Uganda, who had chaired the Ugandan Constitutional Review. And at Raila's request, Nigeria's President Obasanjo sponsored a visit to Kenya by the late Justice Akinola Aguda, an eminent Nigerian and erudite jurist, who had also served as Chief Justice of Botswana.

Through the Indian High Commission, Raila obtained details of the review then underway in India. From South Africa, he engaged Cyril Ramaphosa, who had chaired the Constitutional Assembly of the South African review process. He also read widely on the Namibia, Ethiopia under Meles Zenawi, and the Tanzanian reviews.

After this extensive effort, the Raila-led PSC produced a draft bill reducing the number of Commissioners from 25 to 15. Importantly, they were to be appointed on merit after a national advertising campaign. But, sensitive to Kenya's Provincial set up, there would be no more than two Commissioners from each Province. The word: stake-holders, was also removed from the draft Act.

The opposition parties remained opposed to the process as Parliament passed the Act. President Moi had no difficulty in signing it into law.

The PSC advert for Commissioners received applications from which 14 were selected, leaving the problem of who would chair the review process. Raila realized that the issue of the Chair must be handled carefully. He knew that any Kenyan, however eminently qualified, would be labelled as either a KANU or NDP sympathizer. To reduce this problem, Raila decided to find a non-resident Kenyan, to chair the Commission .

Raila knew of Professor Yash Pal Ghai, a brilliant Kenyan Asian lawyer, through his brother Dharam Ghai. Raila and Dharam had been teachers at the University of Nairobi in the 1970s where they shared accommodation with Dharam occupying the main house and Raila, a bachelor, in the guest house. In those days, Yash Pal Ghai was teaching at the University of Dar-es-Salaam. Raila found Ghai's book on the constitution of Kenya, interesting and knew he was involved in constitutional review in a number of countries.

Raila asked Attorney-General Amos Wako, about possible candidates for the Chair of the review process. When Raila mentioned Ghai, Wako was reportedly excited as he knew Ghai who had been his teacher in Dar-es-Salaam. He agreed to propose Ghai's name to Moi. Raila knew that if he mentioned Ghai's name, it would be a kiss of death as Moi was suspicious of non-KANU loyalists, especially Raila.

As planned, they approached Moi who agreed to Ghai's appointment without hesitation. Moi asked Wako to trace Ghai and make him an offer. Neither Raila nor Amos Wako knew where Ghai was. The best information was that he was teaching in a University in Hong-Kong and was on sabbatical at the University of Wisconsin.

Ghai agreed to return to Kenya to spearhead the process on the condition that he would be given a chance to reconcile the two different approaches to constitutional review, ie the parliamentary process and the Ufungamano process. He had been taking keen interest in the debate and had been briefed by both the late Ooko Ooki Ombaka as Chair of the People's Review Commission, and Willy Mutunga.

The PSC agreed to this condition. Yash Pal Ghai persuaded the Ufungamano group to join efforts with the PSC-led process by appointing 12 more Commissioners.

Raila had pushed in all directions to break the stalemate on the review process. He succeeded by using the Parliamentary Select Committee as a vehicle. His efforts had involved much liaison between a wary Moi and the Ufungamano group. He used to advantage, Moi's wish for an alliance with the NDP. He pushed for the constitutional review to provide a level playing field for Kenyan politics. Phoebe Asiyo noted:

> "Raila worked hard in going round all the groups, including President Moi negotiating the way forward. Moi became hard pressed on the reconciliatory moves Raila had made with the Ufungamano group. Raila had been a blessing to the process that resulted into a National Conference. It was a convention in the Kenyan parliament that the mover of a motion Chairs the Committee that resulted from the motion. So, under the KANU regime, Raila was Chair of the

Parliamentary Select Committee on Constitutional Review. However, he was out-voted by members of the government he is part of. The removal of Raila as Chair of the Select Committee stems from two things: Leadership jealousies and the fact that some of the other leaders would not trust him. Some people had ideas to remove some of the positions that the people of Kenya wanted. They knew Raila would not have been party to the thwarting of the views of the populace. They had to look for the right person to do the job. Raila had worked hard throughout the entire process and knew the views of all the leaders. Paul Muite had not had that privilege."[34]

Professor Wanjiku Kabira had a similar view:

"Raila handled the Constitution review well. He was the buffer between Moi Government that wanted to kill the process and CKRC. He made sure Government did not jettison it."[35]

Failure to Reach Consensus

The NARC Government that had promised a new Constitution within its first 100 days in office dragged its feet on assuming office. But under pressure from Raila and LDP members of NARC, delegates re-assembled for a deliberative process on April 28, 2003. They met and for almost a year, and reviewed every aspect of the draft published by the CKRC in September 2002. This process produced a revised draft for debate by the plenary of the 629 delegates on February 13, 2004. Most of the provisions of the draft were agreed by consensus. However, devolution of power; the structure and powers of the executive; the transition clause and Khadhi's courts remained very controversial.

After canvassing of the views of Kenyans, the CKRC concluded that Kenyans wanted the Provincial Administration system abolished. This was also the position of Kibaki's Democratic Party when in opposition. But no sooner had Kibaki come to power, than his lieutenants like Murungaru argued to retain the structure.

Consequently, the Devolution Committee at Bomas was one of the most contentious. So, when its Chairman, Dr. Crispin Mbai, was killed on September

---

[34] Interview, July 2, 2003.
[35] Interview, February 21, 2003.

14, 2003, many Kenyans associated the killing with his role in the Committee. Late Mbai was one of the few trusted brains in an informal Think-Tank advising Raila. He was also a close friend and ally who died without being able to hand-over results of research he had done with another colleague who had also died. Matters were not helped when a police video of the interrogation of the three of Mbai's alleged four killers, pointed at a close ally of Kibaki's as the one who financed Mbai's assassination.[36] Resolving the murder of Dr. Mbai became as difficult as reaching a consensus on devolution.

As we have seen, the struggle to reduce presidential powers began when President Kenyatta started to concentrate power in his office, at the expense of Parliament and the Judiciary. However, although in opposition, Kibaki and his Judicial and Constitutional Affairs Minister, had wanted a reduction in the powers of the presidency in favour of an Executive Prime Minister, they rejected any such structural change, after taking power.[37] This problem became more serious because Raila had been promised the post of Prime Minister in the MoU and President Kibaki had made a tacit decision not to honour this agreement. So, Raila's campaign for deconcentration of presidential power in favour of a Prime Minister, was generally seen as him trying to achieve constitutionally, what he had failed to get through the MoU. Raila could not shed this image even when he announced that he was no longer interested in the MoU, and did not want to become Prime Minister.

Linked to this problem was the wish of Minister Murungi to protect a phantom term of office for Kibaki by insisting that the reduction in presidential powers should take effect in 2012. Apparently, Kiraitu had concluded that Kibaki would

---

[36] For details on the video on Mbai's killing, see, *Sunday Standard,* September 28, 2003, pp. 1 & 11ff. For details on the accusation and the denial in parliament, see, East African Standard, Thursday October 9, 2003.

[37] Perhaps the most sincere politician on this issue was John Michuki, who as the Minister for Transport had argued on television that his people [the Kikuyu] had thought President Moi would not vacate power and so they decided to put pressure on him to relinquish some power in favour of a Prime Minister so that they could share power with him. He then wondered about why it should still be necessary to share power when a good man was now the President. In stating this position, he offered what could comically be called the "liver theory" of politics. He had asked the TV reporter if he ever went to buy liver in a butchery and tried to hold it. When the reporter responded in the negative, he stated that it was not possible to hold liver and be still as the person holding must constantly juggle the liver or it would fall. For him, politics should be seen as the art of juggling.

contest for and win re-election in 2007. How else can one explain a refusal to restrict the protection of the current presidential powers until his contract with Kenyans expires in 2007. Although he is allowed another five years after 2007, there should be no reason why Kibaki should stand for President again, if he felt the powers had been curtailed beyond what he would like to enjoy. No one could stop him from being Prime Minister if he preferred that office. That was exactly what Meles Zenawi did in Ethiopia.

Kiraitu threatened Bomas delegates that the Government would walk out of the entire process if his position was rejected. In response, delegates decided to set up a small group to work out a consensus position. The Bishop Philip Sulumeti Consensus Committee hammered out a deal that was overwhelmingly rejected by the delegates in a vote on March 15, 2004. At this stage, the Government delegation, led by Vice-President Awori, walked out on its people. Raila, Balala and Ayacko, as Cabinet Ministers, remained, and Raila, in a spirit of magnanimity tabled a motion that would ensure that President Kibaki would enjoy his powers for the term he had been elected for, i.e., until 2007. But the delegates were unconcerned by the Cabinet walk out, arguing that there was no delegate at Bomas called "government."

The largely GEMA delegates, buoyed by the support of a few cabinet members from other parts of Kenya went ahead with all attempts to stop the consideration of the draft Constitution by the Parliament as demanded by the Constitution of Kenya Review Act. They succeeded by having the judiciary ban the formal handing of the draft Constitution to the Attorney-General for onward transmission to Parliament.[38] In a judicial activist mode, the majority in a three-judge bench led by Justice Aaron Ringera, went beyond Justice Ransley's initial injunction, in another case brought by eight people including retired Presbyterian Reverend Timothy Njoya. They ruled that Parliament had no powers to enact a new Constitution and that only a referendum by Kenyans could enact the Constitution. This despite the fact that the current Constitution and all amendments to it had never been done through a referendum.[39] The Ringera judgement ruled for a referendum although there was no law in place for this purpose. Kibaki made a broadcast on

---

[38] See, the injunction to this effect that was granted by Justice Philip Ransley on Monday March 22, 2004 as reported in *East African Standard,* Tuesday, March 23, 2004, pp. 1 & 3.
[39] On the Ringera led three Bench split decision, see, *Daily Nation,* Friday, March 26, 2004 and *East African Standard* of the same day.

the same day immediately after the court decision, urging the need to focus on national interest and stressing reconciliation. He called on Kenyans to work towards consensus on the contentious issues in the draft constitution.[40]

Thus the ethnic struggle over dominance in Kenya, found its way into constitution-making. The judicial intervention postponed the struggle but did not abate it.

President Kibaki chose the opening of the third session of the 9th Parliament, to pass the buck, by asking MPs to come up with consensus on a new constitution. But it was clear that consensus would not be easily reached. In effect, the wish of the Kibaki Administration to continue to govern under the old constitution was unchallengeable.

However, towards the end of June 2004, a group of former Bomas delegates, got together and christened themselves "Bomas *Katiba* Watch." *Katiba* is the Kiswahili word for constitution. They swore to ensure that the Bomas draft became the new constitution of Kenya, and called a rally on July 3rd. They invited party leaders to address the rally and Raila agreed to speak.

The *Katiba* Watch group which included Martin Shikuku, went ahead with plans for their rally at Uhuru Park. In response, another group decided to hold a rally at Kamukunji grounds in support of the "consensus" position of the Kibaki Government. The police decided to cancel both rallies. The Kamukunji group led by Maina Kamanda, MP for Starehe and Assistant Minister for Local Government, and a staunch ally of President Kibaki, agreed to call-off their rally. But the *Katiba* Watch group decided to go ahead with theirs, especially since the other rally was cancelled. [41]

The attempt to hold the Nairobi rally was successfully disrupted by the police. Raila and Musyoka were conspicuously absent among the MPs like KANU's Gideon Moi, William Ruto and Nick Salat; and Peter Owidi; Reuben Ndolo and Otieno Kajwang' of LDP. When the dust had settled, a demonstrator in Kisumu had been shot dead by the police, and many were injured in Kisumu and Nairobi. All Raila could do, was to object publicly to the high-handedness of the police in

---

[40] *See, ibid.*
[41] See, East African Standard, Saturday, July 3, 2004, pp. 1-3.

calling off the rally. He went further to support a referendum, and distanced himself from the consensus call by President Kibaki.[42] He said: "Let the draft come to Parliament, if they are genuine about dialogue...Then we will amend the Act to provide for a referendum."[43] The response from NAK MPs was to call for Raila's sacking. Though the President had been frequently asked to dismiss Raila, he ignored such calls, even though Raila had once dared the President to sack him. He had retorted that if sacked, he had a home to go to. But he would not resign from Government because LDP was an equal partner in putting Kibaki in office.

The stalemate on the Bomas draft continued as efforts continued to find a consensus bill to allow the draft to be debated in Parliament. After several consultations at the William Ruto led Parliamentary Select Committee (Ruto had replaced Muite), the Constitution of Kenya Review (Amendment), Bill, 2004 was presented to Parliament. NAK MPs joined LDP and KANU colleagues on August 5, 2004 by voting for the bill, losing sight of the need for a 65% vote for any amendment to the Bomas draft. The Bill was presented to the President on November 8. Wasting no time, the President refused assent on the following day. He sent the bill back asking Parliament to cure the "defect" of requiring a 65% majority to amend a draft that was, according to him, not yet a Constitution. For him, this was contrary to the Constitution of Kenya.[44] With the Kibaki new Parliamentary majority resulting from the Government of National Unity, all was set to deal the LDP a blow. But LDP walked out on the subsequent voting on the Bill that cured the problem raised by the President. Presidential assent was announced by *The Standard* on January 25, 2005.

At a retreat at the Sopa Lodge, Naivasha, November 4-7, 2004, the Ruto led Parliamentary Select Committee reached agreement on many of the issues that were regarded as contentious in the Bomas draft.[45] For instance, it was agreed among other issues that the Kadhi's Courts provision would be left as in the

---

[42] See, *ibid.,* pp. 1 & 3.

[43] *Ibid.,* p. 3.

[44] See, the President's Memorandum titled: "Refusal to Assent to the Constitution of Kenya Review (Amendment) Bill, 2004, 9th November 2004, pp. 2-4.

[45] On details, see, Ninth Parliament – Third Session - 2004, The Parliamentary Select Committee on Constitutional Review, "Summary of Report of the Retreat, Sopa Lodge, Naivasha, November 04-07, 2004."

current Constitution as negotiations continue with all stakeholders on the status of Kadhi's courts.[46] On devolution, there would be two levels: National and County with current districts retained as operational units.[47] On the most contentious issue of the executive, it was agreed that: "the Executive authority of the Republic of Kenya will repose in the President, the Prime Minister and the Cabinet... That the President shall appoint as Prime Minister the person who is the leader in Parliament of the Party or coalition of Parties with the majority support in Parliament and shall submit the name of the appointed Prime Minister to Parliament for approval by at least 50% vote of all Members of Parliament."[48] The Prime Minister was expected to share power with the President in harmony. He/She shall be the Leader of Government Business in the National Assembly. Parliament would be crucial in the dismissal of the Prime Minister. Such a move, introduced by either the President or a third of the Parliament in a vote of no confidence would require a fifty per cent vote in the Parliament. An agreement in the PSC to publish a bill to allow for an amendment of section 47 of the current Constitution to allow for the replacement of the current Constitution with a new one was abandoned.

Nonetheless, by the fourth session of the ninth Parliament, Norman Nyaga, the NARC Chief Whip in Parliament decided that only Government friendly MPs would be members of the PSC. Colleagues of Raila were removed. The decision of the LDP to protest by quitting all together and seeking the support of KANU was rebuffed by Uhuru Kenyatta who appeared to have visited State House and presumed to have reached some understanding with President Kibaki. When it was clear that LDP was going to be left out, Raila agreed to return. KANU that thought it would have the Chairmanship of the PSC was disappointed when the NAK MPs insisted on having Simeon Nyachae. With a majority on the Nyaga re-arranged PSC, the Kibaki group had their way. It was now the turn of KANU to walk out and it was pay back time as LDP stayed on.

Nyachae led his PSC majority without KANU and LDP members to a retreat at Kilifi where they reversed some of the agreements reached in Naivasha.[49] On

---

[46] *Ibid.*, p. 3.

[47] *Ibid.*, p. 4.

[48] *Ibid.*, pp. 5-7

[49] See, *The Standard,* Wednesday, July 20, 2005, p. 4. for a detailed comparison of the Bomas Draft, Naivasha Accord and the Kilifi Draft.

devolution, it was agreed that there would be only the national and district levels. On the Executive, it was recommended that Executive authority be vested in the President only. It was also recommended that, "the Articles on the election and impeachment of the President and the power and functions of the Prime Minister be reconsidered."[50]

On July 19, 2005, as Nyachae presented his Kilifi draft with the Naivasha accord and Bomas draft in Parliament, people who had been called to arms by LDP and KANU leaders as well as civil society groups went on demonstrations in Nairobi, Kisumu and Nakuru protesting the attempt to avoid the Bomas draft. In spite of the protests of Raila, Kalonzo, Ruto etc., and paralysis from mayhem and the killing of one person in Nairobi, Parliament went on with its deliberation. The members of Parliament were expected to either adopt or reject the draft and pave the way for the Attorney-General to single handedly play the role of Moses in the Bible and give Kenya a Constitution.

Two days later, Parliament voted on the controversial changes to the Bomas draft. The Government rounded up its MPs and won the day by a vote of 102 to 61 to adopt the Nyachae recommendations Raila broke ranks with the Cabinet as he courageously led three other Ministers: Prof. Anyang' Nyong'o; Najib Balala and Ochilo Ayacko to vote against the Kilifi report.[51] Uhuru Kenyatta and William Ruto as KANU Chairman and Secretary-General respectively, joined the LDP in condemning and voting against the Nyachae draft. Kalonzo Musyoka was conveniently absent. He later stated that it was not worth his time to participate in a "fundamentally flawed process."[52]

From this time on, the die was cast. The public show of solidarity from President Kibaki by visiting Nyanza province and proclaiming Raila as his friend as he promised a number of developmental projects in support for his decision to seek re-election that he announced during the three-day tour at the end of July did not change the animosity over the Constitution. Raila had started his mobilization for the referendum as the only way left to counter President Kibaki and his group.

---

[50] *Ibid.*

[51] For more details, see, *The Standard,* Friday July 22, 2005.

[52] See, Kalonzo's explanation in *The Standard,* Saturday July 23, 2005, p. 3.

Meanwhile, the Attorney-General went ahead and came out with his own draft that was named after him as the Wako draft.[53] The Attorney-General retained the spirit of the Kilifi draft and in addition made it more difficult to impeach the President. He also created other courts for the Christians and the Hindus in addition to the Kadhi's courts. However, the Christians and Hindus were not amused about Wako's gift. While the Catholic and Anglican Churches asked their respective adherents to read the draft and make up their minds, some other Christian denominations and Muslims, in the large part, promised to vote against the draft.

President Kibaki, even before the draft Constitution was made public, jumped the gun by stating that he would lead the campaign for a 'Yes' vote on the new Constitution.[54] Murungi, was later to make it clear that the drive for 'Yes' vote was a Government project for which all State resources would be deployed.[55] In a rally in Meru, he pointed out that the battle lines for the referendum on the Wako draft was between President Kibaki and Raila Odinga. As he stated: "Those who will vote 'No' will be backing Raila Odinga in 2007 whereas those for 'Yes' will stick with Kibaki."[56] He urged the people to vote for "Banana" the symbol given to 'Yes' as opposed to Orange, the symbol of the Raila led 'No' group. Raila with his colleagues accepted the gauntlet.

The collaboration of LDP, KANU and some members of FORD-People and FORD-Kenya they tagged the "Orange Democratic Movement" and announced that the movement would be a vehicle for further relationship towards the 2007 elections. The initial five Ministers on the campaign trail: Raila; Kalonzo; Nyong'o; Balala and Ayacko were subsequently joined by Linah Jebii Kilimo, the State Minister for Immigration who defected from the Banana group and William ole Ntimama of the Office of the President.

The campaigns were marred by some level of intolerance and violence that resulted in the police killing eight people, four in Kisumu and another four in Mombasa. School children were among the dead in the Kisumu violence.

---

[53] See, *Kenya Gazette Supplement No. 63,* Nairobi, 22nd August, 2005.
[54] See, Daily Nation, Wednesday, August 10, 2005, pp. 1-2.
[55] This point was not only made a few times, the President and many of his Ministers announced a number largesse that were aimed at wooing voters. Salary increases, land titles were given as many new districts were announced during many organised visits to State House.
[56] *The Standard,* Saturday, September 10, 2005, p. 1.

The referendum took place peacefully on November 21, 2005. Orange led the vote with 3,548,477 as against Banana that realized 2,532,918 votes. The Wako draft was resoundingly defeated by 57% of total votes cast. The Orange Democratic Movement triumphed in 7 of the 8 provinces that make up Kenya. They lost overwhelmingly in President Kibaki's ethnic base, Central Province.

Though the President immediately accepted the statement from the people, he proceeded to sack his entire Cabinet and prorogued Parliament. His Vice-President, who was among many leaders like Nyachae, who lost the vote in their respective constituencies, announced that the thank you rallies that the Orange group had planned for the whole country were banned as they were a threat to 'national security.' The thank you rally that took place at the Uhuru Park on Saturday November 26, had attracted a huge crowd. The Government became jittery of the possibility of an African orange revolution and decided to avoid additional rallies. Of course, unperturbed about whether he was re-appointed into the Cabinet, Raila swore that the rallies would take place as he and colleagues declared that the Government order was unconstitutional and high-handed. Raila called on the President to resign and dissolve Parliament for a fresh mandate.

Chapter 19
Private Accummulation

It is not a crime to be wealthy. We should encourage that under a free enterprise system. The problem arises when people use office to accumulate.

Raila Amolo Odinga, on "The Summit," Kenya Television Network, 21 November 2002.

Jaramogi Oginga Odinga, before Raila, had recognized the importance of business not only as a basis for proving that Africans can perform, but more as an avenue for wealth accumulation to pursue political goals. He made the point very clearly in his autobiography:

"I was convinced that to start the battle against White domination we had to assert our economic independence. We had to show what we could do by our own effort. We had had it drummed into us that the Whites had the brains to give the orders and it was for Africans to carry them out. We had to show we were capable of enterprise and development in fields beyond our *shambas*. It was no good bridling at accusations of our inferiority. We had to prove our mettle to the government, to the Whites."[1]

Raila saw some of his father's companies disappear as he fell from the political order in Kenya. He decided to build his own businesses. The stories of the challenges he faced and his determination to succeed, are as interesting as the political role he has played.

It was not unusual for mischievous people to construe Jaramogi Oginga Odinga's nationalism as communist rabble-rousing. Nothing could be farther from the truth about a man who dreamt of black enterprises as a key route to decolonisation. As a teacher, he kept a small poultry farm from which he saved the profits, and with a few colleagues purchased a truck from army surplus stocks to move goods between Kisumu and Nairobi. This project failed. During those teaching years,

---

[1] Oginga Odinga, *Not Yet Uhuru*, (Nairobi: East Africa Educational Publishers, 1967), p. 76.

he also joined a savings association that floundered. But Jaramogi was not deterred. He learned from the experience and set up the Luo Thrift and Trading Corporation. He began a chain of enterprises that included Posho Mills; Printing Press; Sugar Farming; Bus Services to different parts of Kenya, Uganda and Mwanza in Tanzania; and an Export-Import Clearing and Forwarding Company.

Raila and his brother Oburu were born when their father was trying his hands at various private initiatives. Raila tried to manage his father's enterprises when Jaramogi was incarcerated after the 1969 Kisumu massacre.[2] Jaramogi's partners resisted having Raila on the boards of the companies, insisting on power of attorney from Jaramogi for Raila to act in his place. While seeking power of attorney, the Bus Company failed as the banks called for re-payment[3] Unable to meet such demands, the buses were sold at throw-away prices.[4]

Raila's wish to earn a living to support his father's family, saw him eagerly accept a post at the University of Nairobi's Mechanical Engineering Department. He readily got accommodation and took on some consultancies.

As chance would have it, Raila was introduced by a Deputy Director of Industries, Maina, to Franz Schineiss, a German seeking approval to set up business in Kenya. Schineiss had been in Rhodesia (the ex-name of Zimbabwe) but wanted to start anew in Kenya.

Schineiss was excited to find a capable and qualified engineer, who also spoke German. The duo agreed on a consulting engineering partnership in which Raila would be a 'sleeping partner', given his University employment. They set up office in Caltex House. Schineiss had specialized in boilers and Raila in pressure vessels (container drums for oil storage). Raila's Masters Thesis was on pressure vessels and in Germany, he had gained practical experience with a company that made pressure vessels for oil companies. Schineiss had experience in consulting for oil companies in Rhodesia. With this new partnership, they were well placed to handle contracts on containers for oil companies.

---

[2] The Kisumu massacre will be treated in some detail later.
[3] The Odinga family, in general insist that re-payments demand were instigated by the government as they were not due at the time.
[4] Interview with Raila Odinga, February 15, 2004.

Then one morning, an Asian friend of Raila's who headed the Electrical Laboratories at the University of Nairobi, I.G. Desai, told him of an Asian who had been expelled from Uganda by Idi Amin. The Asian had transported his metal working machines from Jinja to Nairobi and was trying to sell them to fund air tickets for his family to go to London.

Seeing the machines, Raila realized he could use them to set up a mechanical workshop. The asking price for the machinery was 20,000 Kenyan shillings (the equivalent of today's 3000 dollars.) Raila offered 12,000 shillings and a deal was struck. But Raila knew he had no money.

Raila had no relationship with any bank in Kenya. But he took his chance and asked to meet Mr. Jai, General Manager of the Bank of India, who had been a friend of his father and had handled Jaramogi's finances in Kenya and abroad. He asked Jai for a loan of 20,000 shillings to buy the machines, pay the lease on a property to serve as a workshop in the industrial area, and buy immediate furniture needs. Mr. Jai listened but did not give him the money, asking him to return to the bank after dark at 7 pm, and showed him how to knock on the window of Jai's office.

Raila knocked at the scheduled time and Jai opened the window and threw the money at him. He had received a huge amount without signing any documents and without security. But Jai told him that he would ensure that Raila repaid the money.

Raila paid the Asian for the machinery, and with Schineiss, rented a 5,000 square feet warehouse in Nairobi's Industrial Area. This warehouse ("go-down" in Kenyan parlance) was on what was then known as Kingston Road and is now Kampala Road.

Subsequently, he learned that the petrol company, AGIP had started bottling Liquefied Petroleum Gas (LPG), and needed 5,000 cylinders. He successfully negotiated an order with AGIP, and instead of making quick money by importing the cylinders, opted for production. He negotiated with his bankers to raise a loan to buy presses, lathes etc, and when the machines were acquired, production of cylinders started. The name Standard Processing Equipments Construction and Erection (Spectre) was chosen for the company. When Spectre started in

1971, the plant could produce about 36,000 cylinders per year. Three decades later, it can make 150,000 cylinders per year.

But building Spectre was not a smooth experience. It was difficult to raise working capital. They needed money to buy the machinery to make the cylinders. Raila approached Joan Kodhek, wife of the late Foreign Minister, CMG Argwings-Kodhek, whose parents and Raila's had been friends. She provided 20,000 shillings.

The path to growth for the company started when Raila attended a function at the German Embassy in Nairobi and met Theo Schroll, Economic Advisor to the Kenya Industrial Estates (KIE), and funded by a German government technical assistance programme, aimed at promoting African industrial entrepreneurship. Schroll told Raila that he was in Kenya to recruit and train Africans as future entrepreneurs. They were giving loans to budding entrepreneurs to achieve their dreams of industrialization. Enterprises could be funded up to 80% if the African could find the 20% balance to trigger a loan. The KIE was a subsidiary of the Industrial and Commercial Development Corporation (ICDC).

Raila briefed Schroll on Spectre. Schroll was delighted to meet someone on the route to industrialization in Kenya. He visited Kingston Road the following day and concluded that Spectre met the conditions for KIE assistance. He invited Raila to meet the Managing Director, Kipng'eno Arap Ng'eny, a Kalenjin, trained as a Structural Engineer, first in Pakistan and then with Jaramogi's help in the Soviet Union. As one of the first Kalenjin graduates, he joined the ICDC and was seconded to KIE as Managing Director.

Ng'eny and Schroll were impressed and worked with Raila on a proposal for the expansion of Spectre, including acquiring more modern machines from Germany. The KIE agreed to value the achievement of Spectre and use the result as part of its contribution to the 20% required. KIE would inject new funds to purchase the machines.

A feasibility study suggested that 500,000 shillings would be needed. Spectre was valued at 48,000 shillings, so 52,000 shillings was to be raised to meet Spectre's 20% commitment to trigger the release of 400,000 shillings. Jaramogi was released as negotiations were underway, and he lent the money to Spectre. This loan was subsequently converted into equity when Spectre could not repay it.

As Spectre developed its relationship with KIE, East Africa was added to its name. This showed that the company would now meet the demands of Uganda and Tanzania. Ngesso Okolo, a friend of Raila's whom he had met in Germany where Okolo studied Mechanical Engineering, was appointed as a Director. Two years before Raila, after his studies, he had returned to Kenya to teach at the University of Nairobi before going for further studies at the University of Berkeley in California. On return, he worked for East Africa Spectre for about a year before pursuing a new career with Caltex.

Setting up of Standards for Kenya

As East Africa Spectre grew, it faced the biases of multinational corporations towards local companies. It was difficult to accept that a local company could produce cylinders. A campaign began that East Africa Spectre's products did not meet international standards, as they had not been tested by competent experts, and they were declared dangerous. This campaign, according to Raila, was led by Shell.[5]

This campaign forced the Kenyan Government to suspend local production of cylinders for safety reasons. Raila had made Spectre cylinders to British standards. They were required to manufacture some for testing in the presence of all major oil companies at the Ministry of Works. The samples passed the tests, but the oil multinationals demanded that samples be sent to the British Atomic Energy Commission Testing Laboratories at Wolverhampton in the UK.

After the cylinders were sent at EA Spectre's expense, results were not received for six months. But again, they were positive and the oil companies agreed to give EA Spectre orders. The company had operated for a year maintaining a workshop and paying salaries before they received their first orders.

The oil companies insisted that as Kenya had no standards, EA Spectre must have testing done by such entities like Lloyds or Bureau Veritas. East Africa Spectre contacted both companies. Lloyds wanted to station a European in Nairobi at EA Spectre's expense. But Bureau Veritas, had a representative, John Edon, in

---

[5]   Interview, February 15, 2004.

Mombasa whose only cost would be for testing visits to Nairobi. Bureau Veritas got the order. But it was still a cumbersome procedure involving production of a batch of cylinders, suspending production until Edon could do the testing and issue certificates to accompany batch deliveries to customers.

Knowing that this process was unsustainable, Raila petitioned the Government to set up a Kenyan Bureau of Standards. The response by James Osogo, the Minister of Commerce and Industry was positive. A protégé of Jaramogi, Osogo had moved from teaching into Parliament. After Jaramogi broke up with KANU, Osogo remained sympathetic. Raila was invited to work with the Ministry to set up the Kenya Bureau of Standards (KBS). The Bill that came out of this exercise was passed by Parliament.

The Superintendent of Weights and Measures, Francis Maiko, was the first Director of KBS which had a Board chaired by Kipng'eno Arap Ng'eny. Although they advertised for provisional officers, the low civil service salaries did not attract anyone. At the second advertisement with increased scale, Raila, who had resigned from the University to run EA Spectre, decided to go and initiate the writing of standards, including on LPG cylinders. With six others, he joined KBS in 1975 as Group Standards Engineer, the second highest post.

With Engineer Owino Okwero, Raila received specialized training at the British Standards Institution in London. On return, he prepared, among others, Kenya Standards KS 05/06 of 1975 on LPG cylinders.

With these standards, LPG cylinders could be tested locally without Bureau Veritas. Raila also helped to start the Department of Testing within KBS. Persuaded to stay on, he received additional training at the United States National Bureau of Standards in Washington D.C. and the University of Denver in Colorado. He was promoted to Deputy Director of KBS. He initiated construction of KBS Headquarters and the setting up of laboratories and a training programme for young Kenyan graduates to operate the laboratories. He also initiated technical cooperation on standardization between Kenya and Germany. KBS developed a working relationship with the Indian Standards Institution which sent personnel to train Kenyans and received Kenyans in India on exchange programmes.

Raila's stay at the KBS was halted by his detention by the Moi regime.[6] The effort he had put into EA Spectre ensured that the company he had nurtured on a part time basis survived his detention.

The Nairobi Industrial Area attests to the high failure rate of many KIE-supported entities of three decades ago. Many were started based on political connections by people lacking the necessary know-how. There was also competition with imports which EA Spectre also faced. When Raila was detained by Moi, some of his political adversaries, were licenced to import cylinders, which they did in collaboration with some Kenyan Asians.[7] Some KIE projects were taken over in joint ventures by the foreigners. But EA Spectre succeeded against all odds under Raila's determined leadership.

But the EA Spectre success story would not be complete without mentioning that Oluande K'Oduol in an unpublished autobiography claims to have played a vital role before being paid off after a court battle.[8] Then there was the dedication of Israel Wasonga Agina[9] and Ida Odinga, whose relationship with EA Spectre began immediately after her marriage to Raila. The company was a safe haven for a newly-married under-graduate, to study away from the disturbances at home, on Sundays and public holidays when the library was closed. Almost a decade later, Ida had responsibility at EA Spectre unexpectedly thrust on her, when Raila's first arrest coincided with Jaramogi, the Company Chairman being put under house arrest, and Agina, the Technical Manager, fled into exile. With Spectre's management on the run or in detention, Ida was asked to put in some time at Spectre. She took charge of the company's administration and finance, spending her evenings and most Saturdays there. With the death of Jaramogi in 1994, Ida gave up active service at FORD-Kenya, and moved into Spectre as full time Director of Finance.[10] She became the Acting Managing Director in February 2004.

---

[6] Details on this is in this volume.
[7] Interview with Raila Odinga, February 15, 2004.
[8] For details, see, B.F.F. Oluande K'Oduol, *Cultural and Political Evolution in Kenya: an autobiography,* unpublished manuscript dated 12/12/1994, pp. 86-88.
[9] Israel Wasonga Agina who joined East Africa Spectre in May 1973 is a business associate of Raila. See Chapter 9.
[10] Interview with Ida, Nairobi, June 11, 2003.

Applied Engineering Services

Raila, and Engineers James Owino, Owino Okwero and Charles Aloo, operated Applied Engineering Services Limited (AESL) which started in 1978 with Mirulo Okello, one of its engineers, working on water projects. AESL helped to set up, and gave accommodation, to Professional Consultants, a group of young engineers trying to find their feet. They included Alex Karanja, George Mak'Odawa and Jude Loveday, a Kenyan of Goan origin. AESL sometimes worked on project consortiums with Professional Consultants.

AESL specialized in industrial engineering consultancies. Their services included project identification; feasibility studies; engineering design; plant design; resource mobilization; construction; installation; and commissioning. It was also involved in other fields like the provision of municipal engineering services including water and sanitation, irrigation and flood control. The consultancy also handled mechanical and electrical services especially air-conditioning systems.

AESL's clients included the Ministry of Water Development, National Irrigation Board; the United Nations and Brollo Kenya Limited. Professional Consultants remained one of the major indigenous consulting firms in Kenya; but AESL failed. When Raila was detained, the fortunes of the company deteriorated. Consultancy contracts depended on profile. AESL was adversely affected as contracts ceased and Raila's colleagues could only complete those won before his problems with the Moi regime began.

Molasses

Raila's foray into wealth creation did not end with the manufacture of cylinders. In June 1996, with a company named Spectre International Limited, he acquired the Kenya Chemical and Food Corporation, an agro-chemical energy and food complex in Kisumu.

The project, based on molasses processing, was conceived in 1977[11] in response to the 1970s oil crisis. The idea was to produce 20 million litres of ethanol (power

---

[11] The account here has depended on a report prepared for the board of the Kenya Chemical and Food Corporation, in April 1981 and accompanying Foreword to the report by Pierre Delville, Chairman Eximcorp, S.A., Managers of the Kisumu Complex. Interviews with Raila, Kajwang' and the newspaper accounts after Assistant Minister Maina Kamanda accused Raila's family of grabbing the Molasses plant on July 25, 2004, have also been useful.

alcohol) from molasses. As 1 litre of ethanol would yield 1.35 litres of petrol when blended, it was calculated that the project would reduce the cost of Kenya's fuel imports. Savings of 170,000 barrels at $42 per barrel would be U.S.$7 million a year. Other products like potable alcohol, citric acid, yeast, vinegar, oxygen, sulphuric acid, ammonium sulphate fertilizer, gypsum, carbon dioxide and methane gas would make total net savings of US$16 million a year, projected to rise to US$20-30 million a year by the mid-1980s. Kenya was said to be lifting itself by its own boot straps.

The project that was to become operational by August 1981 was abandoned when no more funds were forthcoming. It was 90% completed and spent over US$106 million of foreign loans arranged by the Madhvani Group and Eximcorp and contributions by the Kenyan Government which took 51% equity, to foreign investors' 49% (Chemfood Investment Corporation, S.A. and Advait International, S.A.). The Madhvani Group (Asian Managers), the organizer of the venture was the major investor in Advait International. It demonstrated the lack of transparency and accountability in industrial ventures by developing countries' governments from the 1960s to the 1980s, and in many, to date.

The benefit of the project was to be more than mere cost cutting. Employment was to be created for many Kenyans. The production and sourcing of the main raw material (sugar cane) would have had a major multiplier effect, far beyond the 240 acres on which the plant stood in Kisumu. This multi-purpose complex would spur chemical industrial growth in Kenya.

Government's investment in the project was made with a loan from Kenya Commercial Bank (KCB). When the Government stopped servicing the loan, the KCB put the project into receivership. This was followed by plans to sell the project assets as scrap.

Attempts were made to revitalize the project, one by the late Dr. Robert Ouko, in whose parliamentary constituency, the project was situated. He was murdered in February 1990, in circumstances that some linked to his attempts to expose to the public, the corruption that killed the project.[12]

---

[12] The Gor Sunguh Parliamentary Select Committee is currently examining the circumstances in which Robert Ouko was assassinated. This attempt under a new government is taking place after the Moi regime stopped a Judicial Inquiry that was trying to get to the bottom of Ouko's death.

Dalmas Otieno, Minister of Industry in the Moi regime, carried out a feasibility study on the project using a 3 million shillings grant from the American EximBank. The study concluded that the molasses project was not viable.[13]

Raila, saw the advertisement to sell the project assests, and made an inspection tour. He noted that everything had been given lot numbers for auction. The project that was to create so much employment was now going to scrap dealers and others searching for components and equipment. Although the global price of oil had stabilized, Raila saw possibilities to use the plant for alternative production and decided it could be revived.

Raila was joined at a meeting at the Nairobi Club to discuss the revival of the plant,[14] by Prof. Peter Anyang' Nyong'o, Joab Omino and Orwa Ojodeh, all MPs from Nyanza Province. They decided to raise money internally and seek an international investor to buy the project and realize the dream that started it.

Raila was determined to stop the project from being auctioned piece-meal. Several companies attended. As well as many Kenyan companies (some representing foreign interests), there were one each from the United Kingdom, Sweden and South Africa. Raila had decided to enter the fray with three companies with three different persons to bid. There was Spectre International that he would represent; Nam Development Corporation (NADECO) to be represented by Prof. Anyang' Nyong'o; and Hon. Orwa Ojode's Metro Agencies Ltd was to be represented by Israel Agina.

The auctioneers had made clear that equipment and not land was to be sold. The auction condition was for the highest bidder to pay 25% on the fall of the hammer.

Raila had reasoned that he and others on his side, could persuade the Government to give the land in furtherance of the goal of providing employment for Kenyans. After all, the Government had obtained the land from the community for peanuts on the understanding that the community would benefit from employment to be realized from the project.

Interview with Dalmas Otieno, February 21, 2003.
See, Anyang' Nyong'o's statement as reported in *Saturday Nation,* August 7, 2004, p. 40.

Spectre International's winning bid of five hundred and sixty million shillings, was then about ten million dollars. Raila knew he could not raise that amount in ten days. So, the following day, he sent the auctioneers two cheques of a million shillings each as a sign of commitment and asked them to confirm that the title to the 240 acres of land would pass to Spectre International. He argued that since the buildings had been marked as lots, they could only be used on the land on which they stood.

There was a swift response that the plant was sold without the land, and the cheques were returned. The two runners up in the bidding process began to put pressure to acquire the plant. They knew that Spectre International could not raise the money.

Raila sought a court injunction to prevent the sale to anyone else, until the question of title to the land was resolved arguing that Spectre International would be cheated if its interest in acquiring the buildings on the land was pushed aside before a court ruling. He was granted the injunction.

With time on his side, Raila moved to politicise the whole issue. He argued that the project had been used with public funds and that land had been bought cheaply from the community on the Government's promise that the people would reap social benefits including jobs for their children from the plant. He started to mobilize funds for the project by forming Kisumu Development Trust to receive investments for the project.

Political Workings on Molasses

Raila was obviously buying time and was determined to raise money to buy the plant. But he also saw a political dividend. His sensitisation of the people to struggle to prevent the plant from being removed from Kisumu, endeared him more to the people. He was fighting a major battle in the interest of many communities whose hopes had been raised by promises of multiplier effects from the plant.

The 1997 Elections were just around the corner. Raila had problems popularising himself for his contest as a presidential candidate. KANU's control over the Provincial Administration would not make the campaign easy for opposition parties in many parts of the country. But they could not stop Raila's movements all over the country claiming to be raising funds to purchase the Kisumu plant. He had borrowed a leaf from the itinerant movements of his father in East Africa to collect funds for the Luo Thrift and Trading Corporation and to strengthen the Luo Union and foster anti-colonialism in Kenya.[15]

Otieno Kajwang', one of Raila's collaborators, elaborated on the political benefits of the molasses project. He stated:

"When we formed NDP, we had very little political space. KANU would not allow us have meetings. The molasses project was useful in two ways. We managed to travel throughout the country speaking the politics of investment and politics of the day at the same time. The molasses was used to popularise the NDP and it gave Raila a higher visibility. It also united Luos to feel that they can own some productive enterprise that could translate into jobs in agriculture and services and profit."[16]

Beyond this, Raila achieved the main objective of stopping the Moi government from dismembering and selling the molasses plant as scrap. This was an important achievement given that the Government was then against Raila as an opposition leader. Raila postponed the evil day and bought valuable time that was to come in handy later.

Raila's effort was also successful in galvanizing many Kenyans to ensure that a 90% complete project was not sold-off at 10% of its paper value. Many Kenyans in the country and in the Diaspora understood this, and supported, Raila's zeal. They sent messages of support to the media.

Funding the Molasses Project

Raila's attempt to attract mass funds to pay for the bid failed. The plant was more of an emotional disappointment to Luos who could see the wasting structures on the Busia-Kisumu Road and from the Lake. The Luo elite was in the Universities and lacked the resources available to some of their Kikuyu and Kalenjin

---

For details on this, see, Oginga Odinga, *Not Yet Uhuru,* (Nairobi, East African Educational Publishers, 1967)

Interview with Otieno Kajwang', Nairobi, April 11, 2003.

counterparts who had cornered national resources under Presidents Kenyatta and Moi. Raila received only phantom pledges that were never met.

By October 1996, the Kisumu Development Trust had raised only Ksh 1.844 million.[17] By April 1998, mobilization costs, returned cheques and bank charges stood at about Ksh 980,000. After an additional receipt of KSH 145,000 was added, the balance amounted to about KSH 1 million, a far cry from the sum needed for the acquisition of the plant.

For a long time, no major investor took interest in Raila's offer of a joint venture. The project was deemed unviable. The arguments were that:

1. It made no sense to invest in a project situated on a land whose title was with a Government unwilling to release it.
2. The plant was deemed larger than the molasses that could be made available
3. The projected available sugar-cane as raw materials was deemed inadequate
4. Since it was established in a city and not next to a sugar plantation, the transport costs would be huge.
5. The cost of completion would be enormous.
6. The plant was technologically obsolete.

But characteristically, Raila would not give up. As part of his party's warming to the Moi Government after the 1997 Elections, and the subsequent merger with KANU,[18] Raila paid and wrested title to the land from the Government.

He went back to the drawing board. As the plant was deemed by its receivers, not to have been sold in 1996, Raila, now with a favourable disposition from the Moi government and serious negotiations with KCB, persuaded the receivers to re-open the bid.

For transparency, the Receivers wrote to the three highest bidders asking if they were still interested in acquiring the plant and if so, to make an offer. The secon

---

[17] This information is based on the balance of payments statement that Raila provided on May 2004. Otieno Kajwang' had corroborated this figure by approximating total collection to million shillings in an interview with the author in Nairobi on April 11, 2003.
[18] The move towards the merger is in this volume.

highest bidder in 1996 was Equip Agencies Ltd, a Kenyan company which had represented a Swedish company. The Swedish company had lost interest. The third highest bidder Nam Development Corporation was also not interested.

Revitalization of the struggle to rejuvinate the project, began in earnest in November 2003. Raila persuaded a Canadian investor, Diamond Works Limited to buy a 55% controlling stake for US$2 million.

As rehabilitation at the plant continued, in the wake of Raila's call on some of his cabinet colleagues allegedly involved in the Anglo Leasing and Finance scandal,[19] to resign as investigations took place, the MP for Starehe and Local Government Assistant Minister Maina Kamanda told the press after a church service on July 25, 2004, that Raila had "grabbed" the molasses plant and the land on which it stood. He reportedly produced a letter dated November 21, 2003, from the Commissioner of Lands Mrs. J. Okungu, stating that the title to the 240 acres and had been issued to Spectre International Ltd. Kamanda described the transaction as fraudulent. He asked: "Why are you press people describing some people as clean? Is this not corruption"?[20] The next day, he claimed that Raila had made his Canadian partner in the project, sole supplier of bitumen to Raila's Roads and Public Works ministry.

Oburu Oginga as Chairman of Spectre International Limited, and in the absence of Raila at the Democratic Party Convention in Boston, responded swiftly to Kamanda's allegation, saying: "We do not want to introduce politics into business which is about to take off. I think it is very malicious to do so. He should come and join us instead of hitting us below the belt."[21] Asserting that the transaction was above board, he asked: "How can you grab something given for a particular purpose"?[22]

As part of the normal division within the NARC ruling coalition, the Minister for Lands and Housing, Amos Kimunya stated that the cabinet was studying the circumstances under which the land was acquired in the report of a presidential

---

The Anglo Leasing affair will be examined later.
See, *East African Standard,* Monday July 26, 2004, pp 1.
Daily Nation, Monday July 26, 2004, p. 1.
Ibid., p. 2.

commission to examine illegally acquired lands. His Assistant Minister Joshua Orwa Ojodeh responded that there was nothing wrong as all procedures had been followed. Prof Anyang' Nyong'o joined in on August 6 when he called for a halt to the adverse publicity for the project. He noted that many white elephant projects had been abandoned under the KANU administration and said: "Any investor prepared to revive such projects to boost employment and economic growth, has the full support of the Government."[23]

Even before Anyang' Nyong'o's comment, Raila dismissed Kamanda's charge as an inconsequential red-herring. He argued that the Government does not sell land but leases it for particular purposes. He asserted that the Government took the land from the people of Kisumu on the understanding that the plant would give them employment, and that he was trying to realize that goal. He would not be diverted by claims from the Kamandas of this world.[24] On his return to Nairobi on August 3, Raila described Kimunya's claim that the Cabinet was investigating acquisition of the land as "absolute nonsense." He claimed he was being accused to divert attention and cover up corruption in Government.[25] Threatening to sue Kamanda for defamation, he said that Spectre had offered the Government 12 million shillings for the plant and the offer was accepted when no other company showed interest. A letter of allotment on the land had been issued on September 4, 2001 and all premiums and charges were paid. He asked:

> "For those suggesting that there was any error – even corruption – in the allocation of the land, which was surrendered by the people of Kisumu for this project, I pose the question: Is it now the policy of the government to repossess all land which has been allocated to the various projects undertaken in this country since independence"? Is it an issue with only Kisumu molasses plant land"?[26]

Raila denied the claim that the Canadian company in the molasses project was supplying bitumen to his ministry and gave a list of suppliers. He went further note that all suppliers of bitumen had been appointed before he assumed office

---

[23] See, *Saturday Nation*, August 7, 2004, p. 40.
[24] Telephone interview with the author while Raila was in London on August 2, 2004 on his way Nairobi after a visit to the United States.
[25] See, *East African Standard*, Wednesday August 4, 2004, p. 1.
[26] See, *Daily Nation*, Wednesday, August 4, 2004, pp. 1-2.
[27] *Ibid.*, p. 2.

However, the Head of Public Service, Francis Muthaura entered into the fray in a letter he wrote on August 17, 2004 to the Inspector General of Corporations, Mr. Johnson Otenyo. Muthaura asked Otenyo to give him a report on how the Kisumu molasses plant ended up in the hands of the present owners. Two days after this instruction, Lawyer George Oraro, on behalf of Spectre International challenged the power and authority of Muthaura to interfere in a private transaction and wondered about when the molasses plant became a Statutory Corporation.[28]

Otenyo, however, continued with the probe and apparently submitted a report to Muthaura on November 17, 2004, to the effect that the deal on the transfer of the plant and the land on which it stood were clean.[29] Otenyo stated that Spectre International paid KSH120 million for the movable assets of the plant and was allocated the land on which the plant stood by the Government in January 2001. After Spectre had paid KSH3.6 million for the allocation, titles for the land were issued in February 2002.

The determined effort of Raila in making a success of a molasses plant that had been ruined by kleptomania was an additional kudos to the zeal of a bold entrepreneur in industry. He exercised courage where many faltered and doggedly searched for an answer in a manner that showed his power in thinking out of the box.

---

[28] For details, see, East African Standard, Friday, August 20, 2004, pp 1-2 and *Daily Nation,* Friday August 20, 2004, pp 1 & 4.

[29] See, *The Standard,* Monday, February 21, 2005, pp. 1 & 4.

Chapter 20
Public Stewardship

Raila Odinga first became a member of Kenya's cabinet under President Moi. He was initially appointed to the Ministry of Energy taking charge of electric power and energy from hydro-carbons. The charge for electric power was later separated from his responsibilities and handed to another Minister. Under President Kibaki, he was re-appointed into cabinet, holding the portfolio of Roads, Public Works and Housing. How has Raila performed in public office?

Daniel arap Moi's Minister

As noted earlier, Raila was named Minister of Energy by President Moi on June 11, 2001. This Ministry had two components: electricity and petroleum. These two components had been in different ministerial hands. While Yekoyada Francis Masakhalia, KANU MP for Butula constituency in Busia District, was Minister of Energy but concentrating on electricity, Francis Pollis Loile Lotodo, a close ally of President Moi and KANU MP for Kapenguria constituency in West Pokot District concentrated on Petroleum.

Francis Lotodo died in office on Wednesday November 8, 2000 and he was not immediately replaced. There was a general pressure on President Moi by the Breton Woods multilateral institutions to reduce the number of ministries and ministers. In addition, Raila's understanding during the negotiations for his appointment was that he would hold the two components and become the super Minister of Energy. Indeed, he was so appointed. As a result, Raila also acquired overall supervisory powers over the six public corporations – parastatals in Kenyan parlance – under the Ministry of Energy. These were: National Oil Corporation; Kenya Pipeline Corporation; Kenya Oil Refinery; Kenya Power and Lighting Company (KPLC); Kengen (electricity generating entity) and the Electricity Regulatory Board (ERB).

Raila embarked on a tour of familiarization with the activities of the Ministry and the parastatals under him in order to acquire a proper picture before implementing policy changes for improvement. This effort included an engagement with the private sector stake-holders (multinational and indigenous oil marketers as well as independent power producers of energy) with respect to energy. He realized that Kenya lacked a national energy policy. He decided that he would host a national conference that was to come up with short, medium and long-term plans that would result in a comprehensive strategic plan.

The World Bank that had been interested in public sector reforms in Kenya readily agreed to fund Raila's idea of a national conference. But he claimed that the Permanent Secretary (bureaucratic head) in his Ministry, Professor Mwangi and the Head of Public Service, situated in the Presidency, Dr. Sally Kosgei were hostile to his plan. Raila stated that his Permanent Secretary summoned all Senior Officers in the Ministry and instructed them not take direct instructions from the Minister and that they must go through himself as the Permanent Secretary. Any civil servant who violated the instructions was to face disciplinary action including transfer from the Ministry.[1]

Raila decided on the need for the conference a month after his appointment and speedily proceeded to assemble a task force on the conference he wanted to take place in November of the same year. He secured financial support for the conference in August. However, the position from the Permanent Secretary and Dr. Sally Kosgei in the Office of the President was that the time was too short as they felt experts should be engaged to plan the conference against 2002. To cut Raila to size, a cabinet reshuffle in November 2001 saw the electricity component of the Ministry of Energy hived away off him as Chris Okemo, erstwhile Minister of Finance felt demoted as he was announced as co-Minister of Energy.

But before the reduction in his responsibility, he had been shown that he was expected to be a figure-head in the Ministry of Energy as major decisions were being taken in the State House in consultation with his Permanent Secretary. An illustration was the dismissal of the entire (including Caroli Omondi, the Secretary, who had been trained at some considerable expense by the World Bank) Moses Wetangula headed Electricity Regulatory Board without reference to the Minister.[2] The Electricity Regulatory Board was meant to be an important parastatal with

---

[1] Interview with Raila, Nairobi, March 7, 2004.

[2] On some of the events at the Electricity Regulatory Board when Raila was in charge, see, Jaindi Kisero, "Spare a thought for poor Mr. Bondet," *Daily Nation,* Wednesday February 25, 2004, p. 8.

the technical expertise to fix the tariff for electricity produced by a power producer and to be paid by the distributor, in this case, KPLC. George Mitine led a succeeding Board to that of Wetangula. However, George Mitine as chairman and the rest of his board were appointed, again, without any consultation with Raila the serving Minister in spite of the fact that the Constitutive Act of the parastatal had expressly stated that the Minister was to appoint Board Members and the chairman was to be appointed by the President on the recommendation of the Minister.

For Raila, the main push against the Wetangula Board resulted from the fact that a non-performing officer with close relationship with the State House had been sacked. The Wetangula Board had rejected pressure to reinstate the sacked woman. The George Mitine Board also resisted the reinstatement of the same woman. On a fateful day, George Mitine had gone to seek the support of his Minister (Raila Odinga) in resisting the imposition to the very end. But unknown to the Minister and George Mitine, as he was speaking at the Ministry of Energy, he had been fired. George Mitine returned to his office, but "he was surprised to find a hefty-looking man comfortably sitting on his chair and sipping tea."[3] On his query, his assistant politely informed him that the hefty man, Mr. Jeremiah Muriithi, had been appointed as his replacement.

However, before the reshuffle, and in spite of his figure-head status, Raila put a lot of emphasis on rural electrification. For him, rural electrification in Africa should not be treated as an investment subject to the calculus of return on capital but must be seen as a public good infrastructure that is like road construction. A commercial calculus, for Raila, would show that rural electrification was not viable. But the spin-off from rural electrification in terms of economic activities that would generate employment and wealth would rapidly alleviate poverty, according to Raila.

Rural electrification, though paid for by Government was sub-contracted to the KPLC. Raila regretted that the KPLC was inefficient with respect to this contract from the Government. He wanted to set up a separate parastatal devoted to the sole purpose of rural electrification to benefit and encourage *Jua Kali* (small and middle scale) business. Though he could not achieve that goal, he used lines of

---

[3] *Ibid.*

credit from the Spanish and French Governments to push for the rural electrification projects that took power to Marakwet, West Pokot, Gathondo village in Karatina, some places in Ukambani and Kinango village at the Coast. In Western Kenya, he paid attention to electrification along the many beaches in lake Victoria to enable fishermen set up cold storage facilities and some markets in the Western province.

With respect to energy from oil, its operations had been liberalized in 1994. Hitherto, and at the height of the oil crisis of the 1970s, a National Oil Corporation had been established as a parastatal to fix the price at which oil was sold ostensibly to, among other things, avoid exploitation of consumers. But for Raila,[4] the National Oil Corporation (NOC) failed to be effective as it lacked the necessary financial capability to match or compete with the multinational entities that controlled the downstream aspects of oil distribution. Nepotism in appointments also denied NOC competent management.

Besides, the private indigenous marketers had their grouse on their relationships with the multinationals and the rules governing it. For instance, oil marketers were required to import a certain quantity of crude if they were to be allowed to import refined products. Such crude were to be processed by the State owned refinery in Mombasa. While this was not a problem for multinational oil companies, many indigenous marketers did not have such financial capacity. They were also more likely to be harassed by the State security forces on the accusation of low standards of products.

After listening to the multinationals and the indigenous marketers, Raila engaged consultants from within Kenya to look into the issue. They concluded that the multinationals were making hyper-profits in Kenya as compared to places like South Africa (which is farther from the major sources of crude oil) and Zambia that is landlocked. Both countries had lower pump prices in comparison to the situation in Kenya. The multinational corporations, according to the result of the Raila sponsored studies, also avoided taxation. With facts, he was able to engage the multinational entities in a dialogue that emphasized the need for them to be self-regulating in order to avoid the re-introduction of Government controls.

---

[4]   Interview with Raila, March 7, 2004.

Raila also revitalized oil exploration, which had become moribund after oil was struck in the Sudan and oil exploration companies shifted their gears to that country. On the basis of available geological survey, Raila knew that Kenya had had little prospecting as compared to the situation in most countries where oil had been struck. He had gone to the Sudan to understudy prospecting there when he was condemned for wanting to import "bloody oil" from Sudan. This condemnation was a reaction to the feeling that the Sudanese Government was using proceeds from oil to fight and suppress the southern Sudanese people. But Raila's focus was different. He learnt that the Sudanese authorities, with assistance from the Chinese Government, had established facilities like a "state of the art laboratory" in Khartoum that made it possible to process satellite images and thus reduce areas of the search for oil and thereby reduce risks.

From the totality of his experience, he put together what he saw as an attractive package on profit sharing and went to offer oil prospecting companies. On this basis, Delta Oil Company from Britain and another company from Australia signed for off-shore prospecting.

Raila as Mwai Kibaki's Minister

As part of the pre-election working relationship, Raila was asked to express his preference for a ministerial post. His options were either Transport and Communications or Roads, Public Works and Housing. If Raila were to have had his way, he would actually have preferred to combine Transport and Roads as an integrated ministry. For him, this would have allowed better planning as the two compliment each other. Inland transportation comprises decrepit railway system and road transportation. Raila would have liked to pursue an integrated infrastructure development that reverses the present situation whereby 75% of all cargo imports go by road and only 25% by rail. For him, the statistics should be the other way round in order to change the excessive pressure on the roads.

However, the preference of the new order that President Mwai Kibaki led was to make Raila the Minister for Roads, Public Works and Housing. His predecessor, William Cheruiyot Morogo, former Member of Parliament for Mogotio constituency whose father had been a close friend of President Moi had presided over the same portfolio as he also had housing as part of his responsibility. However, during his tenure, housing was completely ignored resulting in acute shortage and mushrooming of slums.

Raila decided that he would aim at implementing the promises on infrastructure development that NARC made to the electorate. He was under no illusion on the import of an efficient roads network for economic development. For him:

> "roads are to an economy what the blood vessel is to the body. Dilapidated and inefficient roads infrastructure impedes economic development. It affects agriculture when produce cannot get to the market on time. It affects investments in rural areas, it affects business and school-going children."[5]

He had inherited a dilapidated road network of 150,000 kilometres. 63,000 kilometres of this network are classified roads. The classification is in terms of international highways; national highways; national trunk roads and rural access roads. Out of these classified roads, only 9,000 kilometres are tarred while the rest are gravel or earth roads. From Raila's assessment after taking over the mantle, only 57% of the 63,000 kilometres of the network are maintainable. The remaining 43% had collapsed and required total re-construction. In addition, there are 87,000 kilometres unclassified village roads that had been constructed through community self help.[6]

The sorry state of the roads in Kenya could be traced to the duality of the shortage of internally generated funding, donor boycott, and a high level of corruption in the sector.

On funding, the government could only access the fuel levy that was raised locally. This was meant for the maintenance of existing roads, but due to lack of development funds, the money was also used to pay pending bills to contractors, hence a deterioration of existing roads. However, even this was used as opportunity to enrich government officials and those Raila called "cowboy contractors" (they were so christened because they operated without rules as in the wild west of America) as government diverted the fuel levy into many over-inflated prices for road reconstruction.

These cowboy contractors colluded among themselves during bids for government contracts. They decided which amongst them got which contract and at what

---

[5] Interview with Raila Odinga, Nairobi, March 28, 2004.
[6] Much of the information that follows is based on *ibid.*

price. As soon as the contracts were awarded, they returned to exploit the variation clauses that they had colluded with ministry officials to insert in their respective contracts. This was agreed as normal because they then compensated their political god-father from such over inflated variation costs. This practice also involved Engineers, Architects and Quantity Surveyors in the ministry some of who were also contractors. As Raila found out, it was not unusual for an Engineer in the ministry to advertise for tenders on a particular road construction, adjudicate on all tenders received and award the contract to his company and then proceed to supervise the "contractor." Furthermore, he also approved variations to himself.

A deliberate policy of not paying bills as due (some of which bills are fictitious) attracted outrageous claims of high rates of interest. As a result of the demand of development partners for restructuring in the style of governance by the regime and the resistance of the regime, many international financial market opportunities for cheap loans were closed to the Moi government.

Raila immediately decided that he must tackle corruption and boost staff morale in order to improve the roads network under his ministry.[7] At a workshop for all Senior Staff in his Ministry, including those at the field, he spelt out his vision in implementing the NARC manifesto. Pointing out the importance of the December 2002 General Elections as a mandate for thorough regime and structural change in the way things are done, he emphasized a zero tolerance for corruption. He called on his staff to either wind-up their respective contracting companies that under the table carried out government business at exorbitant costs or resign and become full time contractors or be ready to go to jail. He explained that their efforts and collusion with those he termed "cow-boy contractors" was the reason why the cost of roads construction in Kenya is twice and at times thrice the comparative cost in neighbouring states. In exchange, he promised not to interfere with sound professional decisions and urged that appointments and promotion be done in a transparent and merit based manner. In this respect, he announced that periodic performance evaluation and appraisal would be used. In his second month in office, he invited consultants and contractors for a similar exchange. He tried to emphasize that the style of doing business had changed.

---

[7] Many of the commentators in the media in Kenya tended to have a mis-conception on the roads under Raila's ministry. This is more so, in Nairobi where the poor state of the city council roads are blamed on Raila.

He appointed a committee led by Engr. Andrew Chepkoiywa Kiptoon, former Member of Parliament for Baringo North constituency and a former Minister in the ministry, to investigate all pending bills. This committee that was given a free hand to come up with an assessment on what government actually owed was to work for three months but only submitted its report at the end of six months. This committee came up with the shocking revelation to the effect that out of the claims of 7 billion shillings, only 250 million shillings was the actual government debt. In addition, it was established that the government itself was owed over 1 billion shillings in payments for jobs not executed.

Another area of corruption that became controversial was the encroachment on road reserves over time. Raila realized that many of the land set aside for future roads development had been paid for by government and proper notices executed as far back as 1975. However, many government operatives collaborated with others to re-acquire such roads at paltry prices in other to build mansions, petrol stations etc., that attracted huge returns as some sold the lands to third parties. There was total dis-regard for the Roads Act that spelt out the spacing distance between roads and building developments for safety reasons. This situation, especially in Nairobi, resulted in heavy man-hour loss in traffic congestions as it became impossible to build road by-passes in order to ease city traffic congestion.

Upon assuming office and realizing the acute nature of the problem, Raila announced that his Ministry would re-possess all road reserves. He gave the formal notice of 30 days as required by law within his first six months in office. Six months later, he started the task of demolitions of such buildings. There was an interesting case of a building occupied by an expatriate whose landlord had grabbed a road reserve. The landlord approached Raila for a deferment of one month to allow the expatriate to seek alternative accommodation. The expatriate himself approached the line Ministry having supervisory responsibility on his organization to seek such extra time. Raila readily agreed. Unknown to him, however, was the fact that the landlord sought such a time extension in order to go to court to receive an injunction to block the demolition. Unfortunately, for the landlord, none of the officials at Raila's Ministry that needed to be served were in the ministry when the process servers visited. Having been alerted on the true intention of the landlord, the officials went into hiding to avoid services as the bull-dozers rolled, only giving the family of the expatriate enough hours to move their property to an alternative accommodation that had in fact been secured.

As at the time of writing, contracts that had been awarded and those being prepared on the re-construction of the Nairobi-Mombassa road and construction of by-passes were yet to come in place.

On Housing, Raila's survey showed acute shortage of housing especially at the lower income level. Since government had pulled out of housing construction about twenty years earlier, the private investors only targeted the high-income levels for housing provision. With this group, they expected higher returns on their investments.

Raila also realized that the Housing Policy that was put in place in 1967 had not been reviewed. He decided on setting about a policy that would be geared towards NARC's manifesto that saw housing as a fundamental human right. A task force that he put together realized a stake-holders seminar in May 2003, that is, five months after he was sworn into office. At this meeting that was declared open by President Kibaki, a Housing Policy document was approved.

The policy document contained a modality for partnership between the public and private sector to meet the needs of 3 million Kenyans in urban housing. The government, in this respect, was to facilitate an environment that would encourage private investment in housing. The National Housing Corporation, a government parastatal was to be developed into an intervention agent for development of public service housing, low cost housing, slum-upgrading projects and infrastructure provision.

On assuming office, the new Minister found out that many of the government houses meant for civil servants had been grabbed by the powerful in society over the last twenty years. He set up another task force to look into the state of government houses. This task force was chaired by Honourable Winston Ochoro Ayoki, former Member of Parliament for Kisumu rural in the 8th Parliament. Serving as the Secretary was Wanyiri Kihoro, former Member of Parliament for Nyeri Town constituency also in the 8th Parliament. On the basis of the recommendations of this committee, the Mwai Kibaki cabinet decided to re-possess government houses that had been irregularly grabbed and validate those occupied by civil servants.

However, the housing portion of Raila's responsibility was removed in the cabinet reshuffle of June 30, 2004. Housing was relocated in the Ministry of Lands.

The public works aspect of Raila's responsibility involved supervision of various stalled projects that all public entities had embarked upon whether housing for staff or provision of offices or construction and maintenance of the State House and Lodges all over the country. The President set up a committee to ensure that funds were available to complete many of these projects that had been abandoned.

President Kibaki relieved Raila of his ministerial responsibility after Raila led the defeat of the President's preferred draft Constitution in the referendum of November 2005.

> Very often I have been accused of behaving like a Messiah and seeing to it that those who politically disagree with me, especially in Luoland, are defeated in general elections. This is not true. I always try to be in tune with what the people treat as the truth. Those who disagree with me disagree with me only in the *second order;* in the *first order* they disagree with the people themselves, with the people they claim to represent. And it is the people who reject them, not Odinga. Odinga's name is only used as a face-saving device. Such people will often be defeated even when Odinga is no more.

Oginga Odinga in H. Odera Oruka, ed., *Oginga Odinga: His Philosophy and Beliefs* (Nairobi: Initiatives Publishers, 1992), p. 40.

The view that Jaramogi Oginga Odinga tried to dispel in the statement above is very real when one listens to Kenyans of all groupings in an attempt to understand the role of either Jaramogi or Raila in politics among the Luo in Kenya. In an examination of the role of Raila in politics in Kenya, it is essential that one attempts an understanding of his larger than life image among the Luos.

To explain Raila's hold on the Luos, one must look at his pedigree. He is a son of Jaramogi who reigned among the Luos for decades. Jaramogi's good deeds and his tribulations had endeared him to the Luos. A popular patent name could be a good starting point in a competition with alternative leaders. Raila's friends and even enemies agree that he has a popular name behind him.

It is generally agreed by the Luos that Raila was not personally chosen as a successor by Jaramogi. As many Luos would argue, Raila is larger than merely being the son of Jaramogi. Furthermore, Jaramogi had many biological and political children. Oburu Oginga, as Jaramogi's first biological child cut his teeth in Kenyan politics before Raila's debut. Peter Anyang' Nyong'o and James Orengo among others would be right in describing themselves as political children of Jaramogi, among the Luos. A reasonable question should be why Raila, among so many potential successors to the political throne?

To start with, Luos were impressed with the acumen that endeared Jaramogi to them that they could see in Raila, even at an early age. This was shown in his bravery both at home and in school. At early adulthood, he was undaunted or shall we say "unbwogable," (term coined by two Luo musicians implying unshakeable, that NARC adopted for its campaign against KANU) as he went in and out of detention, for seeking a better Kenya. So, it has to be accepted that Raila's attributes, beyond being Jaramogi's son, went a long way in endearing him to the Luos.

Therefore, the second explanation of Raila's hold on the Luos has to do with his own leadership qualities. This places his personal drive into focus. His tribulations gave him a large profile as a defender of overall national interest against an oppressive regime. Luos and many other Kenyans, if they could push ethnic animosities aside, see in him a defender of social justice and the human rights of all. Raila recognized this and occasionally challenged other Luo politicians who were against his leadership to show what they had done in furtherance of democracy in Kenya. He once asked: "Where were they during the repressive one-party state when I spent eight and a half years in detention?"[1]

For the Luos, however, there is an additional need for a Raila in a Kenya that had been ethnicised by colonial circumstances as well as the acts of its founding father among others. As Kajwang' argued, "Luos in Kenya are a large and at the same time, a small community. By Luo socialization, they are used to a band leader referred to as the *Ker*. Because Luos are a small, marginalized community both politically and economically, the tendency is to run back into a welcoming mother's and when frightened. That mother being the Luo community and its leadership."[2]

However, James Orengo differed with this perception of the Luos. For him, it would not be correct to see the Luos as normally searching for one leader. "There was a time Jaramogi was called a tribal leader. This was wrong. The Luos were never feudal and had no paramount chief. So, the Luos cannot be the one-leader type. You cannot go anywhere in Luoland and be honoured as a chief. Some families were bestowed with chieftaincies by the colonial order and they were resented."[3]

See, *The Standard,* October 20, 1998, p. 2.
Interview, Nairobi, April 11, 2003.
Interview with Orengo, Nairobi, June 7, 2003.

Orengo argued that Jaramogi, coming from a very humble background, built a strong network with the Luo Thrift and the Luo Union. He showed concern for the plight of the people all over Luoland. There was, according to Orengo, a relationship with the people that he had earned through hard work. "Raila similarly was a good student of his father and he worked very hard to maintain the network. He also suffered in the hands of the Moi regime. When all these are added to name recognition, he got a following within the community."[4] Illustrating the hold of Jaramogi and Raila on the Luo, Orengo stated:

> Odinga had a community with one language, customs and characteristics. The following from the community is so vehement, loyal and fanatical that people referred to Odinga and later Raila as tribal leaders. In elections, other communities vote in different directions. But something in the psyche of the Luo make the whole community committed. Luos are extroverts who tend to be loud and vigorous in their support. The Luos resent any oppressive rule. They were governed by consensus. Even the *ruoth* among the Luos gained prominence during colonial rule and not before. Luo folklore had great fighters, wise-men, magicians etc. But there were no *ruoth* who was domineering in any clan.[5]

He went on to point out that, Jaramogi, in his rise to become a significant person made a struggle against the *ruoth* system a major part of his campaign. The campaign went to the heart of the people. It may be apt to suggest that for the Luos, a leader emerges and people take their time to understand him. When the recognize that he could represent their interest, they give their unflinching support. It is important to note that Raila did not consciously build his leadership among the Luo. He seized the opportunity that arose and showed them he could lead by things he did and they accepted. Phoebe Asiyo, former Member of Parliament for Karachaunyo, in accounting for the status of Raila Odinga among the Luo noted:

> His hold on Luos comes out of his being who he is. He has suffered a lot but that is beside the point. His being himself accounts for why Luos hold him in high esteem. His hard-work, sacrifices for his people and Kenya, the fact that his father played a significant role in the liberation of Kenya and was treated

---

[4] *Ibid.*
[5] *Ibid.*

roughly by the two post-independence regimes, and being unable to make it to the highest post all combine to define his relationship with the Luos. People see how much his father and himself have suffered. Luos will remain with him for always. Anybody knowing Luos well will know how our people feel about their anointed leaders and not leaders who are imposed on people.[5]

Alternative College of Leadership for the Luos

There was the struggle to set up a so-called "Alternative College of Leadership for the Luos" by politicians like: Oloo Aringo, Anyang' Nyong'o, James Orengo, Shem Ochuodho and Joe Donde. Orengo and Donde were the only non-NDP politicians who were elected from Luo Nyanza in 1997. In the case of Donde, he got into Parliament to represent Gem Constituency in the 8th Parliament on the ticket of FORD-Kenya and earned some publicity for sponsoring a bill to curb interest rates in the banking system. As James Orengo explained:

> The idea of an Alternative College of Leadership for the Luos came at the spur of the moment. It was not thought through. Anyang Nyong'o had lost election and Raila's National Development Party was reigning supreme. We thought it was not right for the community to lose capable leaders just like that. The idea started at a meeting in Ugenya and announced the following day in Anyang's constituency. But the idea was still-born.[6]

The fresh idea of an Alternative College of Leadership could not have succeeded given the way the idea came across to the people. Though the leaders were trying to suggest a multi-party oriented political practice for the Luos, it was an idea whose time was yet to come. The Luos felt beleaguered and sought strength in unity. The campaign of the crop of leaders who disagreed with Raila's style to operate from alternative political structures did not sell. It appeared as the leaders campaigning for an Alternative College of Leadership were fighting against other leaders in Luoland rather than wanting to work together for the advancement of the people. As Phoebe Asiyo reminisced on this issue: "The quest for an alternative college of leaders was not going to succeed. May be it was a novel idea at that time. They wanted Luos to be like Kikuyus and elect leaders from different parties.

Interview with Phoebe Asiyo, Nairobi, July 2, 2003.
Interview with Orengo, *op. cit.*

May be not a bad idea except for the way it came across. It appeared that they were fighting Raila."[7]

So, it was not surprising that all these leaders lost in the 2002 General Elections with only Anyang' Nyong'o surviving among those who sought to create an Alternative College of Leadership for the Luos. In his case, he had a long credible role in Kenyan politics like Orengo. But unlike Orengo, he was part of NAK which joined the NARC that Raila was part of. Reacting on why the push for Alternative College of Leadership among the Luos failed, Otieno Kajwang' said: "I do not think you can break Raila's strangle hold by merely complaining that Luo leadership has been in the hands of a family for too long. Nobody elected him Luo leader. Performance in support of the popular desires of the people would be more crucial"[8]

[7] Interview with Phoebe Asiyo, July 2, 2003.
[8] Interview with Kajwang', April 11, 2003.

Chapter 22
Beyond Raila

Those who love Raila, love him too much leading to Railamania and those who are suspicious of Raila are distrustful of him to the extreme causing what I would call Railaphobia.

Michael Kijana Wamalwa, Late Vice-President, Kenya, Mount Kenya Safari Club, Nanyuki, April 5, 2003

During my 5-hour encounter with Raila in 1991 when he was flying back home following a medical check up in Britain (he had just been released from detention by Moi's regime), he came across as a person profoundly sensitive to public welfare. As we sat next to each other (him on the window seat, me on the aisle), I had all the time to study him at close range. Even when I probed him about his ordeals at the hands of his ruthless torturers, he recounted his hair-raising experiences without a whiff of bitterness. He laced his conversation with the view that Kenya could be a great country if only it had a genuinely pro-people leadership and a welfare-enhancing private sector. It became apparent to me that an all-encompassing welfare was a challenge foremost in his mind.

Dr. M.H. Khalil Timamy, "Are Private Finance Initiatives (PFIs) a Cost-Effective Option for Africa?" an unpublished paper, February 3, 2003, p. 6.

I believe there is a lot of talent in this country, which we can tap. My desire is to be a catalyst for change in this country. Together we will build a greater Kenya. We have resources and unmatched manpower and Kenya can be the engine of growth and development in this region.

Raila Amolo Odinga, *Sunday Standard*, April 20, 2003, p. 11.

Politics has always involved the struggles for the achievement of the material needs, desires, fancies and interests of individuals as members of groups and/or classes within society. In Kenya, the struggles on the socio-economic definition of the Kenyan state could largely be divided into two. A struggle to accumulate wealth without morality on the one hand and a counter-reaction that sought to emphasize moral imperatives in the creation/distribution of wealth as accumulation took place. There are few small organizational efforts in the fringes of society that may differ from these major tendencies.

In the push to realize support for the different world outlook, politicians have tended to find it easy to appeal for support from their respective primordial groups. Thus, the politicisation of ethnicity in Kenya could be understood as a consequence of the struggle for ascendancy between the two tendencies on material acquisition in Kenya. Ethnicity becomes an instrument of rallying popular support to buoy the elite convictions as the basis for the organization of society.

However, the paradox of Kenyan politics has been the necessity for the reinforcing of one's ethnic or provincial terrain and the fact that the more one's ethnic terrain is reinforced, the less the appeal to competing ethnic groups. This paradox is more the case with respect to politicians from relatively large or clearly competing ethnic groups.

President Moi, an adept politician in the manipulation of ethnic feelings never failed to claim that he was above ethnicity. But it is important to remember that he started off with a local district party fighting for local parochial interests. When he subsequently entered into a larger party, KADU, at the national level the aim was to protect ethnic or provincial interests of smaller ethnic and racial groups.

After the dissolution of KADU, a year after independence, Moi's game was that of holding on as protector of a collection of smaller ethnic groups with occasional forays into the hold of the larger ones. As he pursued this, he lost no time in defining other leaders as nothing other than leaders of their respective ethnic groups.

Raila Odinga's Fore-runners in Kenyan Politics

The role of Jaramogi in the de-colonisation of Kenya was important but he would be queuing behind such individuals as Dedan Kimathi and others who took up arms to resist colonial oppression. Jomo Kenyatta himself was a participant but also the main beneficiary of such daring efforts for which Dedan Kimathi's blood was shed. However, the post-independence effort to shape Kenya fell into the laps of Jomo Kenyatta, Jaramogi and Tom Mboya. Of course, these individuals had many significant collaborators some of who, as demonstrated in this volume, paid dearly for daring to make a difference.

Not so long into independence and as a result of the ideological differences stated above, President Kenyatta encouraged the young Tom Mboya to undermine Oginga Odinga with respect to leadership in Kenya. Mboya's ambition drove him into the execution of a marginalisation of the Vice-President, an older man from his own ethnic background. Whatever he could have done to further push for change in Kenya was halted by an assassin's bullet. However, Daniel arap Moi as Kenyatta's Vice-President at the time of the death of the later was to acquire power, and he pushed the agenda of his mentor significantly beyond what would have been the wildest dreams of Kenyatta. He built a dictatorial and repressive, constitutionally declared one-party-state apparatus. Jaramogi led the reactions against the Moi agenda among others. At his demise, Raila became a clear successor to the mantle of leadership vacated by his father.

The Imprint of Raila Odinga

Raila has been different persons when examined over the years. As a young man, he combined elements of nationalism with social justice zeal to become a Che Guevara and Castro type of socialist. However, he could not escape the huge passionate influence of his teacher in politics, his father.

He exhibited tremendous organizational capacity as he studied in the German Democratic Republic. Here, his political praxis started as he got involved in students politics and was influenced by developments around the world, especially the role of Fidel Castro in Cuban history and the war in Vietnam. Finding time to be involved in politics in Kenya, he got involved as the Europe representative of the Kenya People's Union led by his father. The shock of the banning of the KPU and the detention of its leadership in the aftermath of the massacre of helpless people in Kisumu represented the defining moment of his entry into Kenyan politics as well as industrial enterprise.

Following in the footsteps of his father to combine private enterprise with politics, Raila had to shed his Castroist ideological orientation even if he retained strong admiration for Fidel Castro. Ideologically, Raila became a pragmatic liberal democrat.

After an education in Germany, Raila started off trying to be an academic. He would probably have made a success as an academic but he took a diversion into the world of business. It is significant that Raila methodically made the best use of the support being offered to make entrepreneurs of Kenyans. He successfully built a company that has produced gas cylinders, not only for Kenya but the whole of East Africa for well over three decades. Many of those who took advantage of similar facilities about the same time faltered. This business effort he has boosted with a later determination to complete a molasses factory that had been abandoned by the Kenyan State for over two decades.

It is also noteworthy that Raila built his fortune by adding value in the production process. This was in sharp contrast to the normal trend on the African continent in which accumulation is through the manipulation of state resources for private accumulation of wealth in one form or the other. This has tended to take the form of politicians actually going into politics as a means of brazen brigandage. In the process, friends and relatives equally benefited through the awards of over-inflated contracts for the procurement of goods and services in the name of the state. Civil Servants (a misnomer as they tended to serve nobody) were normally not left out of such corrupt avenue of wealth accumulation either by secretly or at times openly operating as director of Companies that supply goods and services to the state or take huge cuts from contractors. At other times, common properties, especially land, are privatised at cheap rates or outright gifts and re-commercialised, at huge financial returns to well connected beneficiaries.

More importantly, however, was Raila's building of a standardization institution for Kenya. When he started, Kenya lacked any means of establishing standards for products. A single individual made the difference to the extent that Kenya not only realized a capable Bureau of Standards but, the African Regional Standards Organisation (ARSO) decided to make Kenya its base.

Raila successfully combined his role as Civil Servant and Entrepreneur with a keen involvement in Kenyan politics. His disillusionment with the Kenyan reality pushed him in favour of joining others like Anyona, Salim Lone and his father in trying to set up a social democratic type of party, Kenya African Socialist Alliance (KASA), as an alternative to KANU. However, the Moi regime met this democratic effort with repression by arresting and detaining Anyona. A clause making Kenya a one-party state was then pushed into the constitution.

The closing of the democratic avenue pushed a young Raila into fighting for democracy by any means necessary. Some could say that he toyed with anarchism at this stage of his life. He collaborated with a bunch of young military men who had also come to the conclusion that there was no other way out except to meet violence with violence by overthrowing President Moi. Raila and his father reportedly sacrificed material resources in the furtherance of this attempt even though they were expressly informed by the coup makers that there would be no civilians in their governing council. In effect, contrary to the notion of a megalomania in search of power at all costs, Jaramogi and Raila were willing to put their resources in the hands of others in seeking a change to the repressive order that Moi's Government represented. The fact that many people went on the streets in jubilation with University students on the coup day when people thought it was succeeding showed the mood of the time. However, it would be an unnecessary speculation to deal with whether the coup would have speeded up multi-party democracy in Kenya if it had succeeded. Suffice it to note that the experience in many parts of Africa was actually a worsening of the situation when the military intervened.

However, the courage of Raila as he went through many years stint in jail endeared him to Kenyans. His reflection in prison convinced him to return to his pragmatic liberal democratic option. But then the one-party state constitution that Moi foisted on Kenya must be changed for a liberal democratic order. Raila was not found wanting in the struggle for a multi-party order in Kenya. His activism in this regard saw him return to jail two other times before he briefly fled into exile.

He returned from exile to continue where he left off, that is, with FORD in the struggle for multi-party democracy. When the opportunity came for multi-party contest under FORD-Kenya, Raila demonstrated that he is made of a stronger element than many who claim to be nationalists. He decided to run for elections in the cosmopolitan Langata constituency in Nairobi instead of running to the safety of Luo Nyanza (that is to his ethnic folks) as many Kenyan leaders did.

However, parliamentary contest in a cosmopolitan setting was not enough. As Raila aspired to national leadership, he easily fell into the dictates of the Kenyan social reality of cementing an ethnic base as a means of leverage at the national level. This has made his detractors uncritically label him an ethnic leader without an analysis on whether any politician in Kenya (perhaps with the exception of

Tom Mboya) has successfully done without ethnicity and succeeded in political advancement. As Raila struggled with the varying legacies he was born into or inherited, he became a foremost leader among his primordial group, the Luos. Using this as a spring-board, Raila continued to demonstrate that leadership in a sub-group should not hamper national leadership and the defence of the general interests of all Kenyans. As he puts it: "Nobody chose to be born where he was, but I have always been a nationalist and that is why I resisted the appeals and temptation to contest (a parliamentary seat) in some rural constituency in Kisumu. That is why I am a Member of Parliament for a cosmopolitan constituency."[1]

Nonetheless, Raila's contradictions are more than the problem of keeping an ethnic constituency as well as aspiring to national leadership. He is temperamental and does not suffer fools easily. In fact, his strict definition of party line in the parties he has been associated with has led some to doubt his democratic claims. Raila is hardworking and an overzealous political animal. He is passionate about Kenya. He is a master in propaganda and adept in making use of opportunities as they arise.

Many a competitor with Raila in the political arena would want to emphasize that Raila is a schemer in a negative sense without giving credit to his strategic capability that could go a long way in improving the lot of Kenyans. He is accused of double-speak. The media and many articulate Kenyans automatically assert, without any analysis, that Raila speaks with one voice and makes many lieutenants say the exact opposite. No credit is given for the intellect of those lieutenants. In the course of interviews for this volume, one had the opportunity of listening to two situations that contradicted this popular view.

For instance, on one Sunday, Raila and Sunguh were enjoying some chivas whisky when Joseph Nyagah phoned asking why Raila was allowing Jak'oyo Midiwo, Member of Parliament for Gem and a cousin of Raila's, as well as others to be making smearing allegations against his brother, Norman Nyagah in a press conference in Mombasa, over the killing of Dr. Crispin Mbai. Raila denied any knowledge of whatever was happening in Mombasa. Dropping the phone, Raila was flabbergasted and annoyed. He did not even know where Midiwo was, let alone be the one behind whatever Midiwo was saying in Mombasa. On inquiry,

---

[1] *Sunday Standard,* April 20, 2003, p. 10.

Sunguh told him Midiwo had just called him (Sunguh) from Mombasa and they had agreed on the Press Conference as a prelude to a subsequent Parliamentary question on the killing of Dr. Mbai. Sunguh went on to phone Midiwo and handed the phone to Raila and the conversation took place in Dholuo.

Another instance was on the appointment of Moody Awori as the Vice-President, in succession to late Wamalwa. During an interview for this book that was combined with lunch at the Horseman Restaurant in Karen, an off the cuff question was posed to Raila on who he felt would be best for Kenya as successor to Wamalwa. He did not hesitate before stating that Moody Awori would be best placed to occupy the post in the interest of the country. However, when the announcement was indeed made, some suggested that Raila wanted the post very badly. Others claimed that Otieno Kajwang's commentary on the popular Kiss FM programme: "Crossfire," to the effect that the post should have gone to Musyoka under the MoU was the real position of Raila and that Kajwang' was "his master's voice."

At the individual level, the tendency in Kenyan politics is that Raila has been suffering from three things: The first is the fact that he is the son of Jaramogi, who was a controversial and principled politician. His being a Luo in this struggle has meant passionate following by most Luos and disdains from many a Kikuyu and associated ethnic groups in the elite exploitation of ethnicity.

Though people tend to focus on the name recognition that the circumstances of birth gave Raila, there is the tendency to overlook the other side of that equation. In many instances, he has automatically acquired some of the enemies of his late father. This reality remains one of the major problems that Raila faces in his strive for social justice in the accumulation and distribution of wealth in Kenya.

Another problem that Raila has tended to face is that of peer jealousy. Many of his contemporaries are envious of the public image of Raila whether that public is within his Luo kinship or Kenya at large.

The third problem is similar to the second. It is the fact that he was jailed for so long and he survived. And the fact of having gone through such harrowing experience became a boost to his public image. None of his contemporaries went through such stints. Many other politicians who could not go through his experience resent the fact that his persecution by the Moi regime endears him to the public.

Undaunted, however, Raila continued to strive for a better Kenya as a hub for his pan-Africanist ideal for continental integration. This integration, for him is best built on the concept of four sub-regional entities made up of Western, Central, Eastern and Southern Africa. While welcoming the re-discovery of the East African Community, Raila regarded the destruction of the earlier experimentation as one of the greatest tragedies of the Kenyatta era. For him, a big East African market of 100 million people would be in a better position to attract foreign direct investment flows that could take advantage of economies of scale that follows major projects. The building of these four entities of East, West, Central and Southern Africa into a viable African Union would, for him, address the need of Africa to be a viable member of the necessary, imperative of a globalised world. For Raila, Kenya itself, not to talk of its ethnic constituents is too small for an end game in a globalised world.[2]

With respect to politics at the Kenyan level, Raila had taken risks like moving from FORD-Kenya into NDP and taking NDP into KANU and then destroying the well planned Moi strategy of control over Kenya even in retirement. These successful risks endeared him more to his ethnic community, the Luos as well as many younger elements in the Kenyan polity. The strong bond of loyalty from the Luos has willy-nilly granted him control over them resulting in a successful marginalization of politicians perceived as opposed to him within his community. However, the more popular he became within his ethnic domain, the more resistance he faced within the Kikuyu/GEMA leadership in the struggle for power in Kenya. He is seen as a threat to what is seen as the divine right of the "House of Mumbi" (Kikuyu's legendary ancestral mother) to rule Kenya.

The opportunity to change this divisive approach to politics arose with respect to the succession of President Moi. With the aim of dictating his successor and preventing any parliamentary move against his plan, Moi performed a dis-service to Kenya on October 26, 2002 when he announced that he had dis-banded the Constitution of Kenya Review Commission. This was significant because all the delegates to a National Constitutional Conference at the Bomas of Kenya had assembled in Nairobi for their inaugural meeting scheduled for October 28, 2002. Though there was a debate as to whether Moi had the powers to disband a

---

[2] Raila's views on the necessity of integration of Africa in a globalised world were articulated in an interview on April 4, 2004.

Commission set up by an Act of Parliament, the National Constitutional Conference had been crippled. The opportunity to have an outgoing President to dispassionately nudge the people on to a desired new constitutional order that was not tied to immediate parochial interests of those wanting power was lost.

Raila's challenge to President Daniel arap Moi was another important move. He gave leadership to many who would have otherwise clapped for Moi's thinking that he had the right to impose a successor to what had become his personal throne. Raila not only dared Moi but took the appropriate decision to push for a coalition between his KANU turn-coats christened the Liberal Democratic Party and the Kibaki led National Alliance Party of Kenya (NAK) as the sure answer to put Moi not only out of business but also forestall the desire of the former President to be a puppeteer in the governance of Kenya.

The electoral campaign that followed after the coalition had been realized further depicted Raila as having the stuff a national leader is made of. Even if his selfless support were aimed at being the Prime Minister of Kenya, (and it is not a crime for a politician to want to govern) his hard work could not but be acknowledged with respect to Kibaki becoming the President of Kenya. This was especially so when Raila took over the leadership of the coalition as candidate Kibaki and Wamalwa, his running-mate were checked into the same hospital for treatment in London during the height of electioneering campaign.

The End of Moi's and Beginning of Kibaki's Regime

Raila, as Kibaki and Murungaru had admitted on different occasions, played a most crucial role in seeing an end to the twenty-four year authoritarian rule of Kenya under Moi's watch. However, former President Moi, in spite of much of his authoritarian mis-rule deserved some praise over the way he gave up power. Not only had President Moi maintained relative stability in Kenya in spite of some ethnic clashes and political assassinations during his watch, his final act of putting up no resistance to the overzealous Raila organized swearing-in of Kibaki was salutary. He could very well have tried the Ratzirak option in Madagascar, in which case many lives would have been lost. This point was emphasized by Moi himself. Speaking at Kapsang village in Soy Division, Uasin-Gishu District during the burial of Mzee Gideon Tarus, former President Moi pointed out that the legacy of peace was his greatest gift to Kenyans after his 24 years in power. As he puts it: "The peace existing in the country enables Kenyans to engage in their daily activities in an enabling environment."[3]

With Moi out of the way, the promise by candidate Kibaki that a constitution would be given to Kenya within his first 100 days and the perception of a united elite across the ethnic barrier that had been put in place since the days of Kenyatta raised a lot of hopes. Kenyans felt *uhuru* (freedom) had arrived.

However, as soon as Kibaki got into office, it became clear that most of the promises that the coalition made in its election manifesto and even in the maiden speech of President Kibaki had been pushed aside as Cabinet members battled it out in a war of supremacy on several issues that had its origin in the decision not to respect the MoU. Significantly, there was no desire to realize a constitution within the promised time frame. President Kibaki and his immediate lieutenants, especially Kiraitu Murungi who had initially articulated strong support for the draft that was to have been discussed by the disbanded National Constitutional Conference had changed gear. Their fear over a reduction in the power being enjoyed by President Kibaki led to several stumbling blocks on the path of a free deliberation by delegates who were trying to mid-wife a popular constitution.

Corruption in Public Life

Apart from ignoring the MoU they had signed, President Kibaki's coalition lost the euphoric support that accompanied NARC's campaign in the 2002 General Elections. However there was the obvious success story of the provision of free primary education. By removing school fees at the elementary education level, many who had been outside the education system or could not afford to go to school were able to do so.

Some feeble attempts to address corruption were made, first by removing several judges on the basis of allegations of corruption investigated by a committee led by Justice Aaron Ringera. But the reinstatement by the Akiwumu tribunal of Justice Philip Waki who had challenged his removal, cast doubts on the thoroughness of Ringera's committee. John Githongo, formerly head of Transparency International in Kenya was appointed Permanent Secretary for

---

[3] *East African Standard*, Wednesday, August 6, 2003, p. 10.

Ethics and Governance in the Office of the President. A Commission was appointed to probe the Goldenberg scandal which had been bogged down in the courts for almost a decade. A number of former heads of Government parastatal companies who had put money into a bank – Euro Bank – which then collapsed, were removed from office and taken to court. A 34-member National Anti-Corruption Campaign Steering Committee, under the Chairmanship of the Revd. Mutava Musyimi, Secretary-General of the National Council of Churches of Kenya, was also put in place. In spite of these efforts, however, corruption at the highest level of governance continued unabated under the NARC government.[4]

A major example was the disclosure in Parliament on April 20, 2004, by Maoka Maore, KANU MP for Ntonyiri, who claimed that the Kibaki administration had expanded a passport contract initially costing Sh800 million to one costing Sh2.7 billion. An obscure company, Anglo Leasing and Finance Limited, had been awarded the contract against the bids of more popular companies like De La Rue. Other shady deals like the building of a forensic laboratory were associated with the same company. However, on the passports issue, Home Affairs Permanent Secretary, Sylvester Mwaliko and Treasury Permanent Secretary, Joseph Magari, were suspended and later dropped from office. Also suspended were Ms. Dorcas Achapa, the Chief Litigation Counsel in the Attorney-General's Office, and Dr. Wilson Sitonic, Director of Government Information Technology Services.[5] Mwaliko; Magari; Sitonic were charged in court on February 16, 2005. Zakayo Cheruiyot, the former Internal Security Permanent Secretary faced a court case on the same day over his alleged role in the forensic laboratory scandal. David Lumumba Onyonka and John Agili Alao were civil servants, who like Sitonic allegedly handled the two projects by virtue of their posts in Government were also taken to court.[6]

However, President Kibaki's trusted long-term friend and his Deputy in the Democratic Party, the Minister of Finance, David Mwiraria, who, on October 3,

---

Many Ministers have either been directly accused or have, at the worst, been criminally negligent in the award of substantially inflated contracts. On a fair assessment of the Narc Government, see, a report compiled by the Chamber of Justice, a human rights organization led by Ababu Namwamba titled: *One Year After the Promise.* For an excerpt of this report, see, *Daily Nation,* Wednesday, June 9, 2004, p. 4.

See, *Daily Nation,* Wednesday, May 19, 2004, p. 1.

See, The Standard, Thursday, February 17, 2005, p. 1.

2003, had given Joseph Magari, the Permanent Secretary special authorization to sign the passports contract, argued that he was not responsible even though he was personally expected to sign foreign loans. He argued that he could not be expected to do everything since he had a Permanent Secretary. As he puts it: "My conscience is clean over the matter. I did what others would do."[7]

In a response he thought would reduce the tension, Murungi, the Justice Minister issued a statement in which he claimed that allegations of corruption in government were exaggerations. He wrote:

> "I would like to assure Kenyans that the government remains steadfast in the fight against corruption. The fight against corruption is at the top of our national priorities. Nothing has changed. We have engaged in this fight consistently Ö Cases of corruption against President Kibaki's government are being exaggerated to divert attention from the real war."[8]

However, Kenya's development partners led by the United States and the United Kingdom were not persuaded. At different times they reacted to the rising claims of corruption that appeared neglected by the Government. At a US Independence Day reception, Ambassador William Bellamy, expressed dissatisfaction with the handling of democracy with respect to the stalled constitutional review process and the move away from multipartyism and coalition government. He was stronger on the problem of corruption in Kenya. He acknowledged that the Kibaki administration had set up institutions to deal with corruption. He, however, noted that recent revelations were casting a shadow of doubt on the Government's commitment to fight corruption. He stressed that American business would only invest in Kenya when corruption was brought under control. He urged the Government to put in place systems that could lead to the identification of those who misappropriate public funds and to hold them accountable. Of these people he said: "They must be identified, expelled from positions of public responsibility,

---

[7] *Daily Nation,* Thursday, May 20, 2004, p. 1. As other accusations were made against Mwiraria like on giving a stamp duty waiver to cabinet colleague, Peter Ndwiga, (*Sunday Standard,* January 16 2005, p. 1), Mwiraria insisted that he would not resign and called on those accusing him to show proof of his guilt. See, *The Standard,* Tuesday, February 15, 2005, pp. 1-2.

[8] See, *East African Standard,* Tuesday, May 11, 2004, pp. 1 & 4.

held accountable for their actions and, as appropriate, brought to justice. This is the most urgent task facing Kenya today."[9]

Edward Clay, the British High Commissioner to Kenya had blazed the trail, a day earlier at a reception he gave to mark the Queen's birthday. He went further with a number of other donors that included Britain, the US, Germany, Canada, Japan, Norway, Sweden and Switzerland to issue a statement warning that they would not give money to support Kenya only to have it tapped for private gain. They warned: "Development partners cannot be expected to put their tax-payers funds at the service of Kenya if the country's own Treasury and public resources are tapped for private gains."[10] A similar statement was issued by the Royal Dutch Embassy (as the EU Presidency at that time), on behalf of all EU countries with presence in Kenya. The EU described the government's fight against corruption as being below expectation.[11]

As the Government claimed that investigations were on-going and as Parliament was undertaking hearings through its Public Accounts Committee led by Joseph Magara, FORD-People MP for Mugirango South; the Head of Public Service, Ambassador Muthaura, absolved government officials from blame in the Anglo Leasing and Finance Ltd. affair.

The restiveness among Kenya's development partners came to a head on July 13, 2004 when Edward Clay, chose the opportunity of a speech to the British Business Association of Kenya to analytically expound on the opportunity cost of corruption in Kenya. The speech, which he titled: "Some bread and butter questions," was not only interesting, but represented one of the few frank statements of a diplomat in a host country. Clay calculated the alternative ways in which money corruptly diverted towards private ends under the NARC Administration could have been spent to alleviate the dire state of the Kenyan socio-economic reality. He went on to accuse some of the members of the Government in power of being unashamedly gluttonous. In his words:

See, *Saturday Nation,* July 3, 2004, p. 3. See also, *East African Standard,* Saturday, July 3, 2004, pp. 1-3.

[) *East African Standard,* Tuesday, July 6, 2004, p. 1.

[] *Ibid.,* p. 3.

We never expected corruption to be vanquished overnight. We all implicitly recognised that some would be carried over to the new era. We hoped it would not be rammed in our faces. But it has: evidently the practitioners now in government have the arrogance, greed and perhaps a desperate sense of panic to lead them to eat like gluttons. They may expect we shall not see, or notice, or will forgive them a bit of gluttony because they profess to like OXFAM lunches. But they can hardly expect us not to care when their gluttony causes them to vomit all over our shoes; do they really expect us to ignore the lurid and mostly accurate details conveyed in the commendably free media and pursued by a properly-curious parliament?

Clay went on to point out what would have been the expected responses from the Government in order to lend credence to the claim of fighting corruption:

If the investigations went on and appropriate action followed, we might say that corruption was deplorable, we were sorry it was still going on, but we accepted Kenya was still fighting and winning the battle and that government was genuine in its efforts. Evidence that would be persuasive would be prosecutions; and the standing aside of those names recently mentioned in connection with the current investigations until those inquiries have been completed. However, the signs are otherwise. The old dragon has turned on its tormentors just as used to happen in the previous regime: veiled threats at the media, who should behave 'responsibly'; real red-blooded threats to fix, nobble or even damage those who want to investigate the corrupters; statements whitewashing in a pedantic, lawyerly way those who were not involved in one deal when investigations– not under the control of the Head of the Civil Service – were still under way to find out who else *was* involved in some way, which is much more fascinating. And at the same time, the corrupt are still cutting deals like there was no tomorrow.[12]

For this frankness on the rate and intensity of corruption in the NARC administration, some Kenyans thought the High Commissioner ought to be declared *persona non grata*. For some reason, however, neither President Kibaki nor his Foreign Minister had the courage to move against a man who, though he might have been undiplomatic, was telling things as they were.

---

[12] Many thanks to Sir Edward Clay for authorising the use of his speech in this work.

That the British High Commissioner was not on a personal crusade but reflected the position of his Government, saw him repeat his accusation on corruption in Kenya on a number of occasions. This fact was further driven home when during a visit to Kenya, the then British Minister for African Affairs, Chris Mullin, urged President Kibaki to step up his fight against corruption at all levels.[13]

Other European Ambassadors were equally vociferous. Bernd Braun, the Ambassador of the Federal Republic of Germany threatened that Germany would re-assess its bilateral and multilateral commitments to Kenya if there was no progress on the fight against graft.[14] He went further during his speech at a reception he gave to mark the Day of German Unity on October 5, 2004, in Nairobi. To the chagrin of Newton Kulundu who represented the Kenyan Government at the ceremony and other cabinet Ministers like Kiraitu Murungi, Martha Karua and Assistant Minister and Nobel Laureat Wangari Maathai, the German Ambassador decried corruption at high levels in the Kenyan Government.[15]

In a reaction to these bashings during an address at a Transparency International meeting in Nairobi, President Kibaki, urged Kenya's partners to note that fighting corruption was not an event but a process. He stated: "I will continue to fight corruption, not by shouting from the hilltops, but by tackling the evil from its roots."[16] Again, in his 2004 Kenyatta Day speech, he urged all Kenyans to join the crusade against corruption.[17]

It was a significant relief for the Kibaki administration when the IMF agreed to release KSH 2.8 billion in support of the Government's economic programmes.[18] And Transparency International's global poll on the perception of business people of the comparative corruption levels, ranked Kenya the 16th most corrupt country out of a total of 146 countries polled; an improvement from 9th position of the previous year.[19]

---

[13] See, *Saturday Nation,* October 23, 2004, p. 36.
[14] See, *East African Standard,* Saturday, September 25, 2004, pp. 1-2.
[15] The author was present at the function.
[16] *The Standard,* Wednesday, October 13, 2004, p. 1.
[17] *The Standard,* Thursday, October 21, 2004, p. 5.
[18] See, *East African Standard,* Saturday, September 25, 2004, pp. 1-2.
[19] See, *The Standard,* Thursday, October 21, 2004, pp. 1.

About three months later, however, Sir Edward Clay, returned to his favourite theme: corruption in high places in Kenya. Speaking to journalists at what was billed as a forum to reward excellence among journalists, and in the presence of the Vice President Moody Awori, Sir Edward examined a list of 20 cases he saw as dubious and suggested that the Government was not serious in fighting corruption.[20]

In what appeared like the first fall-out of the new round of accusations by Sir Edward, John Githongo, Kibaki's Permanent Secretary for Governance and Ethics, unceremoniously left the Government. He had gone on official duty to Britain and chose to write a terse letter of resignation from there. His office in Nairobi, in releasing the content of his resignation letter, stated "that he was no longer able to continue serving the Government of Kenya in the capacity of Permanent Secretary, Governance and Ethics."[21]

There followed cries from many including some cabinet members, Kenyan citizens and diplomats for President Kibaki to rise up to the occasion and deal with corruption in Kenya. On February 14, the President filled vacant positions in his cabinet and moved two trusted Ministers. John Michuki, the Minister of Transport exchanged places with Dr. Chris Murungaru the Minister of Internal Affairs in the Office of the President. Two Permanent Secretaries: Dave Mwangi of Internal Security and Sammy Kyungu of defence were dropped.

However, the general opinion by diplomats and Raila, was that this was too little. At a press conference, Raila argued that Kibaki's moves had nothing to do with anti-corruption. He said: "This (reshuffle) is not a response to what we were saying. The President wanted to fill the vacant post in the Ministry of Tourism."[22]

Uhuru is Still Far

In spite of threats to Raila's life, he remained undaunted. There were criminal attacks on two of Raila's sisters, his son and his brother within a few weeks apart

---

[20] See, *The Standard,* Thursday, February 3, 2005, pp. 1-2 and *Daily Nation*, Thursday, February 3, 2005, pp. 1-2.
[21] For details, see, *The Standard,* Tuesday, February 8, 2005, pp. 1-6 and *Daily Nation,* Tuesday, February 8, 2005, pp. 1-5.
[22] *The Standard,* Wednesday, February 16, 2005, p. 2.

in early 2004. He received a number of threats to his life, details of one was published in the *Sunday Standard* of February 29, 2004. His brother led some MPs to allege that members of the Cabinet were unhappy about Raila's support to the defeat of the Government at the Bomas Constitutional Conference and were planning revenge against him. Oburu said "it is [in the] public domain that an assassination scheme has been hatched by some senior members of the Cabinet and sanctioned by the highest authority in the land." [23]

With Musyoka and Mudavadi, Raila was chosen to lead the Liberal Democratic Party into the 2007 General Elections at a rally in Mombasa on Sunday, August 8, 2004, marking the beginning of the party's recruitment drive.

However, it would be safe to conclude that in Kenya, as in most of Africa, *uhuru* is still far. The challenge for Raila, and his contemporaries remains the transformation of an ethnicised Kenya into a nation-state that acknowledges the differences in birth but builds a cohesive entity for the realisation of democratic ideals and socio-economic justice for all. A Kenya that looks at the qualities of leadership in a person as opposed to placing emphasis on his primordial background and minor and parochial cultural differences like circumcision and ethnic stereotypes. A Kenya that uses her beautiful "Garden of Eden" bequeathed by nature, to develop and be an engine of growth in Africa.

---

[23] See, "Cabinet plotting to kill Raila, MPs say," *East African Standard,* Friday, March 19, 2004, pp. 1-2. Chris Murungaru, as Minister of Security, among others have maintained that there is no plot to kill any member of cabinet.

Epilogue
Who is Raila?

During the several interviews in gathering primary materials for this volume, it became interesting to ask several of the interviewees to exchange views on how they saw the personality called Raila Odinga. Some refused to offer any opinion as others shared their views in response to the question: Who is Raila? Without any analyses, a summary of the views, including Raila's own response to the question are as follows:

Fidel Odinga, *Raila's son and first child:*

He is someone I admire. Sometimes I look at him at rallies and don't act like his son but a fanatical supporter. He has that effect on me. He does not fear anything. I have never seen any form of fear in his face. When he wants to do something, he sets about it irrespective of who is on his way.

He is also very supportive. He rarely turns down people who come to him for assistance. He is supportive of so many people. He is very generous.

He is a revolutionist that is for radical change that would turn the entire process from bad to good.

I believe jailing him made him a politician. He is aiming for the top job. I don't know his strategy as he has always kept that to himself until the last minute.

His negative aspects I would put as his temper and impatience.

Ida Betty Odinga, *Raila's wife who had been through a lot of the turbulence of Raila's life:*

As a father, Raila was a symbol of leisure to the kids as he took them out on Sundays, before he was detained. To the children, a good father; he cares, spends and provides for them. A very nice guy. A good person I would not exchange for anybody. At times, I wonder what couples quarrel about. If all husbands could be like Raila, there would be no breakages in marriages. He is a good person. We talk a lot. I do not know if I am the one who has influenced his political views or he mine. He respects my mind. I have never had occasions in which he reacted as if I am speaking rubbish.

Those who know Raila cannot but love him. Those who claim to fear him do so out of political rivalry.

Otieno Kajwang', *Member of Parliament for Mbita constituency in Nyanza Province and a Raila loyalist:*

Raila is a very dynamic and ambitious politician. He is a grassroots organizer with a very strong faith in democracy and the rule of law. For these reasons, he has been in detention several times and has moved from one party to the other in the pursuit of one goal: To see the democratic culture institutionalised and the rule of law entrenched.

He triggers many passions in people in different ways. Those who like him support him in an almost cultic manner and those who resent him are very frightened of what he can do with the apparent power he enjoys from his supporters. He receives exuberant and ecstatic support.

In the ethnic political arrangement of Kenya, he is adored by his Luo community. The larger communities like the Kikuyus detest him as a competitor. Luhyas and Kambas are awed by the support he enjoys among the Luos.

While he has been honest and forthright in his dealings both with his supporters and people he has engaged with, he has been wronged, cheated and let down by a good number. This trend is visible in his relationship with Wamalwa in FORD-K; the Matiba-Raila Alliance before the 1997 election and later the Moi-Raila merger and now the Kibaki-Raila arrangement.

Someone puts the problem as the fact that he has too much grassroots power that makes his allies uncomfortable. Sometimes, I think he is too honest for a politician. He puts his cards on the table, keeps his side of the bargain. He is most unsuspecting and so he has been horrified that people he thought were his friends could turn against him.

Mark Kiptarbei Too, *one time Assistant Minister in the Office of President Moi, former nominated Member of Parliament and former Chairman Lonhro East Africa Company:*

A person driven by national interests in terms of what is good for the people of Kenya and not personal gains. A politician, a leader, organizer, social worker, a negotiator and businessman. Some-one that hardly has any blemish as a leader. He is someone who can accommodate others and be accommodated by them. A leader that has a bigger role to play in a democratic Kenya.

Prof. Wanjiku Kabira, *political activist with a strong gender bent and one of the Commissioners in the Constitution of Kenya Review Commission:*

Raila is a risk-taker. The way he left a strong FORD-Kenya and moved into an unknown party to re-contest his seat was a bold move many Kenyans would never take. Even the risk of moving into KANU and dissolving NDP with full knowledge of the type of person President Moi was, demonstrated enormous courage. Then the risk of handing over power to someone who will have total power on the paper promise of a post that still did not exist showed Raila as easily trusting.

It was important that when he took those risks, his people moved with him. This also shows that Raila is a charismatic person that people respect and follow. Coupled with the charisma is his enormous organizing capacity.

During the last general election, his national image blew to a higher level as he led people like George Saitoti, Kalonzo Musyoka into NARC and then took over leadership as Kibaki went into hospital until victory. The last election confirmed his national appeal as both the Luhya and Kikuyu as well as other Kenyans relied on his leadership capabilities as Kibaki and Wamalwa were in hospital in England. He was confirmed as a nationalist. As he was being marginalized in the new dispensation, he started receiving sympathy.

Raila already behaves like a leader with his dependence on an effective Think-Tank around him.

Mohamed Abdi Affey, *Kenya's Ambassador for Somalia, a former Assistant Minister for Foreign Affairs and former Member of Parliament for Wajir South constituency:*

Raila is a nationalist with a fanatical tribal following. This could be seen as a contradiction, but at the baseline, Raila is a nationalist. Even if he does not become the ultimate leader, he has what it takes to create the leader for the country. When the country was so polarized after the 1997 elections and the Kikuyu, Luo and Luhya were in opposition, Raila had the guts to merge with the ruling party for the sake of the country. He dissolved his own party. At that time, his action was called betrayal by the opposition but it was later proved to be for the common good.

Dalmas Otieno, *former cabinet minister under President Moi who may arguably be described as an adversary.*

Raila is more of a schemer and possibly a brave person. He has displayed bravery in the face of all odds. When the Kalenjins [President Moi's ethnic group] picked Uhuru Kenyatta, Raila told them that they will not choose who will be President and that the people would. He took the chance of throwing everything away.

It takes a certain personality for Luos to see you as their warrior leader. The warrior gets higher credibility with the Luos. Raila is the warrior type.

Raila is the best propagandist in Kenya. No other person can match him. His communist training has helped him. He is able to create an expectation and make people feel it is real. He is able to specify what each person would benefit.

Though he can control Luos, the "Mount Kenya Mafia" say that he could not be entrusted with national power. They argue that he is not a democrat. They point to the way he deals with dissenters in his own party with the use of violence. When he wanted to install Shabir as Mayor of Kisumu, he sent thugs to beat up Councillors that objected. When they went into hiding, the thugs beat up their wives forcing them to disclose the hiding places.

Israel Otieno Wasonga Agina, *Director at Spectre International and Raila's business and political associate:*

Raila, first and foremost is a modern day politician whose major concern is to put in place structures that will entrench social justice and foster rapid economic development to all Kenyans and mankind at large.

Ruth Adhiambo Odinga, *one of Raila's sisters with whom he stayed in Norway while in exile:*

Raila has that Germanic clean, precise and orderly trait in him. For him, 6 O'clock is 6 O'clock and not 5 past 6. He dropped you at the cinema and came back at the exact time to take you home to avoid men talking to you. His sisters were not to be talked to without his thinking about how he met Ida to talk to her. With Oburu, you can manoeuvre, but with Raila, there is no room.

Raila is very generous and kind hearted. He has a lot of feelings and able to provide attention for the family outside of politics.

Raila is like Jaramogi Odinga. He transcends cultures. He is a man of the world.

Mrs. Phoebe Asiyo, *former Member of Parliament for Karachunyo, Commissioner at the Constitution of Kenya Review Commission and UNIFEM good-will Ambassador:*

Raila was brought up differently by his father. His father used to send him to live with elders far away from home. He was sent to spend time with wise-men in Luoland. His father had invested a lot in making friends all over the world and especially all over Kenya. That reality gave Raila a head-start. I remember that Raila and Oburu came to spend time with my dad. He is the only one in Kenya who is able to go to Nigeria and consult with President Obasanjo; Mandela in South Africa and Ghaddafi in Libya. He inherited relationships that other leaders do not have.

Raila, as a person, cares. Listening is hard for leaders. But he does. And he takes the time to refer those seeking his assistance to others when it is not within his province to help.

In the beginning, people thought he was hungry for power and will not give up for anyone. But it's now clear he wanted power shared. He will go down as one man in Africa who wanted real power shared.

Oginga Odinga had stood for the real liberation of Africa. He wanted the Union of Africa. He cannot be compared with Jomo Kenyatta in this respect. I knew Kenyatta fairly well.

Raila is a people's person with a wonderful memory. He can re-call people by their names. He has an inherent energy that Oburu does not have in spite of Oburu's being very nice to people.

Raila reads a lot. He is able to discuss any topic. He is well informed. He consults a lot with all segments of society: women, elders and others across tribes. The hatred some have for him comes out of jealousy over the position he holds in society. That must be so.

What I know about Raila is that he would share power. History will prove that all he wanted was to share power with people who are concerned about the lots of Kenyans and Africans.

His hold on Luos comes out of the fact that he has suffered a lot for causes the Luos believe in. His hard-work, sacrifices for his people and Kenya, the fact that his father played a significant role in the liberation of Kenya and was treated roughly by the two post-independence regimes, and being unable to make it to the highest post all combine to define his relationship with the Luos. People see how much his father and himself have suffered. Luos will remain with him for always. Anybody knowing Luos well will know how our people feel about their anointed leaders and not leaders who are imposed on people.

Prof. E.S. Atieno-Odhiambo, *a Kenyan historian that was a political associate of Oginga Odinga as his speech-writer and comrade at arms with Raila before he went into exile and academic life at Rice University, United States:*

Very clear minded, industrious and visionary leader. A very good listener to people from all walks of life. An exceptionally humble person. The public image of Raila as a man of intrigues is a creation of the police state we have just weaned Kenya from.

His ability to work very hard with coherent determination on those issues he believed in stand in sharp contrast to the majority of men and women of his generation who, I dare say, are not given to thinking through issues in their varying dimensions rather than the Kenyan quick-fix.

Some are scared about him because he has a natural charisma and charismatic leaders always attract all sorts of following and become the envy of all those not so endowed. There is nothing he can do about that heritage that dated to his father.

Engr. Mirulo Riako Okello, *who went to Eastern Europe with Raila and practices in Kenya after several political and professional collaboration with Raila:*

Raila is a hard-working, fearless strategist. A brave schemer who is never deterred by road-blocks. He goes over. Once he is determined to do something, it will take a big horse to pull him out of doing it. At times, he misses opportunities by not listening to advise.

Rosemary Odinga, *Raila's second child:*

He is a dynamic individual able to communicate with different people with different interests and able to bring them together. He simplifies complex issues so that everybody is able to understand. He is a visionary. He can predict the outcome of his visions. He is also a gentle person who listens to everyone keenly and he is supportive of individual needs and needs of society. That's a part of him most people are not familiar with as they know him through the media. He has had bad publicity as being arrogant and aggressive.

Winnie Odinga, *the last child of Raila:*

Raila is a kind politician. He pays hospital bills of many people. I believe Raila is not only a father to his children but to other people as well. He has influenced and changed lives for the better. In that sense I perceive him as a hero.

Tony Gachoka, *a popular journalist and political analyst*

Raila had personally suffered, inherited the family suffering of his father and when all that is viewed within an overall community suffering, Raila cannot but have the support of his community.

Raila is able to maintain his local constituency and at the same time cut an image of a nationalist. His decision to seek an urban constituency in Nairobi instead of returning to his homestead puts him forth as a nationalist. Raila used the 2002 election to show that he could make a sacrifice.

Raila is good at creating expectations that he gets his people to view as political conditionality and he is able to move them along living on shifting expectations.

Raila does not represent change but an understanding of money and power. He is able to give the appearance of being at arms length from mundane things. As a result of his suffering over time, people presume he is innocent.

Dr. Fred Matiang'i, *a University of Nairobi academic who took time off to work with Simeon Nyachae as the Presidential candidate for FORD People party in the 2002 General Elections:*

Raila is arguably the most brilliant politician in Kenya. He is a schemer. He is gifted in everything political. But a politician is better off to avoid him except if he is in jail and such a politician can keep him in control. He has to be on the leash all the time as he thinks too fast and far beyond all his contemporaries.

Wilfred Aput Adhoch, *one of the many Kenyans in the German Democratic Republic at the time Raila was a student there:*

Oginga Odinga is the foundation of our respect for Raila Odinga. From respect on the achievements of the father, there was affect towards the offspring. Raila as a person likes his people. He is strong and a very courageous man. He does things from experience and he is not a loose talker. He means what he says. He likes his people. He likes Kenya. The people of Kenya are bound to gain from his experience and his method of doing things. If the people of Kenya could observe the interest of Kenya correctly, the country could gain a lot from the efforts and interests that Raila is showing.

Joe Donde, one of the few Luos who remained in FORD-Kenya after most moved enmass with Raila into a new party NDP:

Raila is a double-faced human being that is difficult to understand. As Wamalwa used to say: "If you talk to Raila, you have to know what Amolo is thinking and yet it is the same person." Knowing Raila from the 1950s, it is safe to say that what he says is not what he does on the ground. The Kibaki regime will find it difficult to understand Raila. People who want to deal with him in politics must know how to handle such a situation.

Raila plays dirty politics against his competitors. He would pay violent youths to heckle and smash the cars of his rivals at public functions. It's bad to be a rival of Raila in politics because he plays dirty.

Simeon Nyachae, *seasoned administrator and politician who was the Presidential candidate of FORD-People at the 2002 General Election who conceded that he knew Raila's father more than he knew Raila concluded:*

Raila is a very active politician who knows how to coordinate politics.

Oburu Oginga, *Raila's elder brother and Member of Parliament for Bondo Constituency:*

As a brother, Raila is a very accessible and loving person. Between us, we have maintained some openness that has helped our relationship. Our sister, Wenwa Akinyi once said we are the two who quarrel most and love each other deeply because we do not keep grudges. There are times we disagree. When we have crisis, he likes us to seat together and resolve issues.

One weakness of Raila, is his temper. When he is upset, he could go overboard in the immediacy of the situation.

Raila is a very resourceful person. As a leader, he is soft spoken but has strong beliefs. I also know that he does not threaten people. If he tells you he is going to do it, he does. He does not like to fail in anything he does.

As a politician, he masters a lot of things that one would not expect an Engineer to master. He is at home whether it is economics, health, languages, not to talk of politics etc. He is at ease with almost any subject.

He is simple and does not assume. He never leaves any stone unturned when he is organizing. He goes to the extent of even planning up to details about transportation. He is hands-on. That allows him to have strength in organizing people.

He is not very rich but whatever resources are in his hand, he uses rationally.

Cecily Mbarire, *one of the youngest politicians who had started with Charity Ngilu's NPK and eventually got nominated into the 9th Parliament by NARC having lost NARC nomination earlier on in Runyenjes Constituency:*

Raila Odinga is a goal-getter. He is a political wizard. A very courageous and intelligent man. As far as ethnicity is concerned he initially came out as a Luo Chief. But now he has a national image. He has managed to go beyond ethnicity to be a strong party leader. Raila can get along with anybody. He does not have Religious, Class or Ethnic bias. He fits everywhere. During the campaign he interacted everywhere.

He comes out as a strong supporter of women. Much as he speaks strongly for women, we are yet to see him push women from his province into Parliament. Though he supported Phoebe Asiyo a long time ago, there was no woman candidate from Nyanza that he backed last year.

On his shortcomings, once wounded, he hits back very badly. Sometimes, he hurts many people along the way. He has many passionate enemies. His style of politics, has created a lot of fear in his enemies. They think he is over-ambitious and as some-one who has tended to get what ever he wants, they fear him. He lost the Chair of the Parliamentary Select Committee on Constitution review because he took it for granted and the other side organized. He was caught pants down.

What is most scary about his role in politics is how people around him worship him. Other Kenyans wonder on what these people would do if he actually becomes President. In a way he is an extremist. Many Kenyans ask if he could turn out to be a dictator.

Dr. Willy Mutunga, *a Lawyer and activist from the 1970s to date and former Chairman of the Kenya Human Rights Commission:*

Raila is a lot of things. He is an aggressive and astute politician. A great mobilizer and organizer. His capabilities were clear at the NCEC.

He is a nationalist and patriot. He has always struggled against dictatorship and oppression and has been for social justice. Though it may sound contradictory, he is also an ethnic baron. He has not sorted out this contradiction in his life. He uses both nationalist and ethnic cards for the advancement of his political project.

As a Kenyan leader, he would not just be a spineless sycophant. He would insist on dialogue in the pursuit of Kenyan interest. He also has a vision and road map for Kenya unlike other politicians. I am convinced Kenya's transition needs Raila as the president of this country.

Mohamed Farah Maalim, *former Member of Parliament for Lagdera Constituency, Garissa District and foremost opposition to KANU hold over the Somali area of Kenya who fell out with Raila in FORD-Kenya:*

Raila is a very ambitious person. A steam-roller that would stop at nothing when he wants something. He does not like competition. The more brilliant you are, the less he would support you in politics even if he would use your brilliance. He had a contempt for Luo intellectuals until he started using them as a Think-Tank to achieve his desire for a merger with KANU. He is a schemer. Somebody who loves to wield power. Uses and dump people. He is a very powerful and dangerous dictator in the making.

He is not a thinker as such but makes friends around the world importing what had been done in other places without any justification on relevance to Kenya other than it had been done in Nigeria or South Africa.

What he lacks in eloquence and oratory, he makes up for with extreme confidence and passion. As a result, you feel what he is saying must be correct. He is street-wise as he reverts to dismissive arrogance when he cannot debate. In this respect, he is like former President Moi who scolds those trying to reason with him out of their opinion into submission.

However, as an agent of reform, he is very good for Kenya, not through his substance but through his insistence. He is definitely full of energy.

Munir Khan, *a Kenyan Businessman of Asian origin who was born in Kisumu, the provincial capital of Raila's origin and one of the activist supporters of Raila:*

Raila Odinga is forthright, honest and basically trustworthy. He carries a lot of charisma. He is a de-tribalized politician. He is a Luo Tutunkamen. He has political shock absorbers that make it possible for him to turn around and make friends with those who hit at him. His biggest fault is that he trusts many people easily and they take him for a ride.

John Joseph Kamotho, *veteran politician from the 1970s who Raila replaced as Secretary-General of KANU and currently MP and Secretary-General of the LDP fraction of NARC:*

A very intelligent and dynamic individual. He is not as violent as people were made to believe earlier. I admire his energies and commitment he normally has to principles. Those close to him know that he is a good political asset to work with. He happens to come from a community, which is very united and full of brains.

Paul Muite, *veteran politician and Lawyer who struggled for power through FORD and FORD-Kenya before being edged out and currently MP for Kikuyu and leader of Safina party and former Chairman of the Parliamentary Select Committee on constitution review, a post he snatched from Raila:*

Raila is in the same mode as people like Hitler. Some perverted concept of power. He is somebody who would destroy a country if he sees power. However, he is determined to seize power by hook or crook. But he must be stopped from seizing power. He is somebody who knows he is unelectable and therefore would design short-cuts to grab power.

Professor Makau Mutua, *Human Rights Lawyer and activist and Director, Human Rights Centre, University at Buffalo Law School, State University of New York:*

It is difficult to understand Raila without understanding the context in which he became a leader. He is at once a personification of the political ambition of his family and that of the Luo community. A psychosis and psychology that is forged by the Luo conviction that they are outsiders in the Kenyan State that has excluded them and assassinated their most brilliant sons. In Kenya, it is not possible to understand Raila unless one understands that there is no other community that has coalesced behind the leadership of one family and for which any deviation receives sanction without mercy or pity in a total excommunication and banishment from the body politic of the Luo. The Luos, like other Kenyan communities (e.g. Somalis) have been victimized but the Luos have used their victimization to political advantage into a political machine that cannot be denied access to political power.

Raila, like his father is a principled man. While his father was a nationalist deeply driven by the most noble patriotic zeal for a transparent open and democratic state, Raila is driven by a quest for political supremacy in Kenya by any means necessary. He has a proclivity for double speak. He would strike alliances with some of the most vile political actors for short term gain. He lacks commitment to the building of democratic institutions as he took over political parties and discarded them when they no longer served him.

He is extremely talented and he is arguably the best politician in the country. But for the country to harness and harvest political talents, Raila has to operate within an institutional structure of openness for the containment of his proclivities. Left to him, he would destroy democracy. He needs to be contained.

Davinder Lamba, *an activist Kenyan of Asian origin and Executive Director Mazingira Institute:*

Raila is not unusual in Kenya. Being an autocrat, bully, etc., would apply to others. Raila, like many of his colleagues is able to intersect a patrimonial world based on traditional authority without focus on democratic institutions, with the opposite of a world based on modern authority and institutions. Raila, still like his colleagues avoid substantive statements on issues and change but always focus on ploys which really makes them "ployticians" and not politicians.

He went into KANU, and by so doing, marginalized Luos who had been in KANU. By vanquishing them, he got further strengthened. He is not the learning type. His past patterns have shown that he has always ended in the same spot after several summersaults.

Chris J. Kirubi, *a successful Kenyan Industrialist:*

Raila comes from a famous family as he is from a father who fought for Mzee Jomo Kenyatta and Kenyan independence. He aggressively fought for democratic principles in Kenya in the past. But he must now learn to play a more unifying role in Kenya. He is a tribal leader of the Luo community.

Michael Njeru, *businessman, youth activist and a Raila supporter:*

He is like a father, friend and comrade. At his age, he is truly young at heart. He embraces the youth without reservations. This is well illustrated by his ability to be humble and the support he gives young people.

It is easy to share interests with him and above all, he respects one's freedom and privacy. He is a good listener, he shares his experience (on which he is not bitter or personal) with anybody, hence has no enemies.

The last aspect but not the least, he is a person who has a strategy. He takes life in strides and he believes that you cannot walk without raising dust - meaning that, there are ups and downs in life!

Mirugi Kariuki, *Member of Parliament for Nakuru Town and Assistant Minister for Foreign Affairs who represented Raila during his struggles in FORD-Kenya against late Michael Kijana Wamalwa.*

Raila has no ideals in politics. He has no time for idealism. His ideology is power. He would go after power by any means necessary. He is not excited about what type of society. His is acquisition of power without concern for what he does with such power.

Mutahi Ngunyi, *popular columnist and political analyst.*

Raila is a misunderstood individual. He is a patriot and nationalist. In the 1980s, he spent his waking and sleeping hours shuffling in and out of prisons, not for Luos but for a greater vision of Kenya.

Salim Lone, *former Director of Communications to Kofi Annan and former collaborator with Raila and others in the struggle for an expansion of the democratic space in Kenya.*

Raila is the most dynamic leader we have in Kenya. He has a clear vision of what he wants to achieve and an immense internal strength, character and political drive to fight for what he believes. He is also immensely charismatic. He has most of the qualities of greatness that his father had and like his father, he was always prepared to put his personal safety and freedom on the line for his believes. He is not easily intimidated. I do not want to paint him as an angel. He has his weaknesses. For instance, he comes across as being too aggressive and too much in a hurry. Some people think he would be too tough if he had power and would not seek consensus. But in my view, he would be. Of all the people I know, he is the most competent to run this country after Kibaki's tenure.

Kamoji Wachiira, *an activist who spent some time in jail in the fight for democratic space in Kenya and later moved to Canada*

Raila's history and contribution to politics in Kenya does not fit well in the tradition of such Kenyan militant nationalists of the past as his father. He simply found his father's ample political shoulders, climbed onto them and proceeded to reach upwards. Raila reflects his times, similar across Africa, where the only question for rulers and their opponents is "how can I fastest get to the center of control, to the top and the big prize?" Here no higher principles matter. Little is ever said of the common good or national destiny. What matters is who, by whatever means, gets that prize and the consequent "booty" - for himself, cronies and clan benefit? This is a cut and thrust territory of endless battles - now jockeying, now allying and then quickly re-allying, permanently preparing for the next elections. What results is a state of permanent politicking with no stated benefit for the citizens.

A word on Jaramogi is appropriate as background. Raila's father, was a true African nationalist politician with a set of principles guiding his action at least in the pre-1966 period. In spite of his many complexities, Oginga Odinga led real anti-colonial battles and, much to the disgust of the British and later Kenyatta, he was tactically brilliant and innovative. Like most politicians, Odinga had his questionable moments, but no one can deny him that special attribute of leadership - i.e. the gift to judge the opportune moment, the right point to strike in a battle, the moment that builds momentum and media buzz for the mass movement.

In my opinion Raila is really not an enigma. He is easy to discern. He is a straightforward known entity. A man of remarkable energy and mental acuity, Raila seems to see his destiny as inevitably leading to big and bigger power - one way or another. He may well be right. For him, to get there almost anything goes.

Raila and I spent pleasant evenings debating surreptitiously in Moi's detention wings at Shimo-la-Tewa as we awaited Justice Hancox' fake tribunals. Even then, one had to strain to find a backbone of guiding principles that would inform power once Raila attains it. To wit: his testimony freely offered those days to the prosecution at Njonjos *msaliti* (traitor) trial.

Today one still struggles to understand what his criteria are for choosing friends and allies. Sometimes he seems on power-play mode permanently set on fast-forward. Forget the tedious details of building protracted movements, no, give me power now, in instant form like Nescafe if possible, or I will leave you and your party and move on. This tendency is worrisome.

For these last few reasons Raila unlike his father, has yet to contribute as much as was once anticipated by so many, to the institutional transformation of Kenya. It is perhaps more accurate to say that his energies have been consumed by the tedious in-out chess of alliance making. This is a great loss for the country, perhaps for the continent, as Raila is a truly remarkable thinker and an untiring strategist. I believe many Kenyans are still waiting to see his true contributions to progressive thinking. Their question is, once in power, would Raila be any different from the current and the previous lot?

Peter Marwa, *a retired Colonel from the Kenyan Army who later became an international civil servant with the Inter-Governmental Authority of Development:*

Raila is the greatest political strategist Kenya has had in the recent political period. He was the one who rallied the coalition of individuals, parties and groups that routed KANU from power. However, he has a major weakness among others in his quest to navigate himself into the highest level of authority in Kenya. The main one is the fact that he is Luo. Kenya's ethnic groups could be divided into those who circumcise and those who do not. The former are in the majority. The Luos are in the latter. This divide is very real and had somehow entrenched itself in the minds of Kenyans and reverbrates at the political level. For the ethnic groups who circumcise their male, it is a process of moving from being a child to the status of a warrior. It is a division between those who arfe matured to be leaders and those who cannot.

Lord David Steel, *former Member of the British House of Lords and former leader of the British Liberal Party:*

I first met Raila through his father Jaramogi Oginga Odinga when I was supporting his struggle for multi-party democracy in Kenya. Since then I have got to know him well, and indeed when in opposition he used to stay in my flat on visits to or through London. He has a good political brain and, as his many years in prison testify, a good deal of courage. He also has a nice sense of humour. On one occasion in the 2002 election I addressed with him a huge crowd in one of the muddy slums of Nairobi. I was impressed both by his eloquence and at the manner in which, though coming himself from a relatively privileged background, he identified with the poor and the young. Most of all I admire his capacity to break out of purely tribal politics, something which has bedevilled Kenya. His vision in pulling opposition parties together for the last election, and his generosity in promoting Mwai Kibaki as Presidential candidate has not yet been fully recognised, but I am confident that one day it will be.

Dr. Atul Vadher, *a Consultant and British Liberal Party member:*

Raila Odinga is the most misunderstood politician in Kenya.

His motives are perceived with suspicion, and judgments of his political actions are often extreme. People heap either blame or praise on him but most fail to really understand him.

Raila has an immense amount of political energy and ambition. One pursues a career in politics to serve people. Many of Raila's detractors and colleagues thwart his pursuit and fail to harness his potential. He is only ambitious for Kenya.

There is too much that is good in Raila. He is the least ideological, least ethnically chauvinist, and most gender-sensitive of politicians. He is a most caring man and delightful company. His political instincts and judgements are sound, but he sometimes lacks political finesse. To have so many assets and be lacking in this essential characteristic is a hinderance – but two out of three ain't bad!

I have had privilege to get to know the man as well as the politician. He loves sports, reading, clothes and above all people. For such a man to endure years of prison – a small cell, a bible, one set of clothes, solitary confinement – would have been torture beyond words.

However, such is the magnanimity of Raila that he makes up for the "lost years" with verve, zest and not a hint of bitterness. I am immensely proud and privileged to know Raila and count him as my best friend.

Llyod Pierson, *Assistant Administrator at USAID*

I first met Raila Odinga in the early 1990's when both of us participated in the reconciliation efforts in Mozambique. Raila was extremely effective and consistently encouraged all parties to stay in the democratic process. At a critical time in the post-conflict period, I repeatedly heard members of the political parties say, "Raila said to stay in the system. Raila said not to drop out." I believe he made a difference there and in other situations where he encouraged people to adopt and remain in a democratic process. I am happy to call him my friend.

Raila Odinga on Raila

They say that a human being is a product of the environment and in that regard I am no different. My parents were two very strong personalities who struggled to give us the best upbringing under difficult circumstances. A lot has been written about my father including his own autobiography "Not Yet Uhuru."

As a child, I had an excellent relationship with him and only once did he severely punish me because I defied an order to join others in picking cotton. Although, less has been written about my mother she was the most formative figure of my youth. She was a generous, tough, friendly and hardworking person who was an excellent wife to my father and a mother to thousands of children in Kenya.

My father had written about how my mother caught his attention at an athletics competition in Migwena sports ground when she beat a crowded field of girls in sprints. I believe that I inherited the love of sports from my maternal lineage. Mum was a strict disciplinarian who believed in the motto of 'sparring the rod and spoiling the child'. But her anger was never long-lasting and after punishment, she would even regret her action. She was a good story-teller and used to entertain us with exciting fairy tales.

My formative years were spent in Kaloleni Estate in Kisumu where my father had relocated to start a business having resigned from a teaching profession. Dad was also involved in the freedom struggle in those days and I remember the lengthy political discussions that used to take place in our residence. I was inducted to politics right at infancy. Jaramogi was a loving father who taught us many things about life and who was ready and prepared to discuss all kinds of sensitive issues with his children.

During the school holiday of 1958, dad took me with him on a round trip of Uganda as he raised funds for the construction of Ofafa Memorial Hall in Kisumu. It was a real eye-opener for me as I saw new places and met many people. This and other trips, in which I accompanied my dad, helped me to develop confidence that assisted me when I went abroad at a relatively young age.

I developed a passion for reading and debate. My political awareness and activity became more focused during my stay at the Herder Institute in Leipzig and late at the University in Magdeburg Germany. In Leipzig, my companions included students from Africa, Asia and Latin America; while in Magdeburg, I lived with German students. My wide reading covered Fanon, Lenin, Marx, Nkrumah, Rodney, Mao, Dubois, Garvey as well as Liberal Western thinkers like Galbraith and Adam Smith and it shaped my intellectual and political outlook. Imperialism was the enemy number one and international solidarity of progressive forces was the answer to imperialistic expansion. We believed that collective ownership of means of production was the only way to ensue equitable distribution of wealth, poverty reduction and faster socio-economic development.

Those days, at the height of the cold war, with Vietnam War at its peak, we talked of scientific world outlook. Many changes have since taken place and I have also revised my political outlook. I have witnessed inefficiencies associated with public ownership and management and the ability of entrepreneurship to create wealth. I now believe strongly in the private sector as the engine for faster economic development. But I still strongly believe in the humaneness of our traditional African societies and the need to borrow from the experiences of our forbearers to transform our country. I hold the simple but profound notion that individuals thrive and prosper only when they are supported by strong and active communities.

In long walk to freedom, Nelson Mandela wrote: 'I have taken a moment to rest, to steal a view of the glorious vista that surrounds me, to look back on the distance I have come. But I can rest only for a moment, for with freedom come responsibilities, and I dare not linger, for my long walk is not yet ended'.

Mandela has always been my hero ever since we first demonstrated for his release in the streets of Cairo in 1962. During my days in detention he was a source of inspiration that enabled me to endure the harsh, inhuman conditions.

The post independence developments in Africa have been disappointing. Over the last forty years, the desire to retain political power took the centre stage as the African ruling classes specialized in political repression and the settling of political disagreements in violent and destructive ways. All this has adversely affected possibilities and opportunities for development in Africa. Wars, internal conflicts, internally displaced person, people imprisoned without trials, *coup d' etat,* lack of respect for the sanctity of human life, etc., have all been enemies of progress in Africa. The bloody feuds do not only include the conflicts where guns are drawn and territories fought over. They also include the blood-letting fights for political power using ethnic, religious and territorial chauvinism to divide people in order to rule them, with no agenda for positive and constructive social transformation, but with the single aim of being in power at all costs to the African people.

Kwame Nkrumah observed in *Africa Must Unite* that without a serious commitment to a people-centred development process and collective self-reliance (that he believed socialism was all about), and without political unity at the continental level, neo-colonialism would continue to balkanize and under-develop Africa, and poverty would be perpetuated. I was an ardent student of Nkrumah, and must concede that apart from the discredited public ownership of the means of production, some of his ideas are still valid today.

In Kenya, our long walk is not yet ended but the destination remains the same: modern, democratic, prosperous and developed new nation. To achieve the objective, it is necessary to take cognizance of special circumstances in our society which sometimes might dictate change of strategy or application of new tactics. Sometimes it becomes necessary to make tactical retreat by forming strategic alliances like NDP/KANU cooperation, partnership and then merger in order to surmount ethnic barriers, facilitate constitution review and expand territory.

The elections of 1992/97 revealed both the deep commitment of ordinary Kenyans to the electoral process and their fundamental cynicism about the government's willingness to conduct free and fair elections. The sudden establishment of multi-party democracy had been a panic reaction by the regime to the abrupt cessation of rapid disbursement of aid from the west; it was not based upon a fundamental desire for or understanding of multi-party politics on the part of either the government or the people. It most certainly was not a serious response by the government to the deep-seated anger and dissatisfaction among the masses with political events since the 1982 coup attempt.

Many ethnic chauvinists saw multi-party politics primarily as a means to seize control of the state and the funding it controlled, while President Moi and his ethnic elite group were determined to defend their gains. The introduction of multi-party politics, unfortunately because of opportunism, divided Kenyans into rival, ethnically based political parties. It was in response to this situation that we decided in 1998 to introduce politics of co-operation.

Although I have been criticized for changing political parties, I have maintained that at no time have we compromised our principles. In this regard, I have learnt from Sir Winston Churchill who was forced by circumstances to change parties. In 1923, he announced 'I am what I have always been – a Tory Democrat. Force of circumstances has compelled me to serve with another party.'[1]

Not long before Churchill crossed the floor to join the Liberal Party, he remarked of his (then) fellow conservatives: 'They are a class of right honourable gentlemen – all good, all honest men – who are ready to make great sacrifices for their opinions but they have no opinions. They are ready to die for the truth, if only they knew what the truth was'.

'They say you can rat, but you can't re-rat', Churchill remarked in 1941, referring to changing political parties. He, of course had re-ratted. He is also said to have observed: 'Anyone can rat, but it takes a certain amount of ingenuity to re-rat'. 'A change of party is usually considered a much serious breach of consistency, than a change of view': ratting clearly needed some justification- 'Some men change their party for the sake of their principles; others change their principles for the sake of their party'.

While in an exchange in the commons in 1926 when Churchill was Chancellor of the Exchequer, his Labour predecessor Philip Snowden accused him of switching positions on his budget. Churchill pointed out that there was nothing wrong with change if it was in the right direction to which Snowden countered: 'The honourable gentleman is an authority on that'. Churchill retorted happily: 'To improve is to change; to be perfect is to change often'.

There is no doubt in my mind that every change we have made has advanced the cause of our mission. I can say without fear of contradiction, that the tactical

---

[1] *The Wicked Wit of Winston Churchill*, compiled by Dominique Enright.

manouvres and compromises we have made have been dictated purely by the difficult historical circumstances and not mere opportunism.

As we pause for breath and consult the map, our challenge is to find the common path ahead. And we must always ensure that the compass is pointing at the destination. As governments and economies globalize, no national state can plan rigidly and precisely for the future. We must adjust to the realities of neo-liberal globalization that became triumphant after the fall of Berlin Wall in the late 1980s/early1990s. In this regard, we support political and economic reforms that are in line with liberal democracy along with social justice. In other words, we concur with Francis Fukuyama when he states that, as mankind approached the end of the millennium, the twin crises of authoritarianism and socialist central planning left only one competitor standing in the ring of an ideology of potentially universal validity. This was Liberal democracy, the doctrine of individual freedom and popular sovereignty. This is the ideology upon which our party – The Liberal Democratic Party (LDP) is founded.

I believe that we all owe a duty to each other as well as to ourselves, for human life is a network of social relations. We have to understand this in order to enhance our national unity, to collaborate with each other, and to forge creative partnerships for mutual benefit. We have to believe in this philosophy to avoid destructive competition that can only lead to greed and deception... the two vile characteristics that have seen our nation sick in despair and hopelessness.

It is for this reason that I am committed to building strong communities as cornerstone of our national unity. For I have a vision of a country where everyone recognizes that true national unity is the only option that can create an environment for meaningful development. I have a vision of a nation where every citizen has the dignity and the right to lawfully pursue those ends that will sustain individual and group aspirations and happiness. I envision a free-market economy where citizens can freely and willingly own and dispose of their properties and services, an economy in which both the public and private sectors work in tandem for the benefit of all citizens.

In our view, participatory democracy should be entrenched as the only option for political participation. A small, friendlier but efficient government, that is accountable, transparent and dependable, is our aim. We believe in devolution that will empower the people to meaningfully participate in the decision making process at the grassroots level. Parliament needs to be transformed in such a way to make its working practices simpler; give it more powers to investigate malpractices in government and by public officials, and to make it more responsive to the special needs of women, children disabled and minorities.

The most realistic and efficient way for realizing the desired economic integration remains political. An East African Federation was the dream of the founding fathers of our respective countries. It remains a viable, attainable goal. Likewise, the spirit of Pan-Africanism that inspired Kwame Nkrumah, Mwalimu Nyerere, Sekou Toure, Jomo Kenyatta, Oginga Odinga, Nelson Mandela and Abdel Nasser still throngs and inspires millions of Africans, from Senegal to Madagascar. We must rekindle the Pan-African Unity, not just of the governments as is now the case, but of the African.

Such cultural institutions as the Pan African News Agency, the Festival of African Arts and Culture (FESTAC), and the Association of African Universities, must be given a new Lease of Life. The cue must come from us, from the land of Dedan Kimathi, and Tom Mboya.

Above all, we are internationalist. I believe in the need for international co-operation, and in the desire for the integration of the human race. The most pertinent approach to internationalism at the moment lies in the promotion and propagation of Science and Technology for the emancipation of mankind from scarcity and want, from poverty, ignorance and disease, from ecological and environmental degradation, from cultural and gender biases. Different qualities of Science & Technology obtain from various parts of the world. Thus the exchange of knowledge (ie science) and action (i.e. Technology) has to become a multilateral affair. We must not only think in terms of North to South or South to South transfers: the crucial word is exchange. Technological and economic assistance has in the past been tied up with geopolitics.

My vision is one where African Traditional Healers work together with their Chinese counterparts for the alleviation of physical, mental and emotional pain; where African based research foundations like ICIPE, ILRI, etc, take more peasant knowledge into account and engage our herders and farmers to seek solutions to African Agricultural and Animal Husbandry; where Kenyan, Nigerian, Senegalese and African American Medical researchers work together to eradicate sickle cell/anemia; and where steel research in Tanzania is linked to similar endeavours in Ecuador. In this world of cyberspace, Africans must be seen to be active participants in the quest for Science and Technology as a means of emancipation.

Memorandum of Understanding

WE THE NATIONAL ALLIANCE PARTY OF KENYA AND THE LIBERAL DEMOCRATIC PARTY (RAINBOW) both being registered political parties under the Societies Act, Chapter 108 of the Laws of Kenya AND WE HON MWAI KIBAKI, HON MICHAEL KIJANA WAMALWA, HON CHARITY KALUKI NGILU, HON KIPRUTO ARAP KIRWA, HON STEPHEN KALONZO MUSYOKA, HON RAILA AMOLO ODINGA, HON PROF GEORGE SAITOTI, and HON MOODY AWORI, being members of the said political parties (all collectively and individually referred to hereinafter as "THE SUMMIT") BEING fully cognisant of the overwhelming desire and support of Kenyans for opposition unity in elections and subsequently in government, to promote political and economic changes in Kenya;

FULLY committed to the efforts to achieve opposition unity desired by Kenyans, DO HEREBY AGREE, jointly and severally to enter into this Memorandum of Understanding and undertake and promise Kenyans to do the following:

CLAUSE 1: FORMATION OF THE NATIONAL RAINBOW COALITION (NARC)

a) The parties hereto having reached common agreement collectively and individually **hereby form and constitute** a political and electoral coalition to be known as THE NATIONAL RAINBOW COALITION (NARC) for the purpose of contesting the forthcoming general election and upon being elected by Kenyans to **form, as equal partners,** a GOVERNMENT OF NATIONAL UNITY in the Republic of Kenya as outlined in Clause 2 herein below.

b) THE NATIONAL RAINBOW COALITION will nominate and field single candidates in the forthcoming national civic and parliamentary elections.

CLAUSE 2: COMPOSITION OF GOVERNMENT

a) The Summit has agreed that the GOVERNMENT OF NATIONAL UNITY will be formed as follows;

　i) Hon Mwai Kibaki shall be nominated as the single Presidential candidate in the forthcoming general elections under the aegis of the NATIONAL RAINBOW COALITION and will serve as the President of the Republic of Kenya.

ii)   Upon successful completion of the national Parliamentary and Presidential elections, the President-elect shall immediately convene the Summit in order to discuss the appointment of the Cabinet and the distribution of ministerial duties.

iii) The membership of the Cabinet, to be formed under the GOVERNMENT OF NATIONAL UNITY will be determined on a 50/50 (fifty-fifty) power sharing formula between the two political parties and will be composed of individuals proposed by the respective political parties.

b)   The following positions in the Cabinet shall be allocated to the NATIONAL ALLIANCE PARTY OF KENYA (NAK) to be distributed among Hon Michael Wamalwa, Hon Charity Kaluki Ngilu and Hon Kipruto Arap Kirwa, namely one position of Vice President and two positions of second and third Deputy Prime Ministers.

c)   The following positions in the Cabinet shall be allocated to the LIBERAL DEMOCRATIC PARTY (RAINBOW) to be distributed among Hon Stephen Kalonzo Musyoka, Hon Raila Amolo Odinga, Hon Prof George Saitoti and Hon Moody Awori, namely one position of Vice President, the Prime Minister, the first Deputy Prime Minister and one position of Senior co-ordinating Minister.

d)   The first Deputy Prime Minister shall co-ordinate a class of Ministries to be identified and specified upon formation of Government.

CLAUSE 3: ACTIVITIES TO BE UNDERTAKEN BY THE GOVERNMENT OF NATIONAL UNITY IN THE FIRST 100 DAYS.

The Summit and parties hereto undertake collectively and individually to perform appropriate and requisite actions and activities to achieve the following in the first 100 days of the GOVERNMENT OF NATIONAL UNITY;

a)   To ensure and achieve the full and effective completion of the CONSTITUTIONAL REFORM PROCESS in the Republic of Kenya.

b)   To clearly define and assign the portfolios of Deputy Prime Ministers, and

c)   To design and execute through national participatory process governmental programmes and activities necessary to jump-start the national economic recovery in the Republic of Kenya, such programmes and activities to include the restoration of the World Bank/IMF support, establishment of a merit based civil service, reform of public enterprises, establishment of incentives to assist private sector-led economic growth and judicial sector reform.

CLAUSE 4: OTHER TERMS

a) This Memorandum of understanding shall subsist and remain in force and effective between and amongst the parties until the next general elections.

b) Any disputes or disagreement that any arise regarding the interpretation of implementation of this Memorandum of Understanding shall be submitted for final settlement by a committee comprising the heads of the Catholic Church in Kenya, the Anglican Church in Kenya and the Supreme Council of Muslims in Kenya.

c) In order to achieve the full objectives of this Memorandum of understanding, the parties agree to enter into additional arrangements through the Summit, that they may deem appropriate.

IN WITNESS WHEREOF THE PARTIES HEREINABOVE MENTIONED HAVE EXECUTED THIS MEMORANDUM OF UNDERSTANDING AND THE INDIVIDUALS HAVE HEREUNTO SET THEIR RESPECTIVE HANDS AND AFFIXED THEIR RESPECTIVE SEALS TO INDICATE THEIR AGREEMENT AND COMMITMENT HERETO THIS _____ DAY OF OCTOBER 2002.

SIGNED ON BEHALF OF
THE NATIONAL ALLIANCE PARTY OF KENYA BY

_____

In the presence of;

SIGNED ON BEHALF OF
LIBERAL DEMOCRATIC PARTY (RAINBOW)

_____

In the presence of;

SIGNED SEALED AND DELIVERED BY:
Hon Mwai Kibaki

In the presence of;

_____

SIGNED SEALED AND DELIVERED BY:
Hon Charity Kaluki Ngilu
In the presence of;

_____

SIGNED SEALED AND DELIVERED BY:
Hon Kipruto Arap Kirwa

In the presence of;

_____

SIGNED SEALED AND DELIVERED BY:
Hon Stephen Kalonzo Musyoka

In the presence of;

_____

SIGNED SEALED AND DELIVERED BY:
Hon Raila Amolo Odinga

In the presence of;

_____

SIGNED SEALED AND DELIVERED BY:
Hon Prof. George Saitoti

In the presence of;

_____

SIGNED SEALED AND DELIVERED BY:
Hon Moody Awori

In the presence of;

_____

Pictorial Appendix

L-R: Raila, Rosemary and Ida Odinga

Fidel Odinga

Raila giving pep talk to students at Miranda High School

Younger Raila with Oburu

Okpala, Raila, Ida, Olukanni and Jumoke

Doing what he does best at the final
orange rally

Uhuru, Balala, Raila and Mudavadi

Crowd at final orange rally animated by
Raila

Musyoka, Raila, Ida and Mrs Mwendwa

Raila, Akasa and Marende at
Rosemary's bethrothal

Raila's crowd at Kibera

President Kibaki with Raila at State
House luncheon

Raila at a Diwali party in Kisumu

Temporarily stranded at Namanga
airstrip

Raila, Ida and Wenwa

Raila, President Kibaki and former
President Moi

Nigerian Amb. Omene on Nigeria's
National day, Raila and Ida

Jaramogi Mausoleum

Elder statesman Keen and Raila

Raila in Nigeria with Olugbemi, Mrs Obilana, Raila, Jumoke, Prof. Obilana and author

Raila with George Saitoti

Chinese Ambassador, Raila and Indian High Commissioner

Musyoka, Raila, Kamotho and Ndolo

Index